T0373876

REINVENTING THE SHEIKHDOM

MATTHEW HEDGES

Reinventing the Sheikhdom

*Clan, Power and Patronage
in Mohammed bin Zayed's UAE*

HURST & COMPANY, LONDON

First published in the United Kingdom in 2021 by
C. Hurst & Co. (Publishers) Ltd.,
New Wing, Somerset House, Strand, London, WC2R 1LA
© Matthew Hedges, 2021
All rights reserved.
Printed in Great Britain by Bell & Bain Ltd, Glasgow

The right of Matthew Hedges to be identified as the author
of this publication is asserted by him in accordance with the
Copyright, Designs and Patents Act, 1988.

A Cataloguing-in-Publication data record for this book
is available from the British Library.

ISBN: 9781787385467

This book is printed using paper from registered sustainable
and managed sources.

www.hurstpublishers.com

CONTENTS

NOTE ON SPELLING AND TERMINOLOGY

As a non-Arabic speaker, I have often referred to official sources and references for guidance on spelling. While diplomatic protocol may have unified some spellings and terms, due to varying interpretations in translation and for the sake of uniformity I have utilised the International Journal of Middle East Studies (IJMES) translation and transliteration guide.[1] Where this is not applicable, I have used the Latin spelling from official sources. While I, and many others, do not like the spelling norms of the IJMES, which are often in contradiction to official reporting, I have since implemented them, with a couple of 'recognisability' exceptions listed below. This is justified on the basis of common written format and wider use. In the first reference to an individual I have used their formal title and have shortened this thereafter.

Exceptions include:
Sheikh not Shaykh
Mohammed not Muhammad
Khalifah not Khalifa
Zayed not Zaid

LIST OF ILLUSTRATIONS

LIST OF ILLUSTRATIONS

LIST OF ABBREVIATIONS

ADDF	Abu Dhabi Defence Force
ADDHC	Abu Dhabi Development Holding Company
ADEC	Abu Dhabi Executive Council
ADIA	Abu Dhabi Investment Authority
ADIC	Abu Dhabi Investment Council
ADNOC	Abu Dhabi National Oil Company
AFAD	Air Force and Air Defence
BMBK	Bani Mohammed bin Khalifa
CPC	Crown Prince Court
EDIC	Emirates Defence Investment Company
FNC	Federal National Congress
GCC	Gulf Cooperation Council
IFI	International Financial Institution
IP	Intellectual Property
ISI	Import Substitution Industrialisation
ISP	Internet Service Provider
JAC	Joint Aviation Command
JSOC	Joint Special Operations Command
MENA	Middle East and North Africa
NCO	Non-Commissioned Officer
NCP	Neo-Corporate Praetorianism
NDP	National Development Plan
NESA	National Electronic Security Authority
NGO	Non-Governmental Organisation
NMC	National Media Council

LIST OF ABBREVIATIONS

NOC	National Oil Company
OEM	Original Equipment Manufacturer
OPB	Offset Program Bureau
PG	Presidential Guard
POC	Privately Owned Champion
PPP	Public Private Partnership
PREs	Politically Relevant Elites
RAK	Ras al-Khaimah
SANG	Saudi Arabian National Guard
SAP	Structural Adjustment Package
SIA	Signals Intelligence Authority
SMEs	Small and Medium Enterprises
SOE	State-Owned Enterprise
SPC	Supreme Petroleum Council
SWF	Sovereign Wealth Fund
TOS	Trucial Oman Scouts
TRA	Telecommunication Regulatory Authority
UAQ	Umm al-Quwain
UDF	Union Defence Force
VOIP	Voice Over Internet Protocol
VPN	Virtual Private Network

ACKNOWLEDGEMENTS

Writing the thesis on which this book is based was especially challenging—it is the product of truly extraordinary events. The personal toll has been immense, but its impact on my family, I feel, has been considerably tougher. Initially, I thought that pursuing a doctorate might have been a burden, but it ended becoming far more than that.

I would not have been able to go through nearly five years of academic research without my wife's patience. Here, I want to acknowledge that my research has cost her a lot too. If I had the opportunity to start again, I would not embark on a doctorate—I would not want to put her through the pain I did through my PhD studies. Given that I had already completed the majority of my research when I was arbitrarily detained in the UAE, there was no scenario in which I would not finish it—if only for her. My sincerest gratitude extends also to my father-in-law. He encouraged me to pursue my research and helped me transform every page of my doctorate, from its earliest days, into legible English. Without him, I would still be working on delivering a draft. Mainly, this book is dedicated to them.

Secondly, and without reservation, I want to thank my PhD supervisor, Professor Clive Jones. He not only helped direct my research, but also transformed a rough draft into a document that I was proud to present and share. As if this was not enough, he also supported my wife and worked tirelessly with her to secure my release. Lessons he shared will stay with me forever.

ACKNOWLEDGEMENTS

My experience in undertaking research in an authoritarian state reinforced many of the hypotheses within this book. The disconnect between state authorities and their management of differing portfolios showed me—and I hope others—some of the great dangers of these compartmentalised responsibilities.

FOREWORD

This book represents a comprehensive version of my doctoral thesis, simply edited and refined with no supplementary information. The UAE's State Security Department (SSD) used this document to detain and torture me, and to sentence me to life in prison on the charge of espionage on behalf of the UK Secret Intelligence Service (SIS), also known as MI6. Less than a week after my sentencing, after a high-profile campaign for my release, I was pardoned and returned to the UK. Shortly after, Article 170 of the UAE's Penal Code was adapted to widen the scope of the definition of secrets related to the nation's defence:

1. Military, political, economic, industrial, scientific or social security-related information or other information, which are unknown except to persons who have such a capacity by virtue of one's position or status, and which the interest of the country's defence requires that it remain undisclosed to others.
2. Correspondence, written instruments, documents, drawings, maps, designs, pictures, coordinates, and other things whose disclosure might lead to divulging information such as those referred to in the preceding clause, and which the interest of the country's defence requires that they shall remain classified to persons other than those who are assigned to preserve or use them.
3. News and information related to the armed forces, the Ministry of Interior and security services as well as their formations, manoeuvres, ammunition, supplies, personnel and other things

affecting military affairs, and war and security plans, unless
written permission to publish and announce such things has
been issued by competent authorities.

4. News and information related to measures and procedures
which are adopted to detect crimes provided for in this chapter,
and arrest of culprits as well as news and information related to
the investigation and trial proceedings, if the announcement
thereof, is prohibited by the investigation authority or the competent court.[1]

As will become clear from the evidence and its publicly available
sourcing, the UAE's perception of secretive information reinforces
my hypothesis that the most evident threats to the UAE's regime
arise from internal sources. As much as the publisher allows, all
references are provided to confirm that the information sourced
for this research was publicly available throughout and, as a consequence, could not have been deemed to be secretive. Therefore,
it appears, Article 170 was expanded as a means to legitimise the
state's treatment of me. The UAE has evaded much scrutiny and
investigation due to the lack of academic confidence. This is mostly
due to the fact that academics at large have been co-opted,
employed or intimidated by the state. As a result, this book remains
one of very few in-depth investigations—if not the only one—into
the domestic dynamics of the Abu Dhabi ruling family. Where
historical analysis of past autocratic states provides rich archival
databases, where allowed, the comparison with modern states is
extremely difficult and often dangerous. As a result, research
frameworks must account for diligent sourcing and the limitations
this brings to the analysis.

1

INTRODUCTION

Methods of political governance have been significantly affected by technological developments and social-economic modernisation. While these trends have altered global systems of political interaction, there are still traditional tenets by which many states practise their authority. This is of particular significance for authoritarian states, due to their application of multifaceted methods of control and the lack of formal accountability. For the states of the Gulf Cooperation Council (GCC)—Bahrain, Kuwait, Oman, Qatar, Saudi Arabia, and the United Arab Emirates (UAE)—the evolving task of maintaining control and authority is a complicated challenge as the ruling monarchs balance traditional power mechanisms which legitimise their authority against dynamic sociopolitical conditions. The UAE is regarded as the foremost modern authoritarian state within the Middle East and North Africa (MENA) due to its effective application of overt and covert mechanisms that strengthen the regime's control of society.

Traditional governance systems are defined by their claims to and belief in the 'sanctity of the order and the attendant powers of control as they have been handed down from the past'.[1] Tradition extends the capabilities of a state and, when bonded with identity, provides a powerful platform from which to significantly expand state power. This concept is firmly grounded within the GCC states, who all share the institution of monarchy and continue to operate above society, thus providing multiple avenues from which to extrapolate supplementary power and authority. Their main challenge is how to maintain authority amid an array of evolving threats.

The GCC states have grown as extensions of the households that ruled the region before the formal establishment of their states, and therefore, the sociopolitical dynamics within each state provides exclusive lenses for analysis. The relationship between monarch and society is central to understanding how, and where, pressure is applied to influence domestic power dynamics. The network of factors which support these interactions is deeply ingrained in the tradition of each society. In turn, these unique characteristics have become part of a central strategy for the monarchs to reinforce the fundamental basis upon which their authority is built.

The advent of the Arab Spring altered the ability of regimes across the MENA region to adhere to long-established forms of power, aligning the tradition-focused region with prominent theories of modernisation such as Samuel Huntington's The Third Wave.[2] The plethora of scholarship which emerged in the immediate aftermath of the Cold War, such as Francis Fukuyama's The End of History,[3] hypothesised, that only liberal democracies could survive in the future, arguing that 'as mankind approaches the end of the millennium, the twin crises of authoritarianism and socialist central planning have left only one competitor standing in the ring as an ideology of potential universal validity: liberal democracy'.[4] Why, then, have authoritarian regimes not only survived, but thrived in MENA since the Arab Spring?

While at the peak of the Arab Spring many MENA regimes looked vulnerable and susceptible to institutional change, there has since been a reversal in the progression of authoritarian states, with many reverting to intrinsic, traditional characteristics.[5] Reflecting on the change within MENA, it becomes evident that, apart from Tunisia's successful transition to a functioning democracy, where structural change was demanded through large-scale civil protests, a significant and lengthy period of instability has followed. In contrast, the GCC states were able to successfully contain the ripples of discontent emanating from North Africa. Where disturbances did occur within the GCC—Bahrain, the Eastern region of Saudi Arabia, and northern Sunni dominated areas of Oman—regimes reacted with a mixture of repressive tactics, and, in some cases, increased co-optation. Johannes Gerschewski concurs with this premise and posits three pillars of stability: legitimation, repression, and co-optation.[6] The contrasting responses of the GCC monarchies to the Arab Spring, and the result of such measures, versus that of the republican states of North Africa and the Levant indicate an institutional advantage and capability in monarchy's favour.[7]

Attempts to survey the effects of the Arab Spring on the GCC states[8] often refer to Samuel Huntington's 'King's Dilemma'[9] in their analysis. Huntington postulates that a ruling monarch can practise one of three strategies in the pursuit of modernisation.[10] First, reducing power (potentially abdicating) and continuing to modernise, paving the way for a constitutional monarchy; second, combining monarchical power with popular authority; and third, maintaining the status quo as the sole source of authority and quelling efforts that undermine the regime.[11]

While scholarship focusing on the GCC's symptoms of the King's Dilemma often investigates methods of coercion, and the partial economic and political liberalisation that has taken place since 2011, most analysis has focused on strategic level decisions. This book, however, acknowledges that 'there is no transition whose beginning is not the consequence—direct or indirect—of important divisions within the authoritarian regime itself'.[12] As a result, it is crucial that any investigation into an authoritarian state's management of modernisation incorporates elite dynamics.

This book will present the case study of the UAE to examine how changes following the Arab Spring have been adopted to advance its regime security strategy. Central to this will be the ascension to power of Sheikh Mohammed bin Zayed al-Nahyan and the ways in which he has not only centralised power, but designed a structure that increases his oversight by shortening the agency chain through his direct network of clan and kin. The UAE presents a clear example of a nested dictatorship, like a Russian

doll where each subordinate is closely aligned to his own predecessor but all mimic the ultimate leader.[13] In this case, and since
the Arab Spring, the UAE's supreme leader is Mohammed bin
Zayed al-Nahyan.

Federation: Power or Curse?

The UAE is a member of the GCC. As a state it was founded in
1971, as a federation of seven Emirates—Abu Dhabi, Ajman,
Dubai, Fujairah, Ras al-Khaimah, Sharjah and Umm al-Quwain—
each one having its own relationship with its particular micro-cli-
mate of sociopolitical dynamics. As a result of the overlapping
fabric of social relations and authority, the federal identity of the
UAE has the potential ability to weaken it as a union. This was the
cause of significant tension within the UAE's earlier years, but as
power solidified, so did the state's stability.

While the seven Emirates are technically equal in constitutional
power, Abu Dhabi is the capital Emirate and possesses the vast
majority of the oil reserves that have been used to develop the state
in its image. There is a stark contrast in socioeconomic conditions
between the Emirates, with the capital hosting all major federal
bodies and acting as the central diplomatic hub for foreign relations. Therefore, the management of the state by the Abu Dhabi
ruling family is the single most important factor in the development of the UAE.

The founder of the UAE, Sheikh Zayed bin Sultan al-Nahyan,
carefully managed the relationships between the Emirates and the
collective development of the state. Since his death in 2004, there
has been a seismic shift in political relations. The leadership of his
successor, Sheikh Khalifa bin Zayed al-Nahyan, has faced different
threats, leading to the postulation that governance within the UAE
has also evolved. This book therefore seeks to illustrate the predominant threats to Abu Dhabi's ruling family and analyse how its
members have managed to protect themselves from these issues.

Christopher Davidson,[14] the leading scholar on the contemporary UAE, has written several books analysing in detail the development of Abu Dhabi[15] and Dubai.[16] He builds upon previous

works of Frauke Heard-Bey,[17] Hendrik Van Der Meulen,[18] and Wilfred Thesiger,[19] all of whom analysed the UAE from societal and historical accounts. Yet, it is in a recent monograph[20] that Davidson attempts to challenge the orthodox notions of how the modern day GCC states are reacting to the challenges of modernisation. He postulated that the GCC monarchies 'will be gone in the next two to five years'.[21] While this estimation of longevity has proved to be wrong, the theoretical argument presented throughout the study is strong and built upon a wide breadth of scholarship. Davidson understands that many of the conditions that were apparent in Egypt, Libya, and Tunisia during the Arab Spring are also found, if not magnified, within the GCC states, because of the skewed social contract between the region's monarchs and citizens.

Whilst Davidson examines the macro-trends of the post-Arab Spring GCC, Kristian Ulrichsen examines the case study of Qatar, whose dynamics are somewhat different. His innovative study, *Qatar and the Arab Spring*,[22] observes Qatar's development-focused and political Islam oriented foreign policy ideology, and highlights how this was translated into policy through the turbulent period. Ulrichsen centres his analysis around Qatar's foreign policy, largely overlooking internal issues. What is evident in his thesis, and many other studies about other GCC states,[23] is the absence of analysis of how the mechanisms of power and control are changing to suit a new political reality, leveraging a unique angle that the research seeks to pursue. There is a wide gap in the field of research on the micro-decisions employed by states to protect themselves.

Ulrichsen followed with a book on the UAE, tracing the coaxial development of Emirati foreign and domestic policies.[24] While literature pertaining to the UAE has been limited in scope, Ulrichsen has been able to illustrate the key drivers of the state's united policy, while also explaining the impact of those decisions on the federation's identity. Ulrichsen values the role of formal rational institutions within the UAE, however in doing so it can be said that this approach overlooks many of the informal domestic dynamics that also drive policy decisions within the UAE. While a state-level approach, such as that utilised by Ulrichsen, could be useful when analysing security strategy, the internal dynamics that support a reign within an authoritarian state provide greater influence on issues of governance than their foreign relations. This book, however, acknowledges the fact that 'there is no transition whose beginning is not the consequence—direct or indirect—of important divisions within the authoritarian regime itself'.[25] As a result, it is crucial for an investigation into an authoritarian state's management of modernisation to incorporate elite dynamics.

David Roberts examines the development of the UAE Armed Forces and its effectiveness; however, his study does not provide sufficient evidence for his observations. He states that 'there is little evidence of preferential promotion of royals in contemporary UAE operations. More generally, there is no forging of exclusionary identity-based military'.[26] On the one hand, due mainly to deficiencies in human capital and an acknowledgement of organs which can provide security, it is unlikely that a large portion of ruling family members would seek distinguished roles within the UAE Armed Forces. On the other hand, however, preliminary research shows several examples of ruling family members who have advanced military careers, including Staff Pilot Major General Sheikh Ahmed bin Tahnoon al-Nahyan, the Chairman of the National Service and Reserve Authority;[27] Rear Admiral Pilot Staff Major General Sheikh Saeed bin Hamdan bin Muhammad al-Nahyan, the Commander of the UAE Navy;[28] and Sheikh Zayed bin Hamdan al-Nahyan, who was injured while on overseas operations in Yemen.[29] It is hypothesised that the UAE Armed Forces have come under increased control from the Abu Dhabi ruling family since the Arab Spring, and that this is illustrated by clear changes.

Kenneth Pollack also contributes to the literature concerning the UAE Armed Forces' military effectiveness, and delivers a comparatively thorough and contextually rich analysis. However, like many of his peers, Pollack has avoided topics of sensitivity for the UAE ruling family, namely elite dynamics. Abu Dhabi has heavily invested in the public policy and think tank sector within the United States, and the institution that published Pollack's paper was heavily engaged in lobbying efforts (the fourth most engaged think tank) from UAE Foreign Agents.[30] This would therefore follow a pattern whereby the UAE has been able to co-opt public information and shift analysis away from sensitive areas. As a result, Pollack's study is interesting for as much as what it doesn't include as for what it does.

Therefore, due to the lack of detailed and accurate contemporary case studies, this book will present the case study of the UAE. It aims to complement the current field of scholarship by seeking to address the following research question: to what extent has the UAE's regime security strategy been affected by the Arab Spring? The assumption is that the principal threat to the UAE originates from domestic rather than foreign sources. It illustrates why changes have been made to the UAE's internal governance structure, and in what and whose image. The initial hypothesis is that, since the Arab Spring, there has been an increasing centralisation of the state's power, rising bureaucracy, a move towards a unitary state, and the future of the UAE has been bound to the survival of the Abu Dhabi ruling family; in particular to Mohammed bin Zayed al-Nahyan and his own family clan.

Conceptual Framework

Political administration within the UAE strictly follows traditional dynamics as postulated by Max Weber and later Hisham Sharabi. Central to these dynamics are values of personalism, proximity, informality, balanced conflict, military prowess and religious rationalisation.[31] James Bill and Carl Leiden support this by arguing that the sovereign or leader is the prominent actor within the state and 'he is surrounded by advisors, ministers, military leaders, personal secretaries, and confidants. The one thing that all members of this inner circle share is unquestioned personal loyalty to the leader'.[32] The centrality and supremacy of political leadership within the MENA region is further bolstered by the fact that 'their internal structures remain rooted in the patriarchal values and social relations of kinship, clan, and religious and ethnic groups'.[33] It could be said that neo-patriarchal states can continue to operate in a similar structure to that of past generations, albeit within contemporary mechanisms: an idea that this book builds upon.

John Peterson builds upon the narrative of traditional power mediums influencing the political structure within the MENA by saying that:

> Even though the state has replaced the tribe as the primary political unit, it still relies heavily on various tribal components. The most obvious and most important of these is the ruling family, whose political position is absolute...complementing the family elite is a second elite group composed of the Shaykhly clans from other major tribes in the state.[34]

Peterson's emphasis on the role played by traditional power structures in contemporary politics helps to illuminate formal and informal power networks and dissect ruling coalitions within the state. This understanding has heightened significance across the MENA, and in particular the monarchies of the GCC, as a result of their shared monarchical system of centralised rule and authority.

The concentration of power observed within the UAE, and across the GCC, is according to Brian Job an example of what makes a state weak.[35] In order to balance the blurring of public and private and the lack of a separation of powers, the state has to prepare for a far broader array of threats. It is therefore hypothesised that for the states of the GCC, internal and institutional threats are far more dangerous. As a result, through the monitoring of factors which can affect internal dynamics and the governance structure of the state, any issue can have dire consequences.

At this juncture, a fundamental question arises: within the monarchies of the GCC, whose security is prioritised? The state, the nation or the regime? Due to the fact that each concept has differing security perceptions, this book is framed in reference to the security of the regime. Were it to examine state or national security, a different approach would be required.

Regime Security Strategy Foundation

Due to the combination of the domestic focus of threat construction and the fact that power is disproportionately concentrated within an authoritarian state, it is critical to examine the political and social architecture that houses potentially competing entities.

INTRODUCTION

When observing power structures within a state, there are three predominant locales: the government, the regime, and the state. They are all primarily concerned with the maintenance of their own position within the larger apparatus.

The competing interpretations of security put into evidence a multitude of strategies to achieve the independent goals of the elites and the state; regime security policies are by nature different to national and state security policies. These are also in competition with each other as they attempt to promote their significance to foster their own survival.[36] Thus, unless there is a shift in internal power, the reigning body of authority will continue to undertake measures, predominantly in the short term, to secure its position. Therefore, in an authoritarian state, the security of the regime always supersedes that of the state and the nation. This is further clarified by Job:

> [I]n practice many states become locked into this preliminary status, i.e., with strong despotic and weak infrastructural powers, as a quasi-permanent condition. Either because they prefer this status quo or, more usually, because they are unable to move beyond the raw exercise of coercion to compliance through more peaceful means, regime powerholders sustain themselves through this imbalance of state despotic and infrastructural power.[37]

The predominant focus on regime security being presented as despotic and sultanistic in form is extremely limited, as it isolates physical defence from the broader array of factors that influence the regime's strategic management of affairs. The lack of accounting for the totality of options available to protect and enhance the regime's position in power has resulted in an under-researched topic and an overly simplistic approach to the wider considerations of influencing factors. Regime security is often dominated by the application of a Western and liberal conception of security to non-Western illiberal states and thus ignores the array of the non-kinetic threats that are more prevalent within illiberal states. As a result, Muhammad Mohamedou's typology of regime security is more fitting. 'Regime security is the idiosyncratic set of dispositions, orientations, and strategies of a particular regime as it seeks to maintain its physical presence, establish and perpetuate legitimacy, and further its permanent and ad hoc interests'.[38]

Building upon the hypotheses of Mohamedou and Robert Jackson, this book defines regime security as the array of measures taken to insulate the political elites from an array of internal and external threats, which in turn may have a coercive and non-kinetic character.

Regime Security Application

Regimes implement a wide range of programmes and strategies to insulate themselves from threats. Counterbalancing of state institutions[39] and elite personnel,[40] selective concentration of power within core sectors,[41] effective foreign policy management,[42] co-optation,[43] and the restriction of freedoms,[44] or enforcement of the state's power[45] are all common techniques employed to secure the regime. Opinion on this issue is now split. Scholars such as Gregory Gause argue that the strategic management of foreign relations has ensured the survival of many authoritarian states,[46] whereas those such as Daniel Brumberg hypothesise that there are two domestic components to successful regime security strategies: effective political management and economic management.[47] While Gause's argument has its merits, although debatable,[48] Russell Lucas' more inclusive analysis builds on Brumberg's postulation, indicating that the resources—political, economic, and social—available to a regime, and their utilisation 'provide a key for regime survival'.[49] Joel Migdal contributes to this discussion by explaining that the regime has to provide both 'an elaborate set of institutions to dole out sanctions and material incentives, as well as to package state services and sanctions in a coherent and meaningful set of symbols'.[50] It is on this basis, and because the domestic environment dominates threat construction within weak states, that this book focuses on the changes to the UAE's regime security and not on national or state security.

Gerschewski's three pillars of stability[51]—legitimation, repression, and co-optation[52]—provide the fundamental basis around which this framework and many regime security strategies are ultimately constructed. Legitimacy is a powerful and evocative notion, and when observed within MENA societies, has an augmented

INTRODUCTION

value. The complexity of defining and measuring legitimacy would constitute an unnecessary distraction for this book, especially as, potentially, there are multiple sources of legitimacy across the entire Emirati sociopolitical spectrum; from within the innermost circle of the ruling family[53] through to the state's relationship with expatriates. Additionally, the fragmented and federal structure of the UAE presents the argument that there are competing notions of legitimacy within the UAE. Therefore, this book focuses on the singular regime security strategy of the Abu Dhabi elites, and not any other of the competing interpreters of security.

Regimes view resources and personnel as commodities, over which they have full control.[54] However, this varies according to the distance between the leader and the commodity in question. Therefore, the most effective analysis of a security strategy must concentrate on evaluating the regime's strategic management of personnel and commodities in their pursuit of greater strength. As a result, it becomes essential 'to identify the typology of its actors and their relevance, the dynamics that govern their relationships, the power resources at their disposal and their respective position in society'.[55] Thus, by understanding the complexities of the relationship between regime, society, and resources, there can be an accurate analysis of how each relationship has been co-opted, in order to enforce the UAE's regime security strategy. This will consequently highlight that regimes such as the UAE have two primal concerns: first to physically protect themselves from coercive threats, and second to be able to finance these measures.

Regimes have a structural advantage over their populations due to their ability to structure the inter-relationship between themselves, society, and the resources of the state. This enables regimes to fortify the position of their politically relevant elites (PREs) [all regime personnel are part of the elite][56] to ensure the regime's continuation of power and authority. Therefore, the co-existence between the regime, society, and resources forms the basis of regime security strategy in the UAE, and throughout the GCC.

The parallel strategy to co-optation is repression, with a state's security apparatus being the primary organisation tasked with its enforcement. Regardless of the nature of governance, be it monarchy or republican, power has traditionally gravitated around coercive elements.[57] Nazih Ayubi suggests that the military is one of three poles of power across the MENA, along with the president and the party.[58] The military has traditionally held an elevated position within MENA society and, in some cases, has even been the primary vehicle for state and nation building.[59] The combined observations have witnessed PREs exploiting the institution's sole legitimate ownership of coercion for their own means.

The emphasis placed on the military over other elements within the arsenal of a state's security apparatus indicates academia's priority towards conventional military forces and lack of greater engagement with the wider security architecture. This has resulted in the military being considered an institutionally more significant and dominant actor within the domestic politics of an authoritarian state than it may be in reality. This is supported by the fundamental assertion that 'military forces, trained to fight a foreign aggressor, have always been a dubious instrument for civil-war purposes'.[60] While the military possesses the physical strength and capacity to intervene in politics, and historically more so in authoritarian states, this overlooks the wider range of organisations that can provide comparable intervention and power capabilities. The literature places such organs under the umbrella of state security and their objectives and methods can be vast, from comprehensive surveillance through to domestic terror. Writing within the context of the Soviet Union (USSR), Aleksandr Kokurin and Nikita Petrov define state security by saying that it 'was always broader than the functions of a secret police. It was oriented towards the resolution by extraordinary methods of a whole series of current political or economic tasks.'[61] The challenge is using such terms without the ability to source material that can be used to justify the classification. As a result, the title of 'state security' will not be applied or explored within this work, even if it appears to be suitable. This limitation provides an angle for supplementary research to examine.

This book argues that due to the connection between regime and society, and to the fundamental principle that the regime's power originates from its control of internal sources of contention,

INTRODUCTION

the UAE's regime security strategy rests upon its management of political, economic, and social structures to strengthen its own position. Regimes similar in structure and form to the UAE employ methods to ensure loyalty and allegiance to the regime through a combination of co-optation and intimidation.[62] It can be inferred that there are two prominent strategies aimed at regime security: enforcement of power (control of the coercive apparatus: coup-proofing) and maintenance of power (strategic management of resources: co-optation).

Neo-Corporate Praetorianism

Political, social, and security related factors provide a targeted base from which to observe the location and utilisation of power within a state. Traditional authoritarian states, such as the UAE, empha-sise a neo-patriarchal relationship among political, social, and security related elites. These can further be categorised through what Bill and Leiden postulate as vertical and horizontal layers of social stratification.[63] The former tier accommodates family, tribe, kinship, ethnicity, religious sect, and professional, recreational and political associations. The latter weighs on levels of power, wealth, and prestige. Each filter can be utilised and expanded in its applica-tion towards a case study, however there must be observable and measurable characteristics to support their use. Consequently, there is an acknowledgement that along with the role being fulfilled by the individual, intrinsic characteristics of that individual play a compounding role in their relative power.

The networks of elites that support the rulers of authoritarian states have long been a significant factor in the study of regime secu-rity. However, the recent focus on MENA authoritarian states has built upon a longer trajectory of orthodox theory that has predomi-nantly utilised and compared the region to Western focused values and case studies. These have included comparisons with fascism in Europe,[64] military dominated regimes in former communist states,[65] and Latin America throughout the twentieth century.[66] The role and configuration of elites was rarely a focus within the field of authori-tarianism, however Guillermo O'Donnell's bureaucratic authoritarianism[67] notably illustrated the mechanisms that have invigorated the examination of wider structural inferences.

While traditional authoritarian states embraced a heightened role for the military and security services, they are distinct from their modern equivalents in their embrace of a shared identity across society. Instead of erasing social structures, these linkages become stronger conduits for influence and extrapolation. It is within this image that the unity of society, seen through a neopatriarchal lens, is expanded, to support the functionality of both society and the state. Where ownership is delegated to the regime, this is in turn responsible for the allocation for resources across society. Seen through the lens of rentier state theory, the accumulation of power by traditional monarchies within MENA has promoted the growth of corporate influence within the state; namely that of the regime.

The most defining feature of a corporate state is 'the absence of an autonomous or powerful party'.[68] Amos Perlmutter further explains that, in addition to corporate interests, 'historical and classical corporate institutions'[69] form predominant sections of the state. The combination of traditional power structures within the dynamics of a formal, modern, and somewhat liberal state are illustrated by Perlmutter's Corporate Praetorian model:

> In the corporate praetorian model two structural forms, corporatism and clientelism, converge. The government is the most powerful patron. Composed of military and technocratic groups, it dominates the corporatist social system. The military, the church, and the governmental ministries with their bureaucrats and technocrats are autonomous corporatist groups, while the functional-economic corporations are not.... Although the military, the church, and the technocrats serve as the regime's main source of support, the military is the most powerful, acting as the arbitrator of the corporatist system.[70]

The illustration of power centres within a corporate praetorian state revolves around the two primary strategies within a regime security strategy: enforcement and maintenance of power. In doing so, Perlmutter's hypothesis clearly illustrates how key political portfolios can be manipulated to bureaucratise and minimise levels of influence, and/or empower select institutional organs to increase control.

Attempts to illustrate the structure of political power have largely framed paradigms within modern systems of governance. Whereas some systems have experienced wholescale change, MENA monarchies continue to rule through the same conduits of influence that have supported their reign over generations. Due to the clash of modernity with traditional modes of governance and authority, traditional authoritarians have often responded by increasing their own domestic authority and control. Anthony Giddens argues that the renegotiation of relationships between state and society occurs through what he terms the institutional dimensions of modernity: surveillance, military power, industrialism and capitalism.[71]

Modernity's system of connected governance argues that each dimension is isolated from the political sphere, yet still maintains a direct relationship with each other aspect. When refined and combined with the basic premise of a regime security strategy, the fundamental requirements for survival remain, along with the enforcement and maintenance of power. Industrialism and capitalism are sectors involved in the generation and management of resources that enable a regime to maintain its power while the military and surveillance capabilities allow for the enforcement of power. The fifth category, the religious establishment, is one by which the state can maintain and sculpt its legitimacy and thus enlarge the scope of its dominion. These domains have a heightened profile and significance over other portfolios as a result of their capacity for power. This trend is noted by Perlmutter, who asserts that the 'corporative system is not composed of equally powerful corporations'.[72]

The application and merging of the institutional dimensions of modernity to Perlmutter's corporate praetorian model assists in the construction of a framework identifying the locales of sovereign power within a modern state. This model is called the Neo-Corporate Praetorian (NCP) state.

The NCP state is firmly centred on executive power, and directly managed and overseen by a concise unit of leadership. While the NCP is a modern manifestation, it is a paradigm that

Fig. 1: Author's Neo-Corporate Praetorianism (NCP)

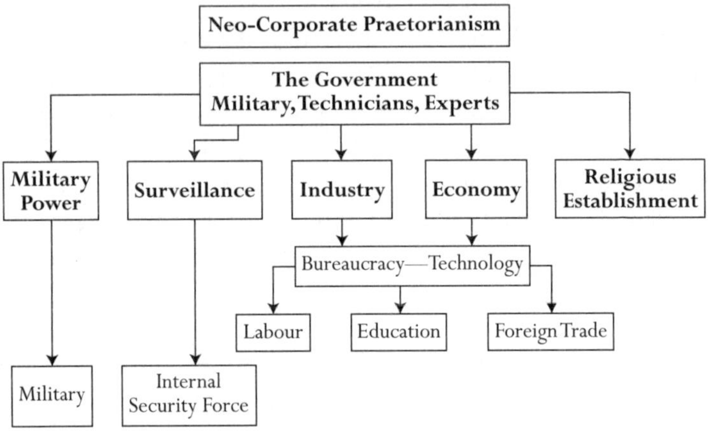

accurately illustrates where and how power is managed by traditional authoritarian leaders within the modern world. This is based upon the assertion that there is a dual-tiered structure of executive power with the five supreme domains of power isolated to ensure the state's maximal power and authority.

Residing at the core of the NCP model is the identity of a traditional state. The government is in the foremost position of power within the state, with the regime exercising ultimate authority. Due to the heightened attributes of neo-patriarchy within traditional authority, the regime's network of control can be tangibly observed through shared bonds of kinship, tribe, and technocratic profession. As a result, by identifying what characteristics institutions and their senior management exhibit, the regime security strategy of the NCP can be identified and highlighted. The implications of these observable changes are analysed to illustrate the drivers of this regime security strategy.

A structural imperative of any traditional and authoritarian society is the monopoly on the utilisation of violence and coercion, aimed at deterring would-be-aggressors from territorial and sovereignty abuses, and directly linked to the surveillance, industrial, and economic dimensions of the state. While the military is predominantly externally focused, due to its significance in matters of national, state, and regime security, the military's personnel and capabilities carry substantial clout. Furthermore, the fragile environment within authoritarian states has prompted many regimes to offset and induce numerous checks and balances into the leadership of the military and the wider coercive apparatus to ensure full compliance and oversight.

The resulting institutional reform has evidenced specialised roles for various aspects of the military. Domestic agencies, such as the Ministry of Interior (MOI), are primary organisations of internal security and surveillance, however various aspects of the military are often drafted into the effort to watch the watchers.[73] The premise for a heightened application of surveillance capabilities within an NCP state is to ensure the direct 'supervision of the activities of subject populations' and maintain a capability that is able to control information.[74] With the advent of modernisation, the surveillance capabilities of a state have been magnified, and thus, have contributed to the militarisation of the NCP state.

There is a long-established link between the military and domestic industrial capabilities, with a strong claim that the military drives domestic innovation. As a tool of coercion, the military is always planning to advance capabilities to overpower adversaries and challengers. Where close cooperation between the military and industry has evolved, tangible results of this relationship have often contributed to the revolution in military affairs (RMA). In order to develop, manufacture, and understand the use of modern applications and platforms, the military and wider coercive apparatus require a constant stream of educated personnel to operate these contemporary systems. This, in turn, demands the prioritisation of higher education and innovation. Through the process of technological modernisation, newly acquired transferable skills also provide the industrial base with added benefits, not only the optimisation of domestic industrial capabilities (also referred to as the military industrial complex (MIC)) but also, as a by-product, an increased influence on the national economy. It is crucial for NCP states to maintain control and ownership of resources, through investments, partnerships, and joint ventures with third-party actors; a common strategy to attract the necessary intellectual property (IP) and technology transfer to build domestic industrial capabilities.

Through the increase in and advancement of productive capabilities, the state can generate a larger volume of revenue. Because the long-term survival of the NCP state is based upon its ability to procure and co-opt capabilities to ensure the status quo of power relations, this is crucial for the selective maintenance of the social contract. The parallel foundations of the NCP state, the enforcement and maintenance of power, therefore remain at the centre of the NCP state and of a coherent regime security strategy.

The inclusion of the religious establishment with an NCP state framework highlights how irrational and emotive propensities directly assist the legitimation of the state within such a context. Religion can often be used directly or indirectly within the state-building process, and can assist the anchoring of society to traditional tenets, thus reinforcing the empowered position of the regime within an NCP state. This, in turn, fortifies the link between the religious establishment and the regime within a state, providing the latter with a substantial power base. The NCP regime must, however, maintain control over religious discourse and impose 'state sponsored "traditional" views' which Brumberg later clarifies, are normally based upon the 'emphasis on state authority and the claims of community'.[75]

The NCP paradigm builds upon cooperative theories to provide accurate and targeted values from which to explore and test in order to explain how the regime security strategy of the UAE has been impacted by the Arab Spring. By acknowledging the heightened role socio-cultural characteristics play within a traditional authoritarian state, this book can focus on the most applicable factors to the regime's utilisation of power conduits. The NCP allows analysis to illustrate how a traditional authoritarian state has incorporated facets of modernity to upgrade its control of society. In turn, the case study of the UAE's regime security strategy conveys an archetype of the modern authoritarian state.

Structure

The book is organised into seven chapters. In this first chapter the theoretical foundation is explored, providing a context to the book. The connection between traditional institutions and their societies focuses attention on the regime and leadership of the state. Of particular note is the exploration of regime security. While this domain lacks rigid and formal theory, my book sets forth the main objectives and practices within a regime security strategy, providing the conceptual foundations for this thesis. The two fundamental tenets of a regime security strategy are the enforcement and the maintenance of power. Based upon these observations, the theory of neo-corporate praetorianism (NCP) is displayed to show how the state manages power.

Once the theoretical framework is addressed, the second chapter explores the historical precedent of regime security set by the founder of the state, Sheikh Zayed bin Sultan al-Nahyan. This enables a contextual foundation for the analysis of the internal security dynamics within the Abu Dhabi ruling family. Building on the cumulative foundation of knowledge, the book will subsequently explore the four pillars of the NCP and the UAE's regime security strategy. It will be broadly split between the enforcement and maintenance of power.

The third chapter assesses how the regime's control of the military has been adapted following the Arab Spring. After this we turn to surveillance, and Chapter Four deals with the evolving tools being employed to increase the state's observation and control of society. Having examined the enforcement mechanisms within a regime security strategy, the following chapters assess how regimes are able to maintain their positions in control. Chapter Five details changes made to the regime's management and political control of the economy, and how this is adapted to optimise continuous revenue generation. Chapter Six will explore how, in-step with the economy, the Abu Dhabi ruling family has managed to control the industrial sector.

By evaluating the changes made to the UAE's regime security strategy through the paradigm of the NCP, this book provides a unique theoretical construct that builds upon contextual nuances, rather than applying an incompatible theory to a specific case study. The application of the NCP to the UAE is furthermore distinctive due to the lack of academic research into the UAE's domestic political relations and the further complication presented by its federal identity.

2

REGIME SECURITY STRATEGY PRECEDENT IN ABU DHABI

The federation of the United Arab Emirates is located at the southern end of the Arabian Peninsula, with coasts on the Persian Gulf and Indian Ocean. The British Empire assisted its development and Zayed bin Sultan al-Nahyan, founder and first President, consolidated its unification. The only noteworthy internal source of contention around Zayed bin Sultan al-Nahyan's rule emerged in the immediate aftermath of his death, when speculation around the selection of his successor complicated power continuity.[1]

In order to show how the modern UAE exploits issues, networks and capabilities to enhance its control, a foundation must explore how previous strategies were implemented. There are three predominant eras of the UAE's political history that will be analysed to highlight the ways in which threats to the ruling elites emerged and the mechanisms used to mitigate them. These eras are al-Nahyan rule in Abu Dhabi during the Emirates' pre-unification period (1761–1968), the process of unification (1968–1971), and the reign of Sheikh Zayed bin Sultan al-Nahyan (1966–2004). This chapter will then discuss how the Abu Dhabi ruling family viewed the Arab Spring (2011).

REINVENTING THE SHEIKHDOM

Pre-Unification Emirates: Al-Nahyan Rule in Abu Dhabi (1761–1968)

Before the formation of the UAE, the Emirates' tribal identities were distinct and often marked by intense levels of competition. Until oil was discovered in the Emirate of Abu Dhabi, the political economy of the Emirates was built on trade and pearling, providing the littoral Emirates of Dubai, Sharjah, and Ras al-Khaimah with significant influence and wealth, attracting people and commodities. Abu Dhabi, the southernmost Emirate, remained remote and isolated due to its location and harsher desert environment. This also explains why—due to Abu Dhabi's land-focused settlements—tribal ties carry more significance than in the maritime and outward-looking maritime empires of the Qawasim and later the Maktoums.

During the era of oil discovery in the UAE, and under the auspices of the British Empire, Emirati society became segmented. Ruling elites could 'identify tribal groups loyal to them in order to define their [geographical] boundaries'.[2] The established limits solidified tribal ties and relationships, and apart from a few standout examples, such as the switch of allegiance of the Zaabi tribe from Ras al-Khaimah to Abu Dhabi,[3] cemented the societal hierarchy that persists to this day.[4] In the period since Zayed bin Sultan al-Nahyan's death, federal sympathies still exist, but the Abu Dhabi ruling family has undertaken a careful strategic programme to centralise political power and social capital within the southern Emirate. The resulting urbanisation of Emirati tribal communities could have prompted a dilution of traditional principles and networks; yet we have seen increased significance of kinship and tribal relations.

Tribal pedigree and legacy continue to hold significant sway in the Emirate of Abu Dhabi where 'among the original tribal population of the UAE the Bani Yas are still the most numerous single tribe'.[5] The Bani Yas is the tribe of which the Abu Dhabi ruling family clan, the al-Nahyans, and the al-Maktoum ruling family of Dubai, form significant sections (or clans). The al-Nahyan is the al-Bu Falah subsection of the Bani Yas,[6] enjoying support from the other subsections due to their leadership in Abu Dhabi. Originating

22

from Liwa and later settling in Buraimi, and more recently Abu Dhabi city, the Bani Yas has been 'one of the most compact and powerful tribes of Trucial Oman; their range is practically co-extensive with the territories of the Shaikh of Abu Dhabi'.[7]

Political Violence Among the UAE Elites

The al-Nahyan family has been at odds with other Emirates' rulers, in particular the Qawasim (Qassimi) families in Sharjah and Ras al-Khaimah,[8] and with tribal rivals from within their own territory and even their own family.

Competition for land has been an ongoing issue for the al-Nahyans. Prominent examples are the Buraimi oasis, Abu Musa, and the Greater and Lesser Tunbs. The al-Nahyan control of Buraimi is especially significant. It represents an emotive and intangible link to the al-Nahyan and Bani Yas, and also enjoys a privileged position in regard to the oil fields of the UAE. Control of the oasis pitted the al-Nahyans against the al-Bu Said Sultan of Muscat as well as the Na'im of Ajman and the Wahhabis of Saudi Arabia.[9]

The al-Nahyans, helped by the British, kept control of Buraimi and the surrounding areas, ensuring geographic integrity and, ultimately, regime authority. Having lived initially in Buraimi and later Al Ain, the founder of the UAE, Zayed bin Sultan al-Nahyan, fostered his charismatic personality, reinforcing the traditional nature of sociopolitical dynamics within the UAE. Clarence Mann stated that 'it is through him [Sheikh Zayed] that Abu Dhabi exerts its influence upon the Bedouin tribes'.[10] While over time there has been an attempt to defer to technocrats, this book will illustrate the renaissance of tribal and kinship relations within Abu Dhabi's executive branch.

The position of the Bani Yas within the UAE's political structure was contested by the Qawasim of Ras al-Khaimah and Sharjah, who had built a substantial maritime empire across the Persian Gulf. An opponent of the British Empire and its enforcement of regional hegemony, the Qawasim's trading monopoly threatened the Bani Yas and the British as they looked to concurrently increase their power and standing in the region, in what is now the UAE's territory. The British, in turn, exploited the threat potential of the Qawasim and, after several raids and subsequent neutering agreements (such as the 1820 General Treaty for the Cessation of Plunder and Piracy by Land and Sea and the 1853 Perpetual Maritime Truce)[11] internal UAE power dynamics firmly swung in favour of Abu Dhabi. Uzi Rabi notes that 'once the power of the Qawasim had been curtailed, that of the Bani Yas—a land power—began to grow correspondingly'.[12]

Al-Nahyan rulers appointed regional representatives across their territory in a tactic aimed at ensuring the continuation of their authority. These representative agents were present at strategic, populated areas such as Dhafrah, Tarif, Jabal al Dhannah, Das Island, Buraimi, and Dalma Island.[13] In the modern day, the ruler of Abu Dhabi maintains official representative offices in the Eastern[14] and Western[15] regions of Abu Dhabi, both of which are staffed by ruling family personnel. It was crucial for Emirati authorities to physically project their leadership and power across society. This form of rule is often referred to as a chiefdom, defined as 'an intermediate political structure between tribe and state, incorporating features of both'.[16]

Because of the numerous threats to the al-Nahyan family, manipulation and fostering of tribal and kinship are crucial for its survival within such a condensed unit of power. Any attempt to disturb power relations (which during the pre-unification UAE were mainly based upon the relationship with other tribes and the British) was the primary and often lethal threat to rulers due to their capacity to restructure those power relations. The weight placed on the family and tribe is the biggest strength and latent threat to the Shaykhs of the UAE.

The al-Nahyan monopoly on power in Abu Dhabi began in the eighteenth century, with the reign of Sheikh Falah providing the foundations for the al-Nahyan legacy. Over the next two hundred years, three rulers died of natural causes while in office, three were deposed by family members (twice by brothers, and once by a son), and eight were murdered—all but one by family members.[17]

The threat posed by family members is noted by Gordon Tullock who states that 'if you look over history, the number of times that a King is known to have been killed by his eldest son is by no means trivial. I frequently say that this is the commonest cause of death of kings'.[18] Likewise, it has been shown that political violence has been a common feature of Emirati politics for generations, and the al-Nahyans are not the only example of inter-family quarrels within the UAE. The last assassination by a fellow family member within the UAE[19] occurred in 1972 when Sheikh Khalid Muhammad of Sharjah was murdered by the ousted Sheikh Saqr who was 'hoping to regain the rulership'.[20] Sheikh Saqr was subsequently exiled, and Sheikh Sultan Muhammad al-Qassimi appointed ruler.[21] Sultan al-Qassimi was later the victim of a coup attempt in 1987 by his own brother, the Sharjah Crown Prince, Sheikh Abdul Aziz Muhammad al-Qassimi.[22]

History demonstrates that threats to Emirati rulers have been more dangerous when originating from fellow ruling family members. Tribal sections were often pragmatic in their support of potential rulers; however, most stayed out of inter-family contests, and instead were more likely to participate in inter-Emirate strife. This was also true for external actors who attempted to exploit tribal factions within the UAE in order to initiate a coup in Abu Dhabi,[23] and to assist the UAE with the potential overthrow of a neighbouring monarch.[24] This period of Emirati history is viewed with scorn by the modern-day authorities and substantial attempts have been made to reconfigure Emirati history and re-write Abu Dhabi's bloody past.[25]

Numerous reports suggest that because of the series of assassinations, the mother of Sheikh Shakhbut bin Sultan al-Nahyan and Sheikh Zayed bin Sultan al-Nahyan, Sheikha Salama bint Butti, demanded her sons pledge an oath 'to refrain from any conspiracy'.[26] It has been noted that this was a factor in the resulting political stability of Abu Dhabi.[27]

Driven by dissatisfaction with Shakhbut bin Sultan al-Nahyan's behaviour and his stiffness against modernisation, the al-Nahyan ruling family[28] lobbied support from the British,[29] and signed a letter on 4 August 1966 that was presented to Glen Balfour-Paul, the acting political agent in Abu Dhabi.[30] Shakhbut bin Sultan al-Nahyan initially rejected the family's call for his resignation, remaining defiant even when his palace was surrounded by troops. A contingent of soldiers entered the palace, escorted him out and put him on a plane to London. Glen Balfour-Paul notes that Sheikha Salama bint Butti was deliberately misinformed of events, and hypothesises that Zayed bin Sultan al-Nahyan was willing to use force to remove Shakhbut bin Sultan al-Nahyan.[31] It is apparent that the history and legacy of previous generations was etched into the mentality of Zayed bin Sultan al-Nahyan and other elite figures within the UAE's leadership when he decided to oust his brother.[32] While the comparison to the modern day UAE may be stark, it is crucial to understand this past in order to understand why some mechanisms are deployed.

Political Opposition

The al-Nahyan rule of Abu Dhabi has carefully managed and exploited traditional principles and values to mediate concerns and qualms. The other Emirates, having been heavily exposed to foreign cultures and peoples from an early period, were more open-minded and thus more accepting in their non-utilisation of tribal and traditional tenants. Therefore, alternate forms of opposition, often organised through formal groupings appeared where concerns and demands could be met. Meanwhile, Abu Dhabi had to contend with influence and subterfuge by competing forces from outside their own neighbourhood; most notably the Wahhabis and Qawasim.

Because of the decline of the pearling industry in Dubai during the middle of the twentieth century, and the perceived dilution of traditional societal morals and identity due to the influx of expatriates and modern education syllabi, political opposition movements emerged within the trading city. The predominant example is the reform movement[33] al-Islah, the UAE branch of the Muslim Brotherhood.[34] Other vehicles of political mobilisation within the Arabian Gulf have rallied around the causes of Pan-Arabism: in the 1970s this included communism (Front for the Liberation of Occupied Eastern Arabia (LOEA) also known as the Popular Front for the Liberation of the Occupied Arabian Gulf (PFLOAG),[35] National Democratic Front for the Liberation of

Oman and the Arabian Gulf (NDFLOAG)), and xenophobia (Dubai National Front).

In the pre-unified Emirates, comparative political organisations were used as extensions of power. A clear example was the reform movement. This was used by Sheikh Mana bin Rashid al-Maktoum in 1929 and 1938, to usurp the British-backed Sheikh Said bin Maktoum.[36] While Mana bin Rashid al-Maktoum partially succeeded in 1929, ruling the Emirate for two days, the British intervened 'with orders from Haworth to cancel Sheikh Mana's appointment'.[37] Later however, in 1938, Said bin Maktoum faced a more serious threat due to his over-indulgence in the appropriation of trading income. Davidson notes that the opposition to Said bin Maktoum became so powerful that they were able to establish a parallel political apparatus including a new majlis.[38]

After several skirmishes, and with assistance from neighbouring Emirates, Said bin Maktoum liquidated the reform movement, and with it, the power of the merchant class.[39] Quietly, however, he amalgamated many of the proposals requested by the reform movement.[40] There were three facets for Said bin Maktoum's success in retaining power: support from the British, emphasis on traditional and tribal ties for leverage,[41] and some of the earliest forms of co-optation, emerging from the initial phases of the UAE's rentier economy.[42]

Regime Security Measures

Threats to the pre-unification UAE were countered by two central strategies: tribal co-optation and external security assistance from the British.

Intermarriage

Marriage between tribes has been a successful and widely utilised tactic within numerous regime security strategies, as the futures of the involved tribes are bound together to vest and increase interest in the other's survival.

One prominent example of the strategic utilisation of marriage bonds is the relationship between the al-Nahyan and the Manasir tribes in Abu Dhabi.[43] The Manasir were very important in Abu Dhabi, especially at the height of the pearl trade, and 'had intermarried with the townsfolk undertaking the responsibility of protecting the town. In return they expected the Shaikh of Abu Dhabi to support them'.[44] Clarence Mann explains, for instance, that Khalifa bin Zayed 'was the most logical choice (for leadership), considering his age and the additional advantage of him being related through his mother to the Manasir tribe'.[45] Therefore, a large degree of the success attributed to Khalifa bin Zayed al-Nahyan originates from his tribal pedigree, and should be seen in context of Sheikh Saqr who failed to forge strong ties with the Manasir and was subsequently assassinated.[46]

Andrea Rugh notes that it was a common and well exploited tactic of the al-Nahyans to foster kinship ties through marriage.[47] The mother of Shakhbut bin Sultan al-Nahyan and Zayed bin Sultan al-Nahyan, Sheikha Salama, was from a prominent commercial family, and several connections can be made with parallel branches of the al-Nahyan ruling family; in particular, the Mohammed bin Khalifa lineage.[48] Sheikh Tahnoon bin Muhammad al-Nahyan, of the Mohammed bin Khalifa line, is the current ruler's representative in the Eastern Region, and based in the tribal heartland of Al Ain, helping to cement al-Nahyan leadership across the Emirate.[49]

Zayed bin Sultan al-Nahyan was noted to have married nine times and fathered at least thirty children, nineteen of whom were male. He was known to have strategically utilised marital agreements to expand his own tribal links, and incorporated women from the tribes of the Bu Shamis, Mishaghin, Bu Smara, Bani Qitab, Manasir, Dhawahir, and the Darmaki. Rugh notes how each marriage, except for Sheikha Fatima al-Ketbi,[50] was largely strategic and political in nature. Each marriage swung the tribal power balance in favour of Zayed bin Sultan[51] and away from other family rivals.

The mother of the Crown Prince of Abu Dhabi, Fatima al-Ketbi, is from the al-Qitab tribe. Descending from Buraimi, they had often disrupted oil explorations, but had traditionally not held much significance beyond this. Due to the power now held by the descendants of Fatima al-Ketbi, there is now a considerable presence of the al-Qitab tribe across the political and military spectrum, and always near the sons of Fatima al-Ketbi. While the al-Nahyan leadership has exploited traditional links for traditional forms of support, they have also fostered a potential threat. As a result, a myriad of new kin-focused ties are emerging to balance and equalise potentially opposing forces within the tribal spectrum.

External British Support

British interest in the security and stability of the UAE, and later in the leadership of the al-Nahyans provided an impetus for the centralisation and prioritisation of regime security around the Abu Dhabi and Dubai elites. The British were predominantly concerned with their commercial supremacy across the Gulf, in particular in securing maritime routes to India, which required an increasing micromanaged approach to the UAE. This led them to manipulate leaders, helping them with resources in a bid to secure British interests within the UAE. The attempt was initially to produce a more egalitarian tribal system, under the authority of London's chosen leaders. In order to ensure the longevity of Britain's regional policy success the British had to, in some cases, intervene directly,[52] and establish permanent representation.[53]

The position of the British was a double-edged sword for the UAE elites. On one hand, in accordance with growing Arab nationalist sentiment, the British Empire was unwanted as its position in the region was seen to have no legitimacy. However, the rulers of the Emirates often relied upon the British for their own survival[54] and thereby weakened their position, setting a historical example of the UAE's insecurity dilemma. A former British military officer, Lieutenant Colonel David Neild, was the commander and founder of both the Sharjah and Ras al-Khaimah defence forces, indicating the necessity of external actors for security assurance. The British were integral at significant points within the UAE's political history (including the 1929 and 1938 coups in Dubai, the usurping of Shakhbut bin Sultan al-Nahyan, and the UAE's ability to hold onto Buraimi/Al Ain in the face of challenges from the Saudis), highlighting how fundamental the British were in maintaining the status quo in favour of the UAE elites.

Unification (1968–1971)

Growing oil reserve discoveries in Abu Dhabi, the looming departure of the Arabian Peninsula's long-term external security guarantor and the progression towards political unity had laid the groundwork for the unification of the UAE. Tribal competition and anxiety, however, proved to be the largest hindrance to the federation's establishment.

The Emirates that would become the UAE identified themselves as separate administrative units, tribally organised around a chief and a ruler, yet the evolving British presence had already started to federalise policy and responsibilities. Two examples of this were the Trucial Oman Scouts and the British Political Resident, who was responsible for establishing the territories of modern-day Bahrain, Qatar and UAE.

Initial steps towards the UAE's unification included the 1952 Trucial States Council[55] and the 18 February 1968 agreement by which Abu Dhabi and Dubai would form a Union covering 'foreign affairs, security, defence, social services, and immigration'.[56] After this agreement, an invitation was sent to the rulers of the other Trucial States and the rulers of Bahrain and Qatar. On 18 February 1968 the rulers of all nine invited states agreed to establish a federation that was to be governed by a supreme council of rulers. This was to be called the Federation of the Arab Emirates.

The short-lived federation collapsed on 21 October 1969. Ibrahim al-Abed claims that part of the reason for the Federation's failure was 'inherent in the charter of the federation itself … its purpose was, in part, to reinforce the respect for each one of them [each emirate] for the independence and sovereignty of the others'.[57] Many insecurities and fallacies were evident in the Emirates' arguments and their perceptions of independence and strength. Most, if not all, were anxious about the role of Abu Dhabi.

The UAE was formed on 2 December 1971, without Qatar, Bahrain, or Ras al-Khaimah, with a provisional constitution that was later made permanent twenty-five years later, in July 1996. The Emirate of Ras al-Khaimah joined a year after the UAE's formation, however vulnerabilities within the federation continue to exist.

Abu Dhabi became the UAE's capital, with federal laws taking precedence over Emirate-level jurisdiction. The UAE is headed by the President and the Vice President (VP), serving five-year terms. They sit below the Supreme Council, composed of the rulers of all seven Emirates, who enact decisions made by the UAE Cabinet.[58] The cabinet is constituted by the Prime Minister, two deputy Prime Ministers, Ministers of the UAE, and General Secretariat[59]— Federal National Council (FNC), and Federal Judiciary Authority. As of May 2021, there are thirty-four cabinet ministers.[60]

Unification Difficulties

During the UAE's formation, Zayed bin Sultan al-Nahyan encountered several substantive problems. These were maintaining the federation's unity, repelling foreign aggression and ensuring security and stability.

Maintaining the Federation's Unity

Zayed bin Sultan al-Nahyan was clearly the leading candidate for leadership within a unified federal state due to his charismatic personality and efficient utilisation of wealth. The Emirate of Dubai was expected to take the lead in the Union, but with Zayed bin Sultan al-Nahyan's unifying presence, he was deemed the paramount leader.

In the pre-oil UAE, the power dynamics and balance of power were somewhat equal. Over time, with more oil wealth, Abu Dhabi centralised its position as the political, economic, and administrative centre of the UAE.[61] Even before the UAE was formed, Abu Dhabi contributed 50 per cent of the budget of the Trucial States Fund in 1967, later increasing to 90 per cent in 1968.[62] Abu Dhabi also makes up 87 per cent of the UAE's territory,[63] lending support to the idea of an Abu Dhabi-centred state. Aqil Kazim highlights this:

> Oil wealth made Abu Dhabi wealthier…this situation provided these small Emirates with a concrete argument for unification. Aside from gaining economic power over the other Emirates, Abu

Dhabi also gained political power in relation to them, as its oil wealth had allowed it to develop its defence and police forces.[64]

There was still a requirement to ensure the agreement of the Emirates rulers to ensure a stable union. Practically this meant the devolution of powers, the representation of each Emirate within national bodies, and the strategic employment of diversified tribal engagement within the UAE's state apparatus. The fundamental challenge for Zayed bin Sultan al-Nahyan was how he would ensure Abu Dhabi's centrality and discourage any inclinations towards independence from the other Emirates.

While Abu Dhabi was the leading actor within the UAE's unification, competition with Dubai and other Emirates over the UAE's constitutional structure severely hampered Zayed bin Sultan al-Nahyan's attempts to ensure the federation's legacy. It is reported that he was close to resigning over his assumed failure to retain the federation's identity.[65] The 1971 federation declaration represented only a temporary agreement. Zayed bin Sultan al-Nahyan had to formalise a constitution that would bind the federation's Emirates and promote Abu Dhabi to a position of leadership.

The UAE's original constitution demanded Zayed bin Sultan al-Nahyan quickly find a way of formalising the long-term unification of the UAE. The first draft of the permanent constitution proposed by Zayed bin Sultan al-Nahyan sought a hard unification where most of the Emirates' powers would be federalised, and the country's President would take on significant powers. To arrest suspicions that Abu Dhabi would become too powerful, Zayed bin Sultan al-Nahyan proposed to empower the FNC[66] and offset Abu Dhabi's perceived dominance. Zayed bin Sultan al-Nahyan assumed he would always succeed in amassing power through the tribes, if necessary, by means of a formal mechanism such as the FNC.[67] His proposal was rejected by Dubai and Ras al-Khaimah, who felt excessive power was being given to Abu Dhabi. To appease some of the other rulers 'he [Zayed] bank-rolled every one of the ruling families—incumbent in their fortresses or modest new palaces—in order for them to maintain their status and respond to ever-increasing demands made on their largesse'.[68] This empowered and elevated the Emirates' rulers within their own domains, and co-opted their position to the leadership of Abu Dhabi.

Following further pressure from the FNC, the rulers of Dubai and Ras al-Khaimah stubbornly resisted overtures to further federalise the UAE. While the smaller and poorer Emirates acknowledged their relative position to Abu Dhabi, the Emirates of Dubai[69] and Ras al-Khaimah stood firm in their conceptions of grandeur and strength and believed they could continue the status quo of relative political equality with Abu Dhabi, while still benefitting from the capital's heightened spending burden.

Initial inter-Emirate competition meant that during the first few years of the UAE's existence, there was a lot of financial waste and duplication of effort. In areas such as immigration and defence, the Emirates were forced to work together, as there was an understanding of the greater combined strength, discovered, if not in regard to external adversaries, then through past competition with each other. Peterson summarises the delegation of powers within the UAE as: 'Areas of sovereignty not specifically assigned to the UAE government fall to the individual amirates [sic], which jealously guard their autonomy. Even when certain powers, such as defence, constitutionally come under the jurisdiction of the federal government, local control persists in practise'.[70]

The delegation of constitutional powers and responsibilities was made clear in articles 116[71] and 122,[72] which, in short, gives control over all matters to the federal level, unless explicitly stated.

Given Abu Dhabi's central role in wealth generation in the UAE, something that has greatly increased over time, the federation has evolved towards Zayed bin Sultan al-Nahyan's original vision of a centrally administered state without much difficulty.

Repelling Foreign Aggression

Aqil Kazim suggests that the British constructed a unique insecurity discourse for Emirati audiences, which securitised the threat of Arab Nationalism, Iran, Oman, and Saudi Arabia to ensure Britain's continued commercial advantage.[73] By manipulating potential threats to the Emirates' rulers, the British could not only solidify the position of their vassal leaders, but also ensure that they united into a federation strong enough to independently repel foreign aggressions. James Onley suggests that the UAE's rulers understood how central the presence of the British was to the continued security and stability of the region and even offered to pay for their continued residence within the GCC.[74]

Kazim's theory of British involvement in threat manipulation can be challenged. On the eve of the United Kingdom's official withdrawal from the Gulf, Iranian troops seized territory claimed by the UAE, and took over the islands of Abu Musa and the Greater and Lesser Tunbs. This event highlighted the vulnerability of the newly formed UAE. Despite this, since Iran's seizure of the UAE's islands, the UAE has not been faced with existential threats.[75] Iran continues to be the UAE's foremost external threat.

The UAE was largely able to secure its geographic integrity,[76] albeit without the seized islands. The presence of the US—replacing the UK as the region's security guarantor—represented a significant factor for the continued security of the Persian Gulf.

Development of the Coercive Apparatus

In 1951, to provide the UAE with an indigenous security capability, the British formed the Trucial Oman Scouts (TOS), initially levied and managed by the British, with its headquarters in Sharjah. Meanwhile, each Emirate continued to possess independent police forces.[77] The TOS were used for an array of tasks that included providing security to rural areas. Upon the looming departure of the British, the TOS were amalgamated into the local police forces (later independent Emirate level brigades), the Ministry of Defence, and in 1971 the Union Defence Forces (UDF).

Following political concerns, the management of the federal military forces was split between Abu Dhabi and Dubai, with the ruler of Dubai being appointed as Minister of Defence. This power-sharing agreement became part of a wider rationale within the federation of the UAE, in an attempt to cater to and appease most tribes, and to avoid formalising the dominance of any single grouping. To ensure Abu Dhabi's legacy and oversight of the military,

Zayed bin Sultan al-Nahyan installed his sons Khalifa bin Zayed al-Nahyan and Sultan al-Nahyan as members of the MOD[78] and the Abu Dhabi Defence Force (ADDF) leadership.[79]

Each Emirate managed the hiring of their independent forces formed of national and foreign personnel.[80] This bolstered the rule of the Emirate's leader in relation to other Emirates as they could develop their forces as they wished. It also allowed the delivery of security and stability and contributed to the repulsion of ideological trends such as the PFLOAG within the UAE. The establishment of the ADDF in 1965 mirrored existing units in Ajman, Dubai, Sharjah, and Ras al-Khaimah, but was a larger and more powerful force than the UDF.

These units were formed to deliver safety and security to the Emirates they were attached to, but they also 'protected the rulers and their families from attempted coups, which more often than not derived from within the ruler's family, as well as threats from their neighbours'.[81] Ali Mohammed Khalifa argues that the seven rulers were hesitant to this process: 'to transfer control over such a force (a centralised and concentrated military) to a higher authority might also mean the transfer, or, at least, the division of loyalty and allegiance of the men involved, something the rulers were reluctant to accept'.[82] It was not until 1976 that the independent forces merged with the UDF into the UAE Armed Forces. Twenty years later, the final independent brigades of Dubai and Sharjah were merged, forming the Central and Northern Commands of the UAE Armed Forces.

Hendrik Van Der Meulen noted that not only did Abu Dhabi fund the development of the UAE's two most important security apparatus, the UAE Armed Forces and the Ministry of Interior, but that the UAE Armed Forces were deliberately constructed heavily in favour of Abu Dhabi. Given Abu Dhabi's control of the military, Zayed bin Sultan al-Nahyan had to very carefully manage the development of capabilities nationally without being seen to overstep his constitutional limitations.[83] Partially because of this lopsided development, the various Armed Forces across the Emirates had to unify as they became less and less relevant: 'Military logic dictated a unity in command and equipment, and for Shaikh Zayid, lack of unity in the armed forces reflected adversely on the unity project as a whole. For this principle, he was willing to renounce his position as President'.[84]

In conclusion, it becomes clear that there was a dual-pronged approach to the delivery of security and stability that would form the template of the UAE's future strategy: to maintain and enforce power.

Post-Unification: Reign of Sheikh Zayed bin Sultan al-Nahyan (1971–2004)

The reign of Zayed bin Sultan al-Nahyan was unprecedented. He was one of the Emirates' longest ever serving monarchs, oversaw the UAE's federation, and secured a stable succession. Much of the success of the modern-day UAE is attributed to him.[85]

Before Zayed bin Sultan al-Nahyan became ruler, Abu Dhabi was desperately poor. His leadership and liberal economic policies encouraged the growth and development of Abu Dhabi and the UAE. Zayed bin Sultan al-Nahyan's reign prioritised the development of infrastructure, building roads[86] and transit hubs, connecting communities, modernising the education syllabi, constructing modern defensive capabilities, leading the development of women's rights and helping to firmly place the UAE on the international scene. Muhammad Abdullah summarises the impact of Zayed bin Sultan al-Nahyan's reign:

> The gigantic growth in oil revenues after 1974 enabled Abu Dhabi, which already provided 90 per cent of the federal budget, to increase her contribution. As a result of which, modernisation has rapidly become a reality in the other Emirates where federal expenditure on roads, schools, houses, clinics, electrification, agriculture, and fisheries has transformed the lives of the people.[87]

The progress of Emirati society delivered by Zayed bin Sultan al-Nahyan prevented the development of any significant threat within the UAE. Andrew Wheatcroft notes that Zayed bin Sultan al-Nahyan faced three predominant challenges to his reign: ensuring a strong union to maintain the UAE's national security, building a strong policy of deterrence, and fostering a strong and positive image of the UAE internationally.[88] Beyond these assertions, Zayed bin Sultan al-Nahyan also faced what Peterson has called structural weaknesses; a rentier economy, a heterogeneous population, an authoritarian governance system, the Iranian threat, and the unequal dispersion of wealth among both citizens and Emirates.[89] Besides, there was yet another threat to Zayed bin Sultan al-Nahyan's reign, as highlighted by Davidson: uncertainty.

In summary, much of the success of the UAE during the unification and development period can be attributed to the guardianship of the Emirates' ruling families and in particular to Zayed bin Sultan al-Nahyan.[90]

Considering Zayed bin Sultan al-Nahyan's crucial role in the stability of the union, the evident question was, what would happen to the stability of the UAE in the period after Zayed bin Sultan al-Nahyan's reign? Given the historical context so far presented, there was apprehension over possible succession issues and the ability of Zayed bin Sultan al-Nahyan's heir to ensure the integrity of the union. Consequently, threats to Zayed bin Sultan al-Nahyan's reign became evident mostly in his last days.

Tribal Completion: The Threat of the Bani Mohammed bin Khalifa

Given Zayed bin Sultan al-Nahyan's skilful management of delicate tribal relations, it was clear that he understood the power held by the tribes of the UAE and the threat they represented. This section illustrates how a parallel branch of the al-Nahyan family, the Bani Mohammed bin Khalifa (BMBK), posed a potential threat to legitimacy, and how Zayed bin Sultan al-Nahyan managed the clan. The BMBK clan were the sons of Zayed bin Sultan al-Nahyan's uncle Khalifa bin Zayed bin Khalifa.[91] They were deemed so powerful that Hendrik Van Der Meulen hypothesises that Zayed bin Sultan al-Nahyan could not have become ruler without their support.[92] This is due to the laws of primogeniture awarding them a stronger claim than Zayed bin Sultan al-Nahyan.

During the early period of Zayed bin Sultan al-Nahyan's reign, there was much uncertainty about how tribal dynamics could either support or weaken his reign. Peterson illustrates this by stating that 'given the weakness of the Bani Sultan (descendants of the father of Shakhbut bin Sultan al-Nahyan and Zayed bin Sultan al-Nahyan), there is considerable speculation that the rival Bani Mohammed might try to wrest away leadership of the al-Nahyan after Zayid's death'.[93] To immediately face the tribal threat posed by the BMBK, Zayed bin Sultan al-Nahyan strategically paired several of his sons with BMBK family members to integrate their bloodline into his lineage.

As a reward for their loyalty, Zayed bin Sultan al-Nahyan kept the BMBK lineage well represented within his leadership; especially as his own immediate family was largely unable to support his position due to death, exile, or, in the case of his sons, excessive youth. This enabled the BMBK to be ever present within Emirati politics. In a bid to offset the potential threat posed by the BMBK, Zayed bin Sultan al-Nahyan installed his eldest son Khalifa bin Zayed al-Nahyan, (twenty at the time) as Crown Prince and Deputy Ruler of Abu Dhabi.[94] This was the first time Zayed bin Sultan al-Nahyan prioritised the promotion of his own line rather than appeasing tribal competitors.

Khalifa bin Zayed al-Nahyan's appointment was an overt move to ensure the security of Zayed bin Sultan al-Nahyan's lineage. As the son of Sheikha Husa bin Muhammad al-Nahyan, a BMBK descendant, the BMBK dynasty could not claim under-representation within Abu Dhabi politics.[95] This was another indication of Zayed bin Sultan al-Nahyan's deep understanding of tribal relations. There were ten marriages between his children and the BMBK line.[96]

Beyond his selective marriage arrangements, Zayed bin Sultan al-Nahyan was acutely aware of parallel al-Nahyan lineages, and of the danger of the BMBK. This resulted in a steady expulsion of BMBK descendants from positions of power in Abu Dhabi throughout the 1970s and 1980s. Zayed bin Sultan al-Nahyan's sons or their allies assumed most newly available positions. This process was finalised on the eve of Zayed bin Sultan al-Nahyan's death, and Khalifa bin Zayed al-Nahyan's ascent, when the last remaining figures of the BMBK lineage, Tahnoon, Surur, and Saeed, were removed from powerful federal positions (the Supreme

Petroleum Council (SPC) and Abu Dhabi Executive Council (ADEC) in particular). Kristian Ulrichsen notes that while Khalifa bin Zayed al-Nahyan neutered family threats upon his political ascension, he 'buttressed his social support by reaching out to influential tribal groups across Emirati society'.[97] This indicates an appreciation on Khalifa bin Zayed al-Nahyan's behalf of the significance in tribal linkages.

Succession Stability

The last remaining challenge for Zayed bin Sultan al-Nahyan was ensuring the peaceful transfer of power to his sons. The growth of revenue from oil and a blossoming relationship with western states, especially with regard to the war on terror, provided the UAE with a stable platform to grow and develop without structural difficulties. Anthony Billingsley states that there are two broad categories of succession practice in the Middle East; 'those that apply primogeniture or a variation of that principle in their succession arrangements and those that, according to Black, are based in traditional Islamic practices whereby "patrimony is divided equally among all sons"'.[98] In Saudi Arabia, with such a vast royal family, primogeniture has traditionally been an easy solution to a difficult problem; the incumbent monarch is fundamentally concerned with the continuation of power to his own blood and kin. This method of succession selection changed in 2017 when Muhammad bin Salman al-Saud bypassed the traditional hierarchy of power to become Crown Prince.

While, for the duration of his tenure, Zayed bin Sultan al-Nahyan attempted to cultivate the leadership of his sons, there were naturally only a few who would stand out as possible successors: Khalifa, Sultan, and Mohammed. Being his three eldest sons, they would seem the obvious choices.

Khalifa bin Zayed al-Nahyan, the eldest, was designated Zayed bin Sultan al-Nahyan's heir from as early as 1966[99] and under Zayed bin Sultan al-Nahyan's reign held the title of Crown Prince of Abu Dhabi, Deputy Prime Minister, Deputy Supreme Commander,[100] Chairman of the Abu Dhabi Executive Council,

Chairman of the Abu Dhabi Investment Authority (ADIA), and head of the SPC. Given his long-term position as deputy to Zayed bin Sultan al-Nahyan, it was generally accepted that Khalifa bin Zayed al-Nahyan would succeed his father. According to Davidson, there were signs suggesting that it would be the third son, Mohammed bin Zayed al-Nahyan who would become President of the UAE.[101]

Before Mohammed bin Zayed al-Nahyan, Sultan bin Zayed al-Nahyan the second son of Zayed bin Sultan al-Nahyan had been highly influential within Abu Dhabi and even commanded the ADDF and later the Union Defence Forces (UDF). Due to 'personal problems',[102] he faded into obscurity and not posing a threat to either his brothers. He died on 18 November 2019.

Mohammed bin Zayed al-Nahyan had also steadily risen through the ranks of the military, progressively gaining their support and loyalty. The ruler of Dubai, Mohammed bin Rashid al-Maktoum, has been the Minister of Defence, but it is Mohammed bin Zayed al-Nahyan who has long held practical control of the UAE Armed Forces. Firstly, as Commander of the Air Force and Air Defence (AFAD) and secondly as Chief of Staff of the UAE Armed Forces. Even from an early age, he possessed his father's charisma and aptitude for leadership. His appointment as Deputy Crown Prince in 2003[103] suggested an intention to streamline his path to leadership.

While Mohammed bin Zayed al-Nahyan had a unique strength that his elders, Khalifa bin Zayed al-Nahyan and Sultan bin Zayed al-Nahyan, could not match, he also, unlike them, was part of a clan referred to as the Bani Fatima that consisted of six full brothers: Muhammad, Hamdan, Hazza, Tahnoon, Mansour, and Abdullah. This meant that naturally, Mohammed bin Zayed al-Nahyan had a stronger base to assume power than either Khalifa or Sultan. Furthermore, and significantly, the Bani Fatima 'have between them gained important control over foreign affairs and parts of the military, domestic intelligence, information services, and other institutions closely connected to national security'.[104]

By imposing themselves within the institutions of power from an early stage, the Bani Fatima quickly became a significant political force in Abu Dhabi. Thus, while Khalifa bin Zayed al-Nahyan's appointment as ruler eventually proved to be smooth, the potential threat of the Bani Fatima provided the rationale for the swiftness in Khalifa bin Zayed al-Nahyan's seizure of power. Davidson notes that it was in fact Khalifa bin Zayed al-Nahyan's position in regard to tribal and kinship alliances that empowered his credentials and ensured his tenure.[105]

Arab Spring (2010)

Zayed bin Sultan al-Nahyan's tenure faced many threats, but the 2010 Arab Spring challenged the UAE in an unprecedented manner. For the Abu Dhabi ruling family, the Arab Spring illustrated how alternative systems of governance threatened incumbent rulers. The downfall of authoritarian leaders, who had previously been seen as untouchable, was a sign that no regime in the region was totally safe. This was magnified when popular uprisings occurred on the Arabian Peninsula. Working through the GCC's Peninsula Shield Force, Saudi Arabia and the UAE deployed military troops and police officers to assist the Bahraini royal family in retaining control. Sectarianism was blamed as the primary motive for the protests,[106] and there was a clear sensitivity around the proximity of developments in Bahrain and the need to issue a collective show of force in response to these protests.

Acknowledging the insecurity dilemma's hypothesis that a regime's most significant threat comes from internal sources, the Arab Spring elevated the danger posed by domestic communities. The UAE's social relations are viewed through two distinct lenses: the hierarchical structure of the native community and the subsequent interaction between the UAE's citizens and its expatriate population. Both communities carry distinctive risks. The Abu Dhabi ruling family addressed them with specific regime security strategies to manipulate them and turn them into pillars of strength. The regime is by its very nature a concentrated faction; in order to survive it must broaden its membership and affiliation by incorporating and integrating a wider network of support; the fewer people have a vested interest in its survival, the more insecure and vulnerable it will become.

Acknowledging the need to drive and maintain new avenues of loyalty and support, the Abu Dhabi ruling family broadcast a key message: the regime consisted of the sons of the Father of the Nation, Zayed bin Sultan al-Nahyan.[107] The message was directed mainly at the native community, but it was also successful in driving the support of the expatriate population. Jean-Jacques Rousseau explains the success of this tactic:

> The earliest of all societies, and the only one, is the family; yet children remain attached to their family only as long as they need him [sic] for their own survival... The family is, then, if you will, the first model of political societies; the leader [sic] is the analogue of the father, while the people are like the children.[108]

Parallel to the development of the UAE's federal identity throughout the reign of Zayed bin Sultan al-Nahyan, the accumulation of wealth and resultant increase in political power held by Abu Dhabi caused considerable disparity across the UAE. This has created tension between the rulers of the seven Emirates, all headed by the families of the most powerful tribes in those regions. The mosaic of identities and affiliations, bolstering traditional legitimacy and authority, converged with a reformed identity of the state. Despite not yet being constitutionally mandated, the Abu Dhabi ruling family secured sovereign control of the state.

The accumulation of capital by the state has positioned the UAE's regime between resources and society, allowing it to manipulate social relations by strategically allocating funds to its population. After exposure to the Arab Spring, 'a real generational gap has emerged between the political elite and the majority of the population'.[109] Notwithstanding the regime's maintenance of power as traditionally relying on subtly appeasing elite figures, the discretion previously enjoyed throughout this process was eroded, exposing how the regime exploited the state.

It is argued that constant generators of support for the regime have been rental income as well as the nurturing of direct interpersonal ties. There are multiple examples of social dynamics being exploited to amplify elite cohesion across the MENA,[110] however, due to the centralised system of traditional governance within the UAE, there is an emphasis on patrimonial relationships. The highly concentrated leadership within the Abu Dhabi ruling family shows a clear preference for blood relations and kinship association, of which the Bani Fatima clan is an evident example. This strategy provides the regime with discreet and flexible protection as it operates within legitimised socio-cultural channels. Alongside the awareness of a wide range of social threats, and their increase during the Arab Spring, the maintenance of elite ties remains the predominant focus.

The Custodian of Abu Dhabi

Following the death of Zayed bin Sultan al-Nahyan on 2 November 2004, his eldest son Khalifa bin Zayed al-Nahyan was appointed President of the UAE.[111] His third-eldest son Mohammed bin Zayed al-Nahyan was appointed as Crown Prince. This partnership has presided over a period of significant growth and stability for the UAE.

Khalifa bin Zayed al-Nahyan led the UAE through the Arab Spring, circumventing major pressures and providing unparalleled stability across the region at the time. The long-term planning and management of the state and its resources allowed the Abu Dhabi ruling family to adapt to the exceptional circumstances. In January 2011 the Abu Dhabi Executive Council (ADEC) announced the hiring of over 6,000 unemployed Emirati nationals[112] in an attempt to ward of discontent and adverse socioeconomic conditions. This is a clear example of the maintenance of power strategy being executed in practice, as the regime was attempting to co-opt a sizeable portion of the native population in reaction to a negative stimulus.

In addition to the UAE's increase in co-optive practices, there was also a surge in repressive measures. The most overt example was the hostility towards organisations that sought to compete with the monarchy; namely the Muslim Brotherhood affiliate, al-Islah. In 2011, in response to a letter signed by 133 people, requesting more representative power, five backers were arrested;[113] they became known as the UAE-5. By the end of 2012, seven members of al-Islah had had their Emirati citizenship revoked[114] and ninety-four members of al-Islah were arrested;[115] many of them had signed the letter the year before. The rapid crackdown on civil society showed the lengths the regime was willing to go to, in order to enforce its power in response to the Arab Spring. The combination of effective maintenance and enforcement of power resulted in a continued period of stability for the UAE. Likewise, Khalifa bin Zayed al-Nahyan was able to stabilise political relations within the Abu Dhabi ruling family. However, on 25 January 2014, Khalifa bin Zayed al-Nahyan suffered a stroke and was largely unable to rule, leading to the unofficial ascension of Mohammed bin Zayed al-Nahyan. To the international audience this was unofficially recognised when Mohammed bin Zayed al-Nahyan travelled to India in 2017 on an official state visit.[116]

The subsequent rule of Mohammed bin Zayed al-Nahyan has been dominated by a security-focused approach. With his military background, Mohammed bin Zayed al-Nahyan has followed a long authoritarian tradition of appointing security elites to significant positions. This supports the regime security strategy pillar of the enforcement of power by means of the military, as a proprietor of quantitatively advanced technology and enforcer of the regime's power, enabling a platform to possess an unequal distribution of power.[117] This has been exploited by the UAE Armed Forces and its ranking leadership who have often found pathways into the political and civilian spheres. Hisham Sharabi expands this hypothesis by arguing that 'the most advanced and functional aspect of the neopatriarchal state is its internal security apparatus, the *mukhabarat*'.[118] Due to the UAE's securitisation of a wide range of issues, the comprehensive security apparatus has enjoyed significant upgrades and investment.

The internal instability illustrated across the MENA provided Mohammed bin Zayed al-Nahyan with a legitimate platform to enhance the power of the military and the wider security apparatus. Having been further legitimised through progressive education initiatives, a new era dominated by technocratic personnel has emerged within the state. The working hypothesis of this book is that key military and technocratic personnel have transitioned into the political elite,[119] thus ensuring a greater control of the state apparatus by the Abu Dhabi ruling family. These actors have been granted elite status through a combination of tribal, kinship and technocratic qualities. Ferran Brichs and Athina Limpridi-Kemou discuss how this strategy is compounded and strengthened by socio-cultural characteristics:

> In the wake of the independence processes, the struggle for state control brought military men to power as well as dominant men from political parties. These men formed very tight-knit, guarded groups. Once in power, these 'clans' ensured their permanence by only allowing other elites to access power if they came from spheres close to their own—the military, political parties, the region, the family, the tribe or the community.[120]

The ascension of Mohammed bin Zayed al-Nahyan to the position of de-facto ruler of Abu Dhabi prompts this investigation to focus on the changes implemented during his rule. By focusing on subsequent changes, this book can effectively highlight how the UAE's regime security strategy has been impacted by the Arab Spring.

Conclusion

The historical context of the Bani Yas legacy helps to highlight not only where threats have surfaced, but also serves as a guide for future generations to circumvent potential pitfalls and continue family rule. The measures implemented by Zayed bin Sultan al-Nahyan—intermarriage, external support, development of coercive apparatus, tribal competition, and succession stability—are reinforced through the region's cultural setting and are complemented by personality traits that bolstered Zayed bin Sultan al-Nahyan's leadership.

The character and aptitude of the ruler has at times also played an integral role in the ability to survive in office. This observation builds upon elite theory as it acknowledges the distinct behavioural characteristics of elites, and in the context of the al-Nahyan family, supports the clear contrast in leadership capability of Zayed bin Sultan al-Nahyan from his predecessor Shakhbut bin Sultan al-Nahyan.

Zayed bin Sultan al-Nahyan clearly understood what was necessary to strengthen and fortify his lineage. He was, however, burdened by his family's bloody past, and this is evident in his attempt to delicately side-line his long-time allies, the BMBK line. As such it is also obvious that Khalifa bin Zayed al-Nahyan prioritises the continuation of al-Nahyan rule over that of a potential BMBK rule. This assessment concurs with traditional tribalism theory such as Ibn Khaldun's *asabiya* which prioritises blood ties.

While modernisation's impact on sociopolitical relations has clearly had a determining effect on threat manifestations, traditional intrinsic dangers to monarchical regimes still endure. Given the historical narrative and context of Emirati history, and subsequent manipulations of personnel and power structures within the UAE, there is clearly an explicit understanding within the mindset of Emirati rulers that the primary threat to regime security is from internal threats; the Arab Spring has magnified this. The same traditional measures employed to insulate the regime from internal threats are still utilised in the modern day. The factors which contributed to the political turbulence caused by the Arab Spring, however, are significantly different to those previously experienced by the UAE's rulers.

Due to the clear clan network Mohammed bin Zayed al-Nahyan commands in contrast to Khalifa bin Zayed al-Nahyan, changes made within his control should be examined in more detail as it is hypothesised that he would make significant modifications in a bid to secure his reign. This will provide the critical point of analysis for examining how the UAE's regime security strategy has been impacted by the Arab Spring.

3

MILITARY CONSOLIDATION

This chapter addresses the military power dimension of the state, which is defined as 'the control of the means of violence'.[1] Rupert Smith advances this definition, which helps to aggregate its application and highlight the dual identity of 'both the physical means of destruction—the bullet, the bayonet—and the body that applies it'.[2] Underlining the differing aspects of military power, the UAE's regime security strategy has optimised multiple coercive elements to strengthen its outlook and control of society. Due to the primary threat a military could pose against a regime, it remains critical that this apparatus is carefully managed so that it is capable of defending the regime while also not being so powerful that it could replace it. Therefore, the strategy to enhance the regime's control of the UAE Armed Forces and its capabilities will be explored to show how this has furthered the UAE's regime security strategy.

The UAE Armed Forces exhibit traits of both a 'tribally dependent monarchy' and a 'dual military', however, as it has developed, there are also examples of 'autocratic-officer politicians' emerging.[3] The self-reinforcing cycle of military-led modernisation empowering the organisation's leadership—who thus promote greater investment and significance in the organisation—signifies how and why the UAE Armed Forces and its personnel have recently grown in stature and significance within the UAE.

Information pertaining to today's UAE Armed Forces is largely limited to limited public interest reports and commercial analysis. In the academic sphere, Victor Gervais,[4] Anthony Cordesman,[5] Zoltan Barany,[6] David Roberts,[7] Hussein Ibish,[8] Athol Yates,[9] and the International Institute for Strategic Studies' (IISS) annual Military Balance[10] monographs are the most significant sources of accurate analyses of the UAE military. It is however in the 2011 PhD thesis of Victor Gervais that an initial analysis of the UAE Armed Forces' development can be found.

Gervais' abridged interpretation of the UAE Armed Forces' chain of command overlooks several entities and over-emphasises others. Missing from his analysis are the Special Forces (SF), Presidential Guard (PG) (or, at the time of Victor Gervais' writing, the Emiri Guard), Critical Infrastructure and Coastal Protection Authority (CICPA), Joint Aviation Command (JAC), and the National Electronic Security Authority (NESA)—renamed the Signals Intelligence Agency (SIA) at an undisclosed time—who manage all the UAE's electronic forms of communications, including the military's. Therefore, through Figure 3, this book proposes

Fig. 2: Author's Translation of Victor Gervais' Interpretation of UAE Armed Forces Structure[11]

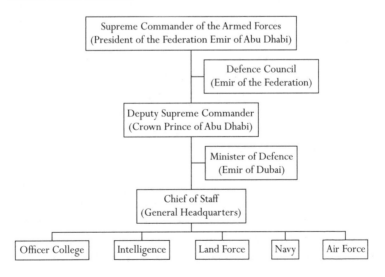

Fig. 3: Military Hierarchy

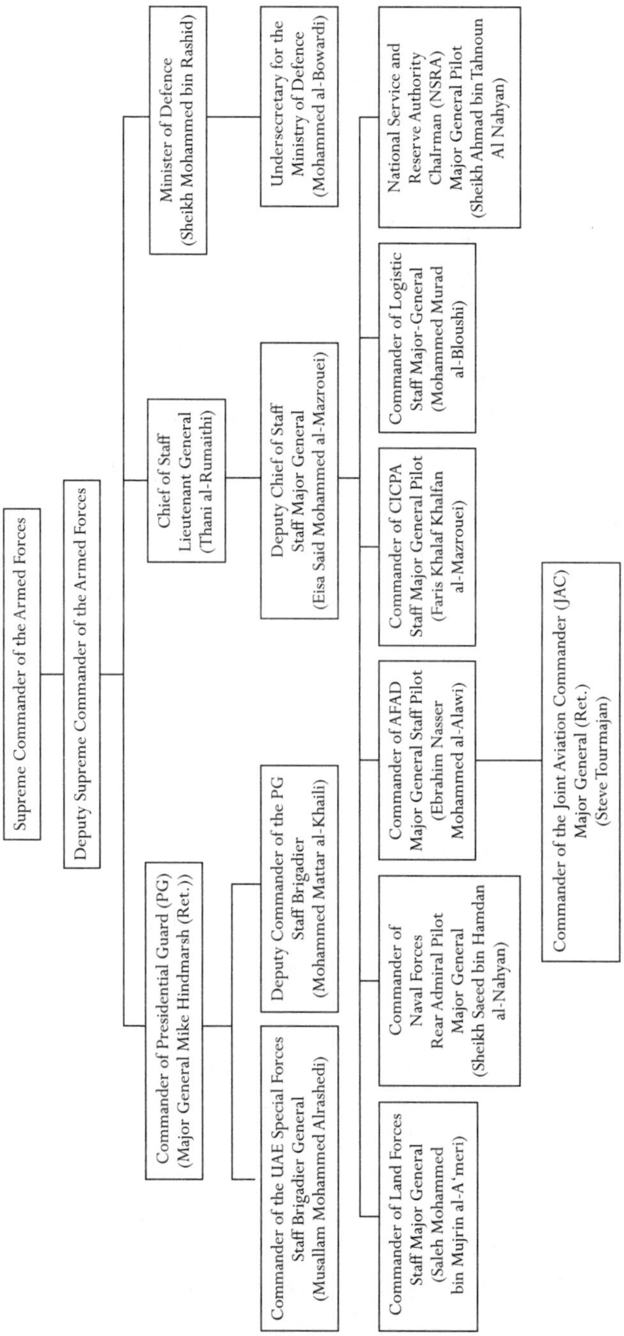

- Supreme Commander of the Armed Forces
- Deputy Supreme Commander of the Armed Forces

- Minister of Defence (Sheikh Mohammed bin Rashid)
- Undersecretary for the Ministry of Defence (Mohammed al-Bowardi)
- National Service and Reserve Authority Chairman (NSRA) Major General Pilot (Sheikh Ahmad bin Tahnoun Al Nahyan)

- Chief of Staff Lieutenant General (Thani al-Rumaithi)
- Deputy Chief of Staff Staff Major General (Eisa Said Mohammed al-Mazrouei)
- Commander of Logistic Staff Major-General (Mohammed Murad al-Bloushi)
- Commander of CICPA Staff Major General Pilot (Faris Khalaf Khalfan al-Mazrouei)

- Commander of Presidential Guard (PG) (Major General Mike Hindmarsh (Ret.))
- Deputy Commander of the PG Staff Brigadier (Mohammed Mattar al-Khaili)
- Commander of AFAD Major General Staff Pilot (Ebrahim Nasser Mohammed al-Alawi)
- Commander of the Joint Aviation Commander (JAC) Major General (Ret.) (Steve Tourmajan)

- Commander of the UAE Special Forces Staff Brigadier General (Musallam Mohammed Alrashedi)
- Commander of Naval Forces Rear Admiral Pilot Major General (Sheikh Saeed bin Hamdan al-Nahyan)

- Commander of Land Forces Staff Major General (Saleh Mohammed bin Mujrin al-A'meri) a more accurate and detailed structure that illustrates the PG as a parallel military vehicle whose principal goal and concern is the protection of the Abu Dhabi ruling family.

The resurgence of the UAE MOD has been largely underplayed within scholarship, with scholars such as Victor Gervais distracted by the ceremonial title of the Minister of Defence for the ruler of Dubai.[12] The common fixation on the symbolic executive leadership of the MOD has caused scholars to overlook the influence and power of the practical elite figures within the MOD. The UAE MOD's return to significance highlights several strategic questions in the post-Arab Spring era: Why has a civilian defence organisation re-appeared after the Arab Spring? Does it have a practical use or is its role designed to limit that of the military? Who are the personnel drafted into the organisation and how much power do they have?

While theoretically thought-provoking, the return to prominence of the UAE's civilian MOD provides the means to reward some elite figures, side-line potential threats, and diversify and proliferate analytical and strategic capabilities. The manifestation of the UAE MOD in Abu Dhabi, within the same physical location as the UAE Armed Forces General Headquarters (GHQ), serves as a signal and declaration by the UAE authorities to reshape the institutional power structure and dynamics of the state's Armed Forces. This reflects an intention to increase competition among the multiple components of the coercive apparatus and thus stem any potential kinetic threat emerging from a power base beyond the direct control of the political elites.[13]

The manufactured competition among the strategic institutions of the UAE Armed Forces has accelerated in the aftermath of the Arab Spring and serves as a key illustration of one aspect of Risa Brooks' interpretation of the maintenance of power.[14] Other strategies postulated by Risa Brooks include the courting of military elites, increased non-military support, and development of extensive counter-intelligence capabilities. These approaches are henceforth analysed to assess how, in response to the Arab Spring, the UAE's regime security strategy has prioritised the careful management of personnel, resources, capabilities, and wider societal support, with the aim of enhancing the military's ability to defend the regime.

Courting of Military Elites

A common strategy employed in regime security is the enhanced courting of elite military figures. Multi-sectarian societies such as Iraq, Jordan, and Syria stand as prominent examples of confessional, and often minority, ownership of the state's security portfolio. Risa Brooks summarises this much-applied strategy through the lens of heightened effectiveness. 'Appointing individuals from the same religious, tribal, ethnic or regional group to key military positions is one of the most persuasive and effective ways by which political leaders secure the support of their armed forces'.[15]

In the context of the UAE, the strategy to court military elites is firmly rooted within the intra-federal and intra-tribal dynamics of the state. Primarily due to the power generated through the concentration of natural resources in the southernmost Emirate, Abu Dhabi has been able to permanently fix the development of the UAE Armed Forces to the strength and stability of the Bani Yas tribe. This has ensured the physical concentration and demographic imbalance of the UAE Armed Forces is tilted in favour of Abu Dhabi's strategic outlook over others from within the federation.[16]

In image and practice, Abu Dhabi is central to the capabilities of the UAE Armed Forces as it hosts the state's Armed Forces GHQ, National Security Council (NSC), and main air, land, and naval bases, ensuring that any significant development can only occur from Abu Dhabi and with the political authorisation from the PREs therein. The resurgence of the MOD, with its primary presence rehoused within the GHQ main building, further distinguishes how, even though the ruler of Dubai is the MOD, Abu Dhabi remains integral to the state's warfare capabilities.

What this means in practice is that, while the UAE Armed Forces are estimated to have around 63,000 active service personnel,[17] at any given time most of these persons are engaged in exercises and administrative duty in Abu Dhabi, further reinforcing the fixed position of Abu Dhabi within the state. The unified identity demon-

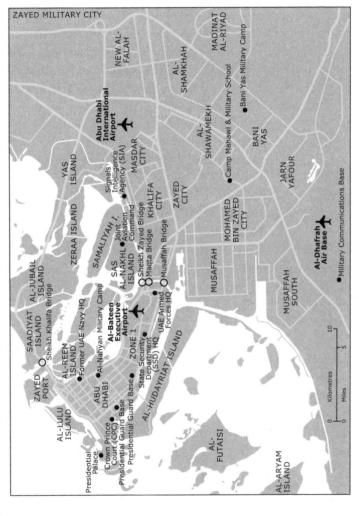

Fig. 4: Map of Abu Dhabi Island Showing Critical Infrastructure, Military Presence, and Political Entities

Fig. 5: Map of UAE Military Installations[18]

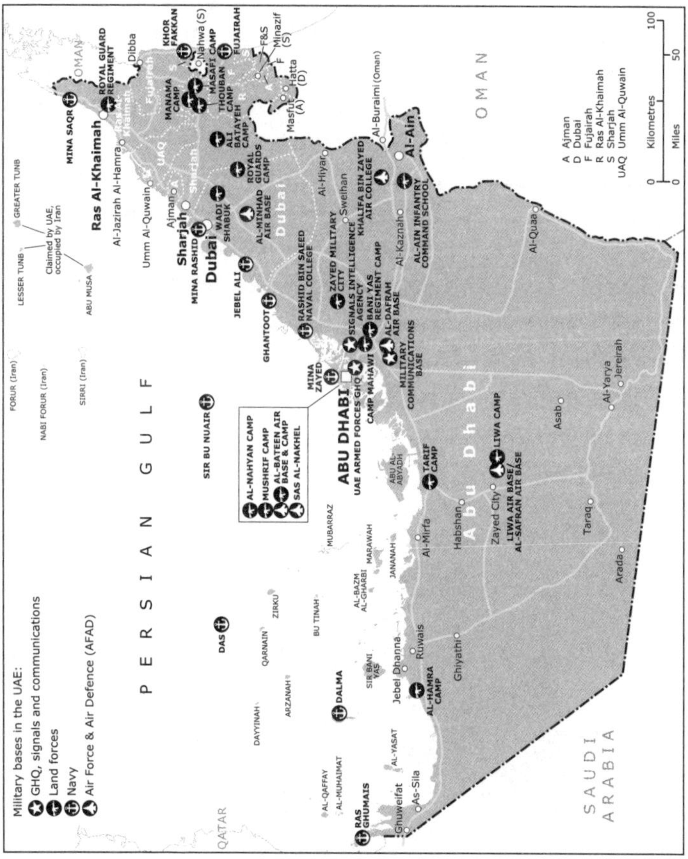

Military bases in the UAE:
- GHQ, signals and communications
- Land forces
- Navy
- Air Force & Air Defence (AFAD)

PERSIAN GULF

QATAR

OMAN

SAUDI ARABIA

ABU DHABI
Abu Dhabi

Dubai

Sharjah

Ras Al-Khaimah

Al-Ain

FUJAIRAH

Umm Al-Quwain

Ajman

LESSER TUNB   GREATER TUNB
Claimed by UAE, occupied by Iran
FORUR (Iran)
NABI FORUR (Iran)
SIRRI (Iran)
ABU MUSA

MINA SAQR
ROYAL GUARD REGIMENT
KHOR FAKKAN
MANAMA CAMP
MASAFI CAMP
THOUBAN CAMP
Dibba
Nahwa (S)
F&S
Minazif (S)
Masfut (A) (D)
ALI BATAYEH CAMP
Al-Jazirah Al-Hamra
MINA RASHID
WADI SHABUK
ROYAL GUARDS CAMP
Al-Hiyar
Al-Minhad AIR BASE
Swelhan
AL-AIN INFANTRY COMMAND SCHOOL
Al-Kaznah
Al-Buraimi (Oman)
SIGNALS INTELLIGENCE AGENCY
ZAYED MILITARY CITY
KHALIFA BIN ZAYED AIR COLLEGE
BANI YAS REGIMENT CAMP
AL-DAFRAM
JEBEL ALI
GHANTOOT
RASHID BIN SAEED NAVAL COLLEGE
MILITARY AIR BASE
MINA ZAYED
UAE ARMED FORCES GHQ
CAMP MAHAWI
MILITARY COMMUNICATIONS BASE

AL-NAHYAN CAMP
MUSHRIF CAMP
AL-BATEEN AIR BASE & CAMP
SAS AL-NAKHEL

DAS

SIR BU NUAIR

DATYINAH
ARZANAH
QARNAIN
ZIRKU
BU TINAH
MUBARRAZ
AL-BAZM AL-GHARBI
MARAWAH
JANANAH
ABU ABYADH
MINA ZAYED
TARIF CAMP
LIWA CAMP
Al-Mirfa
Al-Yarya
Jereirah
Al-Quab

DALMA
SIR BANI YAS
AL-HAMRA CAMP
Jebel Dhanna
Ruwais
Ghiyathi
Habshan
Zayed City
LIWA AIR BASE/AL-SAFRAN AIR BASE
Asab
Taraq
Arada

AL-QAFFAY
AL-MUHAIMAT
AL-YASAT
RAS GHUMAIS
Ghuweifat
As-Sila

A   Ajman
D   Dubai
F   Fujairah
R   Ras Al-Khaimah
S   Sharjah
UAQ Umm Al-Quwain

0   50   100
Kilometres
0   50
Miles

strated by the UAE Armed Forces' position suggests a cohesive organisation (*esprit de corps*) that is capable of meeting, and willing to meet, the demands requested upon it by the state's leadership.

Due to the lack of publicly available information on the social stratification of UAE Armed Forces personnel, information is limited to official statements and reports of military elite figures at events and Emirati military casualties from the war in Yemen.[19] The latter has revealed a trend whereby Emiratis from the poorer and northern Emirates were more likely to be non-commissioned officers (NCOs), and thereby sent to front line action in Yemen.[20]

On the other hand, Emirati military elites often exhibit clear traits of tribal and/or kinship affiliation to senior figures within the al-Nahyan ruling family. This is further strengthened by the presence of al-Nahyan figures within the military hierarchy, with Khalifa bin Zayed al-Nahyan, Mohammed bin Zayed al-Nahyan and formerly Sultan bin Zayed al-Nahyan[21] all holding high-class titles within the Armed Forces.[22]

Fig. 6: Emirati Casualties by Emirate in Yemen Conflict (01 June 2015– 11 November 2017)[23]

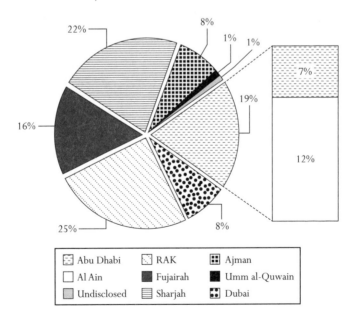

Going beyond the immediate leadership, there are several ruling family members who also wield considerable influence within the UAE Armed Forces. The two most senior serving ruling family members are Major General Pilot Sheikh Ahmed bin Tahnoon al-Nahyan, Chairman of the National Service and Reserve Authority (NSRA)[24] and Major General Sheikh Saeed bin Hamdan al-Nahyan, Commander of the UAE Naval Forces.[25] The appointment of ruling family members to the position of branch commander after the Arab Spring can only extend the notion that a significant component to the UAE's post-Arab Spring regime security strategy is to prioritise the retention of loyalty from the military elites, and it creates 'a constituency with a vested interest in the status quo'.[26] This strategy also has the benefit for the regime of maintaining a live observation of the military's morale and sentiment, thus increasing the chances of foreseeing future issues and challenges to the current political condition.[27]

Assessing the role of tribal affiliation within the UAE Armed Forces and drawing on US State Department intelligence, Hendrik Van Der Meulen notes that:

> the Abu Dhabi ruling family has the command of the Armed Forces firmly in its grip, entrusting the key commands only to members of other Bani Yas clans and its Dahhiri allies ... all key military positions of command of authority under these three Abu Dhabi ruling family members (Sheikh Zayed bin Sultan, Sheikh Khalifa bin Zayed, and Sheikh Muhammad bin Zayed) are held by members of only the Bani Yas and Dhawahir tribes.[28]

Victor Gervais underpins Hendrik Van Der Meulen's analysis, highlighting the fact that the appointment of Vice-Admiral Ahmed Muhammad al-Sabab al-Tenaiji as Chief of UAE Naval Forces in 2007 represented the first appointment of a non-Bani Yas member to serve as commander of the UAE Navy.[29] This trend has been observed within other service branches of the UAE Armed Forces, whereby Bani Yas members have traditionally controlled the Air Force & Air Defence (AFAD)[30] and Land Forces; however, in recent years, members of other tribes have been allowed to infiltrate the highest echelons of authority within the UAE Armed Forces.

While the specialisation of assets and personnel within the AFAD and Navy may explain a possible recalibration of values away from nepotism and towards professionalism,[31] it is unlikely that this would extend to the Land Forces. As the largest branch within the Emirati military, the UAE Land Forces will continue to be led by Bani Yas tribal members and their allies, especially as the Abu Dhabi Emirate is the largest in geographic size and population and is the closest to the most significant land-based threat, Saudi Arabia.[32]

The current commander of the UAE Land Forces is Staff Major General Saleh Muhammad bin Mujrin al-Ameri,[33] a descendant of the *Awamir* section of the Bani Yas, a tribal branch that, as Meulen notes, constitutes 'one of the strongest traditional pillars of support for the Bani Yas tribe in Abu Dhabi'.[34] Other leading figures from the Land Forces include the current Chief of Staff, Lieutenant General Hamad Mohammed Thani al-Rumaithi (*Rumaithat* section of the Bani Yas),[35] who previously served as Deputy Chief of Staff under Mohammed bin Zayed al-Nahyan and as Director of Military Intelligence.

In the newly reformed Ministry of Defence there is Major General Dr. Khalifa al-Rumaithi[36] (brother of the Chief of Staff), who had previously served as Chief of Logistics—while, elsewhere, Major General Muhammad Khalfan al-Rumaithi is the Commander in Chief of Abu Dhabi Police, Member of the Abu Dhabi Executive Council,[37] and Chairman of the National Crisis and Emergency Management Authority (NCEMA). These cases, in combination with other given examples, show the power, influence, and trust placed in the Rumaithat section by the al-Nahyan ruling family.

Other tribes such as the Zaab, Sudan (Suwaidi), al-Bu Muhair (Muhairi), and the Mazari (Mazrouei) are heavily represented across the UAE Armed Forces, and further add weight to the notion that there is a deliberate strategy by the Mohammed bin Zayed al-Nahyan-led al-Nahyan ruling family to court the military elites.

Another observation from the courting of military elites is the close relationship between many of the military elites and Mohammed bin Zayed al-Nahyan, specifically that from when he was Head of the Air Force and later Chief of Staff. While many of those who were in constant professional proximity to Mohammed bin Zayed al-Nahyan have subsequently gone on to leadership positions within the military, many have now been redirected to civilian positions, often with heightened importance and significance.[38] Therefore, the conclusion is that the rule of Mohammed bin Zayed al-Nahyan is evidence of a growing nexus between the Abu Dhabi regime and the military, whereby each one's survival will rest upon the others.

While tribal affiliation had been a determining principle in the promotion and selection of military elites, additional factors such as kinship affiliation and technocracy started to influence military elite membership as early as 2005. The development and modernisation of the UAE Armed Forces during the early twenty-first century suggest that a drive towards professionalism was instigated by the country's leadership, thus amplifying the value of technocracy.

This theory is linked to the development of technology, as the value of technical and logistic units is rising alongside their kinetic counterparts. Where offensive units were able to muster even the most fundamental capability rapidly—and hence were traditionally the primary defensive capability—due to evolving threat developments and the forms in which these threats can manifest, the wider coercive apparatus is equalising its significance alongside their kinetic counterparts. This would explain the professionalism drive in the UAE (and other comparable countries).

As the direct bonds of kinship are moving away from Mohammed bin Zayed al-Nahyan's military tenure, there are novel relationship drivers emerging, whereby a combination of tribal and technocratic values is driving officer succession. The struggle between these two motivations has caused significant tension within the management of the grander military institution; however, due to a wider and more entrenched support base, personnel with a powerful tribal background are still more often advancing to the upper echelons of the UAE military hierarchy.

While the Arab Spring has warranted the development of Mohammed bin Zayed al-Nahyan's military professionalism drive with the aim of providing a capable military force to defend the regime, it has also reinforced the requirement for an enhanced patrimonial selection criterion. A dual structure is increasingly emerging within the UAE Armed Forces; operationally effective entities are being managed by personnel with intimate links to Mohammed bin Zayed al-Nahyan, and those deemed less of an immediate threat are being led by technocrats.

Increase in Non-Military Support

Since the start of the Arab Spring the UAE Armed Forces have significantly grown in prominence; both literally and figuratively. The increasing application of military force, immense escalation in defence spending, and wider civil-military engagement across the UAE, have successfully strengthened the role of the UAE Armed Forces within the post-Arab Spring UAE.

The UAE has recently been referred to as 'little Sparta', a term coined by former US Defence Secretary General James Mattis,[39] due to the state's focus and proficiency in military endeavours. This development can be traced back to the 11 September 2001, terrorist attacks. Since that time 'the UAE has arguably become Washington's closest Gulf ally, with extensive military and intelligence cooperation, and deep economic ties as the largest U.S. export market in the Middle East'.[40]

Exploiting the renewed focus, the UAE became the regional vanguard in overseas military operations, as well as being the first Arab state to deploy combat troops to Afghanistan to join the International Security Assistance Force (ISAF) in 2003,[41] whilst also sending troops to Albania, Eritrea, Iraq, Kuwait, Lebanon, Libya, Mali, Pakistan, Syria, Somalia, and Yemen.[42] The UAE has also initiated the construction of two military bases, in Eritrea and Somaliland[43] as well as additional reported sites in Yemen and its islands, and is also offering direct military cooperation to several countries including Egypt, Somalia,[44] and the Seychelles,[45] having been able to forge greater military relationships across the MENA region.

Regarding the strengthening of the UAE's military engagement with Western powers there is a trend towards more frequent joint operations and training exercises with Australia, France, Italy, South Korea, UK, and the United States. France has formalised its strong relations with the UAE by establishing a naval base in Abu Dhabi,[46] and several other states utilise the many military and logistical bases of the UAE for overseas operations. The UAE's position within the GCC is of heightened significance to the West. This is shown by the deployment of cutting-edge technology to Abu Dhabi instead of other regional states. Washington has a forward operating base (FOB) in every GCC state, but Al Dhafra Air Base in Abu Dhabi 'is the only overseas airbase to host the United States "fifth-generation" F-22 Raptor stealth fighter jet'.[47] Through enhanced military engagements and formal cooperation within the UAE, foreign partners have directly enhanced the image and capability of the UAE Armed Forces.

Under the stewardship of Mohammed bin Zayed al-Nahyan, the UAE has increased its overseas military operations at rapid pace. However, in doing so, it has faced two main challenges: dealing with personnel loss and sustaining a positive image through sacrifice.[48] The UAE's foray into Yemen is a strong example of these challenges, especially as the country's incursions into Afghanistan, Iraq, Libya, and Mali are not covered as broadly or undertaken with the same ferocity.

Following the death of over fifty soldiers from one missile attack in 2015,[49] the UAE initiated an annual Martyrs' Day commemoration to honour fallen soldiers.[50] Anticipating casualties from overseas operations, the UAE Armed Forces would have to appropriately manage how the combatants would be remembered; an especially poignant point within the context of a small Emirati population.

The result of the implementation by the government of this cultural mourning trend includes elite figure visits to martyrs' homes,[51] the construction of and visits to Martyr Monument (*Wahat al Karama*),[52] and subsequent release of songs,[53] publishing of poems,[54] and social media campaigns[55] to generate group feeling and sentiment towards the deceased[56] and the mission they embarked on. Furthermore, the office of the 'Martyr's Family Affairs' was established within the Abu Dhabi Crown Prince's Court, and Sheikh Khalifa Bin Tahnoon Bin Mohammad al-Nahyan (of the BMBK branch) was appointed as director.[57] The domestic tension caused by the political sensitivity of martyrs within Emirati society was reported in GSN when due to a combination of a high death toll and a concentration of casualties coming from the northern and poorer Emirates; 'a brother of RAK Emir Sheikh Saud Bin Saqr was held for a night in Abu Dhabi following what was described as "public dissent" over Yemen'.[58]

Overseas engagement has complicated the task of enhancing the UAE Armed Forces' image due to the high societal cost of Emirati casualties. It has therefore been crucial to resist internal pressures to ease external operations, thus ensuring the continued development of military capabilities. This is based on the assumption that only a capable and united military force will be able to ensure the security of the regime and to act as a key pillar of the UAE's regime security strategy. The requirement for an efficient military has directed the continued investment and prioritising of the UAE Armed Forces and the ecosystem that supports it, thus not only ensuring the institution's sustained capability but also empowering it to present itself as a vehicle of modernisation within the UAE. This has resulted in a vibrant environment of interlocking and supporting entities in both the public and private sectors.

Driving the development of the UAE Armed Forces are consistently high levels of military spending. According to the Stockholm International Peace Research Institute (SIPRI) the UAE's military spending has significantly increased over the last twenty years, while military spending as a percentage of national GDP has also remained high.[59] From 1997–2014, the UAE's actual military spending has quintupled, while spending as a percentage of GDP has slightly decreased. Both values, however, increased following the Arab Spring, and as a result illustrate the importance of the UAE Armed Forces to the UAE's regime security strategy.[60]

The UAE has not only quantitatively increased its defence purchases, but also qualitatively. During the period of increased defence spending, the UAE has imported some of the world's most advanced weaponry, including the F-16 Block-60 (which was at the time of purchase, more advanced than what the US Air Force possessed), Terminal High Altitude Aerial Defence (THAAD), Falcon-

Fig. 7: UAE Military Spending in Real Terms and as % of GDP (produced by author)[61]

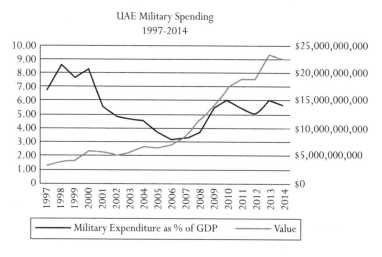

UAE Military Spending
1997-2014

Military Expenditure as % of GDP   Value

eye satellite, and the Predator UAV, and a consistent focus on command, control, communications, computers, Intelligence, Surveillance, and Reconnaissance (C4ISR)[62] showing a determination by the UAE to advance its qualitative edge. This is further illustrated by the Trump administration's approval of a $23bn package which includes 50 F-35A and 18 MQ-9B UAVs: both platforms are at the cutting edge of technological advances and fiercely restricted for export.[63] By maintaining an elevated defence spending level, the Armed Forces receive perceived benefits and 'symbolic rewards'[64] which in turn preserve loyalty and prestige in the strategically important mechanism within the UAE's regime security strategy.

Foreseeing the impending uptick in military spending, the UAE executed an offset policy in 1992 in a bid to augment future defence spending. Since its creation, the Tawazun Economic Council (TEC) (formerly known as the Offset Programme Bureau (OPB)) has successfully 'created over 70 projects in various economic and industrial sectors with a total investment over AED 10bn'.[65] Furthermore, Matar al-Romaithi claims successfully implemented offset projects between 2010 and 2014 created 1,010 jobs, generated US$1.04bn in sales, and encouraged US$1.3bn in investment to the UAE.[66]

The tangible successes of the UAE's offset programme within the defence sector include the Advanced Military Maintenance Repair and Overhaul Centre (AMMROC), Tawazun Dynamics, Etihad Ship Building (ESB), Tawazun Precision Industries (TPI), Abu Dhabi Ship Building (ADSB), and Al Taif, while other commercial and non-defence sector related programmes include Dolphin Gas, Asmak Fish Farm,[67] and the Al Raha Beach Resort in Abu Dhabi.

Further complicating analysis of the UAE's defence spending is the lack of clarity on the state's outsourcing of military capabilities. While arms sales are monitored by governments, non-government organisations (NGOs), and peace activists, the recruitment of foreign personnel for an array of roles within the UAE Armed Forces is not as stringently monitored or recorded. While foreign personnel were previously hired directly by the UAE Armed Forces, a series of legal and contractual mechanisms has now diverted this process through third parties and state-owned entities. While it is alleged that the UAE has hired a contingent of Colombian soldiers to support the UAE's PG,[68] through the online behaviour or several commercial entities, it is clear that many of them, predominantly technical service entities, contract foreign personnel to assist the UAE military.[69] While this provides an enhanced short-term capability for the UAE Armed Forces, unless there is a wider enhancement of the UAE workforce, there will be a reliance on foreign service personnel for future UAE operations.

While there have been obvious industrial and commercial results, military purchase by the UAE Armed Forces has also acted as a means for the development of Emirati society, primarily as an initiator for education, research, and innovation. This has seen heightened engagement between the UAE military, local industry, and local and foreign educational institutions. Masdar University,[70] Khalifa University,[71] Higher Colleges of Technology (HCT), UAE University (UAEU), Abu Dhabi University (ADU), and Zayed University (ZU) are the leading Emirati institutions through which the development of human capital and technology is channelled.

This has directly contributed to the strengthening of Emirati society through the enhancement of technological and engineering capabilities.

As the UAE Armed Forces develops and modernises, so the skills required to succeed evolve. As a result, a supplementary support network and infrastructure that advances in-line with the modernisation of the Armed Forces is required. Therefore, the UAE Armed Forces will continue to exploit and support a society-wide infrastructure that can augment their capabilities and provide a support network that enhances the image of the Armed Forces within the civilian sector.

Development of Extensive Counter-Intelligence (CI) Capabilities

The leading military organisation that provides a CI capability is the UAE Presidential Guard (PG). Like other states within the Middle East, the PG is best described as a praetorian guard in the sense that it adheres to a classical interpretation of the term,[72] or can be seen as a dual (or parallel) military unit whose sole modus operandi is directed inwards, and whose main aim is to safeguard the security of the regime in Abu Dhabi.

The PG's Headquarters are separate from UAE Armed Forces GHQ, and it is additionally the only military base (that is not a branch headquarters) that is situated on Abu Dhabi Island. This is therefore a deliberate physical statement to signify informal intent as to who bears the responsibility of acting as the regime's last line of defence; it clearly acts as a counterweight to conventional forces. PG units are stationed in all of the seven Emirates and therefore illustrate how the praetorian role of the PG is exercised across the UAE's federal landscape.

On the eve of the Arab Spring in 2010, the Emiri Guard was reconfigured as the PG and was designed to mirror the amphibious capabilities of the US Marines and the British Royal Marines. Overseeing its development was the former Commander of Australian Special Forces, Major General Mike Hindmarsh (Retired).[73] While employing a high-level foreigner to manage one of the most sensitive units within the Armed Forces may signal the intention to improve a significant and specialised capability unit, it also highlights how the ultimate guarantee of regime security in the UAE falls to expatriates and not Emirati personnel. This hypothesis would also allow security decisions to be firmly controlled by the political elites. Ibish takes this further by saying that 'the UAE has sought to address its military manpower shortfall by using private security firms and mercenaries'.[74] While a significant number of expatriates, and predominantly Western personnel, were incorporated into the UAE Armed Forces, as of 2014, a reversal of this trend had already started to occur.[75]

Dual military units such as the PG exist to 'counterbalance and watch over the professional armed forces'.[76] While the PG, or its predecessor the Emiri Guard, had existed for several decades, the Emirates of Dubai, Ras al-Khaimah, and Sharjah had each maintained their own independent military brigades in an attempt to operate a constant defensive capability against what was previously a more fractured federation. The dissolution of these Emirate-level Brigades has seen the UAE grow stronger, with the PG evolving away from solely protecting the al-Nahyan ruling family, towards becoming a more specialised entity. This shift has resulted in its deployment to several combat zones—such as Afghanistan and Yemen—to develop expertise and capabilities.

The accelerated development of the PG highlights the strategic intention to rapidly develop a significant capability, especially in contrast to regular branches. The aim is to balance conventional forces and prevent a physical threat from emerging from within the UAE Armed Forces. Due to the critical mission of the PG, an aggressive modernisation policy has been undertaken, which has seen a relatively high budget for greater specialisation, as well as an intensive training programme and elevated exposure to combat, to prepare the PG for emerging threats such as those born out of the Arab Spring across the MENA.

The PG's training has taken place with several foreign states, however, the 2014 US$150 million training deal with the US Marine Corps[77] serves as the most prominent indication of the type of capability being pursued by the Emirati authorities. While there is a multi-branch dimension to the PG, it is predominantly a land-focused branch that has increasingly specialised in counter-insurgency and urban warfare; a sign of how the PG could be used domestically.

While conventional branches of the Emirati military perform at a consistent operational tempo, the PG has a higher drive, prompted by its ideological and professional foundation towards the protection of the Abu Dhabi political authority. The PG has tri-service capabilities; however, it also works alongside its conventional colleagues. A key example is the allocation and management of rotary wing aircraft within the UAE Armed Forces; JAC manages the UAE Armed Forces rotary-wing fleet, however the PG has its own fleet of rotary-wing aircraft and is therefore able to sustain its own operations without wider UAE Armed Forces assistance. This is further supported by the fact that the PG's internal communications run separately to the rest of the Armed Forces; a fact that is extremely significant given the UAE's transition towards C4ISR[78] and development in domestic surveillance capabilities.

The PG's multi-branch capability is further enhanced when it is considered that the UAE's Special Operations Command (UAESOC) falls within its remit. UAESOC retains its own command structure, yet is still managed by the PG. The relationship between the PG and UAESOC is akin to that of US Special Operations Command (SOCOM) and the Joint Special Operations Command (JSOC), with the latter handling what is termed the tier one units, the most specialised and elite units.

The investment and development of the PG firmly attaches the unit to the Abu Dhabi ruling family; specifically, Mohammed bin Zayed al-Nahyan. In turn, its personnel benefit from the intangible reward of membership to its perceived status, and through their membership, illustrate the successful strategy undertaken by the regime elites to co-opted military personnel. While seen as a professional entity, similar neighbouring units, such as the SANG, are predominantly patrimonial in recruitment and design.

Since the Arab Spring, the UAE's regime's security strategy has slightly prioritised capability development and professionalism over nepotism and tribal affiliation. This postulation would explain why the unit with the highest strategic priority—the Presidential

Guard—is led by expatriate personnel, especially if the perceived threat to the regime originated from personnel within the country and political elite.

Military-Led State Building by Mohammed bin Zayed al-Nahyan

The contrasting lack of military engagement by the UAE Armed Forces until 2004, and the subsequent acceleration of overseas operations, supports this book's proposition that since Mohammed bin Zayed al-Nahyan's ascension to political power, the UAE regime has utilised the military to undertake a post-Arab Spring state-building endeavour in Mohammed bin Zayed al-Nahyan's image.[79]

The obvious acknowledgement that the military possesses intrinsic qualities that can sustain the ecosystem of support for the regime and also provide the tools to physically defend the regime, explain why such a high priority has been given to the development of the military. The intimate link between the UAE regime and the military further demonstrates the argument, with leading members of the ruling family and their kin appointed to senior positions across the military.

Besides the already discussed systems, employed to foster elite support and control, there has been a renewed requirement to elicit wider support for the military from Emirati society, i.e., expand subjective control of the military. Tangible results have appeared through formal mechanisms such as military-led economic development and knowledge investment,[80] but also through community-targeted programmes. Central to these has been the image of Mohammed bin Zayed al-Nahyan as the nation's and the military's figurehead. This has resulted in a stronger and more legitimate interpretation of Mohammed bin Zayed al-Nahyan and the UAE regime as the nation's leadership.

While there has been a numerical increase in the platforms employed by the UAE Armed Forces, there has also been a numerical increase in its personnel.[81] This expansion enables the UAE's regime to possess a larger and more capable unit of protection. When the regime can portray the increase of military personnel as a result of the attempt to develop economic, educational, and societal capabilities within the Emirati society, the regime can meet multiple security challenges while still focusing on their own primary concern, regime security.

In a further attempt to foster the military's development and build support and legitimacy across society, on 7 June 2014 the UAE issued Federal Law No.6 to initiate and construct a national military service and reserve force.[82] While aimed at developing social skills and fostering national (note: not federal) sentiment, the national service law was created to evoke greater societal responsibility and understanding: 'The law aims to instil values of loyalty and sacrifice in the hearts of the citizens, linking them with the teachings of religion and the socialisation of different generations in terms of leadership characteristics, physical power and self-reliance, responsibility and discipline, respect of law, and time'.[83]

The centrality of the military as the leader of morality and national character is magnified when oriented towards the geographical and political disposition of the military towards Abu Dhabi. The manufacturing of nationalist and unionist sentiment directly assists the UAE regime security strategy as it can through the process of development, modernisation, and conscription, re-educate and recreate the narrative of a modern-day UAE.

Furthermore, of the nine national service centres (military bases and training camps designated for national service) provided for the seven Emirates, four of the five training centres and three of the four military bases are located within the Emirate of Abu Dhabi.[84] This means that there is a heightened probability that the majority of Emirati males will have to travel to Abu Dhabi for national service and become accustomed to an Abu Dhabi-centric view of the military, and its mission to provide the nation's (and regime's) security. This furthermore enhances society's perception of the military, and therefore increases its legitimacy within society, thus strengthening the UAE's regime security strategy.

The rewriting of sympathies and loyalties from a federal identity to one of a nation not only strengthens the state and the nation, but also the regime as the harbourer of such an identity. The cohesive identity shown within the UAE Armed Forces echoes that of the political endeavour undertaken to transition the UAE from a federal to a unitary state.

Post-Arab Spring Implementation

Since the Arab Spring the UAE has attempted to enhance and fuse the state's and the nation's security culture to one which inherently follows a regime-oriented vision. This is a political-military culture and it 'refers to the subset of the larger political culture that influences how members of a given society view national security, the military as an institution, and the use of force in international relations'.[85]

Central to this process has been the position and role of the UAE Armed Forces. As the domestic institution with the largest threat potential to the incumbent regime, however, it has been critical that the development of the UAE Armed Forces has been for the prioritised purpose of advancing the UAE's regime security over that of the nation and the state.

While elsewhere across the MENA region, militaries have seen heightened engagement in inter-state and intra-state conflict, the UAE has constructed a baseline of positive sentiment towards the state's security issues and established the application of the UAE Armed Forces as the sole owner of legitimate force within the UAE. This observation has developed after years of restructuring and reorganising coercive capabilities with the UAE. Its primary aim is to reduce inter-Emirate competition and thus to strengthen the federal state. Parallel military units such as the PG in the UAE or the SANG in Saudi Arabia exist as a counterweight to the traditional military but are advertised as specialised units to differentiate them from their conventional counterparts.

The result of the nation-building exercise of Mohammed bin Zayed al-Nahyan is the evolution of an Emirati political-military culture that has, in response to turbulent external stimuli, developed the image of a secure but hospitable state. The newly developed Emirati political-military culture has empowered the regime to advance military capabilities whilst also extending political control, actively circumventing traditional and contemporary security challenges. Risa Brooks supports this idea by highlighting the significance of military development in regime security: 'Maintaining social support and eliminating contenders for power can lessen the need for measures detrimental to battlefield efficiency, but does not free these regimes from the need to cultivate military support'.[86]

On the one hand, the UAE Armed Forces' professional drive has warranted a significantly higher operational tempo, at home and abroad, while still maintaining the pursuit of selective appointments and sociological control of elite personnel. As also observed, the reinterpreted political-military culture has sought to publicly securitise security issues and thus legitimise any following reaction. Concurrently, this process has effectively rewritten the UAE's security-focused social facts to align with an Abu Dhabi-focused interpretation.

The legacy of infighting within the al-Nahyan ruling family has affected the political elites' perceptions of their internal vulnerabilities. The Arab Spring compounded the appearance and multitude of domestic threats, and as the primary threat manifestation, the UAE Armed Forces have been the principal and foremost entity within the UAE's post-Arab Spring regime security strategy. This analysis has seen the dual approaches of the maintenance of power and the enforcement of power being applied to the regime's management of the UAE Armed Forces.

4

DIGITAL AUTHORITARIANISM

NEW TOOLS FOR STATE CONTROL

Due to the speed of technical innovation, information is more readily accessible than it has ever been. This has provided avenues for empowerment but also for control. The Iranian Green Movement of 2009 and the Arab Spring have shown how groups have used technological innovation for political gain. The backlash from the Iranian regime and other regional states to these movements illustrates how the state has wrestled back power in times of instability. In an authoritarian state, the regime seeks to maintain control of forces that can potentially threaten its 'absolute authority';[1] in this sense, surveillance can be interpreted as a modern and updated expression of sultanism.

While the regime's control of the military was previously examined, this chapter will explore how surveillance capabilities have developed to maximise the regime's observation of society since the outbreak of the Arab Spring. The illustration of how extensive and effective surveillance is within the UAE will demonstrate why the UAE can be described as one of the vanguards of digital authoritarianism globally.

Initially, the recording of information was, according to Giddens, 'a mode of administration notation'.[2] The single direc-

71

tion of information and its control by the recording administration empowered governors to solidify their authoritative positions. Giddens further clarifies that 'the concentrated focusing of surveillance as "governmental" power is largely, if not completely, a phenomenon of the modern state'.[3] With the advent of the internet and mobile technology, people's access to information and international social interaction has served as a means of empowerment,[4] liberation,[5] and control.[6] The global proliferation of information has even prompted scholars such as John Arquilla and David Ronfeldt to claim that, alongside the political, economic, and military elements of power, information is emerging as an equal factor within the field of national security.[7]

In step with technological developments and the increased scope of information ownership is the concept of surveillance. The field of surveillance is vast, incorporating issues ranging from state-led mass surveillance, through to the collection of individual data required to process institutional requests (e.g. individuals' health records). As a result, surveillance can be viewed negatively, positively, or neutrally.

Negative concepts such as those hypothesised by Jeremy Bentham, Max Horkheimer, and Michel Foucault are often defined through the perceived relationship between information collection, societal discipline,[8] and coercion. At the forefront of this debate is the orthodox perception of panopticon[9]—and its modern reinterpretation superpanopticon[10]—and it is through this lens that Foucault defines surveillance: 'a person that is under surveillance "is seen, but he does not see; he is the object of information, never a subject in communication"'.[11] Within the modern context, Foucault's definition is viewed as a simplification, and the negative connotations of surveillance are an oversimplification of the potential benefits generated by surveillance. Furthermore, the limitation presented by Foucault in this instance critically underplays the understanding that surveillance can be a multifaceted notion; due to technological developments presented by Web 2.0, it is claimed that surveillance now consists of the collection and control of information, and the potentially unintentional behaviour of the individual who owns and distributes such information.[12]

Stuart Armstrong counters and explores the ways and means by which society directly benefits from forms of surveillance.[13] His contextual examples showcase how crime, medicine, research, and even human behaviour can benefit from heightened forms of surveillance. The results of surveillance help humanity to progress, as patterns and relationships captured from large data sets empower researchers to identify causal factors and linkages which can advance society. Furthermore, with more access to more information, subjects can counter and neutralise perceived violations[14] and elicit greater accountability, for example through citizen journalism. Surveillance is therefore understood to have both positive and negative values dependent upon context and relative strength of civil society and commercial sectors.

Giddens builds upon the literature to illustrate both negative and positive aspects of surveillance and does so by defining the concept neutrally; surveillance is the 'control of information and the superintendence of the activities of some group by others'.[15] The neutral notion hypothesised by Giddens firmly adheres to the wide concept of surveillance and ensures that there are both positive and neutral aspects within its capability. The neutral definition postulated by Giddens allows the research to acknowledge both the coercive and constructive dimensions of surveillance, and thus provides a framework which provides a nonaligned observation of the concept.

A further dimension identified within the field of literature pertaining to surveillance is the influence of modernity. In contrast to traditional surveillance[16] Gary Marx defines new surveillance as the 'scrutiny of individuals, groups and contexts through the use of technical means to extract or create information'.[17] Modern and predominantly electronic mediums of surveillance will focus research and evaluate its role of significance to the UAE's regime security strategy.

The digitisation of society has prompted the mass collection of personal data and, accordingly, the speed with which it can be accessed by an increasing number of actors; from state security agencies to local council institutions, through to a wide range of commercial entities who have directly, or indirectly, accumulated information on a user or users. This has provoked a split in academic approaches towards surveillance whereby several approaches have emerged; legal and ethical aspects,[18] technological development,[19] employment tactics,[20] and the perceived motivation for the level of surveillance undertaken.[21]

While it is important to understand the applications and approaches of surveillance, it is equally important to highlight the means of, and restrictions to, collection, access, and use of surveillance data. In practice, this means the degree to which said information can be collected, accessed and used varies dramatically depending on laws and regulations within each state.[22]

Acknowledging the intrinsic limitations within the field of surveillance, this chapter will explore the UAE's surveillance capabilities from the three major academic perspectives of the field: legal, technological, and engagement strategies.

The legal dimension of surveillance provides the just foundation for state capabilities and its pursuit and control of information. With legal justification and legitimacy, the UAE can enhance its surveillance capabilities and as a result enforce its regime security strategy. It is imperative for successful regime security to have the appearance of applying stringent laws to maintain order, and to be seen acting within the same laws it imposes on society.[23] In many cases, the Emirati authorities justify the enforcement of surveillance related laws by appealing to cultural sensitivities, e.g. protection of children,[24] extremism,[25] and immoral sexual conduct.[26]

The ring-fencing of surveillance laws has been complicated by the speed and progress of technological development. While traditional surveillance was physical and required manual effort, technology has enabled the automatic capture, processing, and analysis of information, and thus multiplied the array of surveillance capabilities at the state's disposal. In this vein, it is crucial to examine how the UAE has managed this technological process in order to enhance its regime security strategy.

Analysis of surveillance engagement tactics is a crucial requirement when examining how the UAE has utilised a growing array of surveillance tactics, techniques, and procedures (TTPs) to augment its regime security strategy. This will illustrate how the UAE has incorporated micro and macro approaches to the practice of surveillance to ensure the UAE's regime security strategy stays abreast of technological developments.

This framing empowers analysis to explore the formal and informal mechanisms which are employed to enhance the regime's control of the state's surveillance capabilities. The case study presented of the UAE's adoption and development of digital authoritarian capabilities sets forth a clear argument that surveillance does not have to be coercive in order to achieve its objectives.

Legal Dimension

Since the 11 September 2001 terrorist attacks and the subsequent introduction of legislation such as the 2001 USA PATRIOT Act (Uniting and Strengthening America by Providing Appropriate Tools Required to Intercept and Obstruct Terrorism Act),[27] and the exponential speed at which technology has globally developed,[28] there has been a significant and legal increase in the international community's ability to conduct domestic surveillance.

Where citizens of democratic states assume a degree of legal rights and protections from the state, the state is also held to account for its actions and therefore it faces punishment for illegal engagement. In an autocratic state, these same civil protections do not exist and at the same time, surveillance tends to be more overt.

Attempts have been made to halt and restrict the dilution of personal rights, with an increasing number of interested parties managing daily privacy exposures; regulatory bodies, privacy/pressure groups, technology developers/providers, government policy makers, data controllers, and data subjects.[29] Due to the speed of technology development and its adoption, governments have not been able to effectively manage surveillance legislation, and have more often than not fallen towards either the over-deployment or under-deployment of surveillance legislation.[30] It is noted by Lawrence Lessig that 'governments (democratic and authoritarian alike) can most certainly regulate the internet, both by controlling its underlying code and by shaping the legal environment in which it operates'.[31] In other words, while some states attempted to limit access to the internet others have looked to control what is already accessible online. This observation is further complicated within the UAE due to the state's federal identity; 'national-level initiatives are greatly overshadowed, however, by the e-government efforts of Dubai ... for the most part, other Emirates have failed to match Dubai's stellar progress'.[32]

Building upon Lawrence Lessig's hypothesis, this section will assess the UAE's legal approach to surveillance; firstly, through the state's architecture of control, and secondly, through the domain of legislation.[33]

Architecture of Control

The UAE's approach to electronic surveillance has accelerated since the Arab Spring, though as a global centre of commerce and trade, the control of electronic forms of communication has always been an issue for Emirati authorities. Due to the small expatriate population however, the UAE has been able to effectively manage rights concerns within its borders. As a result of the speed of technological development, it has been nearly impossible for any state to pre-empt cyber vulnerabilities and, instead, many (including the UAE) initially look to institutional forms of control or the architecture of control.

Central to the UAE government's control and dispersion of information is the state's ownership and management of the ICT sector.[34] The state's ownership envelops not only government bodies, ministries, and security establishments, but also media and telecommunications organisations. Through the combined control of information generation and dispersion, the UAE has attempted to ring-fence the parameters to which it believes it can effectively survey society.[35]

Sitting atop of the UAE's electronic surveillance command structure is the Signals Intelligence Agency (SIA). Due to the secretive nature of the UAE's cyber-surveillance sector, it is not entirely clear what mandate SIA has. However, a clearer assessment can be made of its predecessor the National Electronic Security Authority (NESA). It is a 'federal entity responsible for the advancement of the nation's cybersecurity, expanding cyber education and creating a collaborative culture rooted in information technology and innovation'.[36] It is important to note that all electronic forms of communication within the UAE pass through SIA[37]—and previously through NESA. Until the UAE Armed Forces can independently operate their own networks, their communications will also pass through SIA,[38] thus ensuring expanded civilian oversight over the military. Ibish notes that in 2014 the 'country reportedly established a cyber command within the General Headquarters of the national armed forces that runs in parallel to NESA and specifically serves the military'.[39] However, as there has been no formal confirmation of the military's cyber capability, it is assumed SIA will maintain this ability until otherwise stated. As a result of SIA's monopoly on the production of knowledge and the multiplicity of security capabilities available to the state, its manifestation clearly exhibits a coup-proofing mechanism, one which has been created directly in response to the Arab Spring.

The UAE's cyber-surveillance capability was expanded when NESA was formally established on 13 August 2012 through Federal Decree No. 3 of 2012.[40] It was not until 2014 however, that NESA started publishing official policies and standards; National Security Strategy, National Information Assurance Framework, Critical Infrastructure Protection Policy, and UAE Information Assurance Standards.[41] The establishment of a strategic entity immediately after the Arab Spring, and the break between its establishment and its operations, highlights not only the kneejerk reaction to a perceived threat by the Emirati authorities, but that its threat potential to the UAE regime was perceived to be significant.[42] If ICT-based threats were not considered so immediate, the UAE would not have invested as much time and money to combat them.

As noted by Mehran Kamrava,[43] Sheena Grietens[44] and Volker Perthes,[45] there is a requirement and subsequent strategy to ensure the longevity of a regime; one that requires careful management of institutions that can carry a threat.[46] While the strategic management of personnel within the UAE Armed Forces has been previously examined, the Abu Dhabi ruling family has extended this same strategy to NESA. This has materialised in the intimate fusion of regime personnel and PREs. Initially NESA was 'guided by a board of directors elected by the Chairman of the Supreme Council of National Security';[47] however, as the institution has developed, a close-knit operational team has formed that has clear and direct links to Mohammed bin Zayed al-Nahyan. Through the careful maintenance of trusted kin and personnel across the surveillance apparatus, Mohammed bin Zayed al-Nahyan has again co-opted the security focused elites, and is using this platform to help secure his lineage and their eventual tenure of leadership.

According to Federal Decree Law No. 3, which formally established NESA, the organisation was to directly report to the UAE National Security Advisor[48] who, as of 14 February 2016 was Tahnoon bin Zayed al-Nahyan,[49] full brother to Mohammed bin Zayed al-Nahyan. Furthermore, Tahnoon bin Zayed al-Nahyan's deputy,[50] the Minister of National Security, is the eldest son of Mohammed bin Zayed al-Nahyan, Sheikh Khalid bin Mohammed bin Zayed al-Nahyan.[51] The first Director General of NESA was Jassem al-Zaabi, Khalid bin Muhammad al-Nahyan's superior when the pair closely worked together at the Abu Dhabi-based, and Mohammed bin Zayed al-Nahyan-led, SWF Mubadala. The construction of NESA was overseen by the Supreme National Security Council. Its Deputy Secretary General is Ali Mohammed al-Shamsi, who was appointed on 1 November 2013, is an experienced diplomat who had previously served as Ambassador to Afghanistan, Jordan, and Pakistan, and as the UAE representative to the Arab League and the United Nations. Al-Shamsi is an extremely important figure who is amongst the highest ranking non-ruling family officials within the UAE. He holds the rank of Minister and is a constant fixture alongside Mohammed bin Zayed al-Nahyan and Tahnoon bin Zayed al-Nahyan. According to Peter Salisbury, Ali al-Shamsi is the 'UAE's intelligence chief'.[52]

At an unknown point, NESA's first Director General[53] was promoted to the position of Chairman of the Abu Dhabi Executive Office,[54] and subsequently as a member of the Abu Dhabi Executive Council and then as head of its Department of Finance. After the SIA had emerged and assumed the responsibilities of NESA, it was appointed a new Executive Director, Muhammad al-Kuwaiti.[55] He is a Dhawahir tribal member, and therefore has close paternal ties to Mohammed bin Zayed al-Nahyan and the Bani Yas. In addition to his role in SIA, Muhammad al-Kuwaiti was appointed as head of cybersecurity within the government of the UAE, further illustrating his key role within this sector.[56]

The web of interconnecting relationships across NESA's leadership highlights how, since the Arab Spring, the Mohammed bin Zayed al-Nahyan-led UAE has successfully courted political elites, fostering intimate ties within an increasingly concentric circle of trusted personnel. This has helped to secure the regime and is also laying the groundwork for a future Khalid bin Mohammed bin Zayed al-Nahyan-led UAE.

On a federal level, each of the UAE's seven Emirates have their own civilian cybersecurity authorities (in addition to the MOI personnel) that advise and strategise how Emirate-level bodies will manage their own cybersecurity issues. This aligns with James Quinlivan's coup-proofing strategy,[57] as the regime has created multiple security organisations with overlapping responsibilities, ensuring as a result a persistent counter-intelligence capability across the multi-tiered system of governance. This suggests that the fracturing of UAE cybersecurity and surveillance capabilities has been prompted to enhance the UAE's regime security strategy, and to ensure that no security entity beyond the direct control of the Abu Dhabi regime is capable of mounting a significant challenge to the Abu Dhabi-based political elites. Only on occasion have high profile Emiratis criticised the elevated surveillance capabilities of the post-Arab Spring regime security strategy.[58] They have often done so knowingly, and hence, other less public mechanisms are employed to voice certain concerns.

Each of the Emirate-level cybersecurity institutions are subservient to NESA and the Telecommunications Regulatory Authority (TRA). The TRA was established through Federal Law No.3 of 2003[59] and it has two principle aims: 'The role of TRA focuses on two fields: regulating the telecommunications sector, and enabling government entities in the field of smart transformation'.[60] The TRA is thus the leading entity within the governance of day-to-day online engagement across the UAE and is leading the state's development towards wider ICT adoption and development.

Complying with the TRA's governance are the UAE's four tele-communications networks: Etisalat, Emirates Integrated Tele-communications Company (EITC) with its two owned brands Du and Virgin, and Swyp. Any mobile or internet connection is required to subscribe to one of these networks, and in many cases, users cannot choose between networks. Onshore businesses and homes must subscribe to Etisalat, while in free-zone and new-built areas, subscribers must sign to Du. Virgin[61] is a new entity within the UAE's ICT sector, and only offers mobile connections. Swyp is owned by Etisalat and is an age-restricted mobile network that relies heavily on mobile data usage.[62]

Within the field of surveillance, the UAE has opted to enhance its architecture of control through PPPs and SOEs.[63] Leading this effort is Etisalat, the UAE's largest and oldest telecommunications and internet service provider (ISP). Etisalat was created in 1976 and is 60 per cent owned by the UAE Government.[64] Among Etisalat's board members, many hold additional positions within the public sector and are leading actors within the UAE's private sector,[65] and therefore the lack of public/private separation leads to a persistent surveillance of all telecommunication activities within the Etisalat network. The ETIC is the UAE's second licensed telecommunications provider and owns two brands; Du and Virgin. EITC was founded in 2006;[66] its initial offering, Du, was established a year later in 2007 and its second offering, Virgin, was launched in 2017.[67] EITC is 39.5 per cent owned by Emirates Investment Authority (UAE Government), 19.75 per cent owned by Mubadala (Abu Dhabi Government), 19.5 per cent owned by Emirates Communications and Technology (Dubai Holding), and the remaining shares owned by public shareholders.[68] Like Etisalat, many of EITC's board of directors hold additional public-sector portfolios,[69] and further highlight the depth of the regime's control in the state's ICT sector. The state's ownership of the UAE communications sector has not changed since the Arab Spring; however, the number of entities within its portfolio has increased. This suggests this change has been for cosmetic, not organisational purposes.

The UAE's concentrated field of ICT ownership and manage-ment has led Shanthi Kalathil and Taylor Boas to postulate that 'the government of the UAE has sought to maintain control over ICTs for both censorship and financial gain'.[70] This hypothesis is in line with other areas of observation within the UAE's governance system, and it is often through these two lenses that the state's decisions to limit access to the internet, social media, and third-party applications can be understood.

Akin to Giddens' definition of surveillance is the concept of control; both of information and the subject that digests and produces that information. An intrinsic feature of surveillance is the ability to manufacture and limit what information is accessed. Joan Ferrante postulates that 'censorship, surveillance, and sanctions are used to convey and enforce norms',[71] and provides the grounding for an exploration of how censorship and propaganda mechanisms are used to enhance surveillance capabilities.

In parallel with the UAE's ability to control information is its programme to create and propagate information. The media is not only a medium to generate support for the political elites, but 'a vital companion function is to trash and discredit alternatives to the authoritarian status quo',[72] thus ensuring social control and observation of dissident narrative and organisation. In essence, states seek to control the media, so they can 'convey their strength and puff up their claims to legitimacy while undermining potential alternatives'.[73]

Central to this capability is the National Media Council (NMC).[74] Established per Federal Law 1 of 2006, the NMC is a federal government body that monitors what information is published within the UAE, and how it is presented. The NMC is supported by the state's direct and indirect ownership of the leading sources of information to the UAE public. This allows them to potentially restrict or sanction media outlets. A further amendment was made to federal law in 2017 expanding the NMC's capacity to censor electronic publications.[75] The composition of the NMC's board of directors (See Table 1: National Media Council Board of Directors) exhibits the same feature of patrimonialism that seemingly runs throughout the wider state operating apparatus within the UAE. It appears clear that, while the leading members of the NMC hold additional portfolios within other areas of the executive branch, they are assisted by technocrats from federal level entities. In July 2020, the NMC was merged with the Federal Youth Authority into the Ministry of Culture, and the Emirates News Agency, WAM, was transferred to the Ministry of Presidential Affairs.[76] The prompt acceleration of centralised state control of information creation clearly illustrates a strong reaction to potential threats emerging beyond the regime's direct control.

Table 1: National Media Council Board of Directors[77]

Name	Role	Other role(s)	Tribe
Dr. Sultan al-Jaber	Chairman	Cabinet Member and Minister of State and CEO of ADNOC	
Noura al-Kaabi	Chairwoman	UAE Cabinet Member and Minister of Culture and Knowledge Development	Bani Ka'b
Dr. Ali Rashid al-Nuaimi	Board Member	Member of the Executive Council	Na'im
Ahmed al-Jarman	Board Member	Assistant Foreign Minister for Political Affairs	
Mouza Ali al-Hameli	Board Member	Head of Organisational Department at Ministry of Presidential Affairs	Hawamil of the Bani Yas

Amina al-Rustamani	Board Member	CEO of TECOM Group	No tribal connection as family is foreign in origin
Mona al-Marri	Board Member	Director General of the Government of Dubai Media Office	Murrah
Sheikh Sultan bin Ahmed al-Qasimi	Board Member	Chairman of the Sharjah Media Corporation	Qawasim
Mansour Ibrahim al-Mansoori	Director General	Board Member of the Abu Dhabi Tourism and Culture Authority	Manasir

While the UAE-owned print media industry only caters for a daily audience of less than one million (of an estimated population of seven million), the state's controlled ownership of the print sector (prominent pre-digital communication medium) shows how this potential threat medium was controlled for maximal efficiency (See Table 2: UAE-Owned Newspaper Broadsheet Circulation and Ownership). Furthermore, any official government statement or information release is first published by the WAM,[78] thus helping to craft and direct the presentation of information.[79] Foreign print media outlets are permitted to enter the domestic UAE market, but are held prior to entry for censorship review. This results in the full, partial, or non-release of the media format.[80]

The UAE is limited in its ability to monitor and control social media portals and blogs, and instant messaging services. Like many other states it has, on occasion, restricted access[81] and implemented legislation targeting undesirable social media activity.[82] Virtual

Table 2: UAE-Owned Newspaper Broadsheet Circulation and Ownership

Type	Name	Circulation	Ownership
Newspaper	Al-Bayan	105,000	Dubai Government—Dubai Media Incorporated
Newspaper	Gulf News	104,000	Al-Tayer,[83] Al-Rostamani,[84] and Al-Majid[85] families
Newspaper	Al-Ittihad	95,000	Abu Dhabi Government—Abu Dhabi Media
Newspaper	Khaleej Times	90,000	Galadari Printing[86]
Newspaper	The National	80–90,000	International Media Investments (IMI)—Was created by Abu Dhabi Government but now independent
Newspaper	Emarat al-Youm	80,000	Dubai Government—Dubai Media Incorporated
Newspaper	Al-Khaleej	37–60,000	Taryam Omran Taryam and Dr. Abdullah Omran Taryam[87]

Private Networks (VPNs) can mask a user's online activity and, therefore, they present a viable threat to a regime. The UAE's legal perception of VPNs is contradictory as article 1 of Federal Law 12 of 2016 seems to outlaw their use,[88] however later clarification by the TRA illustrated their lawful usage.[89] They are, however, technically difficult to discover and intercept, and therefore weaken the state's legal ability to enforce their restriction. In essence, where possible, the UAE has attempted to halt access to information that goes against the state narrative and mediums of communication beyond its direct control. The process of surveillance enhancement has significantly developed in the post-Arab Spring era, with Ronald Deibert suggesting that a similar process has occurred in other less technically savvy states.[90]

As technology has developed, there have been attempts by the state to re-exert its influence over the broadcast (television) and online sectors. While it is relatively simple to restrict physical newspapers, and the publishing of information therein, restricting and controlling information transmitted live by satellite, or by remote and independent actors online, is a very different endeavour. In a bid to enter and dominate the domain of broadcast media, every federal level government owns an array of media channels, with Abu Dhabi Media and Dubai Media Incorporated, the state's two leading media conglomerates, holding the most diverse portfolios.[91]

The UAE also permits foreign broadcast channels to be received within the UAE; however, through legal and technological restrictions, the state is able to control what is transmitted to UAE audiences.[92] This is a crucial battleground for the regime, and 'state-controlled media must make it a mission to reassure these regime mainstays that the incumbent ruler (or ruling circle) stands secure, making continued unity and loyalty to the regime the "smart play"'.[93] The state's propaganda apparatus has developed a wide array of capabilities across multiple platforms and has illustrated the importance of appealing to emotional and cultural sensitivities, which a patrimonial and traditional political system gains strength from.

Through the strategic ownership and control of the UAE's ICT architecture and the commercial outlets that operate within its domain, the regime is able to efficiently and discreetly manage the 'underlying code'[94] of the state's access to the internet. This ensures that society is exposed to its propaganda and has limited access to information where possible. While a degree of information control has been made possible by the Emirati authorities, the capture of narrative through the controlling array of media ownership ensures the domination of political discourse over the UAE's population.[95]

Since the Arab Spring, the UAE has visibly increased its ownership of the state's ICT architecture. In addition, traditional methods of creating and dispersing information have remained within the gravity of state control. These combined factors have allowed the UAE to expand its domain of surveillance within the post-Arab Spring period.

Domain of Legislation

The UAE's legal system is dominated by its constitution and penal code. Both consider Islamic shari'a law as the main source of law for the state.[96] The UAE has previously struggled to efficiently implement legislation targeting ICT-based threats.[97] ICT-based threats range from state orchestrated espionage through to NGO hacktivists, terrorists, and commercially focused criminals. Since the Arab Spring however, ICT platforms have empowered social activism and opposition to authoritarian states across MENA, and subsequently, there has been a significant uptake in the volume and potency of surveillance legislation. On this basis, ICT and cybercrime threats do envelop a wide range of threats, however, when limited to their impact on regime security, both are focused on the level of direct engagement with the state. This section will therefore assess the extent to which the UAE's post-Arab Spring surveillance legislation has been implemented to strengthen its regime security strategy.

Surveillance is a broad concept that is not fixed in modernity; its modern capabilities have however transformed its potency. Like any state, the UAE has implemented a wide array of laws that have empowered the state's surveillance capabilities; however, as the state has matured and technologies evolved, new legislation has

been created to counter reinterpreted threats. Due to the importance of the UAE's surveillance specific legislation, dated 1971–
present, and across seventeen laws, Table 3: UAE's Surveillance
Legislation lists each law and date of publishing.

Table 3: UAE's Surveillance Legislation[98]

Law	Date
Article 30 of 1971 Constitution	2 December 1971
Federal Law No.15 of 1980 Concerning Press and Publications[99]	16 November 1980
Federal Decree No.3 of 1987 Penal Code	8 December 1987
Federal Law by Decree No.3 of 2003 Regarding the Organization of Telecommunications Sector[100]	15 November 2003
Federal Law No.2 of 2004 Popular Register and Emirates Identity Card Program	29 September 2004
Federal Decree No.1 of 2006 Cyber Crimes Law[101]	30 June 2006
Federal Law by Decree No.5 of 2008 Amending the Provisions of the Federal Law by Decree No.3 of 2003[102]	2008
Cabinet Resolution No. (42/23) of 2008 Session No.3[103] Regarding the Abolition of the Supreme Committee for the Supervision of the Telecommunication Sector and delegating its function to the Board of Directors of the TRA	2008
National Media Council Resolution No.20 of 2010	2010

REINVENTING THE SHEIKHDOM

Federal Decree Law No.3 of 2012[104] Establishment of National Electronic Security Authority (NESA)	13 August 2012
Federal Decree Law No.5 of 2012[105] Combatting Cybercrimes	13 August 2012
National Media Council Chairman's Decision No.35 of 2013 Advertising Content[106]	2013
Federal Decree Law No.7 of 2014[107] Combatting Terrorism Offences	20 August 2014
Federal Decree Law No.2 of 2015[108] Combatting Discrimination and Hatred	15 July 2015
Federal Law No.11 of 2016[109] Competencies of the National Media Council	21 July 2016
Federal Decree Law No.12 of 2016[110]	21 July 2016
Council of Ministers Decree No.23 of 2017[111] Concerning Media Content	2017

While the UAE's 1971 constitution protects free speech, there has been a growing trend of reforms that have tested this right. According to Freedom House,[112] Reporters without Borders,[113] and Human Rights Watch[114] the UAE has significantly enhanced its surveillance capabilities in contrast to the 1971 constitution. As a society structured around Islamic shari'a law, 'officials claim that their sole desire is to censor socially inappropriate material, primarily pornography, although there is some evidence that political sites are also blocked'.[115]

The growing power, and vagueness, of surveillance legislation within the UAE suggests that the Emirati authorities are emphasising the targeting of political dissidents and not just socially inappropriate material; 'far from being made obsolete by the internet, authoritarian regimes are now actively shaping cyberspace to their own strategic advantage'.[116] This observation is clarified by the five most stringent surveillance laws in the UAE, as follows.

Federal Law No.15 of 1980. Prohibits the publishing of criticism directed at the President or the rulers of the UAE, and further limits the broadcasting of sentiment which could offend mainstream social sensibilities.[117] The vague parameters of Federal Law No.15 of 1980 ensure a legal foundation for a wide scope of judicial powers.

Federal Law No.5 of 2012. Focuses on cybercrime targeting security, financial, and individual privacy issues and abuses. The cybercrime law has made significant headlines as its religious and social grounding has influenced stringent defamation laws. Notable examples of the severity of the cybercrime law were the cases of an Indian national imprisoned for filming and uploading to YouTube a video[118] of a UAE government employee assaulting a driver after a driving altercation,[119] and the arrest of an American citizen who had criticised his UAE employer on Facebook.[120] In the former case, the crime the Emirati committed (assault) held a maximum sentence of a year in jail and a AED100,000 fine, while the Indian national who uploaded the video to social media (filming without permission or deformation) faced a maximum sentence of two years in jail or a fine of up to AED20,000.[121] Federal Law No.5 of 2012 increases the judiciary capabilities in combatting online offences and illustrates how within a year of the Arab Spring the UAE had already reacted to the potential from online threats through stringent legislation.

Federal Law No.3 of 2012 established NESA. It illustrates how such a short time after the Arab Spring, the UAE reacted by establishing its own signals intelligence (SIGINT) focused entity. While there is not a great deal of information pertaining to NESA, through Federal Law No.3 and a few publicly available presentations,[122] which heavily focus on the initial period of cybersecurity policy creation, the UAE's cybersecurity and intelligence capabilities have been significantly enhanced. It is also telling that NESA was created in the immediate aftermath of the Arab Spring, further signifying how the state's security capabilities were being upgraded to counter potential threats.

Federal Law No.7 of 2014. Illustrates the vast parameters of what is deemed to be terrorism within the UAE. It is clear from Articles 1, 9, 10, 11, 14, 15, and 34[123] that the counter-terrorism law of 2014 is aimed at more than just conventional terrorist threats. Federal Law No.7 of 2014 also illustrates the state's perception of the hierarchy of authority, placing the serving political elites on par with the state's institutions.[124] This suggests that state and national security are comparable interests to the UAE, yet are subordinate to regime security. With the development of surveillance legislation increasing in the post-Arab Spring era, the reemphasis of the UAE's power structure in favour of the regime supports this book's thesis that surveillance has been a fundamental issue for the UAE's evolving regime security strategy.

The Council of Ministers Decree No.23 of 2017 significantly increased restrictions upon the media sector and ensures that published digital media within the UAE are registered with the NMC, and a content review is exercised prior to publishing.[125] While 'the new regulations do not bring about much tangible change to the regulatory landscape … [t]he key takeaway is that digital media is now very much in scope'.[126] If indeed, decree No.23 of 2017 updates earlier media laws to incorporate digital media, it is unlikely that an effective censorship review programme can be established to monitor, prior to publication, the wide array of online media sources. Although previous laws had supported the notion that the UAE understood how best to construct legal frameworks for an effective surveillance programme, the incorporation of electronic media platforms under the NMC's content review highlights how some challenges are still being met through deterrence.

Figure 8: Timeline of UAE Surveillance Legislation, shows the record of implemented surveillance legislation and the moving average (dotted), both of which illustrate the recent and significant increase in surveillance legislation. The increased pace to which the UAE has implemented legislation that enhances the state's surveillance capabilities is testament to the increased power of the state, its understanding of technological capabilities, and a heightened awareness of vulnerabilities across society. While the implementation of legislation has increased significantly from 2003, the post-Arab Spring period has witnessed a monumental surge in surveillance regulations; every year since the Arab Spring the UAE has introduced legislation that enhances the state's surveillance capability. This suggests that domestic surveillance has formed a critical component in the state's response to the Arab Spring and is subsequently a key pillar of the UAE's post-Arab Spring regime security strategy.

Fig. 8: Timeline of UAE Surveillance Legislation (produced by author)[127]

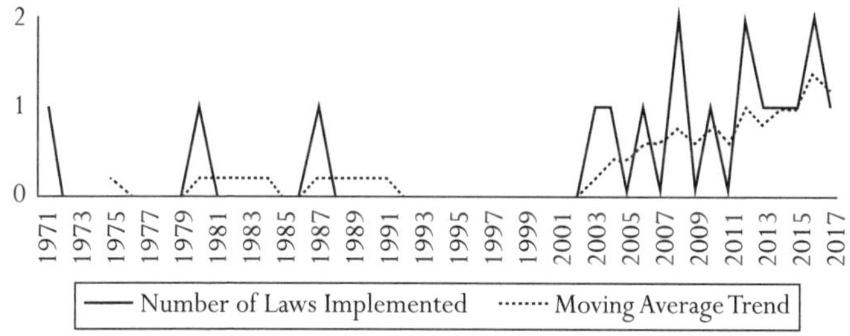

Number of Laws Implemented ⋯⋯ Moving Average Trend

Technological Development

As one of the richest countries in the world, the UAE has been heavily exposed to the speed of technological development. The state's citizens and residents have benefitted from this ecosystem of innovation and are rewarded through unparalleled access to new forms of information and communication. From the state's point of view, it has also infinitely multiplied the array of sensors and mediums through which it can access information, exercise control, and direct behaviour. David Lyon postulates that there are three main forms of data source within the field of surveillance: directed, 'where a human operator obtains the data'; automated, where 'the data are gathered without a human operator intervening'; and volunteered data, that is 'in a weak sense "volunteered" by the user who gives out information'.[128] These three data sources align with Gary Marx's conception of new surveillance, which is defined as 'the use of technical means to extract or create personal data',[129] to illustrate how widely distributed modern sources of information have become.

There are two main concerns when assessing the impact of technological development upon contemporary surveillance capabilities. Firstly, how does a state best manage the increased sources of information; secondly, how have technological developments impacted social and power dynamics within society.[130]

Whenever there has been an advance within a technological domain, there has always been a subsequent degree of control applied to ensure the technology is appropriately managed.[131] What is unique today however is the anarchistic realm within which information is owned, stored, and accessed;[132] the state is no longer the principal proprietor of information. While the state attempts to monopolise ownership of information,[133] and maintain maximal observation of this information, technological developments have inevitably advanced the state's surveillance capabilities.

New surveillance is defined by its low visibility, cost-effective mechanism, remote and often automated extraction, array of mediums surveyed and cross referenced, and the volunteered nature to which the vast array of information is now accessible.[134] This means that larger data sets can now be collected, evaluated, and disseminated within a shorter time frame, and often with a higher degree of accuracy. This field of processing is often referred to as big data.

Due to the high degree of sensitivity and the wide scope of innovative surveillance capabilities, it is inherently difficult to illustrate the UAE's capabilities in this respect. Details of even the simplest surveillance capabilities are registered as state defence secrets as per articles 159,[135] 160,[136] and 170[137] of Federal Law No.3/1987—The UAE Penal Code.[138] Furthermore, in December 2018, article 170 of the penal code was significantly expanded to broaden its definition of classified information.[139] Subsequently, specific UAE surveillance capabilities are principally concealed under the guise of state secrets, and any disclosure of information is predominantly exposed by third-party vendors; i.e. beyond the control of Emirati authorities.

Only on occasion are details of such capabilities formally published within the UAE. Two such programmes stand out as formally publicised surveillance programmes: Dubai 2021 Smart City policy[140] and the Falcon Eye Surveillance system in Abu Dhabi.[141] In Dubai, the first phase of a citywide physical surveillance system has been connected, meaning that 'thousands of CCTV cameras of various Dubai government agencies will now provide live feed to a central command centre'.[142] The centralised command centre will use an automated facial recognition system to monitor known suspects and could potentially be combined with biometric forms of identity to create a fully operational mass-surveillance capability.

Likewise, the Falcon Eye system in Abu Dhabi centralises a citywide network of cameras to enable federal level security authorities to promptly respond to issues. Other instances can be found online to highlight domestic surveillance capabilities;[143] however, only reported cases and successful operations are communicated by local authorities. This therefore obstructs an accurate understanding of the current scope and development of technological surveillance capabilities.

While military purchases are often announced, as a requirement of international legislation and to symbolise the state's power, surveillance platforms are not yet subject to the same international trade laws. Furthermore, by nature, surveillance capabilities are more effective when unknown by the target audience; operational security protocols cannot be tailored to circumvent specific surveillance platforms. This results in the limited ability to illustrate, with certainty, what platforms and systems have been purchased and installed to assist the UAE's evolving surveillance capabilities.

Nonetheless, there are four prominent examples of the surveillance capabilities currently utilised by the UAE authorities. The first is the series of efforts undertaken to observe an Emirati human rights activist, Ahmed Mansour.[144] On three separate occasions, Mansour was a target of electronic hacking attempts. While they can only be alleged to have been conducted on behalf of the UAE authorities, through the illegal disclosure of alleged corporate documents from the company[145] that reportedly executed the exploits,[146] and technical research undertaken by Toronto

University research group, Citizens Lab, there is significant evidence to suggest that the UAE had authorised the deployment of legal interception methods for national security purposes. The high level of capability[147] supposedly sanctioned by the UAE was illustrated through the execution of three previously unknown exploits (zero-days exploit),[148] and led Apple, whose product was targeted for lawful interception, to issue a global security update.[149]

While it is within NESA's legal mandate to conduct lawful interception, the outsourcing of intelligence capabilities to private organisations highlights the determination of the Emirati authorities to leverage modern technological mechanisms for national, state, and regime security matters.[150] This is most clearly highlighted in the development of capabilities by firms such as Darkmatter, Beamtrail, and CyberPoint, and their role in targeting state targets.[151] This strategy also helps to mediate the small pool of naturalised citizens and provides a platform for professional and apolitical actors to engage in matters of security, thus further empowering the UAE's regime security strategy.

In three previous cases, the UAE temporarily blocked the instant messaging platforms provided by Research in Motion's (RIM) Blackberry platform,[152] WhatsApp,[153] and more recently Skype.[154] Firstly, in the immediate aftermath of emerging protests (the Green Revolution of 2009) within Iran, a UAE-wide software upgrade for Blackberry mobile phones was deployed.[155] After the upgrade illustrated critically negative effects on those systems, it was discovered that the upgrade was in fact a spyware programme.[156] As the ongoing political disturbance in Iran was organised primarily by mobile technology and social media, the UAE's reaction of deploying mobile spyware worked as a pre-emptive attempt to increase observation of its population at a moment of heightened regional-wide political sensitivity. This case acts as a precursor for the UAE's reaction to the Arab Spring.

While the UAE claims that it is a national security requirement to have the ability to monitor all forms of communication within the country,[157] more thorough infrastructural mechanisms have been employed to maintain a persistent surveillance of the UAE population. The decision to block instant messaging platforms and voice over internet protocol (VoIP) platforms was intended to secure government access to servers in order in provide the means to intercept what was previously inaccessible to the UAE authorities. Both Blackberry[158] and WhatsApp provided the UAE with the legal and technical means to intercept conversations over their platforms, however this episode showed the difficulty for the UAE in balancing domestic security concerns and membership to international regulatory networks.[159] VoIP remains a highly contested issue within the UAE and in an attempt to reduce dissatisfaction with these restrictions, the UAE authorities have created their own VoIP programmes; however, users at each end of a conversation have to download the UAE created programmes in order for these to work.[160]

While the UAE has on occasion shown an aptitude for acquiring greater information oversight across society, the widely publicised attempts to control independent mediums of information have only resulted in short-term victories.

While the Emirati authorities wrestle with gaining access to currently utilised programmes, new platforms emerge, further multiplying the efforts needed to maintain an authoritative role within society. Christian Fuchs positions this predicament within the Web 2.0 space, explaining that 'the users are producers of information, but this creative communicative activity enables the controllers of disciplinary power to close gain insights'.[161] The creation of Emirati-owned communication platforms shows an understanding of the need to control the means of interaction and mirrors the state's ownership of traditional media entities.[162] This shows that while the UAE has reacted to the potential threat potential of the ICT domain, it reacted with strength, understanding that it can in fact leverage this anarchic field to greater use. The transition in Emirati surveillance strategy shows a maturity that has accepted the uncontrollable pace of technological development, and a willingness to alter the parameters of its control.

Engagement Tactics

Due to the broad nature of surveillance, its contemporary capabilities are vast. From the direct targeting of users[163] through to the mass and automated collection of information,[164] nearly every aspect of modern-day society is encapsulated within some form of surveillance. As previously highlighted, this can either be viewed as a positive development through the enhanced means of access,[165] or negatively through the empowered means to which the state can control information and society.[166] The UAE's embrace and development of technology to boost its surveillance capabilities in the post-Arab Spring era will be herein explored.

Many scholars have discussed how globalisation and modernisation have disrupted the relationship between the state and its citizens. Tim O'Reilly's Web 2.0,[167] Jan Van Dijk's Digital Democracy,[168] and Emma Murphy's ICT and the Gulf Arab States[169] argue that technological advances have eroded the state's position in favour of its population. John Arquilla and David Ronfeldt concur, and argue that technological developments have not only increased sources of information but have drastically altered the relationships of power that result from the changing dynamics presented by technology. This is summarised in simplified terms as 'the shifting from one-to-many broadcast media (e.g. traditional radio and television) to many-to-many interactive media'[170] or, as defined by Manuel Castells, mass self-communication.[171]

The changing power dynamic illustrated by the flow of information has the ability to erode the traditional tenets of power and authority that states such as the UAE rest upon. Foreseeing this issue, many countries have either pre-empted technological evolution where possible, or have utilised the same modern technologies for a conventional purpose. This has ensured the power of the state has not been diluted by the advance of technology and suggests that 'subsequent assertions about the technology's political effects are usually made without consideration of the full national context in which the Internet operates in any given country'.[172] It will in fact be argued that the UAE is encouraging more online engagement in an attempt to control and manage a larger and more interconnected web of information that heightens its regime security strategy.

Underpinned by UAE Government Strategy 2011–2013,[173] UAE Vision 2021,[174] Abu Dhabi Economic Vision 2030,[175] and Dubai Strategic Plan 2021,[176] the UAE has fast become a leading adopter of e-Government.[177] Dating back to 2001, the UAE has been rapidly exploring and implementing avenues for enhanced online government solutions to ensure the state's continued ability to foster innovation, and economic and social growth. This means however that while the population has greater access to governmental services, the state experiences increased levels of exposure. This in turn can make the state vulnerable due to higher degrees of accountability on the one hand or on the other could 'increase citizen satisfaction and further solidify the political regime'.[178]

The state's self-imposed openness is felt within every aspect of its online presence. From federal-level utilities operators, through to official social media profiles of leading Emirati political elites, the UAE state apparatus has emerged online; albeit without a formal online presence for the head of state, Khalifa bin Zayed al-Nahyan.[179] Importantly, while a large portion of government services have migrated online, there is still a requirement for the physical review of documentation and requests by civil servants. On the official website portal of Dubai eGovernment, the most advanced and open e-government structure within the UAE, there is currently a list of 504 government service items.[180] The listing of capabilities is split between Government department, service, and service classification, and each item is further qualified by the documents required to process the request and if the application can be made online.

When the services offered by Dubai eGovernment are compared to other public-sector entities, it is clear that only issues which are perceived to be non-critical and commercially-focused are available for online processing. For instance, and by comparison, the UAE MOI currently offers fifteen online services, which are listed within its crime security database. Clay Shirky suggests that the observation of the UAE's online focus of economic matters is to pre-empt social dissatisfaction.[181] This book however argues that the UAE's reluctance to dilute governance over security related issues is more due to the UAE's micromanaged and stringent approach to regime security.

While there are many e-services offered across the array of online UAE government portals most are handled in Arabic and

Table 4: Government Services Directory[182]

Sr.No	Department	Service	Classification Level 1	Classification Level 2
1	Dubai Municipality	Request of issuance/renewal of Occupational Health Card	Public Health & Safety	Public Health and Safety Services—Individuals
2	Dubai Municipality	Request for Food Export/Food Health Certificate	Public Health & Safety	Certification/Accreditation/Registration
3	Dubai Municipality	Request for Food consignment Releaser permit	Public Health & Safety	Permit/NOC—Food Control
4	Dubai Municipality	Request for Testing of Structural and Construction Materials	Projects & Infrastructure	Laboratory Tests
5	Dubai Municipality	Request to approve releasing of Food consignment for Re-export purpose	Public Health & Safety	Permit/NOC—Food Control

6	Roads and Transport Authority (RTA)	View and Pay Salik Violations	Roads Users	Salik
7	Dubai Police	Request to visit a detainee	Services permits	
8	Dubai Municipality	Request to Permit simple modifications/additions to an existing building(s)	Projects & Infrastructure	Building and Construction Services
9	Dubai Municipality	Request to transfer food consignment from Dubai ports to other Emirates and vice versa	Public Health & Safety	Permit/NOC—Food Control
10	Roads and Transport Authority (RTA)	Request for NOC for Mobility with extra load—weight or dimensions	NOC and Permits	Right of Way
11	Dubai Municipality	Request of Fees for the Hotel facilities & restaurants	Legal/financial services	Financial Services

12	Dubai Municipality	Request for decoration permit	Urban Planning & Construction	Building Permits and Licences
13	Dubai Municipality	Request for the gate level of the entrance to the building	Urban Construction & Planning	Building Permits and Licences
14	Dubai Municipality	Request to approve food Items Destruction	Public Health & Safety	Permit/NOC—Food Control
15	Dubai Municipality	Request for Calibration of Laboratory equipment and instruments	Accreditation & Certification	Laboratory Tests and Calibration Services
16	Dubai Municipality	Request to get a copy of approved engineering drawings	Urban Planning & Construction	Building Permits and Licences
17	Dubai Municipality	Request for planning permits	Urban Planning & Construction	Services/Planning Permits
18	Dubai Municipality	Request for Building permit application cancellation	Urban Planning & Construction	Building Permits and Licences

English, with occasional departments further offering the ability to submit documentation in other commonly spoken languages in the UAE. Government departments that handle predominantly domestic Emirati issues, however, are only published in Arabic.[183] This supports the argument that many of the government transformation plans that have been published by the GCC states (e.g. UAE Vision 2021) are primarily for foreign, not domestic audiences.[184] Domestic audiences and constituents remain serviced by the state in informal and traditional mechanisms so as not to dilute the authority and legitimacy of the regime.

The distinction between policies taken to target domestic and foreign audiences is highlighted further through the comparison of parallel governance strategies taken by the Emirates of Dubai and Abu Dhabi. In the Emirate of Dubai (which is inhabited by a large majority of foreign residents), a fusion of a traditional form of governance has transitioned online through the Mohammed bin Rashid al-Maktoum Smart Majlis.[185] Meanwhile in Abu Dhabi, the traditional tribal heartland of the state's power, the Crown Prince Court (CPC) has sponsored the deployment and engagement of physical majlises across Abu Dhabi in a bid to foster and sponsor Emirati community engagement akin to that of a pre-modern UAE.[186] The CPC also regularly hosts high-level lectures whereby leading political figures and subject matter experts discuss topics to an audience of PREs.[187] The distinction in engagement tactics between the characteristically different and socially contrasting cities of Abu Dhabi and Dubai highlights how superficial the UAE's e-government strategy is and emphasises how the process of modernisation in the country is restricted to non-critical areas of governance.

The development of online government capabilities has significantly increased the volume of information immediately accessible to it. Previously, personally identifiable information (PII) was handled by the data holders of each item, and not fused with other sources due to limitations within the wider state apparatus. At present, though, due to the encouragement of e-government services, and the management by the state in this manner, there are infinitely more opportunities for the state to handle information and analyse society.

Fusing the UAE's e-government strategy with its surveillance capabilities is the advanced identification system that designates ownership of information to a user. Underpinning this system of control is the Emirates ID project. Initiated in 2004 under Federal Law No. 2 of 2004,[188] and later updated by Federal Decree Law No. 3 of 2017,[189] Emirates ID is a federal identification card which stores biometric and personal data. Every resident of the UAE is required by law to own such a card and every public service can request this form of identification. When the biometric attributes are combined with other PII such as passports, resident visas, bank details, telephone numbers, information requests, or complaints, the state can effectively observe, manage, and direct the resident's life remotely.

A prominent example of the potential power wielded by the centralised identity management system is the legal requirement to connect this form of identification to the resident's mobile number(s) (all of which are handled by a majority of state-owned entities). This unifying initiative was launched through the TRA's 'My Number, My Identity' programme on 12 June 2012.[190] The campaign was followed only three months later by the establishment of the UAE's SIGINT establishment NESA, illustrating how the 'My Number, My Identity' operation was evidently a crucial requirement in ensuring the legal mass collection of personal data.

The linking of biometric data to a mobile number is a very powerful source of data, as the PII comprises all activities undertaken by that device to an individual, their location, and wider pattern of life. This means that every mobile phone subscriber can, at a minimum,[191] be located at any given time. The process of information collection and attribution designation was later expanded beyond mobile phones to ISPs.[192] The result is a constant watch over the UAE's residents, and the enhanced ability to observe every aspect of their pattern of life.

While the 'My number, My identity' campaign is a retrospective and live surveillance capability, the UAE also has a preventive online surveillance proficiency. As earlier shown, the internet is heavily controlled within the UAE. Its access, legal enforcement, and information propagation is well documented and aligns with

Elliot Cohen's idea of a four-step strategy for effective state control of the internet; corporatise, sanitise/propagandise, militarise, and globalise.[193] The UAE employs a blocking mechanism to restrict access to websites deemed inappropriate; predominantly pornography but also politically sensitive content. Online activists, anonymous, 'published a list of 24,000 URLs and keywords blocked in the country'.[194] Users are made aware of the censorship with webpage notices reading, 'Access to this site is currently blocked. The site falls under the Prohibited Content Categories of the UAE's Internet Access Management Policy.'

In pursuit of the UAE's attempt to effectively control the internet within its borders, the UAE restricts websites and provides an official source of information and mechanism to broadcast this online. State broadcasts have been forced to transition to digital formats for fear of losing the position of authority.[195] Should a foreign entity disseminate unfavourable stories and information, it is the responsibility of the governing authority to present what it perceives to be the truth.

The UAE has developed a sophisticated strategic communications capability, by which it has unified and extended its online presence through media institutions and social media profiles of government figures, to ensure the continuing domination of narratives. Through combined information campaigns, the UAE is effectively combatting narratives deemed false or contrary to that of the UAE regime. This capability is especially evident in the UAE's recent confrontation with Qatar, as state-owned media outlets, those operating within the UAE, and UAE public figures maintain discourse cohesion in opposition to the neighbouring state. The UAE furthermore blocked access to Qatari-owned media outlets within the UAE and outlawed the online display of support for Qatar.[196] Marc Jones supports this argument by showing how online bots have been deployed to bolster the social media discourse against Qatar, with the hashtag, #AlJazeeraInsultsKingSalman, one example of a reported campaign to spread condemnation against Qatar.[197]

The UAE has demonstrated a clear understanding of how technological development has enhanced the state's surveillance capabilities. In addition to the upgraded offensive surveillance capabilities, the UAE has maximised its passive oversight mechanisms, and has thereby created a larger intelligence database with which to leverage.

Viewing the online domain as another sector within which it can, and should, dominate, the UAE regime has sought to expand its traditional domain of control over a sector that has the intrinsic capability to be easily beyond the state's reach. The increased information demanded from citizens has widened the state's observation of society, legitimised through the veil of government modernisation.

Conclusion

It is clear that, in response to the Arab Spring, the UAE has greatly enhanced it surveillance capabilities. Due to technological developments, and the previous lack thereof, many of these advances have been within the digital domain. Legitimised through a proactive e-government programme, the UAE state apparatus has been able to collect vast streams of private and public data and collate this alongside a network of information provided by state-owned institutions and the wider commercial sector. This has amplified the state's surveillance capabilities as its domination of information and narrative has provided the means for the state to leverage more control over society.

The shift in state surveillance capabilities emerged in the immediate aftermath of the Arab Spring, notably through the creation of NESA. NESA empowers the rapid mass surveillance of UAE society, and is directed by a concentric leadership team that has intimate ties to Mohammed bin Zayed al-Nahyan. Assisting NESA's surveillance capability are the UAE's structural and legal foundation, which further define and solidify the parameters of what the UAE's surveillance capabilities can effectively monitor. The UAE's process of understanding cyber threats has evolved from failed attempts to control small domains through to the redefining of parameters that now provide the state with a platform for effective observation of information and communications.

The propagation of information and the enforcement of an official state message has assisted the authoritative position of the regime as the crafter of this narrative. This favours the ability to enforce a will or produce a deterrence or punishment for whoever disagrees with the party line.[198] In many cases this form of information management reconstructs fact and becomes an effective tool of manipulation; through the delivery of an effective message, national, state, and regime security concerns have been fused for the benefit of the latter. As this restricts the behaviour of society, or provides the context to observe behaviour, the control of the narrative is just as important for the study of surveillance.

Wary of the effects that technology might have upon the UAE's societal dynamics, the Abu Dhabi regime has sought to limit the practical impact of technology upon the most sensitive aspects of the UAE state and society. This has created a two-tier system, whereby issues relating to Emirati citizens remain firmly rooted in interpersonal and traditional relationships. This is to ensure the effective maintenance of the clientelist relationships that solidify the regime's rule, and the societal culture that provides legitimacy for the regime's authority. Technological platforms are being used to elicit support from the Emirati population and are often fused with cultural symbols and messages to maximise strategic messaging campaigns. Where innovation has been more widely employed is generally restricted to areas of commercial and non-critical affairs; sectors which more openly involve the foreign population and as a result are more naturally exposed to external stimuli.

Understanding the inherent dynamism within technological evolution, the UAE has tried to stay abreast of developments controlling the system of architecture through formal institutions and hierarchical personnel structures.[199] While these have so far proved sufficient in supporting the UAE's regime security strategy, their continuing adjustment to technological developments is crucial in their ability to enhance the UAE's regime security strategy in the future.

5

STRATEGIC ECONOMIC MANAGEMENT

The strategic management of the coercive apparatus provides the regime with an ability to enforce its power at will, but it is the primacy of power maintenance[1] that ensures the long-term survival of any political establishment. This chapter will therefore examine the extent to which the Abu Dhabi ruling family has exploited the UAE's economy to strengthen its regime security strategy.

In the wider context, the management of economic resources has increasingly been viewed as a security issue.[2] Barry Buzan and Ole Wæver explain this clearly by stating that 'unless a state is self-reliant in the resources required to feed its population and industry, it needs access to outside supplies. If that need is threatened, the national economy can be clearly and legitimately securitized'.[3] Likewise, Matthew Gray observes 'the blurring of economic and military aspects of security'[4] and makes reference to Peter Moore[5] and Gregory Gause[6] who have also used the framework of a securitised economy in a GCC setting.

Within his hypothesis of institutional dimensions of modernity, Giddens claims that the economy is synonymous with capitalism,[7] defining the latter as 'the insulation of the economic from the political against the backdrop of competitive labour and product markets'.[8] While Giddens adheres to a clear, free market interpretation of the economy, Ian Bremmer reinterprets the role of the economy in the modern day through state-led capitalism, which is defined as 'a system in which the state dominates markets, primarily for political gain'.[9] When Bremmer's hypothesis is coupled with observations of economically-induced societal stratification,[10] widespread corporatism within the Arab world,[11] and the perceived connection between corporatism and authoritarian rule,[12] there is a clear relationship between the management of the economy and the manipulation of societal ties for political gain; a hypothesis that is Weberian in nature.[13] Oliver Schlumberger refers to this trend as patrimonial capitalism.[14]

While as a single entity the UAE clearly symbolises the rentier state classification, the micro-dynamic distribution of rental commodity within the UAE reveals a more complicated perspective. This is because 92.2 billion barrels of the UAE's proven 97.2 billion barrels are located within the Emirate of Abu Dhabi.[15] This concentration of natural and economic resources, in combination with the previously discussed RST provides a strong argument not only for the centralisation of the UAE's power in Abu Dhabi, but also explains why this research focuses exclusively on the strategic management of the UAE by the Abu Dhabi ruling family.[16] Kristian Ulrichsen does note that while oil is concentrated in Abu Dhabi, this only accounted for 28.3 per cent of the national UAE GDP in 2013.[17] This suggests that while oil has enabled the construction of the state in Abu Dhabi's image, there are now additional sources of revenue generation beyond the Emirate's structural ownership.

Implicit within the UAE's federal identity is the requirement for Abu Dhabi to distribute funds generated from oil extraction to the other six Emirates. Nevertheless, there is sufficient evidence to suggest that there is significant economic disparity between Abu Dhabi and the other Emirates.[18] Comparative oil reserve figures may account for the skewed distribution of funds; it should be noted that by controlling the vehicle for revenue generation, the Abu Dhabi elite initiated a process whereby authority would become increasingly centralised.[19] Furthermore, the long-term economic control of the UAE's rental income has allowed Abu Dhabi to build and cement clientelist relationships; both domestically and internationally. The result has seen state-led economic diversification directed by an increasing number of SOEs resulting in PPPs with domestic and international partners, thus serving the dual benefit of revenue generation and co-optative maintenance.

The regime's central role in the development of the economy has empowered it to grow 'accordingly into an inflated, self-perpetuating and self-interested bureaucracy'.[20] The state and the regime can, and has, effectively structured human capital to complement its strategic objectives. However, under healthy financial conditions the state's 'power is still fragile and vulnerable to rapid social changes and economic crises'.[21] Eva Bellin concurs and notes that 'the economic contraction suffered by the Middle East over the past twenty years was triggered by the decline in public investment that followed the fall in oil prices in the mid-1980s'.[22] The focus on the state as the driver of the economy and national growth aligns with the state-led capitalism model. As the directing force of economic development, the state's failure to provide sufficient jobs, growth, and social advancement contributed to the outbreak of the Arab Spring.[23]

Bassam Haddad merges analyses of the state's ownership of resources and the effect that this has on societal relations within MENA, by hypothesising that the clashes witnessed in the Arab Spring were a symptom of the friction between the traditional elites and the newly empowered economic elites.[24] In the GCC context, the relationship between traditional and economic elites[25] has directly contributed to the political tensions in Kuwait[26] and has also provided a platform for extremist groups, such as the Muslim Brotherhood, to grow.[27] By contrast to Kuwait, the ruling PREs of the UAE never relaxed their dominance of the private and commercial sectors. This ensured that there was never a need to establish any power-sharing agreements or mechanisms of coordination with the commercial and economic sector.[28]

Concurrently, due to the reality of the UAE's oil and gas finite reserves, and their turbulent market prices, the UAE's PREs have encouraged economic diversification.[29] This has highlighted an impending challenge; by diversifying the economy away from natural resources, not only does the number of participants in the generation of wealth increase, but this can also potentially reduce the importance of traditional institutions on which the current power structure rests, weakening the position of the current PREs. Thus, it becomes equally important to diversify sources of revenue not only to strengthen revenue generation but also to maintain the state's disproportionate control of resources.

Through the combined aspects of authoritarian governance and tight economic control, there is a potential for the leadership to misinterpret their economic situation. Robert Wade[30] and Chalmers Johnson[31] analyse how economies often suffer as a result of the leadership's separation from society and the false reading they have of their circumstances.[32] It is therefore no coincidence that the GCC's most developed democracy is Kuwait,[33] since in that country 'the private sector is well placed to play an organisational and financial role within the opposition'.[34] This example illustrates how communities that lie beyond the direct control of the state represent a significant threat; an analysis the UAE regime has certainly acknowledged.

While the relationship between the state and the business community is of significant interest and is widely discussed within political economy literature,[35] given the focus of this book on regime security, and not state or national security, there is a greater requirement to look at regime-focused and state-led ventures rather than the micro-dynamics of the wider public-private sector relationship;[36] this is not to argue that the regime and state act unilaterally, but that their perception of interests is significantly different and thus warrants a separate analysis.

With an accurate understanding of state-led economic investment and development, Bremmer's state-led capitalism model provides the adequate framework for this book's research concerns. The theory of state-led capitalism emerged through the combination of failed neo-liberal reforms, high natural resource ownership, and the return to prominence of the big state. While Bremmer's postulation is a new concept for many states, 'the governments of China, Russia, Saudi Arabia and other countries had begun building their own versions of state capitalism long before the Western financial crisis sparked a global recession'.[37] For the

GCC, state-led capitalism has been the optimal model of political economy, as it builds upon rentier state theory to ensure the state's authoritative position within society. Through institutional giants such as those hypothesised by Bremmer—namely national oil corporations (NOCs), state-owned enterprises (SOEs), privately owned champions (POCs), and sovereign wealth funds (SWFs)—the state can continue to direct strategic initiatives that strengthen the fiscal health of the state's economy and provide the platform for human capital development.

The substantive political economy[38] hypothesis provides an additional layer of analysis for the study of the state's relationship with the business community, as it acknowledges the social structure which the power dynamics are based upon.[39] Nonetheless, Ferran Brichs and Athina Limpridi-Kemou contradict this by arguing that, in fact, while pre-rent dynamics are important, through the control of finances and the system that controls them, the ruling authority can remanufacture state relations.[40] With this in mind, it is key to highlight that it is a combination of the historical and contemporary societal dynamics that provides an accurate basis for the understanding of the UAE's political economy.

Due to the ever-changing nature of the economy there is a constant requirement to create and enforce reforms[41] that enhance efficiency and, in the case of an authoritarian state, ensure the state's dominant role.[42] Therefore, in order to understand how the economy has been manipulated to strengthen the UAE's regime security strategy, it is crucial to assess how and why reforms in this respect have been implemented.[43] Since the full array of subsequent changes cannot be foreseen, economic reforms also manifest a significant danger for an incumbent regime;[44] therefore, the state's central position as the owner and distributor of resources supports the focus upon the state.[45] As a consequence, the observation of the UAE as a rentier state combined with its monarchical system of governance, justifies this chapter's focus on the regime's security management.

This chapter will analyse how the UAE's economy has been managed to strengthen the post-Arab Spring regime security strategy through the model of state-led capitalism and the privileged economic network that combine to support the centralised management of the UAE economy. State-led capitalism is defined through its 'four primary actors: national oil corporations, state-owned enterprises, privately owned champions, and sovereign wealth funds (SWFs)',[46] and the privileged economic network is defined as the 'network of business and state actors who collaborate to manage access to economic benefits—disregarding their formal juridical separation into private and public actors'.[47] Ultimately, this chapter illustrates to what extent, since the Arab Spring, the Abu Dhabi ruling family has significantly enhanced the UAE's regime security strategy through effective manipulation of the state's economy.

National Oil Corporations (NOCs)

NOCs (and other resources that empower rentier culture) were established to leverage state-owned resources. As previously discussed, oil and gas revenues have contributed a sizeable amount to the UAE's GDP.[48] Of the UAE's oil proven reserves, 95 per cent are located within the Emirate of Abu Dhabi. The Emirates of Dubai and Sharjah also leverage oil and gas reserves within their territory, however, due to their relatively marginal reserves, these contribute to a considerably lesser degree to the local economy.[49] While Article 23 of the UAE's constitution states that 'the natural resources and wealth in each Emirate shall be considered the public property of that Emirate',[50] it has become abundantly clear that the UAE's federation would have not survived had Abu Dhabi not shared its oil wealth across the state's seven Emirates. Within this context, Abu Dhabi is the predominant focus of the NOC analysis.[51]

An analysis of the political economy of rentier states by definition focuses on the production and exploitation of the resource in question. Michael Herb argues however that 'oil is important—how could it not be in these states? (GCC)—but only as an intervening variable. Oil explains nothing about politics until we understand how it effects existing political institutions'.[52] Using Herb's observation this section analyses the regime's management of oil and gas. The guardianship of Abu Dhabi's natural resources is primarily handled by the SPC and this is described by Davidson as 'Abu Dhabi's highest financial body'.[53] This is primarily comprised of the Abu Dhabi ruling family and their close kin. The 2018 structure of the SPC is as follows:

Table 5: SPC Members as of March 2018[54]

Title	Name	Tribe
Chairman	Khalifa bin Zayed al-Nahyan	Bani Yas
Vice Chairman	Mohammed bin Zayed al-Nahyan	Bani Yas
Member & Vice Chairman of Abu Dhabi Executive Council	Hazza bin Zayed al-Nahyan	Bani Yas
Member & Deputy Prime Minister, Minister of Presidential Affairs, and UAE Cabinet Member	Mansour bin Zayed al-Nahyan	Bani Yas
Member & Managing Director of Abu Dhabi Investment Authority (ADIA) and Member of the Executive Council	Hamed bin Zayed al-Nahyan	Bani Yas
Member & Director of Abu Dhabi Investment Authority (ADIA) and Member of the Executive Council	Mohammed bin Khalifa bin Zayed al-Nahyan	Bani Yas
Member & Chairman of the Department of Transport and Member of the Executive Council	Dhiyab bin Mohammed bin Zayed al-Nahyan	Bani Yas
Member & Minister of Energy	Suhail Muhammad Faraj al-Mazrouei	Bani Yas

Secretary-General	Hamad Mubarak al-Shamsi	Al-bu Shamis—Formerly of the Na'im
Member & ADNOC CEO	Dr. Sultan bin Ahmed al-Jaber	Al-Ali
Member & Secretary General of the Executive Council	Dr. Ahmed Mubarak al-Mazrouei	Bani Yas
Member & CEO Mubadala	Khaldoun Khalifa al-Mubarak	
Member & Chairman of the Department of Finance and Member of the Executive Council	Riyad Abdulrahman al-Mubarak	
Member & Chairman of the Department of Energy and Member of the Executive Council	Eng. Awaidha Murshed al-Marar	Marar—Section of the Bani Yas
Member	Eng. Abdullah Nasser al-Suwaidi	Sudan—Section of the Bani Yas
Member	Suhail Fares Ghanem al-Mazrui	Mazar—Section of the Bani Yas
Former Member[55]	Sultan bin Zayed al-Nahyan	Bani Yas
Former Member	Hamad al Hurr al-Suwaidi	Sudan—Section of the Bani Yas
Former Member	Muhammad Habroush al-Suwaidi	Sudan—Section of the Bani Yas
Former Member & Secretary General	Jawan Salem al-Dhaheri	Dhaheri—Section of the Bani Ma'in[56]
Former Member	Khalifa Mohammed al-Kindi	Sudan—Section of the Bani Yas

Of the sixteen members of the SPC, at least twelve are members of the Bani Yas tribal grouping: both the Chairman and Vice Chairman of the SPC have sons on the board of the SPC, and of the seven present descendants of Zayed bin Sultan al-Nahyan, four are also descendants of Fatima al-Ketbi. The strength of relationship between the ruling family members within the SPC indicates both the significance of the SPC to the ruling family, and who within the ruling family has significant power. This is based on the hypothesis that the Abu Dhabi ruling family is not a monolithic entity and that distinctive cliques can be identified through members' tribal affiliations.

In the post-Arab Spring period the dominant al-Nahyan clan is the Bani Fatima. Their representation has been fortified within the SPC since the Arab Spring and is illustrated through amendments to its membership in 2011 and 2016. In June 2011 Khalifa bin Zayed al-Nahyan appointed Abdullah Nasser al-Suwaidi as Director General of Abu Dhabi National Oil Company (ADNOC)[57] and he was listed among a council consisting of twelve people. Five years later, and two years after Khalifa bin Zayed al-Nahyan's stroke, there was another reshuffle, with Hazza bin Zayed al-Nahyan, Theyab bin Mohammed bin Zayed al-Nahyan, Dr. Sultan al-Jaber, and Khaldoon al-Mubarak appointed to the SPC.[58] Simultaneously, Sultan bin Zayed al-Nahyan, the second oldest son of Zayed bin Sultan al-Nahyan, Hamad al Hurr al-Suwaidi, Muhammad Habroush al-Suwaidi, and Khalifa Mohammed al-Kindli were all relieved of their responsibilities with the SPC. It is noted by GSN that the 2016 appointments illustrate 'the dominance of Crown Prince and Deputy Supreme Commander of the UAE Armed Forces Muhammad Bin Zayed al-Nahyan (MBZ) and his Bani Fatima brothers'.[59] The increased concentration of power among the Bani Fatima within the SPC after the Arab Spring demonstrates how important strategic control of the state's natural resources is for the regime.

Accordingly, while the regime maintains tight control over the strategic management of the SPC, the principal organisation mandated to operate the production of natural resources within the UAE is ADNOC. The Emirates of Dubai and Sharjah also have their own natural resources organisations but these are not comparable to ADNOC's role within the UAE's political economy and will subsequently not be analysed within this work.[60] ADNOC was founded in 1971, following the growth of revenue from oil extraction dating back to 1958.[61] Today, ADNOC is the twelfth largest producer of oil in the world[62] and has onshore and offshore oil and gas exploration and drilling capabilities.

While oil wealth has provided the platform for the Emirate of Abu Dhabi to secure its leading role with the federation and the global stage, there has been a growing transition away from a sole focus on natural resource extraction. ADNOC has been at the forefront of this development, with changes to its leadership team and corporate strategy presenting valuable examples of the innovative policy.

Starting in 2013 and coinciding with the Abu Dhabi Company Onshore Oil Operations (ADCO) concession of 2014,[63] several technocrats and close associates of Mohammed bin Zayed al-Nahyan who were already working within the energy sector had started to rise within the UAE's political arena. The two prominent examples were Suhail Muhammad al-Mazrouei and Dr. Sultan bin Ahmed al-Jaber, who were appointed as Minister of Energy and Minister of State, respectively. Al-Jaber was later, in February 2016, appointed as Director General of ADNOC.[64] Both al-Mazrouei and al-Jaber ADNOC alumni and the Mohammed bin Zayed al-Nahyan-led SWF Mubadala; 'Al-Mazrouei was Al-Jaber's number two at Mubadala'[65] which proves the strength of the relationship between the two leading figures within the UAE's energy structure. Furthermore, it is worth noting that, contrary to the traditionally patriarchal policies across the GCC, both al-Mazrouei and al-Jaber are relatively young for the responsibilities placed upon them.

While Suhail bin Muhammad al-Mazrouei's rapid rise through ADNOC and Mubadala suggests a degree of technocratic weighting, Sultan al-Jaber's rise illustrates the evolution of Emirati natural resource policy.[66] Al-Jaber had led the UAE's engagement with renewable technology as he 'established Masdar, Abu Dhabi's pioneering renewable energy initiative, and served seven years as its CEO, guiding its global contribution to clean technology and sustainable development'.[67] His subsequent rise within ADNOC, and other public-sector institutions such as the NMC and the Abu Dhabi Ports Company (ADPC), illustrates how his evolutionary take on economic, industrial, and energy policy is supporting the UAE's projections for the future.[68]

Al-Jaber's appointment as ADNOC CEO coincided with low oil prices (hovering around US$30 per barrel in February 2016)[69] and demonstrated the new direction Abu Dhabi was going to take with regards to its energy policy. He has since commenced an efficiency strategy, ADNOC Integrated 2030 Strategy,[70] which has identified multiple mechanisms to decrease costs and increase profits,[71] and has also instructed the consolidation of multiple subsidiaries.[72] In addition, al-Jaber has overseen the restructuring of ADNOC's subsidiaries, replacing six chief executives with 'well-regarded internal technocrats to key positions of influence'.[73]

While there have been attempts to optimise oil and gas production in an era of contracted prices, the UAE has initiated a strategy that seeks to ensure the state's future livelihood. Through the appointment of technocratic personnel and empowered by long-term strategic plans, the Abu Dhabi ruling family is attempting to lay the foundations for a long-term and stable future that can survive after its oil reserves are finished. Charles Hankla and Daniel Kuthy explore this enduring vision by suggesting that 'truly stable authoritarian regimes tend to have individual leaders with very long time horizons (far beyond those of stable democratic leaders), providing them with stronger incentives to choose policies, like free trade, that may contribute to long-run economic growth'.[74] This observation is enhanced when the rentier state social contract is applied, as it is crucial for a leader of such a state to provide resources and thus ensure the continuation of legitimacy and authority.[75]

In combination with its lean oil and gas production, the UAE is building the Middle East's first civilian nuclear power station[76] and the world's largest solar panel field.[77] While these programmes will not provide the same financial benefits as their oil and gas counterparts, nor the same rentier state social contract, they demonstrate an understanding of what is needed to support a future state. The UAE's oil and gas reserves will continue to make a sizeable contribution to the state's GDP and government budgets, but they are a finite resource that will deplete within the current leadership's lifetime. Thus, the Abu Dhabi ruling family has initiated the process, following the Arab Spring, to provide the foundation for a post-oil economy, and thus ensure their own long-term longevity. It can be concluded that the enhancement of the state's NOCs is a clear pillar of the UAE's post-Arab Spring regime security strategy.

State-Owned Enterprises (SOEs)

SOEs are defined by the Organisation for Economic Co-operation and Development (OECD) as 'any corporate entity recognised by national law as an enterprise, and in which the state exercises ownership ... enterprises that are under the control of the state, either by the state being the ultimate beneficiary owner of the majority shares or otherwise exercising an equivalent degree of control'.[78] SOEs are prominent across the world as they have enabled planned economies to dictate and lead market share and development. SOEs also provide ample social benefits and support the development of infrastructure whilst also delivering—often subsidised— services to the state's population.[79] As a result, SOEs tend to be judged through a matrix of their value to society and their delivery of financial returns.[80]

Due to the UAE's small population and concentrated group of PREs, the UAE's SOEs are by nature vulnerable.[81] The delivery of service and capability is deemed as necessary as the requirement to generate funds is, and therefore illustrates why most SOEs have a large emphasis on professionalism, technocracy, and profit; i.e. they cannot simply haemorrhage funds. To achieve this, there is often a dual tier of management that directly correlates to national and foreign participation; board level membership is often dominated by Emiratis and the active management is often dominated by foreign employees.[82] This is further clarified by the fact that the state does, in most cases, own the SOEs through one of its SWFs; a more condensed vehicle over which the regime has a greater degree of control. Table 6 shows the SOEs that are owned by the government of Abu Dhabi, and not owned or run exclusively by SWFs.[83]

Table 6: SOEs in Abu Dhabi[84]

State-Owned Enterprise[85]	Ownership vehicle
Abu Dhabi Airports Company (ADAC)	Government of Abu Dhabi[86]
Abu Dhabi Health Services Company (SEHA)	Government of Abu Dhabi[87]
Abu Dhabi Media Company (ADMC)	Government of Abu Dhabi[88]
Abu Dhabi National Exhibitions Company (ADNEC)	Government of Abu Dhabi
Abu Dhabi National Oil Company (ADNOC)	Government of Abu Dhabi[89]
Abu Dhabi Ports [Company] (ADPC)	Government of Abu Dhabi[90]
Abu Dhabi Securities Exchange (ADX)	Government of Abu Dhabi[91]
Abu Dhabi Water & Electricity Authority (ADWEA)	Government of Abu Dhabi[92]
Emirates Nuclear Energy Corporation (ENEC)	Government of Abu Dhabi[93]
Etihad Aviation Group	Government of Abu Dhabi[94]
Etihad Rail Company	Government of Abu Dhabi[95]
First Abu Dhabi Bank	Abu Dhabi Investment Council owns 33.5 per cent, Mubadala owns 3.7 per cent, and other UAE entities and Individuals own 52.1 per cent[96]
National Health Insurance Company	Government of Abu Dhabi owns 80 per cent[97]

In comparison with the UAE's SWFs, the Abu Dhabi-owned SOEs are almost entirely utilities and service-based entities, and thus are not primarily focused on revenue generation. This suggests that the SOEs owned and operated by the government of Abu Dhabi are designed to deliberately subsidise the economy and society so as to ensure its long-lasting attractiveness.[98] Furthermore, as many of these institutions are exposed to internationally competitive markets, they must in turn adapt and enforce internationally accepted governance strategies.[99] Nonetheless 'the federation's [UAE's] largest corporate groups and financial institutions, whether owned by shareholders or directly by the state, are dominated by either the UAE's federal government or a member of one of the seven ruling families'.[100] This is to ensure the continued dominance of the state in the wider economy and exploit structural mechanisms to control every aspect of society.

While there have been incentives and political pressure behind attempts to diversify the domestic economies of the MENA, many 'regimes are loath to privatize public enterprises because these enterprises serve as key sources of state patronage (jobs for the masses, lucrative posts for political cronies) and so are crucial to the regime's strategy of building support at the mass and elite level'.[101] Khaled al-Mezaini takes this further in the case of the UAE by saying that it is crucial for the regime's survival to ensure a relationship dynamic of dependence.[102] This can be expanded to explain why rentier states are often reluctant to diversify their economies, especially as their exposure to international markets significantly increases the potential for criticism of their fiscal performance.[103] Barry Buzan, Ole Wæver, and Jaap Wilde support this idea by explaining that 'although genuine economic security issues are relatively rare, normal and politicized economic activity frequently spills over into other sectors, with security consequences'.[104]

The role played by SOEs in the UAE's economy has ensured that no particular group can emerge from within the commercial sector to rival the power of the state and thus the regime.[105] Should the market swing in favour of private industry, the state would either co-opt them[106] or change the legislative parameters to favour the SOE.[107] Abu Dhabi's monopoly on utilities and critical infrastructure further empowers the state and the regime[108] as they can exploit control of national infrastructure to achieve political gains while also providing a central ability to shape the domestic economy to suit their own strategy and outlook. While there has been no significant change to the domain of SOEs since the Arab Spring, this still reinforces their dominant role within the UAE's regime security strategy.

Privately Owned Champions (POCs)

POCs 'are companies that remain in private hands (though governments sometimes hold a large minority stake) but rely on aggressive material support from the state to develop a commanding position in a domestic economy and its export market'.[109] Bremmer expands by saying that 'the UAE's private sector is dominated so heavily by companies owned directly by various members of the seven families that the concept of national champions doesn't really apply'.[110] While Bremmer's postulation is ultimately accurate, his oversimplification of the UAE's context distracts from an in-depth analysis of the subject in question.

Since the discovery of oil, many GCC states have undertaken aggressive expansion of the private sector, with Adam Hanieh explaining that 'the Gulf capitalist class has emerged rapidly and in "hothouse" fashion—from state-supported and family-based trading groups in the 1960s and 1970s to the domination of a few massive conglomerates in the contemporary period'.[111] While this had led the business community to become a credible threat to the incumbent regime[112] in several GCC states, the UAE has embraced diversification whilst still firmly pursuing a state-led capitalist model.

Due to the significant growth in the non-oil economy of the UAE, the private business community has clearly been prioritised as an enabling force from an early point in the federation's history.[113] This is however a tale of two cities as the Emirate of Dubai has led diversification efforts while Abu Dhabi has been more frugal and has thus ensured that economic growth remains firmly tied to the state;[114] Martin Hvidt claims that initially the Emirate of Dubai had pursued a service economy while the Emirate of Abu Dhabi pursued industrialisation.[115] This meant that while many successful private ventures appeared in Dubai, as in Abu Dhabi, the state maintained control of strategic and infrastructural assets.

A further component that has enabled such a stark contrast between the UAE's two largest Emirates is the provision of free zones. These provide a foreign entity with full ownership rights, as opposed to their comparative 'onshore' alternatives, which require Emirati nationals to own 51 per cent of the commercial entity. To illustrate the contrasting approach to economic diversification and economic liberalism, Abu Dhabi has four free zones[116] whilst Dubai has twenty.[117] It is therefore evident that Abu Dhabi has a more nationalised approach to business within its Emirate given the clear prioritisation of asset retention as a factor in the success of the Emirate's private sector. Providing context to the lack of private sector development in Abu Dhabi, of the top ten largest companies by value traded on the ADX, eight are SOEs.

Table 7: Top 10 Buyers and Sellers on the Abu Dhabi Securities Exchange[118]

Company	Share	Ownership
Dana	74.3%	Foreign Owned
Aldar	8.3%	SOE
Etisalat	1.0%	SOE
National Bank of Abu Dhabi (NBAD)	1.1%	SOE
Abu Dhabi Commercial Bank (ADCB)	0.8%	SOE
Abu Dhabi Islamic Bank (ADIB)	1.1%	SOE
RAKPROP	5.0%	SOE
Union National Bank	1.0%	SOE
ESHRAQ	4.6%	Private, Emirati-owned
TAQA	2.8%	SOE

While the listing on the ADX does not accurately reflect the nature of POCs, it does highlight the deficiency in the development of private institutions within Abu Dhabi. Those private institutions that do exist in Abu Dhabi tend to be, on nearly every occasion, family institutions and, if particularly successful, directly linked to the Abu Dhabi ruling family and/or owned by a member of the Bani Yas.[119] Family businesses are especially common in Abu Dhabi; however, they are rarely publicly listed on the ADX.[120] The National Investor (TNI) published a report in 2008 which evaluated the proportion of tribal members per board seats in Abu Dhabi-based companies.[121] Half of the top ten were Bani Yas affiliates.[122] The concentration of tribal affiliation within the private sector in Abu Dhabi suggests that, within the economy, links to the Abu Dhabi ruling elite still reign supreme.

Specific successes within Abu Dhabi POCs can be identified; however, their apparent collusion and cooperation with the state suggests a form of commercial co-optation. These POCs exist in specific sectors and contribute to a clearly defined predetermined goal. One example is the field of defence, which includes private firms such as Emirates Advanced Investments (EAI),[123] International Golden Group (IGG),[124] and Baynunah Group.[125] All have direct tribal and kinship relations to the al-Nahyan ruling family, whilst also exhibiting clear professional links that would enable these firms to have a definite advantage within the commercial sector.[126] Likewise, the al-Nahyan ruling family have their own private enterprises, which they use to generate greater private finances; these include Royal Group[127] and the Bin Zayed Group.[128] In essence, while the larger POCs may make a significant contribution within certain sectors, they are entirely dependent upon the state for contracts and as a result cannot be deemed to be entirely private.

Abu Dhabi's state-led capitalism strategy for commercial development has ensured that the relationship between the ruling family, tribes, and wider community is not affected by altered dynamics.[129] The reluctance to allow an independent power centre not only secures the hierarchical and authoritative position of the state, but also that of the regime as owner of the resources that direct the development of the UAE economy.[130] As there has been no substantial change to the field of private commercial enterprise within Abu Dhabi, there seems to have been a deliberate campaign to ensure the control of a sector within which a potential adversary could emerge.

Sovereign Wealth Funds (SWFs)

SWFs play an instrumental role for the state as they not only generate economic, political, and social benefits, but also serve as a tool of legitimisation. There are multiple definitions for SWFs,[131] but Andrew Rozanov's original postulation and definition provides the foundations for research into the topic. In summary: "The funds (SWFs) are set up with one or more of the following objectives: insulate the budget and economy from excess volatility in revenues, help monetary authorities sterilise unwanted liquidity, build up savings for future generations, or use the money for economic and social development'.[132]

SWFs differ from other forms of state-owned assets and investments, such as public pension funds, development funds, and state-owned enterprises, due to the objectives and structure of each form. According to Sara Bazoobandi, 'SWFs are usually funded from surplus government income and often held outside their country of origin. In order to protect the sovereign wealth, in most cases, SWFs are managed separately from other types of public investment funds'.[133]

SWFs are, by nature, generally secretive about their investments and 'it is difficult to reliably identify where GCC surpluses have been identified'.[134] This results in the analysis that it is not only impossible to accurately verify the size of SWFs, but that without official declaration it is also impossible to know exactly what SWFs invest in and for what purpose. Andrew Rozanov's definition of a SWF helps to simplify concerns and categorisations of SWF, as he hypothesises that SWFs either prioritise financial and commodity investment or are structured towards societal development. In essence SWFs achieve both but are prioritised towards one or the other.

Due to the UAE's federal identity, SWFs within the UAE are creations of an individual Emirate's government and not a national institution. Given Abu Dhabi's ownership of the state's oil reserves, it was able to establish its SWFs very early. This has allowed Abu Dhabi to strategically invest in projects and mechanisms that enhance the Emirate and the state's economy and help advance human capital to support the objectives of the Abu Dhabi ruling elites. The five SWFs owned by Abu Dhabi are the ADIA,[135] Abu Dhabi Investment Council (ADIC),[136] International Petroleum Investment Company (IPIC), Mubadala,[137] EAI,[138] and Invest AD (also known as Abu Dhabi Investment Company).[139] In the neighbouring Emirate of Dubai, there are, according to Sara Bazoobandi, three SWFs;[140] Dubai World,[141] Dubai Holding,[142] and the Investment Corporation of Dubai.[143] For the purpose of clarification, this chapter will analyse the Abu Dhabi focused SWFs, and not those in other Emirates as they are of peripheral interest to the Abu Dhabi ruling family.

Abu Dhabi Investment Authority (ADIA)

Abu Dhabi's initial engagement of SWFs was through the creation of ADIA in 1976. Its mission 'is to sustain the long-term prosperity of Abu Dhabi by prudently growing capital through a disciplined investment process and committed people who reflect ADIA's cultural values'.[144] According to the Sovereign Wealth Fund Institute (SWFI), ADIA holds US$828 billion worth of assets[145] making it the world's fourth largest SWF.[146] ADIA is funded by the budget surplus of the Abu Dhabi government and contributes to any shortfall when necessary, although it prioritises a longer-term investment strategy.[147] As a result, there is a higher significance in analysing the personnel who make up the leadership of ADIA, rather than the assets in their control, as they oversee and manage the entity which the Abu Dhabi ruling family can depend upon for their future livelihood and security. Hendrik Van Der Meulen concurs and notes that 'the most important decision-making authority under the ruler is the Abu Dhabi Investment Authority (ADIA)... The importance of this fund to the ruling family and the nationals of the Emirate, as well for the country as a whole, is clear'.[148] Davidson further supports this idea by claiming that 'of equal if not greater importance to Abu Dhabi's economy since the 1970s has been the channelling of surplus oil revenues into long term overseas investments'.[149]

The current ruler of Abu Dhabi, Khalifa bin Zayed al-Nahyan, has been the Chairman of ADIA since its creation in 1976.[150] Until 2010, Sheikh Ahmed bin Zayed al-Nahyan had led ADIA as Managing Director, but after his death in 2010, his full brother Sheikh Hamed bin Zayed al-Nahyan took charge.[151] The decision to appoint Hamed bin Zayed al-Nahyan to the position of Managing Director suggests a significant consideration for tribal and family alliances. This is further reinforced through the 2005 appointment of Mansour bin Zayed al-Nahyan to the ADIA board,[152] illustrating the requirement to bolster such a strategically important institution with close family members.

While ADIA has typically reshuffled its directorial board every three years,[153] since the death of Zayed bin Sultan al-Nahyan in 2004, there has been only a marginal change to the membership of the ADIA board. The ADIA board is dominated by sons of Zayed bin Sultan al-Nahyan, and it has increasingly denied access to other tribes. Since 2007 four directors have been removed from the board (See Table 8). It is also telling that changes to the board made in 2013, one year before Khalifa bin Zayed al-Nahyan's stroke, illustrated a degree of stability as they kept the same board members from 2010. Subsequently, changes made to the 2017 board of directors removed three members: Sultan bin Zayed al-Nahyan, Jua'an Salem al-Dhaheri, and Hamad Mohammed al-Hurr al-Suwaidi. This is significant as the incapacity of Khalifa bin Zayed al-Nahyan during this time suggests that his deputy at ADIA, Mohammed bin Zayed al-Nahyan, initiated these changes to suit his own strategy and outlook. Firstly, the removal of Sultan bin Zayed al-Nahyan from the ADIA board of directors removed a potential competitor of Mohammed bin Zayed al-Nahyan and finalised the total eradication of a public profile for Sultan bin Zayed al-Nahyan. Secondly, while Jua'an Salem al-Dhaheri passed away in 2013,[154] Hamad Mohammed al-Hurr al-Suwaidi was appointed as Head of Abu Dhabi Accountability Authority.[155] These changes resulted in five descendants of Zayed bin Sultan al-Nahyan (Bani Yas) manning the ADIA board of directors, joined by two technocrats who are also Bani Yas tribal members. Simply put, this means that the ADIA board is now entirely composed by Bani Yas figures.

Table 8: Evolution of the Abu Dhabi Investment Authority (ADIA) Directors

2007[156]	2010[157]	2013[158]	2017[159]
Khalifa bin Zayed al-Nahyan (*Bani Yas*)	Khalifa bin Zayed al-Nahyan (*Bani Yas*)	Khalifa bin Zayed al-Nahyan (*Bani Yas*)	Khalifa bin Zayed al-Nahyan (*Bani Yas*)
Sultan bin Zayed al-Nahyan (*Bani Yas*)	Sultan bin Zayed al-Nahyan (*Bani Yas*)	Sultan bin Zayed al-Nahyan (*Bani Yas*)	Mohammed bin Zayed al-Nahyan (*Bani Yas*)
Mohammed bin Zayed al-Nahyan (*Bani Yas*)	Mohammed bin Zayed al-Nahyan (*Bani Yas*)	Mohammed bin Zayed al-Nahyan (*Bani Yas*)	Mansour bin Zayed al-Nahyan (*Bani Yas*)
Ahmed bin Zayed al-Nahyan (*Bani Yas*)	Mansour bin Zayed al-Nahyan (*Bani Yas*)	Mansour bin Zayed al-Nahyan (*Bani Yas*)	Hamed bin Zayed al-Nahyan (*Bani Yas*)
Mansour bin Zayed al-Nahyan (*Bani Yas*)	Hamed bin Zayed al-Nahyan replaced Ahmed bin Zayed al-Nahyan following his unexpected death (*Bani Yas*)	Hamed bin Zayed al-Nahyan (*Bani Yas*)	Mohammed bin Khalifa bin Zayed al-Nahyan (*Bani Yas*)
Mohammed bin Khalifa bin Zayed al-Nahyan (*Bani Yas*)	Mohammed bin Khalifa bin Zayed al-Nahyan (*Bani Yas*)	Mohammed bin Khalifa bin Zayed al-Nahyan (*Bani Yas*)	Muhammad Habroush al Suwaidi al-Nahyan (*Sudan of the Bani Yas*)

Muhammad Habroush al-Suwaidi (*Sudan of the Bani Yas*)	Muhammad Habroush al-Suwaidi (*Sudan of the Bani Yas*)	Muhammad Habroush al-Suwaidi (*Sudan of the Bani Yas*)	Khalil Muhammad Sharif Foulathi (*Al bu Falah of the Bani Yas*)
Jua'an Salem al-Dhaheri (*Dhawahir*[160])	Jua'an Salem al-Dhaheri (*Dhawahir*)	Jua'an Salem al-Dhaheri (*Dhawahir*)	
Hamad Mohammed al-Hurr al-Suwaidi (*Sudan of the Bani Yas*)	Hamad Mohammed al-Hurr al-Suwaidi (*Sudan of the Bani Yas*)	Hamad Mohammed al-Hurr al-Suwaidi (*Sudan of the Bani Yas*)	
Saeed Mubarak Rashid al-Hajiri (*Sunni of Iranian origin*)	Khalil Muhammad Sharif Foulathi (*Al bu Falah of the Bani Yas*)	Khalil Muhammad Sharif Foulathi (*Al bu Falah of the Bani Yas*)	

The role of ADIA in ensuring there are sufficient 'financial resources to secure and maintain the future welfare of the Emirate' (Abu Dhabi)[161] clearly acts as the principal mechanism to ensure the regime's long-term maintenance of power. This observation acts as illustration and response to Giacomo Luciani's postulation that 'all states can be autonomous in the short run, but in the longer run their ability to act autonomously from society is linked to their revenue foundations'.[162] Through ADIA's augmentation of oil revenues, the Emirate of Abu Dhabi can ensure its long-term future and security. The adjustment to the ADIA board of directors after the Arab Spring, as well as following the stroke of Khalifa bin Zayed al-Nahyan, shows an enhanced strategy to condense power within a network of closely related personnel and trusted tribal technocrats. Therefore, the adjustment made to ADIA's board showcases a key dynamic of the UAE's post-Arab Spring regime security as it sought to maintain close control of a strategic investment vehicle in time of economic turbulence.

Abu Dhabi Investment Council (ADIC)

Where ADIA's role is to preserve 'some part of the revenues from a depleting resource for future generations and spending needs',[163] and evaluates global opportunities for maximum financial return, the Abu Dhabi Investment Council is tasked with a similar mission but for 'domestic and regional investments'.[164] ADIC was established in 2006, through Article 4 of the Law 16 of 2006, as a breakaway addition to ADIA.[165] ADIC took ADIA's domestic investment portfolio and used this as a basis to expand an interest in the wider MENA region. Like ADIA, ADIC keeps many of its investments a secret. Nonetheless, it has publicised the investment in many SOEs, including National Bank of Abu Dhabi (NBAD), Abu Dhabi Commercial Bank (ADCB), Union National Bank (UNB), Al Hilal Bank, Abu Dhabi National Insurance Company, Abu Dhabi Aviation Company, and the Abu Dhabi Investment Company (also known as Invest AD).[166]

Upon its inception Khalifa bin Zayed al-Nahyan chaired ADIC,[167] and it was noted in 2015 that the ADIC board would be assessed every three years.[168] While there have been three announcements made in reference to the ADIC board, only two amendments have been made. Firstly, the appointment of Mohammed bin Zayed al-Nahyan as ADIC chairman in 2015 and, secondly, the removal of Khalifa Mohammed al-Kindli. In 2018 it was announced that ADIC would be restructured and merged into Mubadala. Before this occurred however, four members of the al-Nahyan ruling family were on the board of ADIC: Mohammed bin Zayed al-Nahyan, Sultan bin Zayed al-Nahyan, Mansour bin Zayed al-Nahyan, and Hamdan bin Zayed al-Nahyan. Joining them were Habroush al-Suwaidi, Eissa Mohamed al-Suwaidi, and Younis Haji Khoori. Due to the significance of the domestic focus of ADIC the non-ruling board members should be further explored.

Habroush al-Suwaidi is a member of the Sudan clan of the Bani Yas and has extensive experience in the finance and investment sector within Abu Dhabi. He was previously the Managing Director of ADIA and member of the Abu Dhabi Executive Council,[169] and is still one of its board of directors. Concurrently, he has also been listed as 'advisor to the President',[170] thus suggesting not only a powerful domestic role but also a close relationship to Khalifa bin Zayed al-Nahyan. Another ADIC board member, Eissa Mohamed al-Suwaidi is also from the Sudan clan of the Bani Yas. He also had a career within ADIA, where he was previously the Director of the Bond and Equity department.[171] He is also chairman of the Abu Dhabi Commercial Bank (ADCB) and Chairman of Emirates Telecommunication Corporation (Etisalat), whilst also being a board member of several SOEs and public-sector institutions.[172] The last figure currently on ADIC's board is Younis Haji Khoori. He is currently the Undersecretary of the Ministry of Finance[173] and is also a board member of the General Pension and Social Security Authority.[174]

While Khalifa Mohammed al-Kindli was removed from the ADIC directors in the 2015 announcement, he remains a very important figure. According to Hendrik Van Der Meulen, the family of Khalifa al-Kindli is 'an important lineage within the Sudan section',[175] also making him a member of the Bani Yas. In 2012, al-Kindli was appointed Chairman of the UAE Central Bank[176] and, given his previous roles as director of the treasury department and as finance director at ADIA and ADNOC respectively, his transition out of ADIC illustrates no significant demotion or fall from favour.

The strategic requirement to offset ADIA's domestic and regional role, and to augment financial returns with societal development shows a more politicised mission for the ADIC. The stable membership of the ADIC board through a time of political turmoil suggests a tightly knit core of trusted and capable people. The transition in leadership to Mohammed bin Zayed al-Nahyan after Khalifa bin Zayed al-Nahyan's stroke and after the Arab Spring, does however further evidence the increased power grab by Mohammed bin Zayed al-Nahyan from an array of strategically important vehicles. This was further demon-

Table 9: Evolution of the ADIC Board of Directors

	2007[177]		2010[178]		2015[179]
Chairman	Khalifa bin Zayed al-Nahyan (*Bani Yas*)	Chairman	Khalifa bin Zayed al-Nahyan (*Bani Yas*)	Chairman	Mohammed bin Zayed al-Nahyan (*Bani Yas*)
Board Member	Sultan bin Zayed al-Nahyan (*Bani Yas*)	Board Member	Sultan bin Zayed al-Nahyan (*Bani Yas*)	Board Member	Sultan bin Zayed al-Nahyan (*Bani Yas*)
Board Member	Mohammed bin Zayed al-Nahyan (*Bani Yas*)	Board Member	Mohammed bin Zayed al-Nahyan (*Bani Yas*)	Board Member	Mansour bin Zayed al-Nahyan (*Bani Yas*)
Board Member	Mansour bin Zayed al-Nahyan (*Bani Yas*)	Board Member	Mansour bin Zayed al-Nahyan (*Bani Yas*)	Board Member	Hamed bin Zayed al-Nahyan (*Bani Yas*)
Board Member	Hamed bin Zayed al-Nahyan (*Bani Yas*)	Board Member	Hamed bin Zayed al-Nahyan (*Bani Yas*)	Board Member	Muhammad bin Habroush al-Suwaidi (*Sudan of the Bani Yas*)

Board Member	Muhammad bin Habroush al-Suwaidi (*Sudan of the Bani Yas*)	Board Member	Muhammad bin Habroush al-Suwaidi (*Sudan of the Bani Yas*)	Managing Director	Eissa Mohamed al-Suwaidi (*Sudan of the Bani Yas*)
Board Member	Khalifa Mohammed al-Kindi (*Sudan of the Bani Yas*)	Managing Director	Khalifa Mohammed al-Kindi (*Sudan of the Bani Yas*)	Board Member	Younis Haji Khoori
Board Member	Younis Haji Khoori	Board Member	Younis Haji Khoori		

strated by the announcement on 21 March 2018 that ADIC was to be integrated with Mubadala.[180] Mohammed bin Zayed al-Nahyan's increased presence in revenue-generating institutions not only seeks to protect his, and his family's, role in the future UAE economy, but to ensure that he can continue to manage those funds to maintain efficient supply of co-optive capital within Emirati society.[181]

Invest AD

Invest AD is a wholly owned subsidiary of ADIC and its aim is to 'to provide excellent returns for investors who increasingly are looking to allocate assets to GCC and MENA markets'.[182] Like other SWFs, there is only a partial array of information available on the investments made by Invest AD. According to Khaled Alsweilem, Angela Cummine, Malan Rietveld and Katherine Tweedie, Invest AD's 'specialisation is in frontier and emerging markets, particularly in Africa and the Middle East'.[183] As Invest AD has gradually ceded influence to the larger SWFs, ADIA and ADIC, Invest AD is not deemed a strategically important SWF for analysis. This is additionally supported by the fact that there are currently no members of the Abu Dhabi ruling family on Invest AD's board of directors.[184]

Table 10: Invest AD Board of Directors

Role	Name
Chairman	Muhammad Ali al-Dhaheri (*Dhawahir*)
Board Member	Mariam Saeed Ghobash
Board Member	Amer Saleh al-Ameri (*Awamir*)
Board Member	Athra Ibrahim al-Zaabi (*Za'ab*)
Board Member	David Beau (*Foreign national*)
Board Member	Dhaen Muhammad al-Hameli (*Hawamil*)
Board Member	Saoud Essa al-Mulla (*Murrah*)

Assuming that the notion of clientelism[185] is rife within the UAE, and that the Abu Dhabi ruling family is central to the state's management and ownership of material resources and their investment,[186] the board of Invest AD exemplifies why they are not as important for the UAE's post-Arab Spring regime security strategy.

International Petroleum Investment Company (IPIC)
and Mubadala

While Mubadala was established in 2002, its forerunner, the IPIC, was founded in 1984[187] and was chaired, since its establishment, by Mansour bin Zayed al-Nahyan. The IPIC was instituted through Emiri Law 3 of 1984, and it was 'initially a 50:50 joint venture between the Abu Dhabi Investment Authority (ADIA) and the Abu Dhabi National Oil Company (ADNOC)'.[188] Like other SWFs, the IPIC sought to utilise Abu Dhabi's oil reserves for long-term investments; however, it focused on the means by which the UAE's natural resources sector could be enhanced. As a result, the IPIC fell 'under the umbrella of the Supreme Petroleum Council'.[189] After Mubadala's creation, it became clear that there was a duplication of effort, often creating unnecessary competition and, as a result, on 21 January 2017[190] the IPIC merged with Mubadala.

Before its fusion with Mubadala, the board of the IPIC clearly depicted the dominance of Abu Dhabi political elites. Its Chairman was Mansour bin Zayed al-Nahyan and its last Managing Director, the current Minister of Energy, Suhail al-Mazrouei,[191] had succeeded Khadem al-Qubaisi in the organisation. Al-Qubaisi was sentenced to fifteen years in prison following a conviction for financial crimes.[192] This is in relation to the 1Malaysia Development Berhad (1MDB) scandal, which saw billions of US dollars stolen from the sovereign fund. As the deputy to Mansour bin Zayed al-Nahyan, the conviction of al-Qubaisi is portrayed as a way to absolve the responsibility of Mansour bin Zayed al-Nahyan and other Abu Dhabi ruling family members who are alleged to have also been involved in the crime.[193] The subsequent incorporation of IPIC into Mubadala could further signify an attempt to protect and insulate the Abu Dhabi ruling family from international investigations. Every member of the board of directors was a member of a tribe from within the Bani Yas (Table 11), a factor that, far from being a coincidence, clearly illustrates the importance of traditional alliances within the structure of strategically important institutions.[194]

Table 11: Last Directors of the IPIC, 2015[195]

Chairman	Mansour bin Zayed al-Nahyan (*Bani Yas*)
Deputy Chairman	Muhammad Dhaen al-Hameli (*Hawamil section of the Bani Yas*)
Managing Director	Suhail al-Mazrouei (*Mazar section of the Bani Yas*)
Board Member	Hamad Mohammed al-Hurr al-Suwaidi (*Sudan section of the Bani Yas*)
Board Member	Nasser Khalifa al-Suwaidi (*Sudan section of the Bani Yas*)
Board Member	Eissa Muhammad Ghanem al-Suwaidi (*Sudan section of the Bani Yas*)

Where IPIC acted as an infrastructure and savings-focused SWF and ADIA 'is a classic example of a savings fund',[196] Mubadala is a strategic investment vehicle whose mandate is to 'support economic diversification through investment and development in strategic sectors ... deliver sustainable financial returns and contribute to social development'.[197] In sharp contrast to the other SWFs, Mubadala is very public with its investment portfolio and strategy as it is through these high-profile endeavours that the organisation can increase its domestic and international standing.

Mubadala is self-referred to as a SOE,[198] but it is better classified as a SWF.[199] Since its creation, Mubadala has been led by Mohammed bin Zayed al-Nahyan and has acted as the vanguard for the modernisation of the UAE. According to Davidson, Mubadala has served as the central focus point for high technology products and ventures and has used its access to vast oil wealth to employ a highly skilled workforce, amongst them a sizeable percentage of Emiratis, so as to capitalise on this concerted effort.[200] An evaluation of the UAE's modernisation effort would suggest that the strategic construction of Mubadala and the subsequent implementation of economic visions such as Abu Dhabi Economic Vision 2030 and UAE Vision 2021 were part of a much longer-term strategy of economic and social development by Mohammed bin Zayed al-Nahyan.

It is evident from the evolution of leadership personnel within Mubadala since 2008 that there has been a clear strategy to build domestic capabilities with foreign personnel and slowly transfer this responsibility to domestic actors. While the board of directors has remained almost exclusively Emirati—with the two foreign nationals assuming the roles of Chief Financial Officer and Chief Legal Consul—the accompanying investment committee and executive management has slowly homogenised. The board of Mubadala condensed, but in a way that condensed ties and kinship amongst a very concentrated group.

Due to the developmental role played by Mubadala domestically, the evolution of the leadership towards an Emirati-dominated board of directors mirrors the wider national developmental strategy promoted by Mohammed bin Zayed al-Nahyan. This has

Fig. 9: Line Graph Showing Evolution of Mubadala Executive Leadership[201]

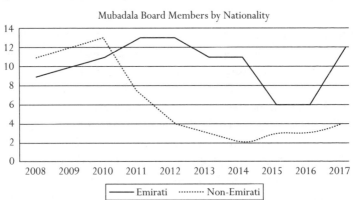

ensured that both Mubadala and Mohammed bin Zayed al-Nahyan, are portrayed as modernising forces that reward technocratic excellence. Additionally, the fact that Mansour bin Zayed al-Nahyan, who is a full brother of Mohammed bin Zayed al-Nahyan and is married to the daughter of Dubai Ruler Mohammed bin Rashid al-Maktoum, was appointed the vice chairman of Mubadala following the integration of IPIC and ADIC into Mubadala, signifies both the importance of Mubadala to Mohammed bin Zayed al-Nahyan and the growing power of Mansour bin Zayed al-Nahyan. While Mubadala's board of directors is characteristically less tribal than other strategic entities, this suggests a greater appreciation for the value of professionalism within the developmentally focused SWF.

Tribal affiliation still plays a moderating influence for membership affiliation within Mubadala; however, an increasing trend is emerging which is evidencing the mix of technocratic excellence and kinship affiliation to Mohammed bin Zayed al-Nahyan. Prominent examples have illustrated that this mix has led to the rapid promotion and growth in stature of said individuals; to use Steffen Hertog's observation, this mechanism would be called technocratic clientelism.[202] Five examples highlight this postulation:

The first example is Sultan al-Jaber, who was initially appointed as CEO of the wholly Mubadala-owned subsidiary, Masdar, in 2011[203] and later as CEO of Mubadala Energy. He has since gone on to assume a position within the UAE Cabinet and as Minister of State. Meanwhile he is also Chairman of the NMC, Group CEO of ADNOC, and Chairman of Abu Dhabi Ports Company.[204] His sharp rise should be seen in the context of his relatively weak tribal heritage, as this further supports his political rise on the tangible and commercial successes that he initially mustered during his tenure at Mubadala.

The second example is Homaid al-Shimmari. While, like Sultan al-Jaber, al-Shimmari lacks the tribal heritage to which we might accredit his rise within Mubadala, he has behind him a career within the UAE Armed Forces, specialising in military maintenance, procurement, and logistics and leaving with the rank of Lieutenant Colonel.[205] Al-Shimmari is among the longer serving directors of Mubadala and was initially listed in the 2009 Annual Report as Executive Director for Aerospace.[206] He has since been credited with establishing and driving defence industrialisation within the UAE and has overseen the creation of Mubadala's aerospace and defence arm, and the Emirates Defence Industries Company (EDIC). He is now Mubadala Group Deputy CEO, Chief of Human Capital & Corporate Services, and is also Chairman of EDIC, Abu Dhabi Ship Building (ADSB), and Board Member of Mubadala Petroleum, Abu Dhabi Future Energy Company (Masdar), GLOBALFOUNDRIES and Du—Emirates Integrated Telecommunications Company PJSC.[207]

The third example is Muhammad al-Bawardi al-Falasi. Al-Bawardi is a member of the Dubai-based Bani Yas tribal affiliate, al-Bawardi,[208] which in turn is also a chain of the al-Bu Falasah. He has had a long tenure at Mubadala serving as Mohammed bin Zayed al-Nahyan's deputy and was listed as Vice Chairman of Mubadala from 2008 to 2014, after which he was not listed on corporate Mubadala documentation. In 2014 al-Bawardi was listed as Under Secretary of the Ministry of Defence,[209] and in the twelfth UAE Cabinet reshuffle in 2016, he was listed as Cabinet Minister and Minister of State for Defence Affairs.[210] His relationship with Mohammed bin Zayed al-Nahyan goes back to their shared time in the military; Hendrik Van Der Meulen notes that in 1997 'Muhammad al-Bawardi is the Director of the Private Office of UAE Armed Forces Chief of Staff Lt. General Sheikh Muhammad bin Zayid Al-Nuhayyan'.[211] The close relationship between Mohammed bin Zayed al-Nahyan and Muhammad al-Bowardi illustrates not only the centralisation of power around the former, but also that through an array of institutions under the direct control of Mohammed bin Zayed al-Nahyan, he has been able to cultivate and co-opt a new generation of leaders who will support him during his own future reign.

The fourth example is Jassem al-Zaabi. His tribal pedigree has firmly tied his family's allegiance to the al-Nahyans as, in 1968, Sheikh Zayed bin Sultan al-Nahyan invited the al-Za'ab tribe to relocate to Abu Dhabi from Ras al Khaimah, in a bid to readjust the domestic tribal dynamics of the UAE in Abu Dhabi's favour.[212] As a result, the al-Za'ab are well represented within public sector offices. During al-Zaabi's time at Mubadala, going back to 2008, he had been responsible for the firm's ICT-related investment. During this period, he worked closely with Mohammed bin Zayed al-Nahyan's eldest son, Khalid bin Mohammed bin Zayed al-Nahyan, and their close working relationship has been reflected in the wider public and security sector. As far back as 2013, al-Zaabi was noted to have become Director General of NESA and, as per its mandate, it would defer to the National Security Advisor and his deputy. In the case of the latter, this was Khalid bin Mohammed bin Zayed al-Nahyan. In February 2017, Khalifa bin Zayed al-Nahyan appointed al-Zaabi a member of the Abu Dhabi Executive Council where he assumed the role of Chairman of the Executive Committee.[213] A further correlation of time spent at Mubadala with a rising public sector career is illustrated through the trajectory of Jassem al-Zaabi.

The last overt example of how a successful career within Mubadala has led to political success and greater responsibility is Mubadala CEO, Khaldoon Mubarak. Due to his position at the helm of Mubadala throughout its growth, Mubarak has likewise risen in significance. He has now assumed the positions of Chairman of the Executive Affairs Authority and member of the ADEC.[214]

Through these five examples a trend is emerging, whereby Mubadala is becoming a significant base for upward mobility within the public sector. The increased emphasis on nationalisation is evidenced through the numerical increase in Emirati board members and reduced presence of foreigners among Mubadala's senior leadership; this trend is markedly distinct from when the Arab Spring erupted. The transition of these figures onto wider political positions further highlights the symbolic role played by Mubadala within the UAE's political community and is also symbolic of the discreet response made by the UAE's political establishment to the Arab Spring. MBZ's careful nurturing of Mubadala since 2002 is a clear example of a method used to pre-empt the Crown Prince's dilemma, as he has used Mubadala as a vehicle for co-option and alliance building, and in this way ensured his smooth ascension to power.

Emirates Investment Authority (EIA)

The EIA is unique in the sense that it is a federal-level entity that 'is mandated to strategically invest funds allocated by the Federal Government to create long-term value for the UAE and contribute to the future prosperity of the country'.[215] The EIA was created through Federal Decree Law No.4 of 2007 and later amended by Federal Decree Law No.13 of 2009. Sara Bazoobandi explains that the state's unequal distribution of natural resources and wealth led to the creation of the EIA. However, due to its low profile and position within Abu Dhabi,[216] the EIA is still regarded as a solely Abu Dhabi-focused entity. It is not pertinent to analyse the EIA further here, taking into account its lack of specific focus on the Abu Dhabi regime.

Effective Privileged Economic Network

Fundamental to the UAE's post-Arab Spring regime security strategy is the manipulation and cultivation of relationships and alliances. This is further exemplified within the state capitalism framework that emphasises 'the existence of close ties binding together those who govern a country and those who run its enterprises'.[217]

In the UAE the relationship between the state and the PREs is extremely close. Khaled al-Mezaini supports this observation by hypothesising that 'the relationships between merchant elites, social elites and the ruling families of the UAE are and have been based on the patrimonial regime, with a political-economic exchange between the political elites and merchant elites'.[218] By means of the state-led capitalist model, the Abu Dhabi ruling family has successfully structured the hierarchy and organisation of the state-society in its favour; in this way, the regime has ensured that not only is its fiscal future secure but that through effective co-optation, there is a long-term strategy to align aspects of society to the ruling family. In other words, the Abu Dhabi ruling family has efficiently exploited the finite resource of oil to permanently structure society in its image.

The state's handling of oil and the economy has created a dual tiered society in which the state remains a monolith within official and corporate sectors and the limited private sector remains fairly open and competitive to a mainly foreign participating environment. At the same time, the development and maintenance of a healthy private sector is a critically important vision for the regime, as it can alleviate the burden of employment, growth, and expenditure. In this vein the state has to maintain a delicate balancing act as foreign nationals desire greater commercial openness and flexibility, while 'many groups who form the core constituencies of these regimes (for example, public sector workers, bureaucrats, army officers, crony capitalists) staunchly oppose economic reform, and embracing it would put the regimes' political foundation at risk'.[219] The aspect of fiscal sociology which separates the interests of national citizens from their foreign counterparts further complicates the potential for a future healthy economy as 'policies that are detrimental to private business hardly affect nationals qua investors'.[220] While within the UAE there is a significant separation between Emirati nationals and foreign citizens, due to the latter's relative insignificance to the UAE's rulers, it is the socioeconomic position and relationship of the UAE's citizens that takes precedent.

It is critically important to highlight the feature of agency within the UAE's management of the economy. In each of the four pillars of the state capitalist model, the Abu Dhabi ruling family has clearly illustrated a degree of pre-meditated control and organisation. The characteristics of the regime-focused economic network are tribal affiliation, kinship relationship to Mohammed bin Zayed al-Nahyan and, increasingly, technocratic success. Within each strategic level entity, it has been shown that these three values have been the factors which the regime has fallen back on to strengthen its grip and control over economic affairs.

Due to the increased concentration of power in the post-Arab Spring era, there are now only a handful of overly powerful entities that manage the UAE's strategic economy; SPC, ADNOC, ADIA, and Mubadala. Through these four institutions, the wider array of state assets and the ecosystems they interact with can be managed by a small team of carefully selected personnel. The micromanagement approach to affairs ensures that this small and trusted team can deal with multiple assets whilst delegating specialist roles to technocratic personnel, ensuring control but also providing support and encouragement to persons who can empower the state's capabilities. This strategy also acts as a mechanism of upward social mobility and evidences a clear series of examples for those who want to show their loyalty to the regime and increase their stature and power within society. In this way, the regime can continue to co-opt the PREs and reward aspects of society for their contribution to assets that enhance the state's economic power.

The network of infrastructural control and management has clearly been enhanced following the Arab Spring. This suggests that it has been a deliberate strategy to retain a tight control over economic activities. The state's dominant role within the post-Arab Spring economy highlights the deliberate central planning and focus on the state. This ensures that state-society relations can continue to be directed in the state's favour, and thus prevent any independent power centre from emerging beyond the direct control of the regime.

6

INDUSTRIAL CONTROL

The stability of the UAE, like that of other rentier states, was deeply shaken by the Arab Spring. Debates surrounding the rentier social contract and the role of the state in social and national development ushered in a period of public accountability and subsequent state response. Where possible, authoritarian states enhanced methods of co-optation; however, this strategy is only possible if the coffers are full. As a result, it becomes a strategic mandate of the state to ensure a sustained lifecycle of fund generation. While the previous chapter examined how the Abu Dhabi ruling family has managed economic resources to strengthen its regime security strategy, this chapter will explore how the development of the UAE's industrial sector has also been employed as a key complementary measure towards achieving the same goal.

According to Giddens, 'modern industry is intrinsically based on divisions of labour, not only on the level of job tasks but on that of regional specialisation in terms of type of industry, skills, and the production of raw materials'.[1] In this regard, and as a clearly defined rentier state, the foundation for the development of the UAE's industry originates from the regime's management of natural resources. This in turn underlines the role of the lens of state-led capitalism in assessing how markets have been used to extend the political and economic leverage of, in this case, the Abu Dhabi ruling family.[2] This is due to the fact that the state's assets are in fact owned and directly managed by the regime, as discussed in the previous chapter.

Industry is a core concept within Giddens' dimensions of modernity, with it described as 'the main axis of interaction of human beings with nature in conditions of modernity'.[3] Industry is thus defined as 'a group of productive enterprises of organizations that produce or supply goods, services, or sources of income'.[4] The management and development of industry is often seen in conjunction with that of the economy, encompassing the commonly understood process of industrialisation. While 'the aim of [economic] diversification is spreading risk by creating a variety of income sources; industrialisation in its broadest understanding is the process of creating these diverse income sources'.[5] Scholars such as Matthew Gray,[6] Peter Moore,[7] and Gregory Gause,[8] have discussed how economic issues are increasingly becoming viewed as traditional security threats, and therefore are being interpreted in a more conventional way. It is within this context that this chapter seeks to examine how the strategic management of industrial development has been used to develop the UAE's economy and, in turn, its regime security strategy.

Global industrial development has occurred asymmetrically, with the MENA region being classified as one of the late developers.[9] To crudely illustrate this trend within the UAE context, it is claimed that 'in early 1966, the capital [Abu Dhabi] had about 30 vehicles'[10] while it is reported that in 2010 there were 2,260,000 cars registered in all of the UAE.[11] The UAE's underdeveloped industrial sector is dependent on foreign support for its development, in terms of both technology and manpower. Importantly, however, while 'it is more difficult for the capitalist countries to manage their economies than formerly was the case, given accelerating global economic interdependence',[12] it can be argued that the UAE is making use of the increased international commercial competitiveness for their own strategic benefit.[13] The best example of this phenomenon is the UAE's economic investment in allied states for augmented strategic gain,[14] as it binds these states to the future of the UAE and vice versa. The UAE–USA relationship is the most important for Abu Dhabi. The UAE has directly invested

US$27.6bn into the US while it remains the United States' largest export destination in the Middle East.[15]

Observing the broader MENA context, many of the region's states are classified as rentier states due to their dependence on the sale of natural resources for a significant portion of their funds; these states are thus required to develop the necessary infrastructure that allows them to exploit the available raw resources. In this vein, it is now common for every form of large-scale public sector procurement to extrapolate some form of reinvestment in the local industry. David Becker expands by explaining how states maximise profits for domestic and political gain:[16]

> The underlying mechanism is the production for exportation of mineral products, conducted such that a portion of the earned surplus is captured by the local state. The surplus share accruing to the state is distributed thus: to support the state apparatus financially, to develop other economic sectors related distantly or not at all to mineral production; and to provide economic benefits to mobilized, vocal societal elements in hopes that they will refrain from challenging the existing structures of political domination and social control.[17]

There are also formal legal and commercial contracts that ratify the state's strategy of financial redistribution and contract augmentation. These are commonly known as offsets and are defined as 'one way of industrializing while at the same time conserving on foreign exchange, and perhaps even reducing the overall financial burden'.[18] Offsets are a central mechanism within the UAE's large-scale state purchases, most regularly employed in the aviation and defence sector and have in recent times been used to structure industrial development.

The UAE's industrial development is best examined through the same prism of state-led capitalism that was explored in the previous chapter. This places national oil corporations (NOCs), state-owned enterprises (SOEs), privately owned national champions (POCs), and sovereign wealth funds (SWFs) as the vanguards of industrial development.[19]

State-led capitalism is distinct from state capitalism due to the regime's inherent ownership of resources; while many previously communist states were state capitalist, state-led capitalism is distinct because of the direct involvement, ownership and manipulation of the economy by the regime. This is due to the neo-patrimonial nature of authoritarian society that is inherent within state-led capitalism. As previously noted, neo-patrimony is a 'style of leadership where a sovereign—a monarch or a president—is at the center of an elite web, with subordinate elites that are submissive to the leader but between which the leader encourages competition'.[20] State-led capitalists exploit their rentier dimension to structure power to the benefit of the regime, and it was shown in the previous chapter that the Abu Dhabi ruling family is no different in this guise.

Due to the long-term generation of funds and capabilities through industrial development, this sector is crucial to a regime's security strategy. This not only improves the literal accumulation of finances, but is also 'used by state élites for the purposes of "state-building"'.[21] This observation assists the analysis of industrial development as a pillar of the UAE's regime security strategy[22] because 'state capitalists see markets primarily as a tool that serves national interests, or at least those of ruling elites'.[23] In essence, state-led capitalist systems such as the UAE, do use the veneer of state or nation-building to construct new forms of legitimacy whilst maintaining a priority on buttressing their own security interests.

There is a careful balancing act required to ensure that the development of the economy and industry does not endanger the incumbent regime. Matthew Gray explains that there is 'a recognition that more active and entrepreneurial state capitalism can assist in providing state longevity ... regimes are taking a more considered and strategic look at their longer-term roles as well as their weaknesses and survival strategies'.[24] As a result, there are differing strategies employed to develop industrial and economic assets whilst still continuing the requirement to ensure the regime is continually insulated. Nazih Ayubi highlights this policy dilemma by explaining that 'the state appears to be obliged to sacrifice one of its two pillars of legitimacy: welfarism or developmentalism'.[25] Consequently, it is a political requirement for an autocratic regime, such as the UAE, to sustain developmental programmes that both develop the capacity to incur finances whilst also providing a social platform that manages forms of legitimation. Whilst numerous scholars have discussed evolutionary forms of rentierism, this book postulates that the UAE is attempting to move towards a more diversified economy that remains micromanaged by the regime but is exploited to generate additional streams of legitimation beyond direct handouts. This chapter will therefore highlight how industrial development and its many accompanying strategies have worked to maximise political control across society.

National Development Plans (NDPs)

NDPs are a common trend across the GCC, given that all of the concerned states face similar vulnerabilities and threats. According to Matthew Gray, 'most of these states set strategic goals and visions rather than seek to centrally plan or manage the economy'.[26] Fundamentally, the primary difficulty encountered by GCC states in this respect is implementing a successful transition from a resource-dependent economy to a more diversified one. NDPs illustrate the strategy that these states will undertake in assisting their efforts towards economic diversification. The most prominent example of an NDP in the region is Saudi Vision 2030,[27] but the UAE had initiated its own roster of NDPs over a decade before.

The UAE's NDPs have included UAE Vision 2021,[28] Abu Dhabi Economic Vision 2030,[29] Dubai Strategic Plan 2015[30] & 2021,[31] and Abu Dhabi Urban Planning Vision 2030.[32] More recently, in November 2018 at the second annual government meeting, seven new NDPs and one hundred initiatives were unveiled. These NDPs not only illustrate the UAE's economic growth targets, but were also aimed at showing tangible evidence of the progress made thus far in the country's development.[33]

There has been a steep increase in the number of NDPs created in the UAE since the Arab Spring, leading to the hypothesis that this is due to the regime's acknowledgement of the economic vulnerabilities the state faces. It is important to note that, while NDPs illustrate a roadmap for progress, they do not guarantee success, an observation corroborated by Kristian Ulrichsen.[34] Many of the NDPs have been composed in particular economic circumstances, becoming irrelevant after a short time. The most prominent examples of short-term strategic NDPs are the Qatar Vision 2030 and the Qatar National Development Strategy 2011–2016.

Due to the political and economic nature of such programmes, NDPs are attached to the individuals or institutions who generate them. It was Saudi Crown Prince Muhammad bin Salman al-Saud who led the Saudi Vision 2030, while Dubai ruler Mohammed bin Rashid al-Maktoum has often been the public face of economic and societal development within the UAE.[35] Through the state-led capitalism model, it is clear that NDPs have been constructed to expand the state's reach, increase scope of co-opted persons, and develop the state and society in the image of a person or persons. However, Abu Dhabi has adopted a subtler approach, wherein the state, as opposed to a specific individual, is for the most part the figurehead of development. This is part of a carefully manufactured nation building strategy that seeks to generate support around the UAE as a singular nation and state, with Mohammed bin Zayed al-Nahyan as its figurehead and father. This ensures a greater emotional link with the regime and whomever its sitting ruler is.

The highest authority responsible for structuring the UAE's and Abu Dhabi's development is the Abu Dhabi Executive Council (ADEC). The Abu Dhabi Executive Council is 'like a council of ministers, with the Chairman of the Executive Council effectively a Prime Minister';[36] a description Davidson agrees with.[37] The ADEC is an indicator of tribal and, more recently, kinship dynamics around Mohammed bin Zayed al-Nahyan, who, since 2007, has demonstratively reorganised the ADEC around his own power base.

The appointment in 2019 of two of Mohammed bin Zayed al-Nahyan's sons, Khalid and Theyab, to the ADEC illustrates the shift in dynastic lineages from Khalifa bin Zayed al-Nahyan's to Mohammed bin Zayed al-Nahyan's descendants; a dramatic change in power dynamics between the two brothers. By contrast, in 2019, only one son of Khalifa bin Zayed al-Nahyan, Mohammed bin Khalifa al-Nahyan, is still part of the ADEC.[38] This move puts in evidence Mohammed bin Zayed al-Nahyan's lineage expansion, growing influence and power in the ADEC, and thus in the industrialisation and economic development of the UAE.

Moreover, through his management of personnel on the ADEC, Mohammed bin Zayed al-Nahyan has balanced tribal and kinship principles to craft a platform that supports his own agenda. As a starting point, Mohammed bin Zayed al-Nahyan has resorted to endorsing tribal links as a means of dominating the ADEC. At the same time, it is important to note that there has been a decrease, proportionally, in the number of Bani Yas members on the ADEC.[39] In combination with this, while there were five sons of Zayed bin Sultan al-Nahyan on the ADEC in 2007, they were of mixed maternal heritage. By 2019, not only were there four sons of Zayed bin Sultan al-Nahyan in the ADEC, but they were all from the same power bloc, the Bani Fatima. This shift demonstrates Mohammed bin Zayed al-Nahyan's strategy of monopolising the ADEC with figures from his own kin, thereby increasing his control and influence.

Understanding the potential risks originating from within his family, Mohammed bin Zayed al-Nahyan has supplemented what would have previously been limited to tribal alliances for kinship and technocratic ability. Due to their lesser—sometimes non-existent—power within the ruling elite, these figures do not represent a threat to the regime. Their positions rely on their success and allegiance to the regime and their directives; should they fail, they are easily replaceable by others with similar technical capacities. Notable non-ruling family figures exemplifying the implementation of this strategy are Jassem al-Zaabi, Saif al-Hajeri, Falah Muhammad al-Ahbabi, Sara Awad Issa Musallam, Khaldoon Khalifa al-Mubarak, and Muhammad Khalifa al-Mubarak, all of whom are members of the ADEC and who have professional history at Mubadala where Mohammed bin Zayed al-Nahyan is the Chairman. This demonstrates a direct link between having a strong relationship with Mohammed bin Zayed al-Nahyan and a successful career as a technocrat within the UAE.

Furthermore, the shrinking and expansion of the ADEC, before and after the Arab Spring, signals a deliberate strategy to initially consolidate and then fortify the political power which has been generated by the political establishment. The ADEC shrank from eighteen members in 2007, of which fourteen were Bani Yas members, down to fourteen members in 2010, of whom only nine were from the Bani Yas. It was then expanded by one member in 2016, before being expanded to nineteen members in 2019—twelve Bani Yas figures are currently part of the council. The dynamics of personnel appointment to the ADEC illustrate the transition of power to Mohammed bin Zayed al-Nahyan, establishing him as ADEC's locus.

From looking at the evolution of the ADEC, it is possible to identify that there has been a dominant influence of tribal and kinship factors in the development of the ADEC. Furthermore, the reduction in size of the ADEC at the height of the Arab Spring before a gradual increase in its membership from 2016 shows how ruling family members are aware of the potential competitive threat from other elites and are extremely selective about their admission to such strategic entities. The singular factor that illustrates the development of the ADEC is the rise of Mohammed bin Zayed al-Nahyan and his use of the ADEC for the development of his own power base.

By controlling the body that directs the development of strategy, the regime can keep a constant oversight of development and progress, shifting goalposts to suit their own agenda across a wide array of sectors. The dynamic observed within the ADEC is also noted by Matthew Gray, who explains this strategy saying that it 'serves both the practical aim of maintaining the political status quo, and the simultaneous appearance of being consultative with society'.[40] This underpins a neo-patrimonial system of governance that controls economic and industrial concerns; one which is structured vertically with the principal at the top. This is best shown through the state-led capitalist model as it places the regime centrally through each entity.

National Oil Company (NOC)

The UAE's financial base was built on the sale of its natural resources. Investment flooded the UAE to develop the production and export of its petroleum products. The strategic management of the National Oil Company (NOC) and its domestic ramifications was previously discussed in Chapter 5. This section will assess how the NOC has been used to facilitate the development of infrastructure, human resources, and financially productive assets.

While the aim for the Abu Dhabi ruling family is to diversify away from oil, which is intrinsically an unstable asset, it continues to be the backbone of the state's economy. This is formalised within the still-enforced 1979 Federal Industrial Law[41] which, as summarised by Fatima al-Shamsi, was centred around the base of profits derived by the oil and gas sector; '1. For the Government to prepare a productive base capable of allowing manufacturing industries to thrive and thereby reduce the reliance on oil'.[42]

The predominant NOC within the UAE is ADNOC, and within its conglomerate are multiple entities that provide both upstream and downstream services. According to the 2015 ADNOC sustainability report, there are '20 diversified and integrated group companies',[43] illustrating how developed ADNOC is. Moreover, ADNOC employs 'nearly 65,000 employees',[44] of whom it was reported in 2014, ADNOC wanted 75 per cent to be Emirati nationals.[45] Presumably, this is in response to the ADNOC sustainability report highlighting that only 34.1 per cent of the workforce were Emirati nationals.[46] While this is a relatively low figure, given the low numbers of Emiratis in the country (less than ten per cent of the total population), those employed by ADNOC represent a substantial proportion of the total Emirati population in the country.

In contrast with strategic level entities such as the SPC, the ADNOC board of directors is made up of technocrats. This contrasts with the common and heightened value that tribal and kinship features play under Mohammed bin Zayed's reign and illustrates the absent features of tribalism and kinship shown so predominantly elsewhere in the country's industrial arena.

The lack of tribal or kinship relationships among the ADNOC board of directors denotes an emphasis on technocratic ability. This reflects how important it is for the Abu Dhabi ruling family to have an efficient and working NOC that can deliver regular funds to

151

support the development of the state and thereby shield the regime.[47] This observation is supported by Steffen Hertog[48] and Matthew Gray.

Table 12: ADNOC Executive Management as of 12 March 2019[49]

Role	Name
Chief Executive Officer (CEO)	Dr. Sultan Ahmed al-Jaber
Director, Upstream Directorate	Abdulmunim Saif al-Kindy
Director, Downstream Directorate	Abdulaziz Abdulla al-Hajri
Director, Marketing, Supply & Trading Directorate	Khaled Salmeen
Director, Executive Officer Directorate	Omar Suwaina al-Suwaidi
Director, Finance and Investment Directorate	Matar Hamdan al-Ameri
Director, Business and Commercial Support Directorate	Rashed Saud al-Shamsi
Director, Human Capital & Administration Directorate	Ghannam al-Mazrouei
Chief Legal Counsel, Legal, Governance and Compliance	Salem Muhammad al-Darei
Manager, Health, Safety & Environment	Abdulla al-Marzooqi
Manager, Audit & Assurance	Ahmed Abujarad

It is within this context that the appointment of Sultan al-Jaber as Chief Executive Officer (CEO) in 2016[50] indicated an acknowledgement of the required changes for ADNOC and the UAE to diversify and evolve its industrial capabilities. According to Sultan al-Jaber, the mission entrusted to him by Mohammed bin Zayed al-Nahyan was to initiate a 'step-change, comprehensive transformation'.[51] This was heralded as a seismic event for the UAE as al-Jaber had previously made a career at Mubadala, where he was Head of Energy and launched the renewable energy company Masdar. The combination of al-Jaber's background and the slump in global oil prices illustrated the path the UAE would be navigating in regard to its dependency on oil production. In July 2020, Sultan al-Jaber was appointed as Minister of Industry and Advanced Technology, a new organisation designed to foster and initiate the UAE's industrial development.[52] Due to al-Jaber's career trajectory it becomes clear that his symbolic rise is an illustration of the regime's attempt to increase its control and leadership of industrial development.

ADNOC has attracted a series of investments from foreign firms into the UAE's oil and gas sector. This has come from renewing onshore concessions,[53] awarding new offshore concessions,[54] issuing a US$3bn international bond,[55] listing of ADNOC distribution,[56] competitive block licensing,[57] and a US$550m investment for US firm Baker Hughes for a 5 per cent stake in ADNOC drilling.[58]

The decision taken by Sultan al-Jaber, as head of ADNOC, to generate supplementary revenue streams from asset sales and partnership agreements is one which runs counter to its previous policy, and thus highlights a novel approach to the management of the NOC.[59] With oil at a lower sustained price, it was crucial for ADNOC to attract sizeable funds to ensure long-term profitability. In this mindset, ADNOC was able to successfully spread its risk and exposure to the international market. This means that the foundations of the UAE's financially productive resources remain stable, and thus are able to provide the regime with the enduring capability to deliver funds for even the most basic public services.

Furthermore, ADNOC is seeking to modify its profile to accommodate demand and spread risk. This is coming mainly in the form of investment and development within the petrochemical sector. ADNOC CEO Sultan al-Jaber estimates that by 2050 the petrochemical industry within the GCC region will grow by 60 per cent.[60] It is clearly not only an objective for ADNOC to invest in the petrochemical market, but also for the wider industrial sector within the UAE. This was heavily stressed by a cooperation agreement that granted to 'build on Mubadala's diverse portfolio of refining and petrochemicals assets and support ADNOC's international Downstream investment ambitions'.[61]

This should be seen in connection with investments made both domestically and abroad by ADNOC, into the petrochemical sector. In the UAE, ADNOC announced in May 2018 a US$45bn investment to develop 'the world's largest integrated refining and petrochemicals facility'[62] in Abu Dhabi. In the accompanying statement by ADNOC, the company estimated that this single investment would contribute 1 per cent annually to the UAE's GDP.[63] Apart from investing in the petrochemical industry directly, there are additional benefits such as the creation of homes, jobs, and development of the wider non-oil sector that will assist the UAE's diversification.[64] The US$45bn investment also seeks to enhance and accelerate the UAE's production of oil, increasing its daily capacity by more than 65 per cent.[65]

Looking abroad, ADNOC took an equal 50 per cent share in a partnership with Saudi Aramco for an investment to jointly develop the Ratnagiri refining and chemicals complex.[66] When assessing the decision by ADNOC to invest in a foreign market, the factors of leadership, the state of the current economic market, and strategic foresight indicate a long-term plan to fortify ADNOC's investment in the oil and gas sector. While India had not been a close partner of the GCC states, its recent warming of relations has generated enormous commercial potential and has, in this case, prompted the development of the UAE's petrochemical industry. As one of the world's largest markets and one that is situated in close proximity to the UAE, it only makes sense to strengthen the position of ADNOC as a leading producer of petrochemicals for the Indian market and beyond.

ADNOC has a large responsibility to develop infrastructure within the UAE and this has only increased since the Arab Spring. In an attempt to fortify its own domestic and international position within the natural resources market, ADNOC has attracted and dedicated funds to boost its development. This has seen an influx in investment towards petrochemicals and has aided the development of public infrastructure in rural areas.[67] While the UAE seeks to diversify its own energy sources, it must still continue to exploit its own oil reserves.

While fundamentally oil and, in particular, ADNOC have provided the basis for the initial and constant contribution of funds to the UAE's industrial sector and economy, they have also provided the backbone for further investments across the UAE's investment network.[68] This is evidenced by the state-led capitalism model.

It has been shown by the array of investments made by ADNOC, and through its partnerships that the oil and gas sector is being used as a conduit for wider industrial development and diversification. While oil prices have dipped momentarily, they will naturally increase again as demand grows and resources dry up.[69] ADNOC is therefore positioning itself to be able to contribute to the UAE's revenue stream in times of both high and low prices, and thus expand the regime's financial fortification; this enables the prolonging of the rentier bargain that secures the Abu Dhabi ruling family.

While ADNOC leads industrial development within the natural resources market, the UAE has also continued its pursuit of a civilian nuclear programme. This was initiated before the Arab Spring in 2008 with the establishment of the Emirates Nuclear Energy Corporation (ENEC).[70] The consistent trajectory suggests that the UAE's nuclear policy has not been affected by the Arab Spring. The Barakh power plant came operational and connected to the UAE's national electric grid in 2020.[71] It is important to note that this development symbolises an attempt to extract additional legitimacy from the state's population through its sponsorship and advocacy of high-tech and progressive technologies.[72] This is further illustrated through other such high-technology focused strategic programmes such as Etihad Rail, Masdar, and the UAE Space Agency.

The direction of development for the UAE's natural resource management since the Arab Spring has been one of investment, diversification, and modernisation. This is to ensure that while the regime has been able to insulate themselves from future instability with price fluctuations, it will always be able to ensure the fundamental maintenance allowances are met. In such a strategic sector, the regime will continue to dominate, balancing a micromanaged approach to the modernisation of the sector.

State-Owned Enterprises (SOEs)

The state is a key driver of industrialisation, as it is the main channel of capital through its sale of natural resources. The UAE has stood out from many fellow states within the GCC due to its business-focused image. Scholars such as Davidson,[73] Herb,[74] Nabil Sultan, Beverly Metcalfe, and David Weir[75] have all discussed the business first approach taken by the UAE, often positioning this strategy as an attempt to depoliticise the population, but on that has actually politicised the business arena due to the regime's control. The Emirate of Dubai is often heralded for its diversification and its assertive business image. The rest of the UAE has often fallen by the wayside in these regards to SOEs within industry; however, in recent years there has been a concerted effort to streamline commercial operations in a bid to maximise revenue and capability.

Since the Arab Spring there has been an orchestrated strategy by the Abu Dhabi ruling family leading to a process of commercial consolidation occurring across the UAE. The first substantial merger was between the National Bank of Abu Dhabi (NBAD) and First Gulf Bank (FGB) into the First Abu Dhabi Bank (FAB) in 2017.[76] It is now reported that FAB is now one of the largest Middle Eastern banks by total asset value.[77] The second major merger was between Abu Dhabi Commercial Bank (ADCB), Union National Bank (UNB), and Bank Al Hilal[78] in January 2019. The third was the unification of Khalifa University, Petroleum Institute, and the Masdar Institute in 2016.[79] The consolidation of significant financial and education assets not only reduces competition, making it easier for the Abu Dhabi ruling family to control the market economy, but also strengthens the SOEs throughout a period of economic downturn. The strategy implemented by the Abu Dhabi ruling family illustrates the prioritisation of efficiency and performance, whilst never relenting their grip on the strategic financial sector which supports the management of the state.

Focusing attention in the banking sector is crucial for the UAE's regime security strategy as large parts of the UAE's diversified economy are positioned within the financial sector. The UAE has become a global hub for the transit of finance, and while the UAE dirham is pegged to the US dollar, the development of the UAE's banking sector can strengthen the state's economy through the collection of assets and attraction of funds. Through this endeavour, the SOEs can lend money cheaply for domestic projects and contribute to the development of Emirati society. Indeed, the UAE has highlighted the banking sector as a crucial target for Emiratisation. As a result, the banking sector is not only employed to develop industrial capabilities, but also to provide the basis for the development of human capital.

While consolidation has occurred, with the state maintaining control of several assets, it has also initiated a process whereby the state is seeking to reduce its ownership of several assets and enterprises. This was observed through the establishment of the Abu Dhabi Development Holding Company (ADDHC) in March 2018.[80] It was later reported that its portfolio would include seven service-based state-owned enterprises; Abu Dhabi Airports, Abu Dhabi Ports, Abu Dhabi National Exhibition Centre, Abu Dhabi Media, Abu Dhabi Power Company, Khalifa Industrial Zone Abu Dhabi, and Abu Dhabi Health Services Company.[81] Through the recalibration of several marque services from public to, possibly and eventually, private institutions, the regime is slowly looking to move away from direct responsibility for these services. The fact that the aforementioned institutions are predominantly tertiary industries shows how the government is looking to distance itself from such simplistic capabilities. By contrast, the Emirates Nuclear Energy Corporation (ENEC) is a fully fledged SOE that maintains its position as a symbol of modernisation.

The ADDHC was created as a public joint stock company and was initially chaired and vice-chaired by Jassem al-Zaabi and Theyab bin Mohammed bin Zayed al-Nahyan. It was later publicised that Tahnoon bin Zayed al-Nahyan was appointed as Chairman of the ADDHC.[82] While Mohammed bin Zayed al-Nahyan has his second son as Deputy Chairman of the ADDHC, the former chairman is a longstanding ally in Jassem al-Zaabi, and the current chairman is Mohammed bin Zayed al-Nahyan's full brother Tahnoon bin Zayed al-Nahyan; thus, further illustrating the immense weight Mohammed bin Zayed al-Nahyan places on kinship and tribal relations. This is further supported by the remaining board members of the ADDHC, all of whom again illustrate the same traits seen throughout the administration of Mohammed bin Zayed al-Nahyan's tenure.

Table 13: Abu Dhabi Development Holding Company Board of Directors[83]

Dr. Mugheer Khamis al-Khalil	Chairman of the Department of Community Development and member of the Abu Dhabi Executive Council
Major General Muhammad Khalfan al-Rumaithi *Rumaithat—Section of the Bani Yas*	Commander-in-Chief of Abu Dhabi Police and former member of the Abu Dhabi Executive Council
Sheikh Abdullah bin Muhammad al-Hamed *Qubaysat—Section of the Bani Yas*	Chairman of the Health Department and member of the Abu Dhabi Executive Council
Dr. Ali Rashid al-Nuaimi *Na'im*	Chairman of the Abu Dhabi Department of Education and Knowledge (ADEK) and former member of the Abu Dhabi Executive Council
Owaida Murshid al-Marrar *Murar—section of the Bani Yas*	Chairman of the Department of Energy and member of the Abu Dhabi Executive Council
Saif Muhammad al-Hajeri	Chairman of Economic Development and member of the Abu Dhabi Executive Council
Falah Muhammad al-Ahbabi *Ahbab*	Head of the Department of Urban Planning and Municipalities

Muhammad Khalifa Ahmed al-Mubarak	Director General of the Abu Dhabi Finance Department
Muhammad Sultan Ghanoum al-Hamli *Hawamil—Section of the Bani Yas*	Managing Director
Muhammad Hassan al-Suwaidi[84] *Sudan—Section of the Bani Yas*	Chief Executive Officer Ex-Mubadala

The development of SOEs within the UAE since the Arab Spring has shown a clear strategy to reduce waste and competition, whilst also centralising management to retain a tighter control of affairs.[85] This allows a more coherent structure to remain under the direct observation of state elites. It is crucially important for the regime to maintain tight control over SOEs due to the fact that they are designed to be financially profitable entities, but also because they are exposed to international financial currents. This means that SOEs are not able to operate exclusively like they do in their own state, but by international norms and laws. As a result, there is a delicate balancing act for authoritarian regimes, such as the UAE, to ensure tight control over financial affairs whilst also exploring avenues for financial gain. This observation explains why there has been a tightening of the ownership and management in SOEs, thus reinforcing the patrimonial power structure of the UAE regime's traditional power base.

SOEs are obvious strategic vehicles for authoritarian states such as the UAE, who are exposed to delicate population dynamics, to leverage greater control over affairs with as little requirement for direct oversight. They lead domestic industrial affairs through the subsidised execution of contracts which support regime allies through preferential contract awards. The Abu Dhabi ruling family has however largely forgone direct management of SOEs since the Arab Spring and has instead merged multiple assets into larger entities. The amalgamation of assets demonstrates how the regime security strategy principle of control has been applied to the domain of SOEs to further the regime's control of affairs.

Privately Owned National Champions

Due to the large-scale investment and development of the state within the industrial sector, primarily through SOEs and SWFs, there does not tend to be much room for private actors to enter the sector. Khaled al-Mezaini notes that 'defining the boundaries between what is private and what is public in the UAE is challenging, owing to a lack of clarity in the state structure'.[86] The Abu Dhabi ruling family has, in this case, effectively closed the space for large-scale private enterprises to grow, only empowering those which it can directly control. This has created a warm relationship between the regime and several merchant elite families such as the al-Otaibas, al-Rumaithis, and the al-Muhairis.

The intimate relationship between successful private businesses and the state is strengthened through affiliations with the local ruling family in the Emirate of establishment.[87] The UAE Ministry of Economy stated that 'the SME sector represents more than 94 per cent of the total number of companies operating in the country and provides jobs for more than 86 per cent of the private sector's workforce'.[88] While these figures illustrate that the bulk of private businesses within the UAE are SMEs by nature, the fact that the most successful SMEs are those owned by merchant families isn't discussed. This is because of both their longevity in the market and their privileged legal position within the UAE.

Private Emirati entities play an important role for the regime as they are an important outlet through which the regime can distribute benefits in a relatively economical way from the state's accrued rent in an attempt to prolong the rentier bargain. These benefits can come in the form of preferential contracts, greater access to state officials, specific licences, and other commercial advantages that are not applicable to foreign entities. By appeasing the business community, the regime can depoliticise any competition through co-optation, maintaining the UAE's image of what Davidson termed, 'economy first politics second'.[89] It is within this vein that SMEs and potential POCs play a vital role in a successful regime security strategy.

As it has been highlighted the UAE is one case in which the concept of successful POCs does not particularly align. The selective co-option of private entities by the regime is, however, a key strategy for authoritarian states to maintain their ability to manage matters of economic and industrial concern. To a great extent there are no large-scale private companies within the UAE that engage, at the strategic level within the industrial sector, mainly as a result of the state maintaining a monopoly over large public sector contracts. As a result of the disconnect between private entities and public sector development and the former's exposure to market forces, private sector involvement in the process of industrialisation has been fairly stagnant since the Arab Spring. Khaled al-Mezaini suggests 'this is because SMEs are excluded from policy-making processes, and well-connected large family businesses always win government contracts'.[90] Therefore, while the co-optation of private industrial firms and organisations can be an important strategic option for the regime, it has not been one employed by the Abu Dhabi ruling family as part of its targeted post-Arab Spring regime security strategy.

Sovereign Wealth Funds (SWFs)

Central to the UAE's industry strategy is the role played by SWFs. Sara Bazoobandi notes that 'the government of Abu Dhabi has particularly focused on diversification of the national economy from the oil sector, via transfer of technological development for the domestic non-oil sector, as one of the core investment strategies for its various SWFs'.[91] By understanding that the Abu Dhabi ruling family channels its process of industrialisation through SWFs, where domain of control was described in the previous chapter, it remains crucial to understand how this process has developed and whether it changed in any particular way after the Arab Spring under Mohammed bin Zayed al-Nahyan's tutelage.

As previously mentioned, the UAE's largest SWF, ADIA, does not publicise its investments and therefore it is impossible to independently verify what involvement it has had in the evolution of the UAE's industrial sector. Instead, the domestic role played by Emirati SWFs has been largely led by Mubadala, with defence-sector focused firms such as Tawazun and EDIC also supporting the industrialisation effort.

A key trend that is clearly visible within the SWF's industrialisation drive is the 'further emphasis on joint venture investments'.[92] While the UAE SWFs can directly engage in joint ventures with foreign firms, offsets have become a key vehicle for the UAE as they encourage and demand joint cooperation among projects.

Within the UAE, offsets were handled by the OPB. The use of defence sales for economic diversification was acknowledged by Mohammed bin Zayed al-Nahyan and has since led the development of offsets and their related projects. Pattarawan Nanakorn concurs and states that 'the OPB was initiated and chaired by the Crown Prince of Abu Dhabi, and functioned independently except for the formal coordination with the GHQ'.[93] Given the fact that Mohammed bin Zayed al-Nahyan has a strong professional and personnel link to the security services within the UAE, it is important to highlight the fact that he used this relationship to initiate his diversification plan. In 2012 the OPB was renamed the Tawazun Economic Council (TEC), and it is affiliated to a domestic, defence and industrial focused SWF named Tawazun, with nearly all of its business units developing from offset related projects.[94]

While there have been several changes to the UAE offset law, most recently in 2010[95] and 2015,[96] there has been a concerted attempt to align the offset policy to NDPs such as Economic Vision 2030. This is highlighted in the offset agreement:

1.3 Objectives of Tawazun Economic Program:
1. Create Knowledge based economy;
2. Diversify the UAE's economy;
3. Grow the Industrial Base of the UAE;
4. Create business opportunities for UAE private sector;
5. Generate exports;
6. Produce employment opportunities for UAE Nationals in high-tech fields.[97]

It becomes clear that there is a widescale policy by state-managed entities to publicly drive industrial development. The offsets within the UAE will remain, at least in theory, a key vehicle for diversification as it is assumed that the UAE will maintain high levels of defence spending.

The OPB was instrumental in the initial development of the UAE's SWFs. In 1997 Dolphin Energy, which is a gas pipeline from Qatar to the UAE and Oman, was established.[98] Figures such as Khaldoon Mubarak (Mubadala CEO) drove the UAE's SWF-led industrialisation, firstly through Dolphin Energy, and later through the establishment of Mubadala in 2002.[99]

Mubadala has made strong process in the diversification drive since its creation, nevertheless, since the Arab Spring there has been more of a process of consolidation rather than expansion within the domain of industrialisation. This is illustrated through the amalgamation of IPIC and ADIC into the Mubadala Investment Company and the establishment of the EDIC in 2014. Other such acquisitions included Yahsat's procurement of Thuraya in 2018,[100] the merger of Dubai Aluminium (DUBAL) and Emirates Aluminium (EA) into Emirates Global Aluminium (EGA) in 2014,[101] and Mubadala's absorption of Advanced Technology Investment Company in 2011.[102] Due to the state's monopoly within the SWF and public sector domains, the decision to merge multiple assets should be viewed as an attempt to increase efficiency and commercial acumen; instead of having three SWFs, all owned and managed by the same entities, competing for the same contract, there will instead be a single large conglomerate managing large scale public sector investments.

There has not been a lot of domestic investment by Mubadala since the Arab Spring, however they have continued to partner with foreign companies and states to expand their industrial portfolio. Prominent examples include the co-investment programme between Mubadala and the Russian Direct Investment Fund (RDIF),[103] establishment of the UAE–China Joint Investment Fund,[104] which dedicated nearly 40 per cent of its $240bn portfolio to investments in the US,[105] intention to establish a US$400m European tech fund,[106] Masdar's GBP£1.5bn investment in an offshore wind farm in the UK,[107] initiation of production at a new oil field in Thailand,[108] Mubadala's investment in mining operations in Spain,[109] and Mubadala Petroleum's acquisition of a 20 per cent interest in an offshore concession in Egypt.[110] By comparison, one of Mubadala's largest investments within the UAE since the Arab

Spring was for AED 82.5m, and 'the funding will be used to accelerate several innovative technology development projects that focus on differentiating concepts from the Fourth Industrial Revolution'.[111] The comparison between domestic and international investment in the industrial sector signifies that while Mubadala is keen to increase its involvement, it is clearly not a sector of large-scale importance.

Instead, Mubadala has paid more attention to delivering its promise of strategic investment and development of human capital. Training programmes target all levels of Emirati society from school children[112] to university students,[113] university graduates,[114] and general Emirati youth.[115] It is clear through Mubadala's strategy that it is hindered by limitations inherent to Emirati society; namely the dearth of human capital. It is crucial for an authoritarian state such as the UAE to develop an industrial base, but not one that is so advanced that it affects the domestic political-economic conditions as this can have a serious impact on the regime's ability to control society.

Offsets, however, will continue to retain their focus on attracting cooperation in the development of the UAE's industrial sector. Due to the fact that offsets are primarily employed within the defence sector, it is here where there has been an advancement in the development of national capabilities. Mubadala, EDIC, and Tawazun are the three main SWF entities that are involved within the UAE's defence sector.

Since their inception, Mubadala and later Tawazun have spearheaded the UAE's defence sector-led industrialisation. Mohammed bin Zayed al-Nahyan is the chairman of both entities and, as it will be illustrated, these organisations have been instrumental in his implementation of strategic industrial development. Throughout their existence, Mubadala and Tawazun have had differing portfolios with separate agendas. Nonetheless, this created unnecessary competition within the already restricted public sector industry in the UAE and, as a result, multiple assets from both entities were merged into EDIC in 2014.[116]

Since the merger, Mubadala has assumed an official position wherein the assets it has held are of significant strategic value to the defence sector and the capability development of the UAE Armed Forces; this is because its most successful companies were all maintenance, repair, and overhaul (MRO) operations servicing the UAE Armed Forces platforms, thus helping to fill a capability void through PPPs. These partnerships included ADSB, Al Taif, AMMROC, and Bayanat.

ADSB was 'founded in 1995 through cooperation between the Government of Abu Dhabi and Newport News Shipbuilding (NNS) … ADSB started as a pre-offset venture'.[117] However, since its inception, ADSB has evolved to the point where it is now able to manufacture and maintain the UAE's naval vessels. ADSB cooperated with French firm *Constructions Mecaniques de Normandie (CMN)* to design and build six Baynunah-class corvettes.[118] With the UAE possessing such a small navy (IISS estimates a strength of 2500 personnel),[119] it has been crucial for the UAE's security capability to develop a broader understanding of naval engineering. Through the successful PPP, ADSB has been able to deliver this, whilst also acting as a platform for which a grander industrialisation and economic diversification process can occur. ADSB has signed memorandum of understanding (MOU) with Babcock in 2013,[120] Strategic Marine in 2017,[121] and most recently, with Leonardo[122] and Fincantieri[123] in 2019, thus highlighting the prolonged importance of ADSB beyond the implementation of the Baynunah corvette delivery.

Al Taif Technical Services is a land-focused MRO company whose primary client is the UAE Armed Forces. It is the product of a joint venture with Dyncorp in 2006[124] whose announcement stated that 'DynCorp International will provide all personnel, equipment, tools, materials, supervision, and services necessary for GMD [General Maintenance Directorate] operations'.[125] This means that while Al Taif is an Emirati-owned entity, through Mubadala, it has outsourced all land-based maintenance operations, with no caveat of limitations, to a foreign and privately owned company. Strategically, this means that while Emirati engineers can be trained to maintain the UAE's land-based platforms, the Abu Dhabi regime can control the development of such capacity by instructing the private firm accordingly.

AMMROC 'is a joint venture company owned by Emirates Defense Industries Company (EDIC), Lockheed Martin Corporation and Sikorsky Aerospace Services (A Lockheed Martin Company)'.[126] AMMROC was established in 2010 and while not formed directly as an offset, Lockheed Martin was awarded offset credits for its crucial partnership in the company. Like ADSB, AMMROC works with the original equipment manufacturer (OEM) to provide MRO capabilities and training for equipment that is supplied by Lockheed Martin (and its present subsidiary, Sikorsky) for the UAE Armed Forces. This covers the majority of both fixed and rotary-wing aircraft including, but not limited to, F-16s, C-130, and the UH-60 Black Hawk. As a result, the UAE's most advanced platforms are maintained by a coalition of experienced foreign personnel, allowing the continuation of capability that is not dependent on a potentially politicised national workforce. Since the Arab Spring, however, AMMROC has not grown or expanded, having only signed one MOU, with BAE systems in 2019,[127] to illustrate any development in capability. The UAE did however go on to acquire Lockheed Martin's 40 per cent stake in AMMROC.[128]

Bayanat is another example of the successful PPP model in the UAE as it evolved from the Military Survey Department (MSD) of the UAE Armed Forces in 2011.[129] By expanding its operations and workforce, Bayanat can follow the example set by others within the defence industry to supplement experienced foreign manpower within a strategic domain that is critically understaffed.

Tawazun, on the other hand, focuses on manufacturing and has developed its array of capabilities through the transfer of technology and intellectual property (IP). Intimately linked to the UAE's offset programme, Tawazun attempted to centralise industrialisation projects within the defence sector, highlighting its desire to work across a broad array of fields; land systems, aerospace, precision manufacturing, munitions, weapons systems, advanced materials, naval systems, and other technologies and systems.[130] It is estimated that between 2007 and 2015 Tawazun 'launched more than 40 joint venture defence, munitions, aerospace, automotive and metals-oriented companies'.[131] This was translated into a series of entities that, whilst demonstrating a degree of capacity, have not proven to be significant commercial or strategic successes; exceptions include Nimr, Abu Dhabi Autonomous Systems Investments (ADASI), and Tawazun Dynamics.

After several years of unnecessary competition between the UAE's publicly held defence sector firms, EDIC was established in December 2014.[132] Within three months, its portfolio had incorporated sixteen companies that were previously held by Mubadala and Tawazun.[133] It was estimated that EDIC held US$871.2m in assets and employed four thousand eight hundred people 'with the workforce expected to rise to 10,000 once the company is fully integrated'.[134] While EDIC served as the central state entity operating within the UAE's defence sector, it did not change the direction in which the process of industrialisation is heading within the UAE.

In contrast, the strategically vital MRO operations handled by EDIC are combined with a wide manufacturing portfolio that is managed by Luc Vigneron,[135] the former CEO of Thales. Above him sits a board which is chaired by Khaled al-Qubaisi. The Vice Chairman is Major General Pilot Fares Khalaf Khalfan al-Mazrouei, and other board members include Badr al-Olama, Lieutenant-General Aqab Shaheen al-Ali, and Matar Ali al-Romaithi. The mixture between military and civilian personnel showcases the desire to prioritise the UAE Armed Forces' requirements whilst also allowing for a degree of commercial activity.

Further illustrating the UAE's attempt to consolidate commercial activities and invigorate defence related activities, a new government company EDGE was inaugurated to absorb and manage all major defence related activities. EDGE took control of EDIC, Tawazun and Emirates Advanced Investments Group (EDIC).[136] The accelerated amalgamation and control of defence related activities enhances the regime's grip on strategic affairs.

While the UAE defence industry underlines its commitment to develop human capital and contribute to multiple NDPs,[137] the core focus remains on maintaining a capability that is in fact in direct competition to those prescribed objectives; to ensure a working capability but with the ability to micromanage who and what is developed.

These organisations all sit under the direct control and observation of Mohammed bin Zayed al-Nahyan and thus further corroborate the hypothesis that the closer an institution is to Mohammed bin Zayed al-Nahyan, the more significant its premise and capability is. The fact that Mohammed bin Zayed al-Nahyan had a professional career within the UAE Armed Forces, and through this vehicle he has used to augment military purchases for industrial development through the entities he chairs, shows that his journey to office has long considered strategic scenarios that have included security, industrial, and economic concerns.

Conclusion

Since the Arab Spring, the UAE has consolidated its industrial sector under a centralised structure that is ever more connected to the regime. This is largely displayed through the domination of the state within this process and the overall lack of private sector entities.

While there have been genuine attempts to develop the UAE's industry, and thus follow through with the publicised NDPs, only marginal progress has been made. Khaled al-Mezaini explains that 'despite these economic changes, the dynamics of the political structure of the UAE have remained authoritarian. This emphasises how economic development and liberalisation have enhanced the survival of the rentier structure'.[138]

While the UAE fits into Matthew Gray's late rentierism and Bremmer's state-led capitalism frameworks, it has been demonstrated that the Gulf state has evolved from these by applying a strategic mandate to its industrialisation process. For example, the role played by SWFs is 'to ensure a source of income after the basic rents that currently sustain it are exhausted, as well as to serve other purposes'.[139] As Matthew Gray leaves space for a debate around what role SWFs can play, the UAE's utilisation of offsets and development of the defence and new technology sectors showcase how the rentier model is only the most basic block for analysis within an increasingly complex and multidimensional environment. As technology evolves and states adopt more modern techniques and methods, there will be a modern evolution of what the rentier state model stands for and how it is applied.

What will not change, however, is the state's control of industrialisation. With specific sectors targeted, the regime has illustrated what it deems important for its own direct security, and which can carry a potential capacity for the fostering of future support and allegiance. As a result, and because of its technical grounding, there is a wider lack of tribal dynamics within the UAE's industrialisation process. Instead, technocratic values and experience is of higher strategic significance; a contrasting value to that seen elsewhere within the UAE's regime security strategy.

7

CONCLUSION

There is no doubt that the UAE's regime security strategy has been developed through a coherent policy following the Arab Spring. At the forefront of this has been the leadership of Mohammed bin Zayed al-Nahyan. However, the fundamental question of this book has been to what extent the Arab Spring has affected the UAE's regime security strategy.

Features of the Arab Spring that have had a determining impact on the UAE's regime security strategy have clearly included economic pressure, changing societal dynamics, and ICT advances. In each pillar of the NCP, there are clear examples of the UAE's reaction to the Arab Spring. The tangible increase in military spending, development of technological capability by the security services, an evident and defined network of personnel linked directly to Mohammed bin Zayed al-Nahyan across the state apparatus, and an increased scope of power by this network, demonstrates that a consistent strategy has been undertaken to enhance the regime's power following the Arab Spring.

As the fundamental pillar of support, the regime's control of the security services has tangibly increased following the Arab Spring. While a series of measures have been implemented to align the focus of these organisations to the regime, they have also been instrumental in the nation building process that has accelerated following the Arab Spring. The securitisation of threat manifestation has legitimised the UAE's rapid development of the armed forces and security services while primarily serving to fortify the UAE's regime security strategy. The careful management of personnel has successfully fortified the relationship to the regime, and has established the groundwork for a long lasting relationship that will continue onto the next generation.

In parallel, while the state has increased its exposure to international markets through economic and industrial diversification, it has retained a tight control of affairs through its strategic layering of manager and ownership dynamics. The strategy demonstrated a clear network of tribal and clan groups who are a blend of technocrat and conviction. Due to its exposed nature, the commercial sphere will have to maintain a delicate balance of controlled growth. Undoubtedly, this will see a less homogenous network develop than in the security field, but, at the highest levels of strategic decision making will continue to be directed by an elite network. The example of the UAE as a nesting dictatorship exemplifies the prerequisite to maintain near direct control of strategic affairs. While evidence has illustrated the regime's increased control of affairs, the relationship with federal level entities has been largely bypassed due to their relative lack of strategic importance.

The UAE regime's perception of the Arab Spring as a threat was most apparent in the dramatic advancement of a security strategy that was previously undeveloped. The UAE's micromanaged, often obscure, response to the Arab Spring meant that only the detailed investigation into the elite's control of affairs—employed by this research—could unveil this strategy.

However, it is equally plausible that the UAE developed a regime security strategy following the ascension of Mohammed bin Zayed al-Nahyan to the role of de-facto ruler. Mohammed bin Zayed al-Nahyan's nurturing of interpersonal ties has had a particularly significant impact on the UAE's regime security strategy—he has become the central pivot to which all power linkages connect. The neo-patrimonial organisation of affairs emphasises the modified character of relations. Mohammed bin Zayed al-Nahyan's administration of security and economic conduits, to which he has long-built considerable power-bases, are now providing him with a strong foundation with which he has expanded, and can continue to do so.

Mohammed bin Zayed al-Nahyan's organisation of societal ties dictates both the enforcement and maintenance of power. He has established groupings obedient to him, and patiently expanded them through similar determining factors. While in essence they have technocratic qualities, there is often a common thread of tribal and kinship affiliation. The most significant discovery within this network is the incorporation of his sons Khaled and Theyab into his own network. The construction of the Bani Mohammed bin Zayed al-Nahyan legacy is what will carry the UAE forward, albeit with different deputies across state organs.

Through his exploitation of alliances, Mohammed bin Zayed al-Nahyan has utilised advances in technical capability to augment the response to perceived security threats. By engaging in such tactics, Mohammed bin Zayed al-Nahyan can entrust a significant image of security through the deployment of relatively overpowered capabilities managed by a compacted section of elites. In parallel, and across the state apparatus, Mohammed bin Zayed al-Nahyan has visibly expanded the state's exposure but has been careful to preserve authority at all costs, either through objective or subjective forms of control. The power of the latter has slowly started to manifest itself through more obvious means, with the federal identity of the UAE evolving into a Mohammed bin Zayed al-Nahyan-led Abu Dhabi-centred nation state.

The Arab Spring certainly affected the UAE's regime security strategy, accelerating the process of consolidation that is transforming the federal image of the state into that of a singular nation. Personnel linkages are of an even more heightened relevance, with proximity to Mohammed bin Zayed al-Nahyan and other regime personnel the measure of a person's significance. In essence, while the dangers of modernisation and development were demonstrated across MENA, the UAE reacted by consolidating the dynamics to its ruling coalition.

APPENDICES

Appendix 1: Sections of the Bani Yas

Bani Yas sections	JB Kelly[1] (1964) 14 major and 6 minor	Heard-Bey[2] (1982) 20+	Van Der Meulen[3] (1997) **8 Major** and *19 minor sections*
Al-Bu Falah **Al-Falahi Al-Nahyan**	Major Section	Al-bu Falah	**Mazari** 6,800
Hawamil	Major Section	Al-bu Mahair	**Sudan** 3,000
Maharibah	**Al-Mehairbi** Major Section	Al-Bu Falasah	**Al-Bu Muhair** 2,500
Mazari **Al-Mazrouei**	Major Section	Rumaithat	**Hawamil** 2,500
Al-Mishaghin	Major Section	Qubaisat	**Maharibah** 2,500
Qubaisat **Al-Qubaisi**	Major Section	Mazari	**Qubaisat** 2,000
Rawashid	Major Section	Hawamil	**Rumaithat** 2,000

Rumaithat **Al-Romaithi**	Major Section	Maharibah	**Al-Bu Falah** 1,000
Al-Bu Falasah **Al-Falasi** **Al-Maktoum**	Major Section	Al-Mishaghin	*Halamah* 1,000
Al-Bu Mahair **Al-Muhairi**	Major Section	Sudan (Suwaidi)	*Qumzan* 1,000
Sudan **Al-Suwaidi**	Major Section		*Rawashid* 1,000
Al-Murur	Major Section		*Al-Bu Hamir* 700
Qumzan **Al-Qamzi**	Major Section		*Al-Bu Amin* 500
Subais	Major Section		*Al-Mishaghin* 500
Al-Bu Amin **Al-Ameemi**	Minor Section		*Al-Sultan* 500
Araifat	Minor Section		*Al-Thuhailat* 500
Duhailat	Minor Section		*Al-Urayfat* 500
Halalmah	Minor Section		*Bani Shikir* 500
Khamarah	Minor Section		*Dhailat* 500
Thumairat	Minor Section		*Khamarah* 500
			Marar 500
			Nuwasir 500

APPENDICES

				Qanaisat 500
				Qasal 500
				Saba'is 500
				Thamairat **500**
				Al-Bu Falasah 0—this is because they are Dubai based

Appendix 2: Transfer of Leadership in Abu Dhabi (1761–Present)[4]

Departure method	Name, date, and method
Deposed	**Shakhbut bin Diab** (1793–1816), deposed by son, Mohammed bin Shakhbut[5]
	Muhammad bin Shakhbut, (1816–1818), deposed by brother Tahnoon with help from father, Shakhbut bin Diab[6]
	Shakhbut bin Sultan (1928–1966), deposed by Zayed bin Sultan al-Nahyan with assistance from the British[7]
Murdered	**Diab Isa** (1761–1793), after killing his Uncle, Zayed Muhammed, Diab was killed by his victim's son, Hazza[8]
	Tahnoon bin Shakhbut (1818–1833), shot and stabbed by brothers Khalifa and Sultan respectively[9]
	Khalifa Shakhbut (1833–1845), killed by a distant cousin, Isa Khalid[10]
	Isa Khalid (1845–1845), killed two months after assuming presidency by the nephew of his victim, Khalifa Shakhbut[11]

	Said Tahnoon (1845–1855), having fled Abu Dhabi, he was killed whilst trying to return[12] **Hamdan Zayed** (1912–1922), murdered by his predecessor, Sultan, and half-brother, Saqr[13] **Sultan Zayed** (1922–1926), Saqr, who assisted Sultan in the murder of Hamdan, invited Sultan to dinner and murdered him. Thereafter Hamdan's son tried and failed to kill Sultan's son, Khalid[14] **Saqr Zayed** (1926–1928), murdered by the family of Sultan[15]
Natural Death	**Zayed Khalifa** (1855–1909)[16] **Tahnoon Zayed** (1909–1912)[17] **Zayed Sultan** (1966–2004)[18]

Appendix 3: Highest Positions of the Bani Mohammed bin Khalifa (BMBK) under Sheikh Zayed

Name	Role
Hamdan	UAE Deputy Prime Minister and Minister of Abu Dhabi Public Works
Mubarak	Minister of Interior
Tahnoon	Ruler's Representative in Al Ain, Member of the Supreme Petroleum Council (CPC), Director of Abu Dhabi National Oil Company (ADNOC), and Deputy Chairmanship of the Abu Dhabi Executive Council
Saif	Chairman of Abu Dhabi Planning Department and Minister of Health
Khalifa	UAE Minster of Hydraulic and Electric Power
Surur	Chairman of UAE Central Bank, and Chairman of ADEWA, Supreme Petroleum Council (SPC), Chairman of Abu Dhabi's Department of Justice, and Chamberlain of the Presidential Court

Appendix 4: *Marital connections between Bani Zayed and Bani Mohammed bin Khalifa*

Bani Sultan bin Zayed	Relationship	Bani Mohammed bin Khalifa
Zayed bin Sultan bin Zayed	Married	Hassa bint Muhammad bin Khalifa
Khalifa bin Zayed al-Nahyan	Son of	Hassa bint Muhammad bin Khalifa
Sultan bin Khalifa bin Zayed	Married	Sheikha bint Saif bin Muhammad
Shammah bint Zayed al-Nahyan	Married	Surur
Sultan bin Zayed al-Nahyan	Married	Shamsa bint Muhammad bin Khalifa

Bani Muhammad bin Khalifa	Relationship	Bani Zayed
Hamad bin Hamdan bin Muhammad "Rainbow Sheikh"	Married	Elizah bin Zayed
Sultan bin Hamdan bin Muhammad	Married	Aishah bin Khalifa bin Zayed
Salamah bint Hamdan bin Muhammad	Married	Muhammad bin Zayed
Shamsa bint Hamdan bin Muhammad	Married	Hamdan bin Zayed
Tahnoon bin Muhammad	Married	Shamsa bint Zayed bin Sultan
Hamad bin Tahnoon bin Muhammad	Married	A daughter of Khalifa
Mansour bin Tahnoon	Married	A daughter of Khalifa

Appendix 5: Partial List of UAE Military Bases

- Air Force & Air Defence (AFAD)
  - Al Dhafra Air Base (AD)[19]
  - Khalifa bin Zayed Air College (AD)[20]
  - Al Bateen Air Base (AD)[21]
  - Sas al Nakhel (AD)[22]
  - Liwa Air Base (AD)[23]
  - Qusaiwera Air Base (AD)[24]
  - Al Safran (AD)[25]
  - Al Minhad (Dubai)

- Land Forces
  - Zayed Military City (AD)[26]
  - Al Nahyan Military (AD)[27]
  - Al Ain Infantry Command School (AD)[28]
  - Baniyas Regiment Camp (AD)[29]
  - Al Hamra Camp (AD)[30]
  - Mushrif Camp (AD)[31]
  - Al Bateen Camp (AD)[32]
  - Mahawi Military Camp (AD)[33]
  - Tarif Camp (AD)[34]
  - Liwa Camp (AD)
  - Manama Camp (FUJ)[35]
  - Wadi Shabuk (Dubai)[36]
  - Royal Guards Camp (Dubai)[37]
  - Thouban Military Camp (Fujairah)[38]
  - Masafi Camp (Fujairah)[39]
  - Royal Guard Regiment (Ras al-Khaimah)[40]
  - Al Batayeh Camp (Sharjah)[41]

- Navy
  - Mina Zayed (AD)[42]
  - Ghantoot (AD)[43]
  - Das Island (AD)[44]
  - Delma (AD)[45]
  - Sir Abu Nu'Ayr (AD)[46]
  - Rashid bin Saeed Naval College
  - Ras Ghumais (AD)[47]
  - Jebel Ali (Dubai)[48]
  - Mina Rashid (Dubai)[49]
  - Khor Fakkan (Dubai)[50]
  - Fujairah[51]
  - Mina Saqr (RAK)[52]
  - Mina Khalid (SHJ)[53]

APPENDICES

Appendix 6: Emirati Martyrs in Yemen

Name	Date	Emirate	Link
Hazim Obeid Khlfan al-Ali*	23–Jun–15	Sharjah	http://www.wam.ae/en/news/emirates/1395283976921.html
Abdul Aziz Sarhan Saleh al-Ka'abi	16–Jul–15	Al Ain	http://www.khaleejtimes.com/region/mena/uae-armed-forces-officer-dies-in-yemen
Saif Youssef Ahmed al-Falasi	20–Jul–15	Dubai	http://www.wam.ae/en/news/emirates/1395283521387.html http://gulftoday.ae/portal/3613f26a-45f2-413d-bd12-88a9761c38d8.aspx
Juma Jawhar Juma Hammadi	08–Aug–15	Abu Dhabi	http://www.wam.ae/en/news/emirates/1395284133772.html http://www.scoopnest.com/user/gulf_news/671190699010875393
Khalid Muhammad Abdullah al-Sehhi	08–Aug–15	RAK	http://www.wam.ae/en/news/emirates/1395284133772.html http://www.khaleejtimes.com/nation/general/friends-for-life-and-in-death
Fahim Saeed Ahmed al-Habsi	08–Aug–15	RAK	http://www.wam.ae/en/news/emirates/1395284133772.html http://www.khaleejtimes.com/nation/general/friends-for-life-and-in-death

181

Name	Date	Emirate	URL
Abdul Rahman Ibrahim Eissa al-Baloushi*	12–Aug–15	Dubai	http://www.wam.ae/en/news/emirates/1395284314194.html https://www.cpc.gov.ae/en-us/mediacenter/Pages/PressRelease_Details.aspx?press_Id_ar=1289&press_Id_en=1289
Mohammad Khaled Mohammad Mamdi	04–Sep–15	Abu Dhabi	http://www.wam.ae/en/news/emirates/1395285009611.html http://www.emirates247.com/news/emirates/45-uae-sons-martyred-in-yemen-nation-mourns-2015-09-07-1.602368
Muhammad Khalid Ibrahim	04–Sep–15	Abu Dhabi	http://www.wam.ae/en/news/emirates/1395285009611.html http://www.emirates247.com/news/emirates/45-uae-sons-martyred-in-yemen-nation-mourns-2015-09-07-1.602368
Muhammad al-Hussein al-Hosani	04–Sep–15	Abu Dhabi	http://www.wam.ae/en/news/emirates/1395285009611.html http://www.emirates247.com/news/emirates/45-uae-sons-martyred-in-yemen-nation-mourns-2015-09-07-1.602368
Suhail Rashid Suhail Hilal al-Mazroeui	04–Sep–15	Abu Dhabi	http://www.wam.ae/en/news/emirates/1395285009611.html http://www.emirates247.com/news/emirates/uae-mourns-martyrs-condolences-pour-in-2015-09-08-1.602740
Mohamad Ali Hassan Ahmed al-Houssani	04–Sep–15	Abu Dhabi	http://www.thenational.ae/uae/government/20150908/sheikh-mohammed-bin-rashid-praises-loyalty-and-dignity-of-uae-heroes-families

Abdulla Saeed al-Kalbani	04–Sep–15	Ajman	http://www.wam.ae/en/news/emirates/1395285009611.html http://www.emirates247.com/news/emirates/uae-mourns-martyrs-condolences-pour-in-2015-09-08-1.602739
Sultan Obaid al-Kaabi	04–Sep–15	Ajman	http://www.wam.ae/en/news/emirates/1395285009611.html http://www.emirates247.com/news/emirates/uae-mourns-martyrs-condolences-pour-in-2015-09-08-1.602740
Abdullah Ali Hassan al-Hammadi	04–Sep–15	Ajman	http://www.reuters.com/article/us-yemen-security-idUSKCN0R40V720150921 http://www.emirates247.com/news/emirates/mohammed-continues-to-offer-condolences-to-families-of-martyrs-2015-09-06-1.602528
Fahd Ali Muhammad Ahmed al-Baloushi	04–Sep–15	Ajman	http://www.wam.ae/en/news/emirates/1395285566116.html
Fahad Ali Muhammad Ahmed	04–Sep–15	Ajman	http://www.wam.ae/en/news/emirates/1395285655523.html
Hazaa Rashid Mohamad Rashid Saleh al-Kaabi	04–Sep–15	Ajman	http://www.thenational.ae/uae/government/20150916/sheikh-mohammed-bin-zayed-continues-solemn-duties-across-uae

Saad Muhammad al-Ahbabi	04–Sep–15	Al Ain	http://www.wam.ae/en/news/emirates/1395285009611.html http://www.emirates247.com/news/emirates/45-uae-sons-martyred-in-yemen-nation-mourns-2015-09-07-1.602368
Butti Ayel Misfer al-Ahbabi	04–Sep–15	Al Ain	http://www.wam.ae/en/news/emirates/1395285009611.html http://www.emirates247.com/news/emirates/45-uae-sons-martyred-in-yemen-nation-mourns-2015-09-07-1.602368
Abdulah Khalifa al-Nuaimi	04–Sep–15	Al Ain	http://www.wam.ae/en/news/emirates/1395285009611.html http://www.emirates247.com/news/emirates/45-uae-sons-martyred-in-yemen-nation-mourns-2015-09-07-1.602368
Abdullah Khalifa Matar al-Nuaimi	04–Sep–15	Al Ain	http://www.wam.ae/en/news/emirates/1395285009611.html http://www.emirates247.com/news/emirates/45-uae-sons-martyred-in-yemen-nation-mourns-2015-09-07-1.602368
Mohammad Saleh al-Ahbabi	04–Sep–15	Al Ain	http://www.wam.ae/en/news/emirates/1395285009611.html http://www.emirates247.com/news/emirates/45-uae-sons-martyred-in-yemen-nation-mourns-2015-09-07-1.602368
Omar Rashid al-Maqbali	04–Sep–15	Al Ain	http://www.wam.ae/en/news/emirates/1395285009611.html http://www.emirates247.com/news/emirates/45-uae-sons-martyred-in-yemen-nation-mourns-2015-09-07-1.602368

Saeed Rashid al-Neyadi	04–Sep–15	Al Ain	http://www.wam.ae/en/news/emirates/1395285513861.html
Saeed Ahmed Obaid al-Marri	04–Sep–15	Dubai	http://www.wam.ae/en/news/emirates/1395285566116.html
Ali Hussein Hassan Abdullah Taher al-Baloushi	04–Sep–15	Dubai	http://www.wam.ae/en/news/emirates/1395285569150.html
Issa Ibrahim al-Badaoui	04–Sep–15	Dubai	http://www.wam.ae/en/news/emirates/1395285570273.html
Walid Ahmed al-Dhanhani	04–Sep–15	Fujairah	http://www.wam.ae/en/news/emirates/1395285009611.html http://www.thenational.ae/uae/emirati-widows-grief-soothed-by-birth-of-son
Muhammad Saeed al-Saraidi	04–Sep–15	Fujairah	http://www.wam.ae/en/news/emirates/1395285009611.html http://www.emirates247.com/news/emirates/uae-mourns-martyrs-condolences-pour-in-2015-09-08-1.602736
Khalifa Abdullah al-Saraidi	04–Sep–15	Fujairah	http://www.wam.ae/en/news/emirates/1395285009611.html http://www.emirates247.com/news/emirates/uae-mourns-martyrs-condolences-pour-in-2015-09-08-1.602736
Khalifa Mohammed al-Yammahi	04–Sep–15	Fujairah	http://www.wam.ae/en/news/emirates/1395285009611.html http://www.emirates247.com/news/emirates/uae-mourns-martyrs-condolences-pour-in-2015-09-08-1.602736

Rashid Saeed al-Yammahi	04–Sep–15	Fujairah	http://www.wam.ae/en/news/emirates/1395285009611.html
			http://www.emirates247.com/news/emirates/uae-mourns-martyrs-condolences-pour-in-2015-09-08-1.602736
Jasim Saeed al-Saadi	04–Sep–15	Fujairah	http://www.reuters.com/article/us-yemen-security-idUSKCN0R40V720150913
			http://www.thenational.ae/uae/government/rulers-emiratis-and-expatriates-continue-to-show-support-for-families-of-martyrs
Saeed Salem Masoud al-Seraidi	04–Sep–15	Fujairah	http://www.wam.ae/en/news/emirates/1395285357487.html
Saud Muhammad al-Saadi	04–Sep–15	Fujairah	http://www.wam.ae/en/news/emirates/1395285570273.html
Ali Hassan al-Shehi	04–Sep–15	RAK	http://www.wam.ae/en/news/emirates/1395285009611.html
			http://www.khaleejtimes.com/martyrs-day-2015/resilience-was-this-martyrs-forte
Obaid Saeed al-Mazouri	04–Sep–15	RAK	http://www.wam.ae/en/news/emirates/1395285009611.html
			http://7days.ae/Families-remember-45-UAE-soldiers-killed-in-Yemen
Muhammad Saeed Balsadriyah al-Khateri	04–Sep–15	RAK	http://www.wam.ae/en/news/emirates/1395285009611.html
			http://www.emirates247.com/news/emirates/45-uae-sons-martyred-in-yemen-nation-mourns-2015-09-07-1.602368

Name	Date		URLs
Rashid Mohammad Matar al-Mosafiri	04–Sep–15	RAK	http://www.wam.ae/en/news/emirates/1395285009611.html http://www.emirates247.com/news/emirates/45-uae-sons-mar-tyred-in-yemen-nation-mourns-2015-09-07-1.602368
Obeid Saeed Rashid al-Mazroui	04–Sep–15	RAK	http://www.wam.ae/en/news/emirates/1395285009611.html http://www.emirates247.com/news/emirates/45-uae-sons-mar-tyred-in-yemen-nation-mourns-2015-09-07-1.602368
Al Shatti Abdullah al-Sayad	04–Sep–15	RAK	http://www.wam.ae/en/news/emirates/1395285009611.html http://www.emirates247.com/news/emirates/45-uae-sons-mar-tyred-in-yemen-nation-mourns-2015-09-07-1.602368
Yousuf Abdullah al-Ali	04–Sep–15	RAK	http://www.wam.ae/en/news/emirates/1395285009611.html http://www.emirates247.com/news/emirates/45-uae-sons-mar-tyred-in-yemen-nation-mourns-2015-09-07-1.602368
Obaid Saeed al-Shamsi	04–Sep–15	RAK	http://www.reuters.com/article/us-yemen-security-idUSKCN0R40V720150912 http://www.khaleejtimes.com/nation/general/he-asked-us-to-give-the-uae-flag-to-his-son
Ahmed Muhammad Ali al-Shehi	04–Sep–15	RAK	http://www.reuters.com/article/us-yemen-security-idUSKCN0R40V720150916 http://www.thenational.ae/uae/government/20150908/sheikh-mohammed-bin-rashid-praises-loyalty-and-dignity-of-uae-heroes-families

Name	Date	Emirate	URLs
Rashid Saeed Rashid al-Habsi	04-Sep-15	RAK	http://www.reuters.com/article/us-yemen-security-idUSKCN0R40V720150916 http://www.thenational.ae/uae/government/20150908/sheikh-mohammed-bin-rashid-praises-loyalty-and-dignity-of-uae-heroes-families
Abdel Saleh Absullah al-Shahhi	04-Sep-15	RAK	http://www.reuters.com/article/us-yemen-security-idUSKCN0R40V720150918 http://www.thenational.ae/uae/government/20150908/sheikh-mohammed-bin-rashid-praises-loyalty-and-dignity-of-uae-heroes-families
Abdullah Omer Mubarak al-Jabri	04-Sep-15	RAK	http://www.reuters.com/article/us-yemen-security-idUSKCN0R40V720150918 http://www.thenational.ae/uae/government/20150908/sheikh-mohammed-bin-rashid-praises-loyalty-and-dignity-of-uae-heroes-families
Ali Hussein al-Baloushi	04-Sep-15	RAK	http://www.reuters.com/article/us-yemen-security-idUSKCN0R40V720150918 http://www.thenational.ae/uae/government/20150908/sheikh-mohammed-bin-rashid-praises-loyalty-and-dignity-of-uae-heroes-families
Adil Saleh Abdullah al-Shehhi	04-Sep-15	RAK	http://www.wam.ae/en/news/emirates/1395285335027.html

Name	Date	Emirate	URL
Sultan Saleh al-Shehi	04–Sep–15	RAK	http://www.wam.ae/en/news/emirates/1395285548932.html
Rashid Muhammad al-Shehi	04–Sep–15	RAK	http://www.wam.ae/en/news/emirates/1395285548932.html
Abdullah Ahmed al-Shumaili	04–Sep–15	RAK	http://www.wam.ae/en/news/emirates/1395285548932.html
Salem Rashid al-Shehi	04–Sep–15	RAK	http://www.wam.ae/en/news/emirates/1395285548932.html
Sulieiman Jasim al-Baloushi	04–Sep–15	RAK	http://www.wam.ae/en/news/emirates/1395285548932.html
Rashid Ali al-Shehi	04–Sep–15	RAK	http://www.wam.ae/en/news/emirates/1395285548932.html
Yousuf Hassan Yusuf al-Obaidli	04–Sep–15	Sharjah	http://www.wam.ae/en/news/emirates/1395285009611.html http://www.emirates247.com/news/emirates/uae-mourns-martyrs-condolences-pour-in-2015-09-08-1.602737
Ahmed Ghulam Abdul Kareem Lengawi	04–Sep–15	Sharjah	http://www.wam.ae/en/news/emirates/1395285009611.html http://www.emirates247.com/news/emirates/uae-mourns-martyrs-condolences-pour-in-2015-09-08-1.602738
Waleed Muhammad al-Yasi	04–Sep–15	Sharjah	http://www.wam.ae/en/news/emirates/1395285009611.html http://www.emirates247.com/news/emirates/uae-mourns-martyrs-condolences-pour-in-2015-09-08-1.602738
Hamed Muhammad al-Baloushi	04–Sep–15	Sharjah	http://www.reuters.com/article/us-yemen-security-idUSKCN0R40V720150913 http://www.thenational.ae/uae/government/rulers-emiratis-and-expatriates-continue-to-show-support-for-families-of-martyrs

Name	Date	Emirate	URL
Muhammad Ismail Yousuf	04-Sep-15	Sharjah	http://www.reuters.com/article/us-yemen-security-idUSKCN0R40V720150913 http://www.thenational.ae/uae/government/rulers-emiratis-and-expatriates-continue-to-show-support-for-families-of-martyrs
Rashid Muhammad Abbas al-Baloushi	04-Sep-15	Sharjah	http://www.reuters.com/article/us-yemen-security-idUSKCN0R40V720150922 http://www.wam.ae/en/news/emirates/1395285241857.html
Jamal Majed al-Muhairi	04-Sep-15	Sharjah	http://www.wam.ae/en/news/emirates/1395285513861.html
Khalifa Bader Jawher	04-Sep-15	Sharjah	http://www.wam.ae/en/news/emirates/1395285513861.html
Saif Issa al-Naqbi	04-Sep-15	Sharjah	http://www.wam.ae/en/news/emirates/1395285570273.html
Rashid Nasser al-Zaabi	04-Sep-15	Sharjah	http://www.wam.ae/en/news/emirates/1395285570273.html
Hassan Muhammad al-Tunaiji	04-Sep-15	Sharjah	http://www.wam.ae/en/news/emirates/1395285570273.html
Rashid Mohammerd al-Baloushi	04-Sep-15	Sharjah	http://www.wam.ae/en/news/emirates/1395285570273.html
Khalifa Bader Suleiman Abdullah	04-Sep-15	Sharjah	http://www.wam.ae/en/news/emirates/1395285570273.html
Ghalib Amir Saleh al-Marri	04-Sep-15	Sharjah	http://www.wam.ae/en/news/emirates/1395285655523.html

Name	Date	Emirate	URL
Ghaleb Amer Saleh Amer Hallabi	04–Sep–15	Sharjah	http://gulfnews.com/news/uae/government/sharjah-streets-to-be-named-after-martyrs-1.1599034 http://www.khaleejtimes.com/martyrs-day-2015/remembering-the-sacrifice-list-of-uae-martyrs-in-operation-restoring-hope
Mohamad Ismail Mohamad	04–Sep–15	Sharjah	http://www.emirates247.com/news/emirates/mohamed-continues-visits-to-families-of-fallen-emirati-servicemen-2015-09-06-1.602445
Saeed Obaid bin Fadil al-Ali	04–Sep–15	Umm al-Quwain	http://www.wam.ae/en/news/emirates/1395285009611.html http://www.emirates247.com/news/emirates/mohammed-continues-to-offer-condolences-to-families-of-martyrs-2015-09-06-1.602528
Essa Ibrahim Hamad Mohamad	04–Sep–15		http://www.khaleejtimes.com/martyrs-day-2015/remembering-the-sacrifice-list-of-uae-martyrs-in-operation-restoring-hope
Ahmed Hebtan Nour Mohamad al-Baloushi	01–Oct–15	RAK	http://www.emirates247.com/news/prayers-for-uae-martyr-ahmed-al-baloushi-2015-10-03-1.605392
Khamis Rashid Al Abdouli	06–Oct–15	Fujairah	http://www.khaleejtimes.com/nation/general/four-more-emiratis-martyred-in-yemen
Ahmed Khamis Malullah al-Hamadi	07–Oct–15	Abu Dhabi	http://www.khaleejtimes.com/nation/general/four-more-emiratis-martyred-in-yemen http://www.khaleejtimes.com/nation/general/martyrdom-is-a-heavenly-gift-say-families

Muhammad Khalfan al-Siyabi	07–Oct–15	Abu Dhabi	http://www.khaleejtimes.com/nation/general/four-more-emiratis-martyred-in-yemen http://www.khaleejtimes.com/nation/general/martyrdom-is-a-heavenly-gift-say-families
Ali Khamis bin Ayed al-Ketbi	07–Oct–15	Al Ain	http://www.khaleejtimes.com/nation/general/four-more-emiratis-martyred-in-yemen http://www.khaleejtimes.com/nation/general/martyrdom-is-a-heavenly-gift-say-families
Yousuf Salem Ali al-Kaabi	07–Oct–15	Fujairah	http://www.khaleejtimes.com/nation/general/four-more-emiratis-martyred-in-yemen http://www.khaleejtimes.com/nation/general/martyrdom-is-a-heavenly-gift-say-families
Abdulsalam Abdulkarim Abdulrahim al-Fuqaha	11–Oct–15	Al Ain	http://www.thenational.ae/uae/government/body-of-uae-service-man-arrives-in-abu-dhabi
Sultan Saeed Mohamad Abdullah al-Mazrouie	11–Oct–15	Sharjah	http://www.uaeinteract.com/docs/Mohamed_bin_Zayed_offers_condolences_to_family_of_martyr_Al_Mazrouie/71691.htm
Hadif Humaid Al Shamsi al-Taher	18–Oct–15	Al Ain	http://www.wam.ae/en/news/emirates/1395286840304.html

Hamoud al-Ameri	24–Oct–15	Al Ain	http://www.wam.ae/en/news/emirates/1395287093172.html
Nasser Hassan Muhammad al-Baloushi	24–Nov–15	Fujairah	http://www.wam.ae/en/news/emirates/1395288426433.html http://www.emirates247.com/news/emirates/mohammed-pays-respects-to-nation-s-martyr-nasser-ali-hassan-al-baloushi-2015-11-29-1.612179
Sultan Muhammad al-Ketbi	17–Dec–15	Sharjah	http://www.wam.ae/en/news/emirates/1395289361259.html
Abdullah Juma Hassan al-Shamsi	14–Feb–16	RAK	http://www.wam.ae/en/news/emirates/1395291573533.html http://www.wam.ae/en/news/general/1395291619858.html
Obaid Salem al-Badwawi	22–Feb–16	Ajman	http://www.wam.ae/en/news/emirates/1395291927565.html
Muhammad Rashid al-Dhahnani	29–Feb–16	Fujairah	http://www.wam.ae/en/news/emirates/1395292203389.html
Muhammad Obaid al-Hmoudi	15–Mar–16	Fujairah	http://www.wam.ae/en/news/emirates/1395292929657.html http://www.thenational.ae/uae/government/sheikh-mohammed-bin-rashid-leads-condolences-for-families-of-the-pilots-killed-in-yemen
Zayed Ali al-Kaabi	15–Mar–16	Sharjah	http://www.wam.ae/en/news/emirates/1395292929657.html http://www.thenational.ae/uae/government/sheikh-mohammed-bin-rashid-leads-condolences-for-families-of-the-pilots-killed-in-yemen

Name	Date	Emirate	Source
Ahmed Muhammad Ahmen al-Zeyoudi	14–Jun–16	Fujairah	http://www.wam.ae/en/news/emirates/1395296720674.html http://www.thenational.ae/uae/sheikh-mohammed-bin-zayed-offers-condolences-to-families-of-pilots-killed-in-yemen
Abdullah Muhammad Saeed al-Yamahi	14–Jun–16	Fujairah	http://www.wam.ae/en/news/emirates/1395296720674.html http://www.thenational.ae/uae/sheikh-mohammed-bin-zayed-offers-condolences-to-families-of-pilots-killed-in-yemen
Ali Muhammad Taresh al-Kaabi	21–Jun–16	Ajman	http://www.wam.ae/en/news/emirates/1395296997277.html
Muhammad Nasser Rashid al-Dhahiri	21–Jun–16	Al Ain	http://www.wam.ae/en/news/emirates/1395296997277.html
Rashid Ahmad Abdullah al-Habsi	05–Sep–16	RAK	http://www.wam.ae/en/news/emirates/1395299616044.html http://gulfnews.com/news/uae/society/martyr-laid-to-rest-in-ras-al-khaimah-1.1892138
Saeed Anbar Juma al-Falasi	22–Sep–16	Dubai	http://gulfnews.com/news/uae/society/emotional-farewell-for-uae-martyr-in-dubai-1.1900672
Rashid Ali Muhammad al-Dhahoori	04–Feb–17	RAK	https://www.khaleejtimes.com/nation/abu-dhabi/two-brave-emirati-soldiers-martyred
Obaid Jowhar Obaid al-Mazrouei	04–Feb–17	Sharjah	http://www.emirates247.com/news/emirates/general-command-of-uae-armed-forces-announces-martyrdom-of-serviceman-2017-02-05-1.647621

Name	Date	Emirate	Source
Nader Mubarak Eisa Soliman	17–Feb–17	Dubai	https://www.thenational.ae/uae/bodies-of-two-uae-martyrs-who-died-in-yemen-arrive-in-abu-dhabi-1.54797 http://wam.ae/en/details/1395302598278
Soliman Muhammad Soliman al-Dhohouri	17–Feb–17	Dubai	https://www.thenational.ae/uae/bodies-of-two-uae-martyrs-who-died-in-yemen-arrive-in-abu-dhabi-1.54797 http://wam.ae/en/details/1395302598278
Khalid Ali Ghareeb al-Baloushi	24–Feb–17	Dubai	https://www.thenational.ae/uae/government/tributes-paid-to-serviceman-killed-in-yemen-ahead-of-al-warqa-funeral-1.29438
Zakaria Sulaiman Obaid al-Zaabi	17–Mar–17	Sharjah	https://www.thenational.ae/uae/government/uae-soldier-who-died-serving-country-in-yemen-laid-to-rest-1.80679
Abdullah Mohammad Eisa al-Hammadi	25–Apr–17	Sharjah	http://gulfnews.com/news/uae/government/uae-soldier-martyred-during-mission-in-the-country-1.2016851
Hassan Abdullah al-Beshr	03–May–17	RAK	https://www.khaleejtimes.com/news/government/UAE-soldier-martyred-in-Yemen
Samir Mohammad Murad Abu Bakr	12–Aug–17	Ajman	http://gulfnews.com/news/uae/government/families-mourn-four-uae-soldiers-martyred-in-yemen-1.2072878
Ahmad Khalifa al-Bloushi	12–Aug–17	Al Ain	http://gulfnews.com/news/uae/government/families-mourn-four-uae-soldiers-martyred-in-yemen-1.2072878

Mohammad Saeed al-Hassani	12–Aug–17	Fujairah	http://gulfnews.com/news/uae/government/families-mourn-four-uae-soldiers-martyred-in-yemen-1.2072878
Jasim Saleh al-Zaabi	12–Aug–17	RAK	http://gulfnews.com/news/uae/government/families-mourn-four-uae-soldiers-martyred-in-yemen-1.2072878
Sultan Muhammad Ali al-Naqbi	12–Sep–17	RAK	https://www.khaleejtimes.com/nation/abu-dhabi/two-uae-soldiers-martyred-
Nassir Gharib al-Mazrouie	12–Sep–17	Sharjah	https://www.khaleejtimes.com/nation/abu-dhabi/two-uae-soldiers-martyred-
Ali Saeed Saif al-Mesmari	17–Oct–17	Fujairah	http://gulfnews.com/news/uae/society/two-uae-pilots-martyred-in-yemen-1.2107963
Bader Yahiya Mohammad al-Marashdeh	17–Oct–17	Sharjah	http://gulfnews.com/news/uae/society/two-uae-pilots-martyred-in-yemen-1.2107963
Saeed al-Kaabi	28–Oct–17	Fujairah	https://www.khaleejtimes.com/news/government/martyred-uae-soldier-saeed-al-kaabi-laid-to-rest-in-fujairah-

APPENDICES

Appendix 7: Partial List of UAE Public Sector Bodies Online

National Government		Ministry of Cabinet Affairs and the Future[54]
		Ministry of Climate Change and Environment[55]
		Ministry of Community Development[56]
		Ministry of Culture and Knowledge Development[57]
		Ministry of Defence[58]
		Ministry of Economy[59]
		Ministry of Education[60]
		Ministry of Energy & Industry[61]
		Ministry of State for Federal National Council Affairs[62]
		Ministry of Finance[63]
		Ministry of Foreign Affairs and International Cooperation[64]
		Government.ae[65]
		Ministry of Health and Prevention[66]
		Ministry of Human Resources and Emiratisation[67]
		Ministry of Infrastructure Development[68]
		Ministry of Interior[69]
		Ministry of Justice[70]
		Ministry of Presidential Affairs[71]

		Ministry of State for Happiness[72]
		Ministry of Tolerance[73]
	Media	Emirates News Agency (WAM)[74]
		National Media Council[75]
	Security	AECERT (Computer Emergency Response Team)[76]
		Federal Authority for Identity and Citizenship[77]
		Telecommunications Regulatory Authority (TRA)[78]
	Telecommunications	DU[79]
		Etisalat[80]
		Virgin[81]
Federal Government		Abu Dhabi Digital Government[82]
		Government of Ajman[83]
		Dubai e-Government[84]
		Fujairah e-Government[85]
		RAK.ae[86]
		Sharjah e-Government[87]
		Umm al-Quwain e-Government[88]
	Security	Abu Dhabi Systems & Information Centre (ADSIC)[89]
		Dubai Electronic Security Centre[90]

APPENDICES

Appendix 8: Etisalat Board Members as of 2016 and their Public-Sector Connections[91]

Position	Name	Public sector positions
Chairman	Eissa Muhammad Ghanem al-Suwaidi	*Managing Director*, Abu Dhabi Investment Council (ADIC) *Chairman*, Abu Dhabi Commercial Bank *Board Member*, ADNOC Distribution *Board Member*, International Petroleum Investment Company *Board Member*, Emirates Investment Authority
Vice Chairman	Sheikh Ahmed Mohd al-Dhahiri	*Vice Chairman*, Abu Dhabi National Hotels Company *Board Member*, Abu Dhabi Aviation *Board Member*, National Bank of Abu Dhabi
Board Members	Muhammad Sultan al-Hameli	*Director General*, Department of Finance *Chairman of the Board of Directors*, National Health Insurance Company *Vice Chairman of the Board of Directors*, Abu Dhabi Commercial Bank
Board Members	Abdullah Salem al-Dhaheri	*Director*, Abu Dhabi National Oil Company *Chairman of the Board of Directors*, National Gas Shipping Company

		Chairman of the Board of Directors, Abu Dhabi National Tanker Company
		Chairman of the Board of Directors, Abu Dhabi National Ports Operating Company
		Chairman of the Board of Directors, Petroleum Services Company
		Board Member, Abu Dhabi National Oil Refining Company
		Board Member, ADNOC Distribution
Board Member	Hesham Abdulla al-Qassim	*Vice Chairman and Managing Director*, Emirates National Bank of Dubai
		Chairman, Emirates Islamic Bank
		Vice Chairman, Dubai Real Estate Corporation
		Board Member, Dubai International Financial Centre
Board Member	Essa Abdulfattah al-Mulla	*Governor*, Dubai International Financial Centre
		Chairman, Dubai Financial Market
		Member, Supreme Fiscal Committee in Dubai
		Member, Supreme Legislation Committee in Dubai
		Board Member, Free Zones Council
Board Member	Abdulfattah Sayed Sharaf	*Group General Manager and Chief Executive Officer*, HSBC Middle East
Board Member	Muhammad Hadi al-Hussaini	*Board Member*, Emirates National Bank of Dubai
		Board Member, Emirates Islamic Bank

		Board Member, Dubai Real Estate Corporation Board Member, Emaar Malls Group
Board Member	Abdelmonem bin Eisa bin Nasser Alserkal	Founder, AlSerkal Avenue Managing Director, Nasser bin Abdullatif Alserkal
Board Member	Khalid Abdulwahid al-Rustamani	Vice Chairman, A.W. Rostamani Group Vice Chairman, Commercial Bank of Dubai
Board Member	Otaiba Khalaf Ahmed al-Otaiba	

Appendix 9: Du Board of Directors and their Public-Sector Connections[92]

Position	Name	Public sector positions
Chairman	Ahmed Bin Bayt	Member, Emirates Investment Authority Member of the Board of Trustees, Mohammed bin Rashid School of Government Member of the Board of Trustees, Zayed University
Vice Chairman	Khaled Balama	Executive Director, Real Estate, Abu Dhabi Investment Council Board Member, UAE Central Bank Board Member, General Pension and Social Security Authority Board Member, Emirates Development Bank
Board Member	Saeed al-Yateem	Assistant Undersecretary, Budget and Revenue Affairs, Ministry of Finance

Board Member	Ziad Galadari	*Chairman*, Galadari Investments Board of Directors, Dubai World Trade Centre
Board Member	Homaid al-Shemmari	*Chief Executive Officer*, Aerospace and Engineering Services, Mubadala *Board Member*, Mubadala Investment Committee *Chairman*, Emirates Defence Industries Company (EDIC)
Board Member	Fadhel al-Ali	*Group Chief*, Customer Experience and Digital Officer, First Abu Dhabi Bank *Board Member*, Dubai Financial Services Authority *Board Member*, Abu Dhabi Capital Group
Board Member	Masood Mahmood	*Chief Executive*, Yahsat *Board Member*, EMEA Satellite Operators Association *Chairman*, Du Investment Committee
Board Member	Abdullah al-Shamsi	*General Manager*, United Arab Shipping Agencies *Vice President*, Dubai Shipping Agents Association Chairman, Dubai Properties Group
Board Member	Muhammad al-Suwaidi	*Executive Director*, Investment, Emirates Investment Authority

Appendix 10: UAE's Surveillance-Based Legislation

– Article 30 of 1971 Constitution, 2 December 1971[93]
– Federal Law No.15 of 1980 *Concerning Press and Publications*, 16 November 1980[94]
– Federal Decree No.3 of 1987 Penal Code, 8 December 1987

APPENDICES

- Federal Law by Decree No.3 of 2003 Regarding the Organization of Telecommunications Sector, 15 November 2003[95]
- Federal Law No.2 of 2004 Popular Register and Emirates Identity Card Program, 29 September 2004[96]
- Federal Decree No.1 of 2006 Cyber Crimes Law, 30 June 2006[97]
- Federal Law by Decree No.5 of 2008
- Amending the Provisions of the Federal Law by Decree No.3 of 2003[98]
- Cabinet Resolution No. (42/23) of 2008 Session No.3, Regarding the Abolition of the Supreme Committee for the Supervision of the Telecommunication Sector and delegating its function to the Board of Directors of the TRA[99]
- National Media Council Resolution No.20 of 2010[100]
- Federal Decree Law No.3 of 2012 Establishment of National Electronic Security Authority (NESA), 13 August 2012[101]
- Federal Decree Law No.5 of 2012 Combatting Cybercrimes, 13 August 2012[102]
- National Media Council Chairman's Decision No.35 of 2013 Advertising Content[103]
- Federal Decree Law No.7 of 2014 Combatting Terrorism Offences, 20 August 2014[104]
- Federal Decree Law No.2 of 2015 Combatting Discrimination and Hatred, 15 July 2015[105]
- Federal Law No.11 of 2016 Competencies of the National Media Council, 21 July 2016[106]
- Federal Decree Law No.12 of 2016, 21 July 2016[107]
- Council of Ministers Decree No.23 of 2017 Concerning Media Content[108]

Appendix 11: Text of Articles Pertinent to Political Targeting Federal Law No.7 of 2014—Combatting Terrorism Offences[109]

Article 1	In implementation of the provisions of the present Law, the following terms and expressions shall have the meanings assigned thereto, unless the context requires otherwise:
	Terrorist Result; Inciting fear among a group of people, killing them, or causing them serious physical injury, or inflicting substantial damage to property or the environment, or disrupting security of the international community, or opposing the country, or influencing the public authorities of the country or another country or international organisation while discharging its duties, or receiving a privilege from the country or another country or an international organisation.

Internationally Protected Persons;

1. Kings and presidents of other states including any member of an organisation that perform the functions of head of state under the constitution of the concerned state, prime ministers and ministers of foreign affairs as the time of presence of any of the aforementioned persons in the state, along with their family members who accompany them.

2. Representatives or public officials of other states or an international governmental organisation, within the period during which such persons, along with their family members supported thereby, receive the prescribed special protection under the international law.

Article 9	Capital punishment shall be imposed on whoever attempts to commit or commits any aggression against the safety of the President of the State, his deputy or any of the members of the Federal Supreme Council, their heir apparents, deputies or family members, or deliberately endangers their life or freedom for a terrorist purpose.
Article 10	Life imprisonment shall be imposed on whoever uses or threatens the use of violence to urge the head of state, his deputy or any of the members of the Federal Supreme Council, their heir apparents or deputies to perform or abstain from performing an act that falls within their legal competence.
Article 11	Life imprisonment shall be imposed on whoever uses violence or threat of it to urge the Prime Minister of any of his deputies, or the ministers, the Chairman of the Federal National Council or any of its members or the members of the judiciary, to perform or abstain from the performance of an act that legally falls within their competence.
Article 14	Capital punishment or life imprisonment shall be imposed on whoever commits an action or inaction intended for threatening the State's stability, safety, unity, sovereignty or security, which contradicts the basic principles underlying the governance system of the State, or with the purpose of making a coup and taking over the power, illegally invalidating the provisions of the constitution or preventing one of the State's institutions or the public authorities from practising their activities, or prejudicing the national unity of the social security.

APPENDICES

Article 15	Temporary imprisonment shall be imposed on whoever declares, by any means of communication, his opposition to the state, or to the ruling system therein or his non-allegiance to its leadership.
Article 34	1. Temporary imprisonment for no more than 10 years shall be imposed on whoever knowingly promotes or supports a terrorist organisation, person or offence, whether verbally, in writing or by any other method. 2. Temporary imprisonment for no more than 10 years shall be imposed on whoever: a. Knowingly possesses, in person or through someone else, any documents, print or recordings of any kind that encompass promotion or supporting of any terrorist organisation, person or offence if intended for distribution of access by others. b. Knowingly possesses or acquires any printing, recording or publishing mean used or intended to be used, even if temporarily, for the printing, recording, circulating or publishing any of the aforementioned.

Appendix 12: Evolution of Mubadala Leadership 2008–2018[110]

2008[111]		2009[112]		2010[113]		2011[114]		2012[115]	
Chairman	MBZ	Chairman	MBZ	Chairman	MBZ	Chairman	MBZ	Chairman	MBZ
Vice Chairman	Muhammad Ahmed al-Bowardi	Vice Chairman	Muhammad Ahmed al-Bowardi	Vice Chairman	Muhammad Ahmed al-Bowardi	Vice Chairman	Muhammad Ahmed al-Bowardi	Vice Chairman	Muhammad Ahmed al-Bowardi
Member	Hamad al-Hurr al-Suwaidi	Member	Hamad al-Hurr al-Suwaidi	Member	Hamad al-Hurr al-Suwaidi	Member	Hamad al-Hurr al-Suwaidi	Member	Hamad al-Hurr al-Suwaidi
Member	Nasser Ahmed Khalifa al-Sowaidi	Member	Nasser Ahmed Khalifa al-Sowaidi	Member	Nasser Ahmed Khalifa al-Sowaidi	Member	Nasser Ahmed Khalifa al-Sowaidi	Member	Nasser Ahmed Khalifa al-Sowaidi
Member	Ahmed Ali al-Sayegh	Member	Ahmed Ali al-Sayegh	Member	Ahmed Ali al-Sayegh	Member	Abdulhamid Muhammad Saeed	Member	Abdulhamid Muhammad Saeed
Member	Muhammad Saif al-Mazrouei	Member	Muhammad Saif al-Mazrouei	Member	Muhammad Saif al-Mazrouei	Member	Mahmood Ebraheem al-Mahmood	Member	Mahmood Ebraheem al-Mahmood

Group CEO and Managing Director	Khaldoon Khalifa al-Mubarak	Group CEO and Managing Director	Khaldoon Khalifa al-Mubarak	Group CEO and Managing Director	Khaldoon Khalifa al-Mubarak	Group CEO and Managing Director	Khaldoon Khalifa al-Mubarak	Group CEO and Managing Director	Khaldoon Khalifa al-Mubarak
Chief Operating Officer (COO)	Waleed al Mokarrab al-Muhairi	Chief Operating Officer (COO)	Waleed al Mokarrab al-Muhairi	Chief Operating Officer (COO)	Waleed al Mokarrab al-Muhairi	Chief Operating Officer (COO)	Waleed al Mokarrab al-Muhairi	Chief Operating Officer (COO)	Waleed al Mokarrab al-Muhairi
CFO	Carlos Obeid	CFO	Carlos Obeid	CFO	Carlos Obeid	CFO	Carlos Obeid	CFO	Carlos Obeid
Executive Director, Strategic Planning and Portfolio Management	Alexej Ogorek	Chief Legal Counsel	Samer Halawa	Chief Legal Counsel	Samer Halawa	Chief Legal Counsel	Samer Halawa	Chief Legal Counsel	Samer Halawa
Executive Director	Derek Pozycki	CEO, Mubadala Oil and Gas & Executive Director, Energy & Industry	Maurizio La Noce	Executive Director, Finance	Moiz Chakkiwala	Executive Director	Homaid al-Shemmari	Executive Director, Aerospace	Homaid al-Shemmari

Executive Director, Acquisitions	Hani Barhoush	Executive Director, Real Estate	John Thomas	Executive Director, Group Treasury	Matthew Hun	Executive Director	Hani Barhoush	Executive Director, Industry	Ahmed Yahia
Executive Director, ICT	Jassem Muhammad al-Zaabi	CEO, Mubadala Infrastructure	Rod Mathers	Executive Director, Construction Management Services	Rod Mathers	Executive Director	Suhail Mahmood al-Ansari	Executive Director, Information and Communications Technology (ICT)	Jassem Muhammad al-Zaabi
Executive Director, Real Estate and Hospitality	John Thomas	Executive Director, Services Ventures	Laurent Depolla	Executive Director, Structured Finance and Capital Markets	Derek Rozycki	Executive Director	Ahmed Yahia al-Idrissi	CEO and Executive Director, Mubadala Petroleum	Maurizio la Noce
Executive Director, Communications	Kate Triggs	Executive Director, Aerospace	Homaid al-Shemmari	Executive Director, Group Communications	Kate Triggs	Executive Director	Jassem Muhammad al-Zaabi	CEO, Masdar	Sultan Ahmed al-Jaber

Suhail Moahmood al-Ansari	Abdulla al-Shamsi			
Executive Director, Mubadala Healthcare	Vice-President, Mubadala Real Estate and Infrastructure			
Ali Eid al Mheiri	Maurizio la Noce	Laurent Depolla		Ibrahim Ajami
Executive Director	CEO, Oil	Executive Director		Executive Director
Ajit Naidu	Suhail Mahmoof al-Ansari	Hani Barhoush		Laurent Depolla
Chief Information Officer	Executive Director, Healthcare	Executive Director, Mubadala Capital & Mergers and Acquisitions		Executive Director, Mubadala Services Ventures
Jassem Muhammad al-Zaabi	Mark Erhart	Hani Barhoush		Moiz Chakkiwala
Executive Director	Executive Director, Healthcare	Executive Director, Acquisitions		Executive Director, Finance
Laurent Depolla	Mark Erhart	Matthew Hurn		Maurizio La Noce
Executive Director, Services	Executive Director, Healthcare	Executive Director, Group Treasury		Executive Director, Energy & Industry, CEO, Mubadala Oil and Gas

Sultan Ahmed al-Jaber	CEO, Masdar
Ahmed Yahia al-Idrissi	Executive Director, Mubadala Industry
Maurizio la Noce	Executive Director, Mubadala Energy & Oil and Gas
Homaid al-Shemmari	Executive Director, Mubadala Aerospace
Peter Wilding	Executive Director, Real Estate & Hospitality
Jassem Muhammad al-Zaabi	Executive Director, Mubadala ICT
Derek Rozycki	Executive Director, Project & Corporate Finance
Kate Triggs	Executive Director, Group Communications
Ajit Naidu	Chief Information Officer
Rod Mathers	CEO, Mubadala Infrastructure

	2013[116]		2014[117]		2015[118]		2016[119]		2017[120]	
	Chairman	MBZ	Chairman	MBZ	Chairman	MBZ	Chairman	MBZ	Chairman	MBZ
	Vice Chairman	Muhammad Ahmed al-Bowardi	Vice Chairman	Muhammad Ahmed al-Bowardi					Vice Chairman	Mansour bin Zayed
	Member	Hamad Al-Hurr al-Suwaidi	Member	Hamad Al-Hurr al-Suwaidi	Group CEO & Managing Director	Khaldoon Khalifa al-Mubarak	Group CEO & Managing Director	Khaldoon Khalifa al-Mubarak	Board Member	Muhammad Ahmed al-Bowardi
	Member	Nasser Ahmed Khalifa al-Sowaidi	Member	Nasser Ahmed Khalifa al-Sowaidi	Deputy Group CEO & CEO Emerging Sectors	Waleed al-Mokarrab al-Muhairi	Deputy Group CEO & CEO Emerging Sectors	Waleed al-Mokarrab al-Muhairi	Member	Suhail Muhammad Faraj al-Mazrouei
	Member	Abdulhamid Muhammad Saeed	Member	Abdulhamid Muhammad Saeed	CEO Technology & Industry	Ahmed Yahia al-Idrissi	CEO Technology & Industry	Ahmed Yahia al-Idrissi	Member	Mahmood Ebraheem al-Mahmood
	Member	Mahmood Ebraheem al-Mahmood	Member	Mahmood Ebraheem al-Mahmood	CEO Energy	Dr Sultan al-Jaber	CEO Energy	Amed Saeed al-Calily	Member	Abdulhamid Muhammad Saeed

Khaldoon Khalifa al-Mubarak	Group CEO & Managing Director	Khaled Abdulla al-Qubaisi	Chief Human Capital Officer	Khaled Abdulla al-Qubaisi	Chief Human Capital Officer	Khaldoon Khalifa al-Mubarak	Group CEO and Managing Director	Khaldoon Khalifa al-Mubarak	Group CEO and Managing Director
Waleed al-Mokarrab al-Muhairi	Deputy Group CEO & CEO, Alternative Investments and Infrastructure	Homaid al-Shimmari	Chief Executive Officer, Aerospace and Engineering Services	Homaid al-Shimmari	Chief Executive Officer, Aerospace and Engineering Services	Waleed al-Mokarrab al-Muhairi	Deputy Group CEO and CEO Emerging Sectors	Waleed al-Mokarrab al-Muhairi	Deputy Group CEO and CEO Emerging Sectors
Homaid al-Shimmari	Deputy CEO, Chief of Human Capital and Corporate Services	Samer Halawa	Chief Legal Counsel	Samer Halawa	Chief Legal Counsel	Sultan Ahmed al-Jaber	Chief Executive Officer, Energy	Sultan Ahmed al-Jaber	Chief Executive Officer, Energy
Ahmed Saeed al-Calily	Chief Strategy & Risk Officer	Carlos Obeid	Chief Financial Officer	Carlos Obeid	Chief Financial Officer	Homaid al-Shemmari	CEO, Aerospace & Engineering Service	Homaid al-Shemmari	CEO, Aerospace & Engineering Service
Hmed Yahia al-Idrissi	CEO, Technology, Manufacturing & Mining					Khaled Abdulla al-Qubaisi	Chief Human Capital Officer	Khaled Abdulla al-Qubaisi	Chief Human Capital Officer

APPENDICES

Chief Legal Counsel	Samer Halawa	Chief Legal Counsel	Samer Halawa		Mussabbeh al-Kaabi — CEO, Petroleum & Petrochemicals
CFO	Carlos Obeid	CFO	Carlos Obeid		Khaled Abdullah al-Qubaisi — CEO, Aerospace, Renewables, and ICT
CEO Technology & Industry	Ahmed Yahia al-Idrissi				Hani Barhoush — Executive Director
					Samer Halawa — Chief Legal Officer
					Carlos Obeid — Chief Financial Officer

213

Appendix 13: Evolution of the Tribal and Kinship Dynamics within the Abu Dhabi Executive Council (ADEC)

ADEC members 2007[121]	ADEC members 2010[122]	ADEC members 2016[123]	ADEC members 2019[124]
Chairman of ADEC Mohammed bin Zayed al-Nahyan *Bani Yas*	Chairman of ADEC Mohammed bin Zayed al-Nahyan *Bani Yas*	Chairman of ADEC Mohammed bin Zayed al-Nahyan *Bani Yas*	Chairman of ADEC Mohammed bin Zayed al-Nahyan *Bani Yas*
Saeed bin Zayed al-Nahyan *Bani Yas*	Vice-Chairman of ADEC Hazza bin Zayed al-Nahyan *Bani Yas*	Vice-Chairman of ADEC Hazza bin Zayed al-Nahyan *Bani Yas*	Vice-Chairman of ADEC Hazza bin Zayed al-Nahyan *Bani Yas*
Tahnoon bin Zayed al-Nahyan *Bani Yas*	Hamed bin Zayed al-Nahyan *Bani Yas*	Hamed bin Zayed al-Nahyan *Bani Yas*	Tahnoon bin Zayed al-Nahyan *Bani Yas*
Diab bin Zayed al-Nahyan *Bani Yas*	Muhammad bin Khalifa al-Nahyan *Bani Yas*	Muhammad bin Khalifa al-Nahyan *Bani Yas*	Hamed bin Zayed al-Nahyan *Bani Yas*
Hamed bin Zayed al-Nahyan *Bani Yas*	Sultan bin Tahnoon al-Nahyan *Bani Yas*	Sultan bin Tahnoon al-Nahyan *Bani Yas*	Muhammad bin Khalifa al-Nahyan *Bani Yas*
Sultan bin Khalifa al-Nahyan *Bani Yas*	Secretary-General of the ADEC Muhammad Ahmed al-Bowardi	Secretary-General of the ADEC Ahmed Mubarak al-Mazroui	Khalid bin Mohammed bin Zayed al-Nahyan *Bani Yas*

APPENDICES

	Al Bu Falasah of the Bani Yas	*Mazar—Section of the Bani Yas*	
Muhammad bin Khalifa al-Nahyan *Bani Yas*	Khaldoun Khalifa al-Mubarak	Khaldoun Khalifa al-Mubarak	Theyab bin Mohammed bin Zayed al-Nahyan *Bani Yas*
Ahmed bin Said al-Nahyan *Bani Yas*	Ahmed Mubarak al-Mazroui *Mazar—Section of the Bani Yas*	Mugheer Khamis al-Khalil	Sultan bin Tahnoon al-Nahyan *Bani Yas*
Sultan bin Tahnoon al-Nahyan *Bani Yas*	Deputy Secretary-General of the ADEC Hamad al-Hurr al-Suwaidi *Sudan section of the Bani Yas*	Saeed Eid al-Ghafli *Ghafalah*	Secretary-General of the ADEC Ahmed Mubarak al-Mazrouei *Mazar—Section of the Bani Yas*
Secretary-General of the ADEC Mohammad Ahmad al-Bowardi[125] *Al Bu Falasah of the Bani Yas*	Nasser Ahmad al-Suwaidi *Sudan section of the Bani Yas*	Ali Majeed al-Mansoori *Manasir*	Khaldoun Khalifa al-Mubarak
Khaldoon Khalifa al-Mubarak	Abdullah Rashid Khalaf al-Otaiba[126]	Muhammad Khalfan al-Rumaithi *Rumaithat of the Bani Yas*	Jassem Muhammad Buatabh al-Zaabi *Za'ab*
Rashid Mubarak[127] Al-Hajeri *Sunni of Iranian origin*	Major General Obaid al-Ketbi *Bani Qitab*	Riyad Abdul Rahman al-Mubarak	Mugheer Khamis al-Khalil

Jou'an Salem al-Daheri *Dhawahir*	Mugheer Khamis al-Khalil	Abdulla bin Muhammad bin Butti al Hamed al-Qubaisi *Qubaysat of the Bani Yas*	Abdulla bin Muhammad bin Butti al Hamed al-Qubaisi *Qubaysat of the Bani Yas*
Hamad al Hurr al-Suwaidi *Sudan section of the Bani Yas*	Majid Ali al-Mansouri *Manasir*	Ali Rashed al-Nuaimi *Na'im*	Awaidha Murshed al-Marar *Al-Marar of the Bani Yas*
Nasser Ahmad al-Suwaidi *Sudan section of the Bani Yas*		Oweidah Murshed al-Murar *Al-Marar of the Bani Yas*	Saif Muhammad al-Hajeri
Major General Saeed Obaid al-Mazroui *Mazar—Section of the Bani Yas*			Falah Muhammad al-Ahbabi *Ahbab*
Abdullah Rashid al-Otaiba			Muhammad Khalifa al-Mubarak
Ahmed Mubarak al-Mazroui *Mazar—Section of the Bani Yas*			Major General Faris Khalaf al-Mazrouei *Mazar—Section of the Bani Yas*
			Sara Awad Issa Musallam

NOTES

NOTE ON SPELLING AND TERMINOLOGY

1. 'IJMES Translation and Transliteration Guide', *International Journal of Middle East Studies*, available online, https://www.cambridge.org/core/journals/international-journal-of-middle-east-studies/information/author-resources/ijmes-translation-and-transliteration-guide, date accessed 4ᵗʰ June 2021.

FOREWORD

1. S Salama, 'UAE widens scope of penal code to fight corruption', *Gulf News*, 5ᵗʰ December 2018, available online, https://gulfnews.com/uae/uae-widens-scope-of-penal-code-to-fight-corruption-1.60767814, date accessed, 15ᵗʰ June 2019.

1. INTRODUCTION

1. M Weber, *The Theory of Social and Economic Organisation*, trans. AM Henderson & T Parsons, The Free Press, Glencoe, 1947, p.341.
2. SP Huntington, *The Third Wave: Democratization in the Late Twentieth Century*, University of Oklahoma Press, Norman, 1993.
3. F Fukuyama, *The End of History and the Last Man*, Hamish Hamilton, London, 1992.
4. Ibid, p.42.
5. F Halliday, *After the Sultans*, Saqi Books, London, 2001. D Lerner, *The Passing of Traditional Society: Modernizing the Middle East*, Free Press of Glencoe, New York, 1958. S P Huntington, *Political Order in Changing Societies*, Yale University Press, London, 2006. M W Svolik, *The Politics of Authoritarian Rule*, Cambridge University Press, Cambridge, 2012. JP Filiu, *From Deep State to Islamic State: The Arab Counter-Revolution and its Jihad Legacy*, Hurst & Co, London, 2015.
6. J Gerschewski, 'The Three Pillars of Stability: Legitimation, Repression, and

Co-optation in Autocratic Regimes', *Democratization*, Vol.20, No.1, 2013, pp.13–38.

7. A statement supported by Yom. SL Yom, 'Understanding the Resilience of Monarchy During the Arab Spring', *Foreign Policy Research Institute*, April 2012.

8. SL Yom and FG Gause, 'Resilient Royals: How Arab Monarchies Hang On', *Journal of Democracy*, Vol.23, No.4, October 2012, pp.74–88.

9. SP Huntington, *Political Order in Changing Societies*, p.177.

10. It is assumed that a monarchy will inevitably modernise because of globalisation.

11. SP Huntington, *Political Order in Changing Societies*, p.177.

12. G O'Donnell and P Schmitter, *Transitions from Authoritarian Rule: Tentative Conclusions about Uncertain Democracies*, John Hopkins University Press, Baltimore, 1986, p.19.

13. V Lazarev and PR Gregory, 'Commissars and Csars: A Case Study in the Political Economy of Dictatorship', *Journal of Comparative Economics*, Vol. 1, 2003, pp.1–19 in PR Gregory, *Terror by Quota, State Security from Lenin to Stalin (An Archival Study)*, Yale University Press, New Haven, 2009, p.60.

14. C Davidson, *The United Arab Emirates: A Study in Survival*, Lynne Rienner, London, 2004.

15. C Davidson, *Abu Dhabi: Oil and Beyond*, Hurst & Co, London, 2011.

16. C Davidson, *Dubai: The Vulnerability of Success*, Hurst & Co, London, 2009.

17. F Heard-Bey, *From Trucial States to United Arab Emirates*, Longman, London, 1982.

18. H Van Der Muelen, *The Role of Tribal and Kinship Ties in the Politics of the United Arab Emirates*, PhD Thesis, Tufts University, 1997.

19. W Thesiger, *Arabian Sands*, Penguin, London, 2007.

20. C Davidson, *After the Sheikhs: The Coming Collapse of the Gulf Monarchies*, Hurst & Co, London, 2012.

21. C Davidson, *After the Sheikhs*, p.vii.

22. KC Ulrichsen, *Qatar and the Arab Spring*, Hurst & Co, London, 2014.

23. DB Roberts, *Qatar: Securing the Global Ambitions of a City-State*, Hurst & Co, London, 2017. D Held & KC Ulrichsen (eds.), *The Transformation of the Gulf: Politics, Economics and the Global Order*, Routledge, London, 2011.

24. KC Ulrichsen, *The United Arab Emirates; Power, Politics, and Decision Making*, Routledge, London, 2016.

25. G O'Donnell and P Schmitter, *Transitions from Authoritarian Rule: Tentative Conclusions about Uncertain Democracies*, John Hopkins University Press, Baltimore, 1986, p.19.

26. DB Robert, 'Bucking the Trend: The UAE and the Development of Military Capabilities in the Arab World', *Security Studies*, Vol.29, No.2, 2020, p.30.

27. 'Chairman of the National Service and Reserve Authority Lecture', *National Defence College*, 19th February 2018, available online, http://www.ndc.ac.ae/en/chairman-of-the-national-service-and-reserve-authority-lecture, date accessed, 20th August 2020.

28. 'UAE Naval Forces Commander, Pakistani counterpart discuss cooperation', *WAM*, 22ᵗʰ July 2019, available online, http://www.wam.ae/en/details/ 1395302775675, date accessed, 20ᵗʰ August 2020.

29. 'UAE Leaders welcome Sheikh Zayed bin Hamdan home after Yemen injuries', *The National*, 19ᵗʰ February 2018, available online, https://www.thenational. ae/uae/government/uae-leaders-welcome-sheikh-zayed-bin-hamdan-home-after-yemen-injuries-1.706108, date accessed, 20ᵗʰ August 2020.

30. KM Pollack, Sizing Up Little Sparta, Understanding UAE Military Effectiveness, *American Enterprise Institute (AEI)*, Washington DC, October 2020, p.8.

31. J Bill and R Springborg, *Politics in the Middle East*, Addison Wesley Longman, New York, 2000, p.118.

32. JA Bill and A Leiden, *The Middle East Politics and Power*, Allyn and Bacon, Boston 1974, p.106.

33. Ibid, p.8.

34. JE Peterson, 'Tribes and Politics in Eastern Arabia', Middle East Journal, Vol. 31, No.3, Summer 1977, pp.306–307.

35. BL Job, 'The Insecurity Dilemma: National, Regime and State Securities in the Third World', BL Job (ed.), The Insecurity Dilemma; National Security of Third World States, p.19.

36. Barry Buzan, however, suggests that in fact the differing interpretations of security are in fact, differing priorities of state security. The three components of a state are; idea of a state, physical base of a state, and the institutional expression of a state. B Buzan, *People, States & Fear; An Agenda for International Security Studies in the Post-Cold War Era*, Pearson Longman, Harlow, 1991, p.65.

37. BL Job, 'The Insecurity Dilemma: National, Regime and State Securities in the Third World', BL Job (ed.), *The Insecurity Dilemma; National Security of Third World States*, p.18.

38. M Mohamedou, *State-building and regime security: A study of Iraq's foreign policy making during the Second Gulf War*, PhD Dissertation, City University of New York, New York, 1996, p.111.

39. SR David, 'Explaining Third World Alignment', *World Politics*, Vol. 43, No.2, January 1991, pp.233–256.

40. M Herb, *All in the Family*, 1999.

41. S Greitens, *Coercive Institutions and State Violence Under Authoritarianism*, PhD Thesis, Harvard University, Boston, 2013.

42. G Gause, 'The Persistence of Monarchy in the Arabian Peninsula: A Comparative Analysis', in J Kostiner (ed.), *Middle East Monarchies: The Challenge of Modernity*, p.168.

43. JM Powell, *Coups and Conflict: The Paradox of Coup-Proofing*, PhD Thesis, University of Kentucky, Kentucky, 2012.

44. SL Yom, 'Understanding the Durability of Authoritarianism in the Middle East', *The Arab Studies Journal*, Vol 13/14, No 2/1, Fall 2005, pp.227–233.

45. E Bellin, 'Reconsidering the Robustness of Authoritarianism in the Middle East', *Comparative Politics*, Vol.44, No.2, January 2012, pp.127–149.

46. "the success and failure of monarchy in the Arabian Peninsula in the twentieth century had more to do with the position of Arabian countries in the regional security picture and the international political economy than with their particular domestic characteristics", G Gause, 'The Persistence of Monarchy in the Arabian Peninsula', p.168. There is a prominent argument within literature that hypothesises that the survival of authoritarian regimes is inherently linked to external security assistance. This was applied when the GCC was under the tutelage of the British and more recently under US influence, however, this book focuses on internal rather than external strategic issues. For research on this topic, see C Spencer, 'The Middle East: Changing from External Arbiter to Regional Player', in R Niblett (ed.), *America and a Changed World*, Chatham House, Wiley-Blackwell, London, 2010; K Ulrichsen, *Gulf Security: Changing Internal and External Dynamics*, The Centre for the Study of Global Governance, Kuwait Programme on Development, Governance, and Globalisation in the Gulf States, London School of Economics (LSE), London, 2009; K Selvik and S Stenslie, *Stability and Change in the Modern Middle East*, I B Tauris, London, 2011.

47. D Brumberg, 'Authoritarian Legacies and Reform Strategies in the Arab World', in R Brynen, B Korany, and P Noble (eds.), *Political Liberalization and Democratization in the Arab World, Volume 1, Theoretical Perspectives*, Lynne Rienner Publishers, 1995, p.235.

48. It can be argued that the lack of US support for Hosni Mubarak swung the pendulum in favour of the popular uprisings in Egypt, and ultimately led to his overthrow, however, decades of isolation for North Korea's regimes have proven Gause's postulation invalid.

49. R Lucas, 'Monarchical Authoritarianism: Survival and Political Liberalisation in a Middle Eastern Regime Type', *International Journal of Middle Eastern Studies*, Vol. 36, No.1, 2004, p.111.

50. JS Migdal, *Strong Societies and Weak States: State-Society Relations and State Capabilities in the Third World*, Princeton University Press, Princeton, 1988, p.208.

51. This is not to be confused with Francis Fukuyama's three pillars of stability (modern and strong, obey the rule of law, and to be accountable) F Fukuyama, *The Origins of Political Order*, Farrar, New York, 2011.

52. J Gerschewski, 'The Three Pillars of Stability: Legitimation, Repression, and Co-optation in Autocratic Regimes'.

53. Ibn Khaldun discusses legitimacy within tribal Arab culture at great length throughout *The Maqqadimah* Chapter 3 in particular.

54. Gregory Gause's postulation that the success of regime security in the GCC has rested upon foreign relations (G Gause, 'The Persistence of Monarchy in the Arabian Peninsula: A Comparative Analysis') is in fact contradictory because,

in order to secure your position, you reduce your own sovereignty. This book argues that in fact the aim of regime security is to increase power and control.

55. F Brichs & A Lampridi-Kemou, 'Sociology of Power in Today's Arab World', in F Brichs (ed.), *Political Regimes in the Arab World*.

56. "the Gulf's Kings and Emirs rule at the head of large families that share in executive authority through cabinet and other positions. The ruler cannot simply replace the Prime Minister when discontent rises, either because he is the Prime Minister (Saudi Arabia and Oman) or the Prime Minister is his nephew, uncle or cousin. About one-third of the Cabinet positions of each of the GCC states, including many of the most important ones, are held by ruling family members", G Gause, *Kings for all Seasons: How the Middle East's Monarchies Survived the Arab Spring*, p.27.

57. D Lutterbeck, 'Arab Uprisings, Armed Forces, and Civil-Military Relations', *Armed Forces & Society*, Vol.39, No.1, 2013, p.30.

58. N Ayubi, *Política y Sociedad en Oriente Próximo. La Hipertrofia del estado árabe*, Bellaterra, Barcelona, p.300–301 in F Brichs and A Lampridi-Kemou, 'Sociology of Power in Today's Arab World', in F Brichs (ed.), *Political Regimes in the Arab World*, p.24.

59. L Anderson, 'Dynasts and Nationalists: Why Monarchies Survive', in J Kostiner (ed.), *Middle East Monarchies: The Challenge of Modernity*, p.55.

60. H Arendt, *The Origins of Totalitarianism*, Penguin Books, London, 2017, p.549.

61. AI Kokurin and NV Petrov (eds.), *Lubianka, VChK-OGPU-NKVD-NKGB-MGB—MVD-KGB 1917–1960 spravochnik*. Moscow: MFD, 1997, p.10 in PR Gregory, *Terror by Quota, State Security from Lenin to Stalin (An Archival Study)*, Yale University Press, New Haven, 2009, pp.4–5

62. H Albrecht & O Schlumberger, '"Waiting for Godot"; Regime Change Without Democratization in the Middle East', *International Political Science Review*, Vol.25, No.4, 2004, p.372.

63. JA Bill & C Leiden, *The Middle East: Politics and Power*, p.58.

64. C Moore (ed.), *Authoritarian Politics in Modern Society*, Basic Books, New York, 1970. W Laquer, *International Fascism, 1920–1945*, Harper & Row, London, 1966.

65. LJ Cohen & JP Shapiro (eds.), *Communist Systems in Comparative Perspective*, Doubleday, New York, 1974. PR Gregory, *Terror by Quota, State Security from Lenin to Stalin (An Archival Study)*, Yale University Press, New Haven, 2009.

66. SM Lipset & A Solari (eds.), *Elites in Latin America*, Oxford University Press, Oxford, 1967. A Stepan, *The Military in Politics: Changing Patterns in Brazil*, Princeton University Press, Princeton, 1971. A Stepan, *Authoritarian Brazil: Origins, Policies, and Future*, Yale University Press, New Haven, 1973.

67. G O'Donnell, *Modernization and Bureaucratic-Authoritarianism: Studies in South American Politics*, Institute of International Studies, University of California, Berkley, 1973.

pp. [14–24] NOTES

68. A Perlmutter, *Modern Authoritarianism, A Comparative Institutional Analysis*, Yale University Press, New Haven, 1981, p.38.
69. Ibid, p.38.
70. Ibid, p.43–44.
71. A Giddens, *The Consequences of Modernity*, Polity Press, Cambridge, 1990, p.59.
72. A Perlmutter, *Modern Authoritarianism, A Comparative Institutional Analysis*, Yale University Press, New Haven, 1981, p.266.
73. Paraphrasing Satires who said 'Sed quis custodiet ipsos custodies?', or, who will guard the guards themselves? Satires, *Juvenal*, Satvra VI, 347–348, P Labriolle and F Villeneuve, trans., Belles Lettres, Paris, 1967, p.72.
74. A Giddens, *The Consequences of Modernity*, p.58.
75. D Brumberg, 'Democratization in the Arab World? The Trap of Liberalized Autocracy', *Journal of Democracy*, Vol. 13, No.4, 2002, p.63.

2. REGIME SECURITY STRATEGY PRECEDENT IN ABU DHABI

1. CD Davidson, 'After Shaikh Zayed: The Politics of Succession in Abu Dhabi and the UAE', *Middle East Policy*, Vol.13, No.1, Spring 2006, pp.42–59.
2. AB Rugh, *The Political Culture of Leadership in the United Arab Emirates*, p.12.
3. The evolution of the Zaabi tribe and its allegiance from the Qawasim in RAK to the Al-Nahyan's in Abu Dhabi is a key example.
4. Not only are the rulers of each Emirate head of the family, and thus head of the most important tribe in that area, but also, those surrounding the monarch form similar groupings and relationships that have not changed. Kazim notes that the driver behind this strategy was for the British to maximise oil concessions and weaken institutional capabilities and so strengthen foreign hegemony within the region. AA Kazim, *Historic Oman to the United Arab Emirates, from 600 A.D. to 1995: An Analysis of the Making, Remaking and Unmaking of a Socio-Discursive Formation in the Arabian Gulf, Part 1*, PhD Thesis, The American University, Washington D.C., 1996, p.513.
5. F Heard-Bey, *From Trucial States to United Arab Emirates: A Society in Transition*, p.27.
6. Hereafter simply referred to as the al-Nahyan.
7. JG Lorimer, *Gazetteer of the Persian Gulf, Oman, and Central Arabia*, Superintendent Government Printing, Calcutta, 1915, p.1932.
8. JB Kelly, *Eastern Arabian Frontiers*, p.60.
9. Ibid, p.61.
10. C Mann, *Abu Dhabi, Birth of an Oil Sheikhdom*, p.109.
11. U Rabi, 'Oil Politics and Tribal Rulers in Eastern Arabia: The Reign of Shakhbut (1928–1966)', *British Journal of Middle Eastern Studies*, Vol.33, No.1, May 2006, pp.37–50.
12. Ibid, p.39.
13. F Heard-Bey, *From Trucial States to United Arab Emirates*, pp.103–112.

14. Sheikh Tahnoon bin Muhammad al Nahyan in Al Ain, Eastern Region http://erd.ae/en/portal/20ac468d-ae7f-4bf1-a74f-58daeca461bc.aspx

15. Sheikh Hamdan bin Zayed al Nahyan, Madinat Zayed, https://www.abudhabi.ae/portal/public/en/departments/department_detail?docName=ADEGP_DF_135812_EN&_adf.ctrl-state=17lcvf3y2r_4&_afrLoop=1572475 5292232468#

16. U Rabi, 'Oil Politics and Tribal Rulers in Eastern Arabia: The Reign of Shakhbut (1928–1966)', p.40.

17. A Rugh, *The Political Culture of Leadership in the United Arab Emirates*, pp.220–227. Appendix 2: Transfer of Leadership in Abu Dhabi (1761–Present).

18. G Tullock, *The Social Dilemma of Autocracy, Revolution, Coup D'Etat, and War*, p.84.

19. The UAE's first foreign minister, Saif Ghubash, was accidently assassinated in 1977 when a gunman missed his target, the Syrian Foreign Minister, Abdel Halim Khaddam.

20. AB Rugh, *The Political Culture of Leadership in the United Arab Emirates*, p.156.

21. RS Zahlan, *The Origins of the United Arab Emirates: A Political and Social History of the Trucial States*, The MacMillan Press, London, 1978, p.196.

22. AB Rugh, *The Political Culture of Leadership in the United Arab Emirates*, p.156. Another branch of the Qawasim line, the Qassimis of RAK, have also experienced considerable political turbulence. The former Crown Prince of RAK, Sheikh Khalid bin Saqr al-Qassimi, was removed from the line of succession by his father and ruler of RAK, Sheikh Saqr bin Muhammad al-Qassimi. Sheikh Khalid has made several attempts to reassert his claim to power ('RAK Ruler's Death to Test Saud's Leadership', *Gulf States Newsletter (GSN)*, Vol.34, No.888, 29th October 2010.

23. During the political turmoil of 1818–1820, the Sheikh of Bahrain and Sultan of Muscat were deeply involved in the political wranglings of Sheikh Muhammad and Sheikh Tahnoon bin Shakhbut. C Mann, *Abu Dhabi, Birth of an Oil Sheikhdom*, p.26.

24. When Sheikh Khalifa bin Hamad al-Thani of Qatar was deposed by his son Sheikh Hamad bin Khalifa in 1995, while residing in Abu Dhabi, he attempted to regain power through a counter-coup, but ultimately failed. Sheikh Zayed was accused by Doha of assisting Sheikh Khalifa in his attempts to regain power.

25. In official documentation, while there is mention of Abu Dhabi's bloody past, this is often overlooked with the deliberate strategic direction of alternate discourses. See, JMA Al-Hajji, *Qasr al-Hosn, The History of the Rulers of Abu Dhabi 1793–1966*, Centre for Documentation and Research, Emirates Printing Press, Dubai, 2004, AM el Reyes (ed.), *New Perspectives on Recording UAE History*, Ministry of Presidential Affairs, National Centre for Documentation & Research, Abu Dhabi, 2009. In a tribute book to Zayed edited by Land, previous accounts of Emirati history are reimagined. Diab who by previous accounts was murdered by his cousin, Hazza, was according to Land simply '*succeeded by his eldest*

son'. S Land (ed.), *Zayed: A Man Who Built a Nation*, Media Prima, London, 2004, p.26.

26. C Mann, *Abu Dhabi, Birth of an Oil Shaykhdoman Oil Sheikhdom*, p.81.

27. Lienhardt notes that 'to kill a brother is considered as only slightly less shameful and disastrous than to kill a father'. P Lienhardt, *Shaikhdoms of Eastern Arabia*, A Al-Shahi (ed.), Palgrave, London, 2001, p.179.

28. Andrew Wheatcroft notes that 'according to Shaikh Zayid, he was compelled, with the full approval and encouragement of the family, to replace Shaikh Shakhbut'. A Wheatcroft, *With United Strength, H.H Shaikh Zayid bin Sultan Al Nahyan, the Leader and the Nation*, Emirates Center for Strategic Studies and Research (ECSSR), Abu Dhabi, 2013, p.138.

29. Hendrik Van Der Meulen and Frauke Heard-Bey both concur that opposition to Shakhbut within the family reached a point of no return as Shakhbut's behaviour had started to upset tribal alliances to the al-Nahyan, thus Shakhbut was removed to appease and stabilise the political balance of tribal support to the al-Nahyans. F Heard-Bey, 'The Gulf States and Oman in Transition', pp.20–21 in H Van Der Meulen, *The Role of Tribal and Kinship Ties in the Politics of the United Arab Emirates*, pp.48–49.

30. PRO, FO 371/185527, Foreign Office to Certain Missions, 6th August 1966, in U Rabi, 'Oil Politics and Tribal Rulers in Eastern Arabia: The Reign of Shakhbut (1928–1966)', p.49.

31. PRO, FO 371/185527, Political Agency, Abu Dhabi to HG Balfour-Paul, Bahrain Residency, 14th August 1966, U Rabi, 'Oil Politics and Tribal Rulers in Eastern Arabia: The Reign of Shakhbut (1928–1966)', p.50.

32. Several factors have been highlighted for Shakhbut's dismissal; however, it was his inability and reluctance to utilise the oil wealth for the development of Abu Dhabi that contributed to his demise.

33. AA Kazim, *Historic Oman to the United Arab Emirates, from 600 A.D. to 1995: An Analysis of the Making, Remaking and Unmaking of a Socio-Discursive Formation in the Arabian Gulf, Part 1*, pp.454–474.

34. M Hedges and G Cafiero, 'The Future of the Muslim Brotherhood in the GCC'.

35. Elsewhere across the region the PFLOAG had caused considerable instability and while its socialist gravitating ideology was evident within some sections of the Emirati population, Zayed bin Sultan al-Nahyan's management of the UAE economy and society repelled its ideological attraction. It is noted that because of the UAE's commercial and financial prosperity, as well as political and security capabilities, the PFLOAG was not able to significantly inject itself into Emirati society.

36. AA Kazim, *Historic Oman to the United Arab Emirates, from 600 A.D. to 1995: An Analysis of the Making, Remaking and Unmaking of a Socio-Discursive Formation in the Arabian Gulf, Part 1*, p.465.

37. S Yanai, *Transformation of Gulf Tribal States; Elitism and the Social Contract in Kuwait, Bahrain and Dubai, 1918–1970s*, Sussex Academic Press, Brighton, 2014, p.82.

38. C Davidson, *Dubai: The Vulnerability of Success*, Hurst & Co, London, 2008, p.33.

39. In contrast, the Kuwaiti Royal family failed to blunt the power of the merchant class, which now forms a substantial formalised opposition bloc to the Emir.

40. AA Kazim, *Historic Oman to the United Arab Emirates, from 600 A.D. to 1995: An Analysis of the Making, Remaking and Unmaking of a Socio-Discursive Formation in the Arabian Gulf, Part 1*, p.473.

41. MM Abdullah, *The United Arab Emirates: A Modern History*, Croom Helm, London, 1978, p.128.

42. C Davidson, 'Arab Nationalism and British Opposition in Dubai, 1920–66', *Middle Eastern Studies*, Vol.43, No.6, 2007, p.890.

43. The Manasir is not part of the Bani Yas, however, according to Van Der Meulen, is their closest tribal ally. H Van Der Meulen, *The Role of Tribal and Kinship Ties in the Politics of the United Arab Emirates*, p.153.

44. JMA Al-Hajji, *Qasr Al Hosn*, p.227.

45. C Mann, *Abu Dhabi, Birth of an Oil Sheikhdom*, p.77

46. Ibid, p.229.

47. A Rugh, *The Political Culture of Leadership in the United Arab Emirates*, p.136.

48. H Van Der Meulen, *The Role of Tribal and Kinship Ties in the Politics of the United Arab Emirates*, pp.99–100.

49. Sheikh Tahnoon bin Muhammad al Nahyan Biography, available online, http://erd.ae/en/portal/C55827FB-8FAE-496D-82E4-BFCB990BA5A3.aspx, date accessed, 27th December 2016. Sheikh Tahnoon was Chairman of the powerful Abu Dhabi National Oil Company (ADNOC) and a member of the Supreme Petroleum, however was removed prior to the death of Sheikh Zayed, along with other Mohammed bin Khalifa descendants in July 2004, to ensure the uncontested continuation of power from Sheikh Zayed to his sons, and not to other branches of the Emirati ruling family.

50. 'This presumably made theirs a love marriage [Sheikh Zayed and Sheikha Fatima] but given Zaid's tendency to marry wives from strategically important tribes, this could not have been a bad marriage in the late 1950s when he was still Wali of Buraimi'. AB Rugh, *The Political Culture of Leadership*, p.84.

51. AB Rugh, *The Political Culture of Leadership*, pp.82–87.

52. For example, the 11–14 November 1809 battle at Ras al-Khaimah.

53. A political officer in Bahrain, and later in Abu Dhabi and Dubai.

54. J Onley, 'Britain and the Gulf Shaikhdoms, 1820–1971: The Politics of Protection', *Centre for International and Regional Studies, Georgetown University School of Foreign Service in Qatar*, Doha, 2009, p.12.

55. KG Fenelon, *The United Arab Emirates: An Economic and Social Survey*, p.21.

56. Ibid, p.22.

57. I al-Abed, 'The Historical Background and Constitutional Basis to the Federation', E Ghareeb and I al-Abed (eds.), *United Arab Emirates: A New Perspective*, Trident Press, London, 1997, p.108.

58. 'Federal System', *UAE Cabinet*, available online, https://uaecabinet.ae/en/federal-system, date accessed, 30ᵗʰ December 2016.

59. 'Cabinet', *UAE Cabinet*, available online, https://uaecabinet.ae/en/about-the-cabinet, date accessed, 6ᵗʰ March 2021.

60. Federal Government Entities, *UAE Cabinet*, available online, https://uaecabinet.ae/en/federal-government-entities, date accessed, 30ᵗʰ December 2016. Ministry of Defence (MOD), MOI, Ministry of Presidential Affairs (MOPA), Ministry of Finance (MOF), Ministry of Foreign Affairs and International Cooperation (MICAD), Ministry of Culture and Knowledge Development (MCKD), Ministry of Cabinet Affairs and the Future (MOCAF), Ministry of Economy, Ministry of Community Development (MOCD), Ministry of Education, Ministry of Health and Prevention (MOHAP), Ministry of Human Resources and Emiratisation (MOHRE), Ministry of State for Federal National Council Affairs (MFNCA), Ministry of Justice (MOJ), Ministry of Climate Change and Environment (MOCCAE), Ministry of Energy and Industry (MOEI), Ministry of Infrastructure Development (MOID).

61. Al-Tabtabai notes that in the 1950s, when the UAE was at its least developed, the poorer Emirates maintained little to no contact with the outside world and lived in something like isolation. A al-Tabtabai, *Al-Nizam al-ittihadi fi al-imarat al-arabiyya: Dirasa muqarana* [The Federal System in the UAE: A Comparative Study], N.p. 1978, p.383, in M Herb, *The Wages of Oil: Parliaments and Economic Development in Kuwait and the UAE*, p.86.

62. MM Abdullah, *The United Arab Emirates; A Modern History*, p.139.

63. F Heard-Bey, 'The United Arab Emirates: Statehood and Nation-Building in a Traditional Society', *Middle East Journal*, Vol.59, No.3, Democratization and Civil Society, Summer 2005, p.359.

64. AA Kazim, *Historic Oman to the United Arab Emirates, from 600 A.D. to 1995: An Analysis of the Making, Remaking and Unmaking of a Socio-Discursive Formation in the Arabian Gulf, Part 1*, p.740.

65. A Wheatcroft, *With United Strength, H.H Shaikh Zayid bin Sultan Al Nahyan, the Leader and the Nation*, Emirates Center for Strategic Studies and Research (ECSSR), Abu Dhabi, 2013, p.108.

66. Because of a weak civil society and limited political power outside of official channels, the FNC has never had significant power. The UAE's ruling families were not only distinct from expatriates at an early period but were also invested in local matters through commercial activity, and as such have always been able to direct policy to suit their own strategic imperatives, thus the FNC has always been only a veneer of participatory politics.

67. M Herb, *The Wages of Oil: Parliaments and Economic Development in Kuwait and the UAE*, p.124.

68. F Heard-Bey, *The United Arab Emirates: Statehood and Nation-Building in a Traditional Civil Society*, p.363.

69. Sheikh Rashid's deteriorating health weakened his opposition to a strong union and enabled Sheikh Zayed to unite the federation.
70. JE Peterson, 'The Future of Federalism in the United Arab Emirates', in HR Sindelar and JE Peterson (eds.), *Crosscurrents in the Gulf: Arab, Regional and Global Interests*, The Middle East Institute, Routledge, London, 1988, p.198.
71. 'The Emirates shall exercise all powers not assigned to the Union by this Constitution. The Emirates shall all participate in the establishment of the Union and shall benefit from its existence, services and protection'.
72. 'The Emirates shall have jurisdiction in all matters not assigned to the exclusive jurisdiction of the Union in accordance with the provisions of the two preceding Articles'.
73. AA Kazim, *Historic Oman to the United Arab Emirates, from 600 A.D. to 1995: An Analysis of the Making, Remaking and Unmaking of a Socio-Discursive Formation in the Arabian Gulf, Part 1*, p.739.
74. Abu Dhabi to Foreign Office, 10th January 1968, PREM 13/2209 (TNA, London), citied in Sato, "Britain's Decision to Withdraw from the Persian Gulf, 1964–68", p.108 (n.54); The Times, 22 Jan 1968, p.1; The Times, 26 Jan 1968, p.5, in J Onley, Britain and the Gulf Shaikdoms, p.22 (n.85).
75. Michael Herb agrees and clarifies that while Saudi Arabia's dispute with the UAE over Buraimi delayed Riyadh's decision to acknowledge the UAE until 1974, this did not present a credible threat to the UAE. M Herb, *The Wages of Oil: Parliaments and Economic Development in Kuwait and the UAE*, p.99.
76. Border disputes with Oman and Saudi Arabia have however continued into the modern day. These are not perceived as strategically critical issues by the Emirati authorities.
77. Later the TOS were incorporated into local police forces.
78. MM Abdullah, *The United Arab Emirates*, p.139.
79. H Van Der Meulen, *The Role of Tribal and Kinship Ties in the Politics of the United Arab Emirates*, p.121.
80. A Yates, 'Western Expatriates in the UAE Armed Forces, 1964–2015', *Journal of Arabian Studies*, Vol.6, No.2, December 2016, pp.182–200.
81. JE Peterson, 'The Future of Federalism in the United Arab Emirates', pp.213–14.
82. AM Khalifa, *The United Arab Emirates: Unity in Fragmentation*, Saqi Books, London, 1989, p.80, in K Ulrichsen, *The United Arab Emirates*, p.64.
83. H Van Der Meulen, *The Role of Tribal and Kinship Ties in the Politics of the United Arab Emirates*, pp.97–100.
84. A Wheatcroft, *With United Strength, H.H Shaikh Zayid bin Sultan Al Nahyan, the Leader and the Nation*, Emirates Center for Strategic Studies and Research (ECSSR), Abu Dhabi, 2013, p.209.
85. This is in context of the obvious underutilisation of funds by his predecessor.
86. The construction of the Sheikh Zayed Road that connects the UAE's Emirates

was a highly symbolic gesture which has been recently trumped by the Emirates Road and the Sheikh Mohammed bin Zayed Road.

87. MM Abdullah, *The United Arab Emirates*, p.142.
88. A Wheatcroft, *With United Strength, H.H Shaikh Zayid bin Sultan Al Nahyan, the Leader and the Nation*, Emirates Center for Strategic Studies and Research (ECSSR), Abu Dhabi, 2013, pp.217–19.
89. WA Rugh, 'The United Arab Emirates: What Are the Sources of Its Stability?', *Middle East Policy*, Vol.5, No.3, Sept 1997, p.15.
90. C Davidson, 'After Shaikh Zayed: The Politics of Succession in Abu Dhabi and the UAE', p.43.
91. Sheikh Khalifa bin Zayed bin Khalifa did not however hold rule in Abu Dhabi, even though he was the eldest son of Zayed bin Khalifa.
92. H Van Der Meulen, *The Role of Tribal and Kinship Ties in the Politics of the United Arab Emirates*, p.110.
93. JE Peterson, 'The Future of Federalism in the United Arab Emirates', in HR Sindelar and JE Peterson (eds.), *Crosscurrents in the Gulf: Arab, Regional and Global Interests*, p.204.
94. AB Rugh, *The Political Culture of Leadership*, p.88.
95. H Van Der Meulen, *The Role of Tribal and Kinship Ties in the Politics of the United Arab Emirates*, p.111. See Appendix 3: Highest Positions of the Bani Mohammed bin Khalifa (BMBK) under Sheikh Zayed.
96. See Appendix 4: Marital connections between Bani Zayed and Bani Mohammed bin Khalifa. This contrasts with Sheikh Mubarak bin Mohammed bin Khalifa whose children have not married directly into the Bani Zayed, and thus, are not largely represented within departments of power within the UAE. For a family tree of the Bani Mohammed bin Khalifa (BMBK) and a wider examination of the family group see AB Rugh, *The Political Culture of Leadership*, p.87.
97. 'C.P. Khalifa Holds the Purse Strings as Abu Dhabi's Younger Generations Emerge', *Gulf States Newsletter (GSN)*, Vol. 26, No.683, April 3, 2002, p.5 in K Ulrichsen, *The United Arab Emirates*, p.70.
98. A Black, *The History of Islamic Political Thought: From the Prophet to the Present*, Edinburgh University Press, Edinburgh, 2001, p.53, in A Billingsley, *Political Succession in the Arab World: Constitutions, Family Loyalties and Islam*, Routledge, London, 2009, p.117.
99. H Van Der Meulen, *The Role of Tribal and Kinship Ties in the Politics of the United Arab Emirates*, p.118.
100. Hierarchically senior than the Minister of Defence.
101. C Davidson, 'After Shaikh Zayed: The Politics of Succession In Abu Dhabi and the UAE', p.46.
102. JE Peterson, 'The Future of Federalism in the UAE' in HR Sindelar III and JE Peterson, (eds.), *Crosscurrents in the Gulf*, p.204.
103. 'His Highness Sheikh Mohammed bin Zayed al Nahyan, Crown Prince', *Ruler's Representative Court, Al Ain*, available online, https://aard.gov.ae/en/portal/

1A27AC75-7DE3-4EC5-B624–9EF99A00533B.aspx, date accessed, 10th August 2020.

104. C Davidson, *After Shaikh Zayed*, p.48.

105. C Davidson, *After Shaikh Zayed*, p.46.

106. F Kane, 'UAE and Saudi Arabia send forces to Bahrain', *The National*, 5th March 2011, available online, https://www.thenational.ae/world/mena/uae-and-saudi-arabia-send-forces-to-bahrain-1.425312, date accessed, 24th July 2020.

107. http://www.ourfatherzayed.ae/eng/web.html#The%20Legend%20 Lives%20on, accessed 3rd November 2015.

108. JJ Rousseau, *The Social Contract and the First and Second Discourses*, S Dunn (ed.), Yale University Press, New Haven, 2002, p.156.

109. V Perthes, 'Politics and Elite Change in the Arab World', p.4.

110. S Heydemann, *Authoritarianism in Syria: Institutions and Social Conflict, 1946–1970*, Cornell University Press, Ithaca, 1999. A Baram, 'Neo-Tribalism in Iraq: Saddam Hussein's Tribal Policies 1991–96', *International Journal of Middle East Studies*, Vol. 29, No.1, February 1997, pp.1–31. SE Baroudi, 'Sectarianism and Business Associations in Postwar Lebanon', *Arab Studies Quarterly*, Vol.22, No.4, Fall 2000, pp.81–107.

111. 'His Highness Sheikh Khalifa bin Zayed al Nahyan', *United Arab Emirates, The Cabinet*, available online, https://www.uaecabinet.ae/en/details/federal-supreme-council/his-highness-Shaykh-khalifa-bin-zayed-al-nahyan, date accessed, 10th August 2020.

112. 'Abu Dhabi's Job Move "Historic": Writer', *Gulf News*, 18th June 2011.

113. M Hedges & G Cafiero, 'The Role of the Muslim Brotherhood in the GCC', p.138.

114. S Kerr, 'UAE confirms move against Islamist group', *Financial Times*, 22nd December 2011, available online, https://app.ft.com/content/f33e0200–2c8a-11e1-aaf5–00144feabdc0, date accessed, 11th August 2020.

115. O Salem, '94 Emiratis charges with compromising UAE security', *The National*, 28th January 2013, available online, https://www.thenational.ae/uae/government/94-emiratis-charged-with-compromising-uae-security-1.458803, date accessed, 11th August 2020.

116. 'India–UAE Joint Statement during State visit of Crown Prince of Abu Dhabi to India (January 24–26, 2017)', 26th January 2017, *Ministry of External Affairs, Government of India*, available online, https://mea.gov.in/bilateral-documents. htm?dtl/27969/India++UAE+Joint+Statement+during+State+visit+of+C rown+Prince+of+Abu+Dhabi+to+India+January+2426+2017, date accessed, 10th August 2020.

117. In Russia this is seen in the guise of the *Siloviki*. The term *siloviki* comes from the phrase *silovye struktury* (force structures) and refers to the bodies that control the coercive power of the state. *Siloviki* refers to individuals of these organisations who have entered politics along with Vladimir Putin. I Bremmer and

S Charap, 'The Siloviki in Putin's Russia: Who They are and What They Want', *The Washington Quarterly*, Vol. 30, No.1, Winter 2006–7, pp.83–92.

118. H Sharabi, *Neopatriarchy: A Theory of Distorted Change in Arab Society*, Oxford University Press, Oxford, 1992, p.7.

119. Bellin discusses the common patrimonial linkages between the military and political elites in; E Bellin, 'The Robustness of Authoritarianism in the Middle East: Exceptionalism in Comparative Perspective', *Comparative Politics*, Vol. 36, No.2, January 2004, pp.139–57.

120. FI Brichs and A Limpridi-Kemou, 'Sociology of Power in Today's Arab World', p.32.

3. MILITARY CONSOLIDATION

1. A Giddens, *The Consequences of Modernity*, p.58.

2. R Smith, *The Utility of Force, The Art of War in the Modern World*, Penguin, London, 2006, p.6.

3. M Kamrava, 'Military Professionalization and Civil-Military Relations in the Middle East', p.71.

4. V Gervais, *Du Pétrole à L'Armée: Les Stratégies de Construction De L'État Aux Émirats Arabes Unis*, Institut de Recherche Stratégique de l'Ecole Militaire, No.8, 2011.

5. AH Cordesman, *Iran and the Gulf Military Balance*, Center for Strategic and International Affairs (CSIS), Washington DC, 4th October 2016, available online, https://www.csis.org/analysis/iran-and-gulf-military-balance-1, date accessed, 8th July 2017.

6. Z Barany, *Military Officers in the Gulf: Career Trajectories and Determinants*, Center for Strategic & International Studies (CSIS), 5th November 2019.

7. D Roberts, 'Bucking the Trend: The UAE and Development of Military Capabilities in the Arab World', *Security Studies*, Vol.29, No.2, 2020, pp.301–334.

8. H Ibish, *The UAE's Evolving National Security Strategy*, The Arab Gulf States Institute in Washington (AGSIW), Washington DC, 6th April 2017.

9. A Yates, *The Evolution of the Armed Forces of the United Arab Emirates*, Helion & Company, 2021.

10. *Military Balance 2021*, International Institute for Strategic Studies (IISS), Routledge, London, 2021.

11. V Gervais, *Du Pétrole à L'Armée: Les Stratégies de Construction De L'État Aux Émirats Arabes Unis*, p.117.

12. While the ruler of Dubai has always been the UAE's Minister of Defence, his position has little to no power within the actual security apparatus. This is illustrated by the lack of involvement by Mohammed bin Rashid al-Maktoum within security-orientated displays and engagements.

13. Gaub warns however that if 'armed forces are not capable of acting or thinking collectively, they will lack the first necessary ingredient to be a political actor

(and will be inefficient security actors)'. F Gaub, *Guardians of the Arab State: When Militaries Intervene in Politics, from Iraq to Mauritania*, p.7.

14. R Brooks, *Political-Military Relations and the Stability of Arab Regimes*.

15. Ibid, p.32.

16. Barany concurs by explaining that 'aspiring officers in most GCC states go through a rigorous vetting process that is focused more on political reliability— e.g., the proven allegiance of one's relatives and clan to the ruling family—than on intellectual, physical, or psychological, suitability'. Z Barany, *Military Officers in the Gulf: Career Trajectories and Determinants*, p.2.

17. *Military Balance 2021*, p.371.

18. See Appendix 5: Partial List of UAE Military Bases.

19. Due to the authoritarian nature of governance within the UAE, the collection of information pertaining to the social stratification of the UAE Armed Forces is difficult. This means that only generalised statements can be made when referring to the social and tribal makeup of the UAE Armed Forces.

20. 'Rising Death Toll in Yemen Raises Tough Domestic Questions for Abu Dhabi', *Gulf States Newsletter (GSN)*, Vol.40, No.1,022, 22nd September 2016.

21. Sheikh Sultan bin Zayed al-Nahyan was previously Chief of Staff, however he was removed from all Federal and Emirate-level positions in the mid 1980s. JE Peterson, 'The Future of Federalism in the UAE', in HR Sindelar III and JE Peterson (ed.), *Crosscurrents in the Gulf*, p.204, in H Van Der Meulen, *The Role of Tribal and Kinship Ties in the Politics of the United Arab Emirates*, p.121. Van Der Meulen also notes that 'Sheikh Sultan bin Zayed reportedly has considerable popularity amongst the most important tribes of the Emirate [Abu Dhabi]'. H Van Der Meulen, *The Role of Tribal and Kinship Ties in the Politics of the United Arab Emirates*, p.128.

22. The participation and career of MBZ within the UAE Armed Forces prepared him for his future leadership position as head of the Abu Dhabi and UAE Ruling family. His charisma and professional attitude enabled him to develop a strong following within the UAE Armed Forces, and with the contrasting image of his brothers Khalifa and Sultan within the UAE Armed Forces, MBZ is perceived as the UAE's 'strong man'.

23. Author composed with information from Appendix 6: Emirati Martyrs in Yemen.

24. *WAM*, 'Ahmed bin Tahnoun receives members of Youth National Service Council', 12th April 2017, available online, http://wam.ae/en/details/1395 302608348, date accessed, 15th July 2017.

25. *WAM*, 'UAE's Hamdan bin Zayed inaugurates ADNOC's Central Control Centre on Das Island', Zawya, 10th October 2017, available online, https://www. zawya.com/mena/en/story/UAEs_Hamdan_bin_Zayed_inaugurates_ ADNOCs_Central_Control_Centre_on_Das_Island-WAM20171010 112050113/, date accessed, 10th November 2017.

26. R Brooks, *Political-Military Relations and the Stability of Arab Regimes*, p.32.

27. Gaub notes how this strategy ensured the survival of King Hussein of Jordan in the 1957 crisis. F Gaub, *Guardians of the Arab State: When Militaries Intervene in Politics, from Iraq to Mauritania*, p.67.

28. H Van Der Meulen, *The Role of Tribal and Kinship Ties in the Politics of the United Arab Emirates*, pp.96–97.

29. 'Il est le premier commandant émirati de cette branche à n'être ni lié aux Bani Yas ni originaire d'Abu Dhabi', V Gervais, *Du Pétrole à L'Armée: Les Stratégies de Construction de L'État aux Émirats Arabes Unis*, p.146.

30. The AFAD was under the stewardship of Lieutenant General Mohammed bin Zayed between 1986 and 1990, Major General Khalid bu-Ainnain (Mazari section of the Bani Yas) between 1998 and 2006. Thereafter, as in the Navy, non-Bani Yas members assumed positions of leadership. H Van Der Meulen, *The Role of Tribal and Kinship Ties in the Politics of the United Arab Emirates*, p.144.

31. The fact that the Navy is now commanded by a member of the UAE ruling family suggests that any future attempt to instil values of professionalism will likely be led by members of the royal family.

32. The issue of professionalism within the Armed Forces presents a difficult situation for a regime as on the one hand, while a professional military would be more capable of countering threats, it also becomes a threat to the regime (especially as the process of professionalising moves the personnel away from social and informal ties to which many regimes rest upon). If, however, professionalism was slowed within the Armed Forces, the tactical effectiveness of the military and the regime security strategy would be lower.

33. WAM, 'UAE Armed Forces observe 41st Unification Day Anniversary', 6th May 2017, available online, http://wam.ae/en/details/1395302612461, date accessed, 16th July 2017.

34. H Van Der Meulen, *The Role of Tribal and Kinship Ties in the Politics of the United Arab Emirates*, p.160.

35. Ibid, p.144.

36. 'UAE Talks with US Transport Chief', *The National*, 2nd February 2015, available online, https://www.thenational.ae/uae/government/uae-talks-with-us-transport-chief-1.27759, date accessed, 16th February 2017.

37. 'Major General Mohammed Khalfan al Rumaithi', *Abu Dhabi Executive Committee*, available online, https://www.ecouncil.ae/en/ADGovernment/Pages/MemberDetail.aspx?mid=19, date accessed, 16th July 2017.

38. Examples include; UAE Ambassador to Australia, Obaid al-Ketbi, former Deputy Commander in Chief of Abu Dhabi policy and leader of UAE military operations in Bosnia, Iraq, and Afghanistan; UAE Ambassador to South Africa, Mahash al-Hamli, former Director of Security Cooperation at UAE MOFA and Former Head of Military Intelligence and Security, GHQ.

39. R Chandrasekaran, 'In the UAE, the United States has a Quiet, Potent Ally Nicknamed "Little Sparta"', *Washington Post*, Al Dhafra Air Base, Abu Dhabi, 9th November 2014.

40. 'UAE-US Economic Relationship', *Embassy of the United Arab Emirates in Washington* DC, available online, http://www.uae-embassy.org/uae-us-relations/key-areas-bilateral-cooperation/uae-us-economic-relationship, date accessed, 8th July 2017, in H Ibish, *The UAE's Evolving National Security Strategy*, p.6.

41. SA Makakhleh, 'UAE Troops Spare No Effort to Bring Peace to Afghanistan', *Gulf News*, 24th August 2011, available online, http://gulfnews.com/news/uae/general/uae-troops-spare-no-effort-to-bring-peace-to-afghanistan-1.856240, date accessed, 22nd July 2017.

42. 'Armed Forces', *UAE Government*, available online, https://government.ae/en/information-and-services/justice-safety-and-the-law/armed-forces, date accessed, 10th November 2017. C Lussato, 'MALI. La France un peu moins isolée… Un peu', *L'Obs*, 21st January 2013, available online, http://tempsreel.nouvelobs.com/monde/guerre-au-mali/20130121.OBS6101/mali-la-france-un-peu-moins-isolee-un-peu.html, date accessed, 22nd July 2017, 'An Enduring Partnership for Peace and Stability: The U.S.–UAE Defense and Security Relationship', *U.S.–UAE Business Council*, February 2015. 'Why is the UAE Building a Military Base in Somaliland', *BBC*, 22nd February 2017, available online, http://www.bbc.co.uk/news/av/world-africa-39051551/why-is-uae-building-a-military-base-in-somaliland, date accessed, 22nd July 2017.

43. 'The Gulf's "Little Sparta": The Ambitious United Arab Emirates', *The Economist*, 6th April 2017, available online, https://www.economist.com/news/middle-east-and-africa/21720319-driven-energetic-crown-price-uae-building-bases-far-beyond-its, date accessed, 22nd July 2017.

44. 'Somali PM Visits UAE Military Training Centre in Mogadishu', *WAM*, 4th November 2017, available online, http://wam.ae/en/details/1395302644025, date accessed, 4th November 2017.

45. 'UAE, Seychelles Sign Accord for Military Cooperation', *WAM*, 21st December 2009, available online, http://gulfnews.com/news/uae/government/seychelles-opens-coast-guard-base-built-with-uae-support-1.929203, date accessed, 22nd July 2017.

46. 'UAE is France's Major Trading Partner in the Region: French President', *WAM*, 24th May 2009, accessed online, http://wam.ae/en/details/1395228377358, date accessed, 22nd July 2017.

47. D Majumdar, 'The F-22 Raptor is the World's Best Fighter (And it Has a Secret Weapon That is Out in the Open)', *The National Interest*, 29th November 2016, in H Ibish, *The UAE's Evolving National Security Strategy*, p.19.

48. 'military values such as discipline, bravery, obedience, honesty, political impartiality are generally valued in society', F Gaub, *Guardians of the Arab State: When Militaries Intervene in Politics, from Iraq to Mauritania*, p.82. Gaub suggests that increased military engagement has a detrimental effect on the image of a state's military (ibid, p.80). This book postulates, however, that the deployment of

233

the UAE's Armed Forces is designed to enhance their image, and thus contribute to the post-Arab Spring regime security strategy.

49. On 4th September 2015 Houthi-Saleh forces fired a Toshka ballistic missile at a military base within the Marib province. The missile hit an ammunition storage facility and killed over 100 soldiers from the Saudi-led coalition. The death of over 50 Emirati soldiers was the largest death toll since the UAE's formation in 1971.

50. 'Martyrs' Day Statement by His Highness Sheikh Khalifa bin Zayed Al Nahyan', *Emirates News Agency (WAM)*, 29th November 2015, available online, http:// wam.ae/en/details/1395288638027, date accessed, 4th August 2017.

51. O Obina, 'Sheikh Mohammed bin Zayed offers condolences to families of martyrs', *The National*, 26th February 2017, available online, https://www.thenational.ae/uae/government/sheikh-mohammed-bin-zayed-offers-condolences-to-families-of-martyrs-in-pictures-1.72908, date accessed, 4th August 2017.

52. https://www.wahatalkarama.ae/?lang=en, date accessed, 4th August 2017.

53. 'Tribute—Heroes of the UAE—Anthem Ft. Adel Ebrahim & Musicians of World Official', 1st December 2015, available online, https://www.youtube.com/watch?v=hZeZynIQW0I, date accessed, 4th August 2017.

54. 'We Salute you, Heroes of the Emirates', 1st November 2015, available online, https://www.youtube.com/watch?v=eprry-lHrRw, date accessed, 4th August 2017.

55. "الله أجرك يا وطن", (May Allah reward you, oh nation), and "#martyrs'_mothers_a_pride_to_the_UAE"

56. M Butti, I Denizli, and T Chelali, '*The Martyr and the Nation: The UAE, Turkey, and Algeria*', Delma Institute, 22nd May 2017, available online, http://delma. io/en/draft/the-martyr-and-the-nation-the-uae-turkey-and-algeria,   date accessed, 4th August 2017.

57. WAM, 'Director of the Martyrs' Families' Affairs Office visits martyrs' families', *Gulf News*, 16th November 2016, available online, http://gulfnews.com/news/uae/government/director-of-the-martyrs-families-affairs-office-visits-martyrs-families-1.1930404, date accessed, 11th November 2017.

58. 'Signs of Strain in UAE Reflected in Abu Dhabi-RAK Tensions', *Gulf States Newsletter (GSN)*, Vol.40, No.1,012, 31st March 2016.

59. Scholars such as Cordesman have noted the unreliability of publicly listed arms transfers and expenditure reports. This means that there are only vague estimations with seminal reports published highlighting aspects of arms purchases.

60. Gaub notes that 'coups are least likely in states with high military spending'. F Gaub, *Guardians of the Arab State: When Militaries Intervene in Politics, from Iraq to Mauritania*, p.32.

61. 'SIPRI Military Expenditure Database', *Stockholm Institute Peace Research Institute (SIPRI)*, date accessed, 22nd July 2017.

62. M Hedges, 'The UAE's C4ISR Transformation', *Defense Procurement International (DPI)*, Winter 2014.
63. 'United Arab Emirates Embassy in Washington, DC Statement on Letters of Agreement for UAE Defense Package', *Embassy of The United Arab Emirates, Washington DC*, 21st January 2021, available online, https://www.uae-embassy. org/news-media/united-arab-emirates-embassy-washington-dc-statement-letters-agreement-uae-defense, date accessed, 2nd June 2021
64. R Brooks, *Political-Military Relations and the Stability of Arab Regimes*, p.26.
65. M Al Romaithi, *Tawazun Economic Council*, Abu Dhabi International Offset Conference (ADIOC), Abu Dhabi, 18th February 2015.
66. Ibid.
67. http://www.asmak.biz
68. M Mazzetti & EB Hager, 'Secret Desert Force Set Up By Blackwater's Founder', *The New York Times*, 14th May 2011, available online, http://www.nytimes. com/2011/05/15/world/middleeast/15prince.html, date accessed, 5th February 2018.
69. 'Ordnance Technician Vacancy', *Lockheed Martin*, available online, https:// search.lockheedmartinjobs.com/ShowJob/Id/104091/Ordnance-Technician/, date accessed, 5th February 2018. 'People who work at AMMROC', *LinkedIn*, available online, https://www.linkedin.com/search/results/people/?facetCu rrentCompany=%5B%221383123%22%5D, date accessed, 5th February 2018. 'Crew Chief (APG)', *Orion Talent*, 12th December 2017, available online, https://www.oriontalent.com/ammroc/#211667554068112, date accessed, 5th February 2018.
70. Masdar was constructed with direct assistance from Massachusetts Institute of Technology (MIT).
71. Before Khalifa University was merged into a partnership with Masdar University and the Petroleum Institute, it was a private institution owned by the current, as of August 2017, Minister of Higher Education, HE Hussein al Hammadi. http://www.kustar.ac.ae.
72. Instead of Amos Perlmutter's modern interpretation, which describes a praetorian state as 'one in which the military tends to intervene in the government and has the potential to dominate the executive'. A Perlmutter, *The Military and Politics in Modern Time*, Yale University Press, London, 1978, p.93.
73. 'Foreign Military Service—MAJGEN M HINDMARSH (RETD)', *Senate Estimates Brief*, FOI 030/18/19, February 2016, available online, http://www. defence.gov.au/FOI/Docs/Disclosures/030_1819_Docs.pdf, date accessed, 13th August 2019.
74. H Ibish, *The UAE's Evolving National Security Strategy*, p.19.
75. Expatriate personnel were often employed in an official capacity as serving officers, retaining their previously held ranks, but were being syphoned off onto private sector contracts from 2014. In the civilian sector, scores of foreign personnel were fired from sensitive positions in 2013. *The Economist*, 'Sending the

Foreigners Home', 13ᵗʰ June 2013, available online, https://www.economist.com/news/middle-east-and-africa/21581783-sacking-foreign-civil-servants-may-become-regional-trend-sending, date accessed, 15ᵗʰ July 2017.

76. M Kamrava, 'Military Professionalization and Civil-Military Relations in the Middle East', p.82.

77. 'United Arab Emirates (UAE)—Blanket Order Training', *Defence Security Cooperation Agency (DSCA)*, 8ᵗʰ January 2014, available online, http://www.i2insights.com/library/fms-dsca-annoucements/fms-2014-united_arab_emirates-uae-13_46.pdf, date accessed, 4ᵗʰ August 2017.

78. M Hedges, 'The UAE's C4ISR Transformation'.

79. Hussein Ibish postulates that this development goes back to the first Gulf War stating that 'the period following Desert Storm initiated a UAE military development drive principally guided by MBZ that has continued, and gained steam, since.' H Ibish, *The UAE's Evolving National Security Strategy*, p.13. While Ibish is not wrong as Mohammed bin Zayed al-Nahyan held tenure as head of the Air Force and Chief of Staff in the years following the first gulf war, it was his appointment to Crown Prince that thrust his hand over the military and drove its development to previously unseen speeds.

80. Military-led modernisation as postulated by Huntington (S Huntington, *Political Order in Changing Societies*, p.203).

81. Florence Gaub notes how smaller militaries are more likely to initiate coups and as a result, the inflation of the UAE Armed Forces is another example of how the UAE's post-Arab Spring regime security strategy is looking to protect itself from future threats. (F Gaub, *Guardians of the Arab State: When Militaries Intervene in Politics, from Iraq to Mauritania*, p.39).

82. 'Khalifa Issues Federal National Service and Reserve Law', *WAM*, 7ᵗʰ June 2014, available online, http://wam.ae/en/details/1395262684433, date accessed, 21ˢᵗ October 2017.

83. Ibid.

84. https://www.uaensr.ae/Pages/default.aspx

85. TU Berger, 'Norms, Identity, and National Security', in CW Hughes & LY Meng (eds.), *Security Studies, A Reader*, Routledge, London, 2011, p.187.

86. R Brooks, *Political-Military Relations and the Stability of Arab Regimes*, p.52.

4. DIGITAL AUTHORITARIANISM: NEW TOOLS FOR STATE CONTROL

1. M Weber, *The Theory of Social and Economic Organisation*, p.347.

2. A Giddens, *The Nation-State and Violence*, Polity Press, Cambridge, 1985, p.41.

3. Ibid, p.49.

4. M Castells, *Networks of Outrage and Hope: Social Movements in the Internet Age*, Polity Press, Cambridge, 2012. J Habermas, *The Structural Transformation of the Public Sphere*, Polity Press, Cambridge, 1962.

5. L Diamond, 'Liberation Technology', *Journal of Democracy*, Vol. 21, No.3, July 2010, pp.70–84. R Deibert & R Rohozinski, 'Liberation vs. Control: The Future of Cyberspace', *Journal of Democracy*, Vol.21, No.4, October 2010, pp.43–57.

6. 'The bottom line is that probable cause can never do enough alone to keep up with the way technology empowers and expands surveillance and concomitantly invades privacy and shifts the balance of power from the citizenry and to the state', P Ohm, The Surveillance Regulation Toolkit: Thinking Beyond Probable Cause, in D Gray & SE Henderson (ed.), *The Cambridge Handbook of Surveillance Law*, Cambridge University Press, Cambridge, 2017, p.495. R Deibert, 'Cyberspace Under Siege', *Journal of Democracy*, Vol. 26, No.3, July 2015, pp.64–78.

7. J Arquilla & D Ronfeldt, *The Emergence of Noopolitik: Toward an American Information Strategy*, RAND, Santa Monica, 1999, p.1.

8. M Foucault, *Discipline and Punish: The Birth of the Prison*, A Sheridan, trans., Vintage, New York, 1977. K Haggerty & R Ericson, 'The Surveillance Assemblage', *The British Journal of Sociology*, Vol. 54, No.4, 2000, pp.605–622, in D Lyon, 'Surveillance, Snowden, and Big Data: Capacities, Consequences, Critique', *Big Data & Society*, 2014, July–December, p.2.

9. J Bentham, *The Panopticon Writings*, M Bozovic (ed.), Verso, London, 1995.

10. M Poster, *The Mode of Information*, University of Chicago Press, Chicago, 1990.

11. M Foucault, *Discipline and Punish*, Vintage, New York, 1977, p.200, in C Fuchs, 'New Media, Web 2.0 and Surveillance', *Sociology Compass*, Vol. 5, No.2, 2011, p.136.

12. 'On the internet, the separation between "objects of information" and "subjects in communication" that Foucault described for historical forms of surveillance no longer exists ... this permanent, creative online activity becomes the object of surveillance'. Ibid, p.140.

13. S Armstrong, 'Life in the Fishbowl', *AEON*, 30th September 2013, available online, https://aeon.co/essays/the-strange-benefits-of-living-in-a-total-surveillance-state, date accessed, 16th February 2018.

14. S Mann, J Nolan, and B Wellman, 'Sousveillance: Inventing and Using Wearable Computing devices for Data Collection in Surveillance Environments', *Surveillance Society*, Vol.1, No.3, 2003, pp.331–355.

15. A Giddens, *The Nation-State and Violence*, p.2.

16. 'Traditional surveillance is limited. It relies upon the unaided senses and was characteristic of pre-industrial societies—information tended to stay local, compartmentalized, unshared and was often unrecorded, or if kept, difficult to retrieve and analyze in depth', GT Marx, 'Preface: "Your Papers Please": Personal and Professional Encounters with Surveillance', in K Ball, KD Haggerty, and D Lyon (eds.), *Routledge Handbook of Surveillance Studies*, Routledge, Milton Park, 2012, p.XXV.

17. Ibid.

18. A Edwards, *Regulation and Repression*, Allen & Unwin, London, 1988.

19. Z Bauman & D Lyon, *Liquid Surveillance*, Polity Press, Cambridge, 2013.

20. D Lyon, *Surveillance Society, Monitoring Everyday Life*, Open University Press, Buckingham, 2002.

21. S Cohen, *Visions of Social Control: Crime, Punishment, and Classification*, Polity Press, Oxford, 1985.

22. Within many states, surveillance information is often unobtainable due to secrecy laws and issues of confidentiality. Furthermore, there are issues of commercial sensitivity and ethical reservations which limit greater and more streamlined access to information. This is an ever-important topic as commercial companies are holding more and more data which can be used by the state. A Holpuch, 'Tim Cook says Apple's refusal to unlock iPhone for FBI is a "civil liberties" issue', *The Guardian*, 22nd February 2016, available online, https://www.theguardian.com/technology/2016/feb/22/tim cook apple refusal unlock iphone-fbi-civil-liberties, date accessed, 17th February 2018.

23. Peter Pomerantsev disagrees and uses the case of Putin's Russia to suggest how authoritarian states mock the state's laws publicly, and thus reassert their position of authority over their competitors and the general public. P Pomerantsev, 'The Kremlin's Information War', *Journal of Democracy*, Vol.26, No.4, October 2015, pp.40–50.

24. D Guha, '20 Do's and Don'ts on Social Media', *999 Magazine*, UAE Ministry of Interior, September 2016, pp.16–23, available online, https://www.moi.gov.ae/DataFolder/magazine2016/Sept/999%20SEPTEMBEr%20-%202016.pdf, date accessed, 16th March 2018.

25. N Al Ramahi, 'Parents Warned Extremists Will Use Internet to Recruit Their Children', *The National*, 28th May 2017, available online, https://www.thenational.ae/uae/parents-warned-violent-extremists-will-use-internet-to-recruit-their-children-1.12760, date accessed, 16th March 2018.

26. S Dhal, 'Cybersex in the UAE', *Gulf News*, 23rd September 2010, available online, http://gulfnews.com/news/uae/crime/cybersex-in-the-uae-1.686035, date accessed, 16th March 2018.

27. S Chesterman, *One Nation Under Surveillance, A New Social Contract to Defend Freedom Without Sacrificing Liberty*, Oxford University Press, Oxford, 2011.

28. In context, in 2000 only 20% of the UAE population had access to the internet, yet by 2016, 91.6% of the population (which had tripled in the same period) had access. 'Internet Growth and Population Statistics, United Arab Emirates', *Internet World Stats*, available online, https://www.internetworldstats.com/me/ae.htm, date accessed, 17th February 2018.

29. CJ Bennett & CD Raab, *The Governance of Privacy, Policy Instruments in Global Perspective*, MIT Press, London, 2006, p.220.

30. R Deibert, 'Cyberspace Under Siege' 'Net Losses: Estimating the Global Cost of Cybercrime, Economic impact of Cybercrime ii', Center for Strategic and International Studies *(CSIS)*, McAfee, 2014, available online, https://csis-prod.

s3.amazonaws.com/s3fs-public/legacy_files/files/attachments/140609_rp_
economic_impact_cybercrime_report.pdf, date accessed, 17ᵗʰ February 2018.

31. L Lessig, *Code and Other Laws of Cyberspace*, Basic Books, New York, 1999, in S
Kalathil & TC Boas, *Open Networks, Closed Regimes: The Impact of the Internet on
Authoritarian Rule*, Carnegie Endowment for International Peace, Brooking
Institution Press, Washington, 2003, p.3.

32. Ibid, p.110.

33. Ronald Deibert concurs with Lawrence Lessig in designating first-generational
controls as the limitation of physical access and second-generation controls as
the legal and regulatory environment in which states can restrict access. R
Deibert, 'Cyberspace Under Siege', p.66.

34. See Appendix 7: Partial List of UAE Public Sector Bodies Online.

35. 'The government of the UAE has sought to maintain control over ICTs for both
censorship and financial gain, though it is more open to information than many
of its neighbours. The state owns virtually all broadcast media and applies guidelines to reporting', Kalathil & TC Boas, *Open Networks, Closed Regimes: The Impact
of the Internet on Authoritarian Rule*, p.108.

36. SIA Overview, *LinkedIn*, available online, https://www.linkedin.com/com-
pany/uaenesa/, date accessed, 20ᵗʰ January 2017.

37. Article 14, Federal Decree Law No.3 of 2012, On The Establishment of the
National Electronic Security Authority, Khalifa bin Zayed Al Nahyan, Abu
Dhabi, available online, http://ejustice.gov.ae/downloads/latest_laws/fed-
eral_decree_law_3_2012_en.pdf, date accessed, 20ᵗʰ January 2018.

38. B Thomas, 'UAE Military to Set up Cyber Command', *Defence World*, 30ᵗʰ
September 2014, available online, http://www.defenseworld.net/
news/11185/UAE_Military_To_Set_Up_Cyber_Command#.
WmM1IyN0fVo, date accessed, 20ᵗʰ January 2018.

39. B Thomas, 'UAE Military to Set Up Cyber Command', *Defense World*, 30ᵗʰ
September 2014, in H Ibish, *The UAE's Evolving National Security Strategy*, Arab
Gulf States Institute in Washington, 6ᵗʰ April 2017.

40. Federal Decree Law No.3 of 2012, On The Establishment of the National
Electronic Security Authority.

41. P MacGloin & M al-Jneibi, 'The Components of National and International
Cyberspace Governance', *RSA Conference 2015*, Abu Dhabi, 4–5 November
2015.

42. The development of the Arab Spring and the manifestation of ICT-based based
threats neuters earlier observations of the UAE's perceived ICT vulnerabilities,
such as that hypothesised by Shanthi Kalathil and Taylor Boas; 'public internet
use poses little threat to the regime's stability'. Kalathil & TC Boas, *Open
Networks, Closed Regimes: The Impact of the Internet on Authoritarian Rule*, p.109.

43. M Kamrava, 'Military Professionalization and Civil-Military Relations in the
Middle East'.

44. S Greitens, *Coercive Institutions and State Violence Under Authoritarianism*.

45. V Perthes (ed.), *Arab Elites: Negotiating the Politics of Change*.

46. R Brooks, *Political-Military Relations and the Stability of Arab Regimes*. JT Quinlivan, 'Coup-Proofing: Its Practice and Consequences in the Middle East'.

47. O Danino, 'Conflict in Cyberspace: The Case of the Middle East', in O Danino (ed.), *Conflict in Cyberspace: The Case of the Middle East*, French Institute for Strategic Analysis, France, 2015, p.291.

48. Articles 6 & 7, Federal Decree Law No.3 of 2012, On The Establishment of the National Electronic Security Authority.

49. 'President Names Tahnoun Bin Zayed as National Security Advisor', *UAE Cabinet*, available online, https://uaecabinet.ae/en/details/news/president-names-tahnoun-bin-zayed-as-national-security-advisor, date accessed, 20th January 2018. 'Tahnoun Appointed National Security Advisor', *WAM*, *Gulf News*, 14th February 2016, available online, http://gulfnews.com/news/uae/government/tahnoun-appointed-national-security-adviser-1.1672367, date accessed, 20th January 2016.

50. WAM, 'Mohammed bin Zayed Attends Official Reception in New Delhi', *Emirates 24/7, 26th* January 2017, available online, http://www.emirates247.com/news/government/mohamed-bin-zayed-attends-official-reception-in-new-delhi-2017–01–26–1.647063, date accessed, 21st January 2018.

51. C Malek, 'Sheikh Khalid bin Mohammed Appointed Head of National Security', *The National*, 15th February 2016, available online, https://www.thenational.ae/uae/government/sheikh-khalid-bin-mohammed-appointed-head-of-national-security-1.197959, date accessed, 20th January 2018.

52. P Salisbury, 'Risk Perception and Appetite in UAE Foreign and National Security Policy', *Chatham House*, 1st July 2020, available online, https://www.chathamhouse.org/2020/07/risk-perception-and-appetite-uae-foreign-and-national-security-policy-0/6-stretched, date accessed, 5th June 2021

53. Jassem al Zaabi's deputy at NESA was Zayed al-Otaiba, the brother of the UAE Ambassador to the US and reportedly a key conduit for American firm's engagement with NESA.

54. 'Chairman of Abu Dhabi Executive Office', *General Secretariat of the Executive Council*, available online, https://www.ecouncil.ae/en/ADGovernment/Pages/MemberDetail.aspx?mid=23, date accessed, 20th January 2017.

55. 'Dr. Mohamed Al-Kuwaiti, Executive Director, Signals Intelligence Agency (SIA)', *RSA Conference*, Abu Dhabi 2017, available online, https://www.rsaconference.com/speakers/dr-mohamed-al-kuwaiti, date accessed, 7th June 2019.

56. 'President approves new structure of UAE Government', *WAM*, 5th July 2020, available online, https://www.wam.ae/en/details/1395302853277, date accessed, 20th August 2020.

57. JT Quinlivan, 'Coup-Proofing: Its Practice and Consequences in the Middle East'.

58. Emirati political scientist, Abdulkhaleq Abdulla was allegedly arrested by Emirati state security officials in January 2017 after he advocated greater freedom of

speech. Another free speech advocate who was arrested after his advocacy work was Ahmed Mansour. In 2018 he was sentenced to 10 years in prison.

59. Federal Law by Decree No.3 of 2003, *Regarding the Organisation of Telecommunication Sector*, in Official Gazette, Edition 411, Year 34, April 2004.

60. 'About TRA/Vision, Mission & Values, *TRA*, available online, https://www.tra.gov.ae/en/about-tra/about-tra-vision-mission-and-values.aspx, date accessed, 21st January 2018.

61. UAE-based franchise of the Richard Branson-owned Virgin Group.

62. 'Etisalat Launches New Mobile Service SWYP Targeting Youngsters', *ITP.net*, 10th September 2017, available online, http://www.itp.net/614624-etisalat-launches-new-mobile-service-swyp-targeting-youngsters, date accessed, 21st January 2018.

63. I Bremmer, *The End of the Free Market: Who Wins the War Between States and Corporations*.

64. Etisalat, *Company Profile*, available online, https://www.etisalat.ae/en/about-us/etisalat_corporation.jsp, date accessed, 21st January 2018. Etisalat, 'Ownership Structure', available online, http://www.etisalat.com/en/ir/corporateinfo/ownership-structure.jsp, date accessed, 21st January 2018.

65. See Appendix 8: Etisalat Board Members as of 2016 and their Public-Sector Connections.

66. EITC, *Emirates Integrated Telecommunication Company PJS (du) Publishes its Financial Results for Q2 2017*, Press Release.

67. Ibid.

68. DU, *Company Overview*, available online, http://www.du.ae/about-us/investor-relations/company-overview, date accessed, 21st January 2018.

69. See Appendix 9: Du Board of Directors and their Public-Sector Connections

70. Kalathil & TC Boas, *Open Networks, Closed Regimes: The Impact of the Internet on Authoritarian Rule*, p.108.

71. J Ferrante, *Sociology: A Global Perspective*, Cengage Learning, Stamford, 2015, p.148, in, S Morley, J Turner, and K Corteen (eds.), *A Companion to State Power, Liberties, and Rights*, Policy Press, Bristol, 2017, p.242.

72. C Walker & RW Orttung, 'Breaking the News: The Role of State-Run Media', *Journal of Democracy*, Vol.25, No.1, January 2014, p.72.

73. Ibid.

74. http://nmc.gov.ae/en-us.

75. 'Mohammed bin Rashid Issues Decision Organising Media Content', *UAE, The Cabinet*, available online, https://www.uaecabinet.ae/en/details/news/mohammed-bin-rashid-issues-decision-organizing-media-content, date accessed, 26th January 2018.

76. President approves new structure of UAE Government', *WAM*, 5th July 2020, available online, https://www.wam.ae/en/details/1395302853277, date accessed, 20th August 2020.

77. 'Board of Directors', *National Media Council (NMC)*, available online, http://

nmc.gov.ae/en-us/Pages/BoardofDirectors.aspx, date accessed, 12ᵗʰ March 2018.

78. http://wam.ae/ar.

79. C Walker & RW Orttung, 'Breaking the News: The Role of State-Run Media'.

80. MN Al Khan, 'Media Matters: Meet The Censors', *Gulf News*, 25ᵗʰ April 2007, available online, http://gulfnews.com/news/uae/general/media-matters-meet-the-censors-1.463677, date accessed, 26ᵗʰ January 2018. Enhanced control of information flows does however create the dictator's dilemma whereby, due to the increased ability to create and source information, the state's narrative is now weaker and 'finds itself called to account for anomalies between its view of events and the public's'. C Shirky, 'The Political Power of Social Media', *Foreign Affairs*, Vol. 90, No.1, January/February 2011, p.36.

81. G Warren, 'Yes, Skype's blocked in the UAE, what now?', *Gulf News*, 2ⁿᵈ January 2018, available online, http://gulfnews.com/guides/tech/yep-skype-s-blocked-in-the-uae-what-now-1.2150373, date accessed, 17ᵗʰ February 2018.

82. M Al Sadafy, 'Dubai Police monitoring social networking sites round the clock', *Emirates 24/7*, 4ᵗʰ April 2012, available online, http://www.emirates247.com/news/emirates/dubai-police-monitoring-social-networking-sites-round-the-clock-2012-04-04-1.452143, date accessed, 17ᵗʰ February 2018.

83. The al-Tayer family are a branch of the Bani Yas tribe which both the Abu Dhabi and Dubai ruling families originate from. The al-Tayer have married into the al-Maktoum dynasty, and many of its members have held senior public-sector positions. H Van Der Meulen, *The Role of Tribal and Kinship Ties in the Politics of the UAE*, p.192.

84. Prominent business family with no intrinsic tribal connections.

85. Arab tribe of non-UAE origin. H Van Der Meulen, *The Role of Tribal and Kinship Ties in the Politics of the UAE*, p.197.

86. Prominent merchant family of Iranian origin. H Van Der Meulen, *The Role of Tribal and Kinship Ties in the Politics of the UAE*, p.199.

87. Abdullah Omran Taryam was the Former UAE Minister of Justice. The Taryam family are members of the al-Ali tribe. In relation to the Emirate of Sharjah, the Taryam family are extremely powerful. H Van Der Meulen, *The Role of Tribal and Kinship Ties in the Politics of the UAE*, p.45, 221.

88. Article 1, Federal Law 12 of 2016, 'Whoever uses a fraudulent computer network protocol address (IP address) by using a false address or a third-party address by any other means for the purpose of committing a crime or preventing its discovery, shall be punished by temporary imprisonment and a fine of no less than Dh500,000 and not exceeding Dh2,000,000, or either of these two penalties', WAM, 'UAE Federal Laws Tackle Media Governance, Cybercrime', *Khaleej Times*, 23ʳᵈ July 2016, available online, https://www.khaleejtimes.com/UAE-federal-laws-NMC-media-governance-cybercrime, date accessed, 17ᵗʰ February 2018.

89. 'Telecommunications Regulatory Authority Issues Statement on the Use of VPN

to Clarify Media Reports', *WAM*, 2nd August 2016, available online, http://wam.ae/en/details/1395298419036, date accessed, 12th March 2018.

90. 'Cyberspace authoritarianism, in other words, has evolved over at least three generations of information controls'. R Deibert, 'Cyberspace Under Siege', p.65.

91. Abu Dhabi Media owns Al Emarat TV, Abu Dhabi TV, Abu Dhabi Sports Channel, Yas, Majid TV, National Geographic Abu Dhabi, and Abu Dhabi Drama.[91] Dubai Media Incorporated[91] owns Sama Dubai,[91] Dubai Zaman,[91] Dubai Sports,[91] Dubai Racing,[91] and Dubai One.[91] 'The media outlets in question may be owned and run by the state, or they may be nominally private but in fact under government control'. C Walker & RW Orttung, 'Breaking the News: The Role of State-Run Media', p.71.

92. Black market satellite boxes are illegal, however, they are still very popular across the UAE. A Ahmed, 'Counting the Cost of Illegal TV', *The National*, 6th March 2015, available online, https://www.thenational.ae/business/technology/counting-the-cost-of-illegal-tv-1.633036, date accessed, 26th January 2018.

93. C Walker & RW Orttung, 'Breaking the News: The Role of State-Run Media', p.74. Domestic Emirati media is heavily focused on cultural references and this suggests this is the prominent target audience for its strategic communications campaigns.

94. L Lessig, *Code and Other Laws of Cyberspace*, Basic Books, New York, 1999, in S Kalathil and TC Boas, *Open Networks, Closed Regimes: The Impact of the Internet on Authoritarian Rule*, p.3.

95. 'Access to information is far less important, politically, than access to conversation', C Shirky, 'The Political Power of Social Media', p.35. EC Murphy, 'Theorizing ICTs in the Arab World: Informational Capitalism and the Public Sphere', *International Studies Quarterly*, Vol.53, No.4, 2009, pp.1131–53.

96. *United Arab Emirates Constitution of 1971 with Amendments through 2004*, Abu Dhabi, Constitute Project, 1971, available online, https://www.constituteproject.org/constitution/United_Arab_Emirates_2004.pdf, date accessed, 26th January 2018.

97. *UAE Security Forum: Bridging the Cybersecurity Talent Gap*, Conference Report, Arab Gulf States Institute in Washington, Washington, Event Report 2, 2016.

98. For a detailed summary of each law, see Appendix 10: Summary of UAE's Surveillance-Based Legislation.

99. Federal Law No.15 of 1980, available online, http://nmc.gov.ae/en-us/NMC/Lists/LawsandLegislationsList/Attachments/55/والنشر20%المطبوعاتانونا.pdf, date accessed, 26th January 2018.

100. Federal Law by Decree No.3 of 2003, Regarding the Organization of Telecommunications Sector, *Telecommunications Regulatory Authority*, Abu Dhabi, Official Gazette, Edition 411, April 2004, online, https://www.tra.

gov.ae/en/about-tra/legal-references/law.aspx, date accessed, 26ᵗʰ January 2018.

101. Federal Law No. (1) of 2006, Electronic Commerce and Transactions, available online, https://www.tra.gov.ae/en/about-tra/legal-references/law.aspx, date accessed, 26ᵗʰ January 2018.

102. Official Gazette, Edition 485, October 2008.

103. 'Legal References', *Telecommunications Regulatory Authority (TRA)*, available online, https://www.tra.gov.ae/en/legal-references.aspx, date accessed, 26ᵗʰ January 2018.

104. Federal Decree Law No.3 of 2012, On The Establishment of the National Electronic Security Authority, Khalifa bin Zayed Al Nahyan, Abu Dhabi, available online, http://ejustice.gov.ae/downloads/latest_laws/federal_decree_law_3_2012_en.pdf, date accessed, 20ᵗʰ January 2018.

105. Federal Decree Law No.5 of 2012, Ministry of Justice, 13ᵗʰ August 2012, available online, http://ejustice.gov.ae/downloads/latest_laws/cybercrimes_5_2012_en.pdf, date accessed, 26ᵗʰ January 2018.

106. 'Media in the UAE', *UAE Government*, available online, https://government.ae/en/media/media, date accessed, 26ᵗʰ January 2018.

107. Federal Decree Law No.7 of 2014, Ministry of Justice, 20ᵗʰ August 2014, available online, https://moj.gov.ae/documents/21128/86231/Federal%20Law%20No%207%20of%202014%20On%20Combating%20Terrorism%20Offences.pdf/d8e6e696-e44b-45eb-8c30-ca2cb2ff6ce5, date accessed, 26ᵗʰ January 2018.

108. Federal Decree Law No.2 of 2015, Ministry of Justice, 15ᵗʰ July 2015, available online, http://ejustice.gov.ae/downloads/latest_laws2015/FDL_2_2015_discrimination_hate_en.pdf, date accessed, 26ᵗʰ January 2018.

109. Federal Law No.11 of 2016, available online, http://nmc.gov.ae/en-us/NMC/Lists/LawsandLegislationsList/Attachments/56/%20تنظيم%20شان واختصاصاته%20المجلس%20واختصاصاته, date accessed, 26ᵗʰ January 2018.

110. 'UAE President Issues Federal Laws', *WAM*, 22ⁿᵈ July 2017, available online, http://wam.ae/en/details/1395298018406, date accessed, 26ᵗʰ January 2018.

111. 'Mohammed bin Rashid Issues Decision Organising Media Content', *UAE, The Cabinet*, available online, https://www.uaecabinet.ae/en/details/news/mohammed-bin-rashid-issues-decision-organizing-media-content, date accessed, 26ᵗʰ January 2018.

112. *United Arab Emirates*, Freedom House, Freedom on the Net 2016.

113. Ranking 2017, *Reporters Without Borders*, available online, https://rsf.org/en/ranking, date accessed, 26ᵗʰ January 2018.

114. 'UAE: Authorities Enhance Surveillance of Critics', *Human Rights Watch*, 12ᵗʰ January 2017, available online, https://www.hrw.org/news/2017/01/12/uae-authorities-enhance-surveillance-critics, date accessed, 26ᵗʰ January 2018.

115. Kalathil and TC Boas, *Open Network, Closed Regimes: The Impact of the Internet on Authoritarian Rule*, p.109.

116. R Deibert, 'Cyberspace Under Siege', p.64.

117. D Bardsley, 'The 1980 UAE Press and Publications Law', *The National*, 17th January 2015, available online, https://www.thenational.ae/uae/the-1980-uae-press-and-publications-law-1.107607, date accessed, 26th January 2018.

118. DesertFoxDubai1, *UAE Dubai Official Beating Indian Driver*, 16th July 2013, available online, https://www.youtube.com/watch?v=JseN0wyClkg, date accessed, 27th January 2018.

119. H Strange, 'Videomaker Arrested After Filming UAE Official Beating Driver', *The Telegraph*, 18th July 2013, available online, http://www.telegraph.co.uk/news/worldnews/middleeast/dubai/10188514/Videomaker-arrested-after-filming-UAE-official-beating-driver.html, date accessed, 27th January 2018.

120. AP, 'American Arrested in UAE After Criticising Employer on Facebook', *The Telegraph*, 6th March 2015, available online, http://www.telegraph.co.uk/news/worldnews/middleeast/unitedarabemirates/11453658/American-arrested-in-UAE-after-criticising-employer-on-Facebook.html, date accessed, 27th January 2018.

121. A clear example of what Larry Diamond called 'Liberation Technology' and Mann defined as Sousveillance. L Diamond, 'Liberation Technology'. S Mann, J Nolan, and B Wellman, 'Sousveillance: Inventing and Using Wearable Computing Devices for Data Collection in Surveillance Environments'.

122. P MacGloin and M al-Jneibi, 'The Components of National and International Cyberspace Governance', *RSA Conference 2015*, Abu Dhabi, 4–5 November 2015.

123. Article texts are in *Appendix 11: Text of Articles Pertinent to Political Targeting Federal Law No.7 of 2014—Combatting Terrorism Offences*

124. Articles 1, 9, 10, 11, 14, 15, and 34 of Federal Law No.7 of 2014.

125. Censorship is a highly utilised tactic within MENA, with Mellor accurately explaining the legislator environment; 'if Egyptians want to know about Egypt, they are better watching Al-Jazeera, while a Qatari is better served by reading Arab newspapers from outside Qatar to keep informed of what is happening inside Qatar'. N Mellor, *The Making of Arab News*, Rowman and Littlefield, Lanham, 2005, p.145, in E Murphy, 'Theorizing ICTs in the Arab World: Informational Capitalism and the Public Sphere', p.1140.

126. 'Digital Media Now Firmly Within the UAE's Regulatory Scope', *Baker McKenzie*, 31st October 2017, available online, https://www.bakermckenzie.com/en/insight/publications/2017/10/digital-media-uae-regulatory-scope/, date accessed, 26th January 2018.

127. Table 4: UAE's Surveillance Legislation.

128. in D Lyon, 'Surveillance, Snowden, and Big Data: Capacities, Consequences, Critique', p.5.

129. GT Marx, 'What's new about the "new surveillance"? Classifying for change and continuity', in SP Hier and J Greenberg (eds.), *The Surveillance Studies Reader*, Open University Press, Maidenhead, 2007, p.85.

130. Ibid, p.5.

131. The appropriate use of a technology is by nature a contextual perspective. Evgeny Morozov explores the management of the internet to explore both national-level and sociopolitical controls. E Morozov, 'Whither Internet Control?', *Journal of Democracy*, Vol.22, No.2, April 2011, pp.62–74.

132. Rob Joyce, the head of the US National Security Agency's (NSA's) Tailored Access operations (TAOs) gave a public presentation where he discussed cyberspace vulnerabilities, making particular reference to third-party weaknesses and subsequent exploitations. USENIX Enigma Conference, 'USENIX Enigma 2016—NSA TAO Chief on Disrupting Nation State Hackers', filmed 27th January 2016, YouTube Video, 34:55, Posted 28th January 2016.

133. One prominent example being the restriction of technological platforms that deny the state arbitrary observation and control. The 2010 dispute between the UAE and Blackberry over the basing of servers illustrates this point. A Hammond, 'UAE Says Blackberry Dispute Resolved Before Deadline', *Reuters*, 8th October 2010, available online, https://www.reuters.com/article/us-blackberry-emirates/uae-says-blackberry-dispute-resolved-before-deadline-idUSTRE6970S320101008, date accessed, 12th March 2018.

134. SP Hier and J Greenberg, 'Editors' Introduction: Contemporary Surveillance Studies', pp.87–88.

135. 'Shall be sentenced to term imprisonment, every public servant, or a person commissioned with a public service, who discloses a secret entrusted to him concerning state defense. The penalty shall be life imprisonment if the crime is perpetrated during war time'.

136. 'Shall be sentenced to term imprisonment: 1. Whoever endeavours to obtain by any illicit means a state defense secret without the intention of delivering or disclosing it to a foreign country or to one serving its benefits. 2. Whoever propagates by any means a state defence secret. 3.Whoever devises or uses a communication means or information technology to attain, deliver or disseminate a state defense secrets (sic). The penalty shall be life imprisonment if the crime occurs during war time.'

137. 'The following shall be considered a state defense secret: 1. Military, Political, Economic, industrial, scientific and security information which are by nature known exclusively to persons having capacity thereto and the state interest requires that such information have to remain secret for others. 2. Correspondence, written instruments, documents, drawings, maps, designs, pictures, coordinates and other items, which disclosure shall reveal the information referred to in the preceding paragraph and for which the state interest requires that they be kept secret from others than those in charge of their preservation or use. 3. News and information concerning the armed forces, the

ministry of interior, the security forces, and their formation, manoeuvres, equipment, supplies, staff and other items which may affect military affairs, war and secret plans, unless a written authorization has been given by the authority in charge of their publication and diffusion. 4. News and information relating to measures and procedures that are adopted to detect the crimes provided for in the present chapter and arrest the perpetrators; as well as news and information relating to the conduct of investigation and trial in case the competent investigation authority or the court prohibits their diffusion.'

138. Federal Law No.3, 1987, UAE Penal Code, Judicial Department, available online, https://www.adjd.gov.ae/sites/Authoring/AR/ELibrary%20Books/ E-Library/PDFs/Penal%20Code.pdf, date accessed, 27th January 2018.

139. S Salama, 'UAE widens scope of penal code to fight corruption', *Gulf News*, 5th December 2018, available online, https://gulfnews.com/uae/uae-widens-scope-of-penal-code-to-fight-corruption-1.60767814, date accessed, 15th June 2019.

140. The Smart Dubai framework is expected to be installed across the nation following its successful implementation in Dubai. https://2021.smartdubai.ae

141. WAM, 'Abu Dhabi Launches New Surveillance System', Emirates 24/7, 13th July 2016, available online, http://www.emirates247.com/news/emirates/ abu-dhabi-launches-new-surveillance-system-2016–07–13–1.635659, date accessed, 29th January 2018.

142. A Al Shouk, 'Dubai CCTV Cameras to use AI, Facial Recognition', *Gulf News*, 27th January 2018, available online, http://gulfnews.com/news/uae/government/dubai-cctv-cameras-to-use-ai-face-recognition-1.2163726, date accessed, 29th January 2018.

143. A Ali, '13 Social Media Accounts Shut Down for Selling Drugs in UAE', *Gulf News*, 15th October 2017, available online, http://gulfnews.com/news/uae/crime/13-social-media-accounts-shut-down-for-selling-drugs-in-uae-1.2106100, date accessed, 2nd February 2018.

144. B Marczak and J Scott-Railton, 'The Million Dollar Dissident', *The Citizen Lab*, 24th August 2016, available online, https://citizenlab.ca/2016/08/million-dollar-dissident-iphone-zero-day-nso-group-uae/, date accessed, 27th January 2018.

145. http://www.hackingteam.it.

146. M Marquis-Boire and E Galperin, 'A Brief History of Governments Hacking Human Rights Organisations', *Amnesty International*, 11th January 2016, available online, https://www.amnesty.org/en/latest/campaigns/2016/01/brief-history-of-government-hacking-human-rights-organizations/, date accessed, 27th January 2018.

147. An example of Ronald Deibert's third-generational control. R Deibert, 'Cyberspace Under Seige', p.68.

148. B Marczak and J Scott-Railton, 'The Million Dollar Dissident', *The Citizen Lab*, 24th August 2016, available online, https://citizenlab.ca/2016/08/million-

dollar-dissident-iphone-zero-day-nso-group-uae/, date accessed, 27ᵗʰ January 2018.

149. D Tynan, 'Apple Issues Global iOS Update After Attempt To Use Spyware on Activist's iPhone', *The Guardian*, 25ᵗʰ August 2016, available online, https://www.theguardian.com/technology/2016/aug/25/apple-ios-update-arab-activists-iphone-spyware, date accessed, 27ᵗʰ January 2018.

150. The targeted surveillance capability illustrated is defined by Ronald Deibert as the third-generation control. R Deibert, 'Cyberspace Under Siege', p.68.

151. C Bing and J Schectman, 'Special Report—Inside the UAE's secret hacking team of US mercenaries', *Reuters*, 30ᵗʰ January 2019, available online, https://uk.reuters.com/article/uk-usa-spying-raven-specialreport/special-report-inside-the-uaes-secret-hacking-team-of-u-s-mercenaries-idUKKCN1PO1A6, date accessed, 7ᵗʰ June 2019.

152. S Shuey, 'UAE Regulator to Suspend Blackberry Services From October 11', *Gulf News*, 1ˢᵗ August 2010, available online, http://gulfnews.com/business/sectors/telecoms/uae-regulator-to-suspend-blackberry-services-from-october-11–1.662333, date accessed, 29ᵗʰ January 2018.

153. MA Droubi, 'UAE Residents Welcome Unblocked Whatsapp Voice Calls', *The National*, 22ⁿᵈ June 2017, available online, https://www.thenational.ae/uae/uae-residents-welcome-unblocked-whatsapp-voice-calls-1.92973, date accessed, 26ᵗʰ February 2018.

154. 'Skype Users in the UAE Urge Rethink of VoIP Policy', *The National*, 31ˢᵗ December 2017, available online, https://www.thenational.ae/uae/government/skype-users-in-the-uae-urge-rethink-of-voip-policy-1.691702, date accessed, 29ᵗʰ January 2018.

155. B Thompson, 'UAE Blackberry Update was Spyware', *BBC*, 21ˢᵗ July 2009, available online, http://news.bbc.co.uk/1/hi/8161190.stm, date accessed, 29ᵗʰ January 2017.

156. Ibid.

157. 'The Authority shall enjoy, in urgent cases, and after consulting the National Security Advisor, the prerogative to monitor, penetrate, process, eliminate, jam, or block the communications network, the information systems, and the communications and email devices that belong to any person or entity that appears to the Authority as having participated in any act that may affect the State's security, doctrine, economy, heritage, civilization, public system, social peace, international and regional relations, or vital utilities altogether with the public and private parties working therein, or that may affect the life or funds of any person in the State, provided that the competent public prosecution is informed of the measure taken by the Authority in such cases within one week, so that it can conduct its affairs in respect of such measure.' Article 14, Federal Decree Law No.3, 2012.

158. A Hammond, 'UAE Says Blackberry Dispute Resolved Before Deadline', *Reuters*, 8ᵗʰ October 2010, available online, https://www.reuters.com/arti-

cle/us-blackberry-emirates/uae-says-blackberry-dispute-resolved-before-deadline-idUSTRE6970S320101008, date accessed, 2nd February 2018.

159. E Murphy, 'Agency and Space: The Political Impact of Information Technologies in the Gulf Arab States', *Third World Quarterly*, Vol.27, No.6, 2006, p.1064.

160. 'Media Statement on Etisalat Launch of Internet Calling Plans', *Etisalat*, 8th January 2018, available online, https://www.etisalat.ae/en/about-us/media_center/press_releases/internet_calling_plans.jsp, date accessed, 29th January 2018.

161. C Fuchs, 'New Media, Web 2.0 and Surveillance', p.140.

162. M Lynch, 'How the Media Trashed the Transitions', *Journal of Democracy*, Vol.26, No.4, October 2015, pp.90–99.

163. R Deibert, 'Cyberspace Under Siege'.

164. Z Bauman and D Lyon, *Liquid Surveillance*.

165. M Castells, *Networks of Outrage and Hope—Social Movements in the Internet Age*, Wiley, Chichester, 2012.

166. C Shirky, 'The Political Power of Social Media: Technology, the Public Sphere, and Political Change'.

167. T O'Reilly, 'What Is Web 2.0'.

168. J Van Dijk, 'Digital Democracy: Vision and Reality'.

169. E Murphy, 'ICT and the Gulf Arab States: A Force for Democracy?'.

170. J Arquilla and D Ronfeldt, *The Emergence of Noopolitik*, p.7.

171. M Castells, *Networks of Outrage and Hope*.

172. S Kalathil and TC Boas, *Open Networks, Closed Regimes: The Impact of the Internet on Authoritarian Rule*, p.2.

173. 'UAE Strategy 2011–2013', *UAE Cabinet*, available online, https://uaecabinet.ae/en/uae-strategy-2011–2013, date accessed 3rd February 2018.

174. https://www.vision2021.ae/en.

175. *The Abu Dhabi Economic Vision 2030*, The Government of Abu Dhabi, Abu Dhabi, November 2008.

176. https://www.dubaiplan2021.ae/dubai-plan-2021/.

177. 'EGovernment deals with facilitating the operation of government and the distribution of governmental information and services', AM Al-Khouri, 'eGovernment Strategies the Case of the United Arab Emirates', *European Journal of ePractice*, No.17, September 2016, p.127.

178. S Kalathil and TC Boas, *Open Networks, Closed Regimes*, p.110.

179. There is a clear appreciation for the potential vulnerability of sousveillance, as postulated by Steve Mann, Jason Nolan, and Barry Wellman. Sousveillance is the reflection of surveillance activities upon those deemed to be under observation. Due to the high exposure of information on PREs, now made possible through their own forays into modern technologies, they are now subject of surveillance by the global public. S Mann, J Nolan, and B Wellman,

'Sousveillance: Inventing and Using Wearable Computing Devices for Data Collection in Surveillance Environments'.

180. 'Dubai Government Service Directory', *Government of Dubai*, available online, http://www.dubai.ae/en/ServiceDirectory/Pages/default.aspx,   date accessed, 29ᵗʰ January 2018.

181. 'a public sphere is more likely to emerge in a society as a result of people's dissatisfaction with matters of economics or day-to-day governance than from their embrace of abstract political ideas', C Shriky, 'The Political Power of Social Media', p.35.

182. 'Service Details', Dubai eGovernment, available online, http://www.dubai.ae/en/ServiceDirectory/Pages/ServiceDetails.aspx?ServiceID=1135&Identity=17134560, date accessed, 29ᵗʰ January 2018.

183. Federal National Council, available online, https://www.almajles.gov.ae/Pages/FNCHome.aspx, date accessed, 29ᵗʰ January 2018.

184. K Ulrichsen, *The Politics of Economic Reform in Arab Gulf States*. Hisham Sharabi's neopatriarchy augments the execution of culturally distinct strategies as the traditional and cultural nuances within Emirati society distinguish them from their foreign counterparts. H Sharabi, *Neopatriarchy: A Theory of Distorted Change in Arab Society*.

185. https://www.mbrmajlis.ae/en#home

186. The emphasis on informal and interpersonal ties is both a form of empowerment for the traditional form of legitimacy that the Abu Dhabi leadership rests upon and the suggestion that 'historical experiences have led Arabs to place far greater trust in information which is transmitted informally'. M Fandy, 'Information Technology, Trust and Social Change in the Arab World', *Middle East Journal*, Vol.54, No.3, 2000, pp.378–394, in E Murphy, 'Agency and Space: The Political Impact of Information Technologies in the Gulf Arab States', p.1068.

187. 'Majlis Mohammed bin Zayed', *Crown Prince Court*, available online, https://www.cpc.gov.ae/en-us/thecrownprince/Majlis/Pages/default.aspx, date accessed, 2ⁿᵈ February 2018.

188. 'Laws and Legislation', *Federal Authority for Identity and Citizenship*, available online, https://www.id.gov.ae/en/emirates-id/laws-and-legislation.aspx, date accessed, 29ᵗʰ January 2018.

189. Ibid.

190. N Hanif, 'Every Mobile Phone User in the UAE Must Re-Register SIM Card', *The National*, 28ᵗʰ June 2012, available online, https://www.thenational.ae/uae/every-mobile-phone-user-in-the-uae-must-re-register-sim-card-1.396199, date accessed, 26ᵗʰ January 2018.

191. Spyware and other legal interception programs can further remotely activate the microphone and camera on smartphone, as well as access electronic data stored on the device and through third-party providers, and thus offer audio, video, and text intelligence at the state's request.

192. C Malek, 'UAE Ministry to Link ID Cards With the Internet to Crack Down on Child Abusers', *The National*, 5th April 2014, available online, https://www.thenational.ae/business/technology/uae-ministry-to-link-id-cards-with-the-internet-to-crack-down-on-child-abusers-1.340210, date accessed, 26th January 2018.

193. ED Cohen, *Mass Surveillance and State Control: The Total Information Awareness Project*, Palgrave, New York, 2010, p.84.

194. M Croucher, 'Hackers List "sites banned by Emirates"', *The National*, 6th July 2012, available online, https://www.thenational.ae/uae/hackers-list-sites-banned-by-emirates-1.603227, date accessed, 29th January 2018.

195. http://wam.ae/ar

196. T AlSubaihi, 'Supporting Qatar on Social Media a Cybercrime, says UAE Attorney General', *The National*, 7th June 2017, available online, https://www.thenational.ae/uae/supporting-qatar-on-social-media-a-cybercrime-says-uae-attorney-general-1.31515, date accessed, 29th January 2018.

197. M Jones, 'Hacking, bots and information wars in the Qatar spat', *Monkey Cage, Washington Post*, 7th June 2017, available online, https://www.washingtonpost.com/news/monkey-cage/wp/2017/06/07/hacking-bots-and-information-wars-in-the-qatar-spat/, date accessed, 26th February 2018.

198. E Noelle-Neumann, *The Spiral Silence: Public Opinion, Our Social Skin*, University of Chicago Press, Chicago, 1993.

199. S Heydemann, *Upgrading Authoritarianism in the Arab World*.

5. STRATEGIC ECONOMIC MANAGEMENT

1. O Schlumberger, 'Structural Reform, Economic Order, and Development: Patrimonial Capitalism'.

2. M Flournoy and R Fontaine, 'Economic Growth is a Security Issue', *The Wall Street Journal*, 26th May 2015, available online, https://www.wsj.com/articles/economic-growth-is-a-national-security-issue-1432683397, date accessed, 4th March 2018. K Zukrowska, 'The Link Between Economics, Stability and Security in a Transforming Economy', *NATO Economic Colloquium*, 1999, pp.269–83.

3. B Buzan, O Wæver, and J de Wilde, *Security, A New Framework for Analysis*, p.105.

4. M Gray, *A Theory of "Late Rentierism" in the Arab States of the Gulf*, p.13.

5. PW Moore, 'Late Development and Rents in the Arab World', pp.8–11.

6. G Gause, *Oil Monarchies: Domestic Security and Security Challenges in the Arab Gulf States*, 1994.

7. A Giddens, *The Consequences of Modernity*, Cambridge, pp.55–56.

8. Ibid, p.59.

9. I Bremmer, *The End of the Free Market*, p.43.

10. TR Dye and JW Pickering, 'Governmental and Corporate Elites: Convergence and Differentiation', *The Journal of Politics*, Vol.36, No.4, November 1974, pp.900–925.

11. NH Ayubi, *Over-stating the Arab State: Politics and Society in the Middle East*, IB Tauris, London, 1995. A Ehteshami and EC Murphy, 'Transformation of the Corporatist State in the Middle East', *Third World Quarterly*, Vol.17, 1996, pp.753–72.

12. A Perlmutter, *Modern Authoritarianism: A Comparative Institutional Analysis*. G O'Donnell, *Modernization and Bureaucratic Authoritarianism, Studies in South American Politics*, University of California Press, Berkeley, 1979.

13. 'On the one hand it is generally possible to go far toward attaining a monopoly of the management of productive enterprises in favour of the member of the class and their business interests. On the other hand, such a class tends to insure the security of its economic position by exercising influence on the economic policy of political bodies and other groups'. M Weber, *Max Weber: The Theory of Social and Economic Organization*, p.426.

14. 'This economic order emerges in environments where political control over the economy is highly concentrated and where informal modes of interaction between state and business dominate over formal rules and laws.' O Schlumberger, 'Structural reform, economic order, and development: Patrimonial capitalism', pp.622–23.

15. 'The UAE and Global Oil Supply', UAE Embassy in Washington DC, available online, http://www.uae-embassy.org/about-uae/energy/uae-and-global-oil-supply, date accessed, 19th January 2016.

16. An analysis of the UAE's political economy is extremely complicated due to the UAE's federal nature, unequal distribution of resources and subsequent generation of finances across the state's seven Emirates, as well as the high proportion of foreign population with no relation to the state's resources. Christopher Davidson has approached this predicament by analysing Abu Dhabi and Dubai in separate volumes. As this book examines the UAE's regime security strategy, an Abu Dhabi-focused approach will direct the analysis into the evolving political economy dynamics.

17. 'IMF Executive Board Concludes 2015 Article IV Consultation with United Arab Emirates', *IMF*, International Monetary Fund Press Release No.15/370, August 4, 2015, in K Ulrichsen, *The United Arab Emirates: Power, Politics, and Policymaking*, p.87.

18. S Chubin, A Litwak and A Plascov, *Security in the Gulf*, The Adelphi Library 7, International Institute for Strategic Studies (IISS), Gower, Aldershot, 1982, p.22.

19. This is supported by literature that postulates a relationship between rentierism and authoritarian governance. See generally ML Ross, 'Does Oil Hinder Democracy', S Huntington, *The Third Wave: Democratization in the Late Twentieth Century*, M Herb, 'No Representation Without Taxation? Rents, Development and Democracy', and E Bellin, 'The Robustness of Authoritarianism in the Middle East: Exceptionalism in Comparative Perspective'. 'Reshuffle allows

MBZ to increase Abu Dhabi's interest in UAE Federal affairs', *Gulf States Newsletter (GSN)*, Vol. 40, Issue 1,010, 18ᵗʰ February 2016.

20. A Ehteshami and EC Murphy, 'Transformation of the Corporatist State in the Middle East', p.754.
21. Ibid, p.756.
22. E Bellin, *The Political-Economic Conundrum: The Affinity of Economic and Political Reform in the Middle East and North Africa*, Middle East Series, Carnegie Papers, No.53, November 2004, p.4.
23. L Guazzone and D Pioppi (eds.), *The Arab State and Neo-Liberal Globalization: The Restructuring of State Power in the Middle East*.
24. B Haddad, 'Syria, the Arab uprisings, and the political economy of authoritarian resilience', *Interface: a journal for and about social movements*, Vol. 4, No.1, May 2012, p.122.
25. PW Moore and BF Salloukh, 'Struggles Under Authoritarianism: Regimes, States, and Professional Associations in the Arab World'.
26. SL Yom and G Gause, 'Resilient Royals: How Arab Monarchies Hang On'.
27. C Freer, *Rentier Islamism: The Influence of the Muslim Brotherhood in the Gulf Monarchies*, Oxford University Press, Oxford, 2018.
28. S Hertog, *The Private Sector and Reform in the Gulf Cooperation Council*, Research Papers, LSE Kuwait Programme, London, 2013. For more on state-business relations; Evans hypothesises a four-pronged framework for the analysis of the state's relationship with the business community: firstly, a requirement to understand the internal structure of the state; secondly, an assumption that the business community can be reshaped by state policies; thirdly, policies that renegotiate the state-business relations weaken the state's relationship with the commercial sector; fourthly, a growing requirement to institutionalise social groups to ensure easier reform implementation. P Evans, 'State Structures, Government-Business Relations, and Economic Transformation', in S Maxfield and BR Schneider (eds.), *Business and the State in Developing Countries*, Cornell University Press, Ithaca, 1997, pp.66–67.
29. The Abu Dhabi Economic Vision 2030, The Government of Abu Dhabi, Abu Dhabi, November 2008. Lessons have been learnt from the turbulence in global oil markets during the 1990s and this has paved the way for subsequent development.
30. R Wade, *Governing the Market: Economic Theory and the Role of Government in East Asian Industrialization*, Princeton University Press, Princeton, 1990.
31. C Johnson, 'Political Institutions and Economic Performance: The Government-Business Relationship in Japan, South Korea, and Taiwan', in FC Deyo (ed.), *The Political Economy of The New Asian Industrialism*, Cornell University Press, Ithaca, 1987.
32. B Haddad, *Business Networks in Syria: The Political Economy of Authoritarian Resilience*, Stanford University Press, Stanford, 2012.
33. A Nosova, *The Merchant Elite and Parliamentary Politics in Kuwait: The Dynamics of*

Business Political Participation in a Rentier State, PhD Thesis, London School of Economics, London, 2016.

34. S Haggard and RR Kaufman, *The Political Economy of Democratic Transitions*, Princeton University Press, Princetown, 1995, p.30.

35. M Valeri and S Hertog (eds.), *Business Politics in the Middle East;* B Geddes, 'Challenging the Conventional Wisdom', *Journal of Democracy*, Vol.5, No.4, October 1994, pp.104–18.

36. This has a greater usage within the UAE's industrial sector where the private sector has a greater influence in matters, than in the state's economy.

37. I Bremmer, *The End of the Free Market: Who Wins the War Between States and Corporations?* p.46.

38. KA Chaudhry, 'Prices, Politics, Institutions: Oil Exporters in the International Economy', *Business Politics*, Vol.1, No.3, 1999, p.334, in, PW Moore, 'Rentier Fiscal Crisis and Regime Stability: Business-State Relations in the Gulf', *Studies in Comparative International Development*, Vol.37, No.1, Spring 2002, p.38.

39. 'to incorporate the pre-rent state-society dynamic into an analysis of post-rent political order and relationships'. M Gray, *A Theory of 'Late Rentierism' in the Arab States of the Gulf*, p.12.

40. 'Once power is gained over income-generating resources, the relation established to citizens is no longer one of collection but of distribution, which enormously weakens the populations negotiation capacity, while strengthen the elites' power and authority [sic]'. FI Brichs and A Limpridi-Kemou, 'Sociology of Power in Today's Arab World', in FI Brichs (ed.), *Political Regimes in the Arab World: Society and the Exercise of Power*, p.26.

41. B Haddad, *Business Networks in Syria: The Political Economy of Authoritarian Resilience*.

42. S Heydemann, 'Networks of Privilege: Rethinking the Politics of Economic Reform in the Middle East', in S Heydemann (ed.), *Networks of Privilege in the Middle East: The Politics of Economic Reform Revisited*, Palgrave Macmillan, Basingstoke, 2004.

43. HJ Barkey (ed.), *The Politics of Economic Reform in the Middle East*, St Martin's Press, New York, 1992.

44. Huntington, SP, *Political Order in Changing Societies*. S Haggard and R Kaufman (ed.), *The Politics of Economic Adjustment*, Princeton University Press, Princeton, 1995.

45. B Haddad, *Business Networks in Syria: The Political Economy of Authoritarian Resilience*.

46. I Bremmer, 'State Capitalism Comes of Age, The End of the Free Market?', p.42.

47. S Heydemann, 'Networks of Privilege: Rethinking the Politics of Economic Reform in the Middle East', in S Heydemann (ed.), *Networks of Privilege in the Middle East: The Politics of Economic Reform Revisited*, p.29.

48. From 60% in the 1980s down to between 34.3% and 20% in 2011–2016.

49. 'The Dubai Supreme Council of Energy (DSCE) oversees Dubai's energy policy development and coordination … Sharjah, which is a minor producer of condensate and natural gas, established a national oil company in 2010'. 'Country Analysis Brief: United Arab Emirates', *U.S. Energy Information Administration*, 21st March 2017, available online, http://www.iberglobal.com/files/2017/emiratos_eia.pdf, date accessed, 10th March 2018.

50. 'Article 23', *UAE Constitution*, 1971.

51. Christopher Davidson analyses in great depth the intra-Emirate politics surrounding the UAE's oil reserves and states that the SPC 'plays a major role in the policymaking process, as it approves all oil-related policies and development projects for the companies falling under the umbrella of the State-Owned Abu Dhabi National Oil Company'. C Davidson, *The United Arab Emirates: A Study in Survival*, p.244.

52. M Herb, *All in the Family*, p.241.

53. C Davidson, *The United Arab Emirates: A Study in Survival*, p.102.

54. 'Supreme Petroleum Council', *ADNOC*, available online, https://www.adnoc. ae/en/about-us/supreme-petroleum-council, date accessed, 9th March 2018.

55. WAM, 'Khalifa Restructure Supreme Petroleum Council', *Emirates 24/7*, 25th June 2011, available online, https://www.emirates247.com/news/government/khalifa-restructures-supreme-petroleum-council-2011-06-25-1.404511, date accessed, 9th March 2018.

56. Hendrik Van Der Muelen notes that the Bani Ma'in originate from Kish island and other surrounding territories in Iran. H Van Der Muelen, *The Role of Tribal and Kinship Ties in the Politics of the UAE*, p.365.

57. WAM, 'President Khalifa Revamps Supreme Petroleum Council', *Khaleej Times*, 27th June 2011, available online, https://www.khaleejtimes.com/article/20110626/ARTICLE/306269986/1002, date accessed, 9th March 2018.

58. A McAuley, 'UAE President Reshuffles Supreme Petroleum Council of Abu Dhabi', *The National*, 29th March 2016, available online, https://www.the-national.ae/business/uae-president-reshuffles-supreme-petroleum-council-of-abu-dhabi-1.159318, date accessed, 9th March 2018.

59. 'SPC Changes Tighten MBZ Grip', *Gulf States Newsletter (GSN)*, Vol.40, Issue 1,012, 31st March 2016, p.7.

60. The Emirates National Oil Company (ENOC) is owned by the Government of Dubai while the Sharjah National Oil Company (SNOC) is owned by the Government of Sharjah.

61. 'Our History', *Abu Dhabi National Oil Company (ADNOC)*, available online, https://www.adnoc.ae/en/about-us/our-history, date accessed, 9th March 2018.

62. 'Strategy 2030', *Abu Dhabi National Oil Company (ADNOC)*, available online, https://www.adnoc.ae/en/strategy2030, date accessed, 9th March 2018.

63. The expiration of the ADCO concession is significant as it marked the point at which negotiations for contract renewals were to take place. As the contract

was later reduced from 65 to 40 years, changes to the leadership of ADNOC around this period illustrated the UAE's reimagined strategy to natural resources governance.

64. 'Khalifa Appoints Sultan al-Jaber as Director General of ADNOC', *WAM Emirates News Agency*, 15th February 2016, available online, http://wam.ae/en/details/1395291637840, date accessed, 10th March 2018. Ulrichsen notes that ADNOC was traditionally an entity close to Sheikh Khalifa, and al Jaber's appointment exhibited another symptom of the power shift from Khalifa bin Zayed to Muhammad bin Zayed. K Ulrichsen, *The United Arab Emirates: Power, Politics, and Policymaking*, p.228.

65. 'UAE Reshuffle', *Gulf States Newsletter (GSN)*, Vol.40, Issue 1,010, 18th February 2016.

66. L Graves, 'Sultan al Jaber: New Man at ADNOC Helm Has the Right Energy Mix', *The National*, 16th February 2016, available online, https://www.the-national.ae/business/sultan-al-jaber-new-man-at-adnoc-helm-has-the-right-energy-mix-1.202477, date accessed, 13th April 2018.

67. 'Masdar Board of Directors', *Masdar*, available online, http://www.masdar.ae/en/masdar/detail/masdar-board-of-directors, date accessed, 10th March 2018.

68. WAM, 'UAE's ADNOC Group to Continue its Transformation, says Al Jaber', *Zawya*, 3rd January 2017, available online, https://www.zawya.com/mena/en/story/UAEs_ADNOC_Group_to_continue_its_transformation_says_Al_Jaber-WAM20170103123040071/, date accessed, 13th April 2018.

69. M West, 'Just How Low Can Oil Prices Go and Who is Hit Hardest?', *BBC*, 18th January 2016, available online, http://www.bbc.co.uk/news/business-35245133, date accessed, 10th March 2018.

70. '2030 Strategy', *ADNOC*, available online, https://www.adnoc.ae/en/strategy2030, date accessed, 10th March 2018.

71. D Munro, 'ADNOC's CEO Institutes Seismic Shift in Corporate Strategy', *Arab Gulf States Institute in Washington Blog*, 1st June 2016.

72. 'UAE Giant ADNOC to Consolidate Three Firms in Efficiency Drive', *Reuters*, 18th October 2016, available online, https://www.reuters.com/article/emirates-adnoc-consolidation/uae-oil-giant-adnoc-to-consolidate-three-firms-in-efficiency-drive-idUSL8N1CO1WX?type=companyNews, date accessed, 10th March 2018.

73. 'ADNOC Restructuring Continues Apace', *The Economist Intelligence Unit (EIU)*, 20th May 2016, available online, http://country.eiu.com/article.aspx?articleid=1544237538, date accessed, 10th March 2018.

74. CR Hankla and D Kuthy, 'Economic Liberalism in Illiberal Regimes: Authoritarian Variation and the Political Economy of Trade', *International Studies Quarterly*, Vol.57, 2013, p.495.

75. U Abulof, '"Can't Buy Me Legitimacy": The Elusive Stability of Mideast Rentier Regimes', *Journal of International Relations and Development*, 2015, pp.1–25.

76. Embassy of the United Arab Emirates in Washington D.C., 'How The UAE is Pioneering Peaceful Civilian Nuclear Energy in the Middle East', *Smithsonian. com*, 3rd January 2018, available online, https://www.smithsonianmag.com/sponsored/uae-pioneering-peaceful-nuclear-power-middle-east-180967322/, date accessed, 10th March 2018.

77. L Graves, 'Construction Begins at Abu Dhabi's Largest Solar Panel Field', *The National*, 4th May 2017, available online, https://www.thenational.ae/business/construction-begins-at-abu-dhabi-s-largest-solar-power-project-1.32040, date accessed, 10th March 2018.

78. OECD, *OECD Guidelines on Corporate Governance of State-Owned Enterprises*, OECD Publishing, Paris, 2015 Edition, p.14.

79. Ibid, p.17.

80. PWC, *State-Owned Enterprises: Catalysts For Public Value Creation?*, April 2015, p.6.

81. SOEs are often criticised for their lack of transparency, inefficient management, and potentially negative burden on the state's economy. Hashem notes an observation of the IMF that 'about 92 per cent of Abu Dhabi's total debt maturing last year and this and beyond comes from its SOEs—Dubai's SOE debt accounts for about 60 per cent of its total. The two emirates represent 90 per cent of the UAE economy (Abu Dhabi 60 per cent and Dubai 30 per cent). If SOEs in both emirates do not do well, the whole economy will be in peril'. E Hashem, 'UAE State-Owned Concerns Must Show the State Forward', *The National*, 28th June 2013, available online, https://www.thenational.ae/business/uae-state-owned-concerns-must-show-the-way-forward-1.288245, date accessed, 24th March 2018.

82. OECD, *OECD Guidelines on Corporate Governance of State-Owned Enterprises*, p.18.

83. As the book and this chapter focus on the UAE regime security strategy and are thus focused on the direct role of the Abu Dhabi ruling family, this section will only focus on SOEs linked to the government of Abu Dhabi. For information on SOEs in other Emirates see S Hertog, 'Defying the Resource Curse, Explaining Successful State-Owned Enterprises in Rentier States', *World Politics*, Vol.62, No.2, April 2010, pp.261–301.

84. The UAE refers to SOEs as Government Related Entities (GREs).

85. Abu Dhabi Accountability Authority, *2015 Accountability Report*, Abu Dhabi, 2015.

86. 'Who we are', *Abu Dhabi Airports Company*, available online, http://www.adac.ae/english/who-we-are/who-we-are/, date accessed, 24th March 2018.

87. 'SEHA 2013 Annual Report, Delivering the Right Care for the Right Patient', *Abu Dhabi Health Services Company*, 2013.

88. 'Khalifa Establishes Abu Dhabi Media Company', *WAM*, 6th June 2007, available online, http://wam.ae/en/details/1395227857102, date accessed, 24th March 2018.

89. 'Our History', *Abu Dhabi National Oil Company (ADNOC)*, available online, https://www.adnoc.ae/en/about-us/our-history, date accessed, 24ᵗʰ March 2018.

90. 'General Directions', *Abu Dhabi Ports Company*, May 2011.

91. 'Overview', *Abu Dhabi Securities Exchange*, available online, Abu Dhabi Securities Exchange (ADX), https://www.adx.ae/English/Pages/AboutUs/Whoweare/default.aspx, date accessed, 24ᵗʰ March 2018.

92. 'Abu Dhabi Water and Electric Authority', *Abu Dhabi Digital Government*, available online, https://www.abudhabi.ae/portal/public/en/departments/adwea, date accessed, 24ᵗʰ March 2018.

93. 'Emirates Nuclear Energy Company (ENEC), *U.S—U.A.E Business Council*, available online, http://usuaebusiness.org/members/emirates-nuclear-energy-corporation-enec/, date accessed, 24ᵗʰ March 2018.

94. 'Etihad Aviation Group', *CAPA Center For Aviation*, available online, https://centreforaviation.com/data/profiles/airline-groups/etihad-aviation-group, date accessed, 24ᵗʰ March 2018.

95. *Etihad Rail Fact Sheet*, available online, https://www.etihadrail.ae/sites/default/files/pdf/factsheets.pdf, date accessed, 24ᵗʰ March 2018.

96. 'Ownership Information', *First Abu Dhabi Bank*, 31ˢᵗ December 2017, available online, https://www.nbad.com/en-ae/about-nbad/investor-relations/shareholders/ownership.html, date accessed, 24ᵗʰ March 2018.

97. 'The National Health Insurance Company', *Abu Dhabi Digital Government*, available online, https://www.abudhabi.ae/portal/public/en/departments/daman, date accessed, 24ᵗʰ March 2018.

98. G Lahn, *Fuel, Food and Utilities Price Reforms in the GCC A Wake Up Call for Business*, Chatham House, London, Research Paper, June 2016.

99. The GCC's airlines are often criticised for perceivably subsidising their airlines and undercutting the global competitive market.

100. I Bremmer, *The End of the Free Market: Who Wins the War Between States and Corporations?*, p.94.

101. E Bellin, *The Political-Economic Conundrum: The Affinity of Economic and Political Reform in the Middle East and North Africa*, pp.6–7.

102. K Almezaini, 'Private Sector Actors in the UAE and their Role in the Process of Economic and Political Reform', in S Hertog, G Luciani, and M Valeri (eds.), *Business Politics in the Middle East*, p.51.

103. G Luciani, 'Allocation vs Production States: A Theoretical Framework', in G Luciani (ed.), *The Arab State*, p.76.

104. B Buzan, O Wæver, and J de Wilde, *Security, A New Framework for Analysis*, p.109.

105. Steffen Hertog supports this by postulating two reasons for the success of SOEs in the GCC; absence of populist mobilisation and the fact the regime and decision-making authority is highly centralised.

106. A prominent example is Hussein Hammadi. His investment firm, Emirates

Advanced Investments (EAI), had made a series of significant purchases, including establishing a high technology university, Khalifa University of Science and Technology. Several of his assets were subsequently incorporated into SOEs and SWFs, and Hammadi was appointed as Minister of Education and Cabinet Member in 2014. 'Cabinet Member', *United Arab Emirates The Cabinet*, available online, https://uaecabinet.ae/en/details/cabinet-members/his-excellency-hussain-bin-ibrahim-al-hammadi, date accessed, 24th March 2018.

107. An example is the telecommunications sector, which has slowly increased its membership to four companies; all of which are majority-owned by the state.

108. Steffen Hertog disagrees and, when speaking generally, he says that 'instead of using them as political tools, they [GCC monarchies] are taking pains to signal that the business of their public sectors is only that: business'. S Hertog, 'Defying the Resource Curse, Explaining Successful State-Owned Enterprises in Rentier States', p.262.

109. I Bremmer, *The End of the Free Market: Who Wins the War Between States and Corporations?*, p.67.

110. I Bremmer, *The End of the Free Market: Who Wins the War Between States and Corporations?*, p.97.

111. A Hanieh, *Capitalism and Class in the Gulf Arab States*, p.2.

112. For example in Kuwait. M Herb, 'A Nation of Bureaucrats: Political Participation and Economic Diversification in Kuwait and the United Arab Emirates', pp.375–95.

113. M Hvidt, 'The Dubai Model: An Outline of Key Development-Process Elements in Dubai', *International Journal of Middle East Studies*, Vol.41, 2009, pp.397–418.

114. C Davidson, 'The Emirates of Abu Dhabi and Dubai: Contrasting Roles in the International System', *Asian Affairs*, Vol. 38, No.1, March 2007, pp.33–48.

115. M Hvidt, 'The Dubai Model: An Outline of Key Development-Process Elements in Dubai', p.378.

116. Two Four54, Abu Dhabi Airport Free Zone, Masdar City Free Zone and Technology Park, and Khalifa Industrial Zone.

117. Dubai Airport Free Zone, Dubai Auto Zone, Dubai Care and Automotive Zone, Dubai Design District, Dubai Flower Centre, Dubai Gold and Diamond Park, Dubai Healthcare City, Dubai Industrial City, Dubai International Academic City, Dubai International Financial Centre, Dubai Internet City, Dubai Knowledge Park, Dubai Logistics City, Dubai Maritime City Authority, Dubai Media City, Dubai Multi Commodities Centre, Dubai Outsource Zone, Dubai Science Park, Dubai Silicon Oasis, Dubai Studio City, National Industries Complex, Dubai Textile City, Energy and Environment Park, International Humanitarian City, Jebel Ali Free Zone Authority, Jumeirah Lake Towers Free Zone, Dubai Production City.

118. 'Top 10 Buyers and Sellers', *Abu Dhabi Securities Exchange*, 24th March 2018,

available online, https://www.adx.ae/English/Pages/Data/ReportandCharts/ ChartCenter/Top10BuyersSellersbySymbol.aspx, date accessed, 24th March 2018.

119. This observation follows Steffen Hertog's islands of efficiency postulation and aligns with a patrimonial understanding of society. S Hertog, *Princes, Brokers, and Bureaucrats: Oil and the State in Saudi Arabia*, p.21.

120. M Kassem, 'Family Businesses Continue to Shun Public Listing', *The National*, 23rd November 2017, available online, https://www.thenational.ae/business/ economy/family-businesses-continue-to-shun-public-listings-1.678270, date accessed, 24th March 2018.

121. 'TNI Market Insight', *The National Investor*, 13th May 2008, available online, https://www.hawkamah.org/uploads/1469026337_578f90218eb7c_ Powermatters.pdf, date accessed, 24th March 2018.

122. Mazrouei, Qubaisi, Suwaidi, Rumaithi, and Muhairi.

123. http://www.eaig.ae.

124. http://www.iggroup.ae.

125. http://www.baynunagroup.com/index.html.

126. K Young, *The Political Economy of Energy, Finance and Security in the United Arab Emirates; Between the Majlis and the Market*, Palgrave MacMillan, Basingstoke, 2014.

127. http://www.royalgroupuae.com/about-us.html

128. http://www.binzayed.com

129. K Young, *The Political Economy of Energy, Finance and Security in the United Arab Emirates: Between the Majlis and the Market*, p.67.

130. S Heydemann, 'Networks of Privilege: Rethinking the Politics of Economic Reform in the Middle East', p.1.

131. 'Sovereign Wealth Funds, Generally Accepted Principles and Practices, "Santiago Principles"', *International Working Group of Sovereign Wealth Funds*, October 2008, 'What is a SWF?', *Sovereign Wealth Fund Research Institute*, available online, https://www.swfinstitute.org/sovereign-wealth-fund/, date accessed, 9th March 2018.

132. A Rozanov, 'Who Holds the Wealth of Nations?', *Central Bank Journal*, May 2005.

133. S Bazoobandi, *The Political Economy of the Gulf Sovereign Wealth Funds*, p.6.

134. A Hanieh, *Capitalism and Class in the Gulf Arab States*, p.95.

135. http://www.adia.ae/En/home.aspx.

136. http://www.adcouncil.ae.

137. https://www.mubadala.com.

138. http://www.eia.gov.ae.

139. http://www.investad.com.

140. S Bazoobandi, *The Political Economy of the Gulf Sovereign Wealth Funds*, pp.98– 102.

141. http://www.dubaiworld.ae.

142. https://dubaiholding.com/en/.

143. https://www.icd.gov.ae.

144. Abu Dhabi Investment Authority (ADIA), 'Mission', *Annual Review 2016: A Legacy in Motion*, 2017, available online, http://www.adia.ae/En/pr/2016/pdf/ADIA_2016_Review_01_FULL.pdf, date accessed, 17th March 2018.

145. Khaldoon al Mubarak however claimed that *'Abu Dhabi has $1 trillion under investment'*. USUAEBUSINESSCOUNCIL (@USUAEBIZCOUNCIL), 27th February 2018, 1340.

146. 'Fund Rankings', *Sovereign Wealth Fund Institute*, June 2017, available online, https://www.swfinstitute.org/fund-rankings/, date accessed, 17th March 2018.

147. 'The Government of the Emirate of Abu Dhabi provides ADIA with funds that are allocated for investment and surplus to its budgetary requirements and its other funding commitments', Abu Dhabi Investment Authority (ADIA), 'Governance', *Annual Review 2016: A Legacy in Motion*, 2017.

148. H Van Der Meulen, *The Role of Tribal and Kinship Ties in the Politics of the UAE*, p.93.

149. C Davidson, *Abu Dhabi: Oil and Beyond*, p.73.

150. H bin Zayed al Nahyan, 'Abu Dhabi Investment Authority Marks 40th Anniversary', *Press Release*, Abu Dhabi, 21st March 2016, available online, http://www.adia.ae/En/pr/ADIA_40th_Anniversary_Open_Letter_Press_Release_English.pdf, date accessed, 17th March 2018.

151. Sheikh Ahmed bin Zayed al-Nahyan had been Managing Director of ADIA for 13 years, however was killed in a gliding accident in Morocco in March 2010. Subsequently, his full brother, Sheikh Hamed bin Zayed al-Nahyan was appointed as ADIA Managing Director on 14th April 2010. B Hope, 'Sheikh Hamed bin Zayed named ADIA Chief', *The National*, available online, https://www.thenational.ae/business/sheikh-hamed-bin-zayed-named-adia-chief-1.531542, date accessed, 16th March 2018.

152. 'Khalifa Appoints Mansour as ADIA Board Member', *WAM*, 8th June 2005, available online, http://wam.ae/en/details/1395227444392, date accessed, 17th March 2018.

153. B Hope, 'Sheikh Hamed bin Zayed Names ADIA Chief', *The National*, 14th April 2010, available online, https://www.thenational.ae/business/sheikh-hamed-bin-zayed-named-adia-chief-1.531542, date accessed, 13th April 2018.

154. A DiPaola, 'Abu Dhabi Investment Authority Director Jauan Al Dhaheri Dies', *Bloomberg*, 5th May 2013, available online, https://www.bloomberg.com/news/articles/2013–05–05/abu-dhabi-investment-authority-director-jauan-al-dhaheri-dies, date accessed, 17th March 2018.

155. 'Two Officials Take Oath Before Abu Dhabi Crown Prince', *WAM*, 6th March 2017, available online, http://wam.ae/en/details/1395302601294, date accessed, 17th March 2018.

156. 'Khalifa Reshuffles ADIA's BoD', *WAM*, 4th January 2007, available online, http://wam.ae/en/details/1395227772438, date accessed, 17th March 2018.

157. 'Board of Directors', *2010 Review: Prudent Global Growth*, Abu Dhabi Investment Authority, Abu Dhabi, 2011, available online, http://www.adia.ae/En/pr/Annual_Review_Website_2010.pdf, date accessed, 16th March 2018.

158. 'Sheikh Khalifa Restructures ADIA's Board', Sovereign Wealth Fund Institute, 9th April 2013, available online, https://www.swfinstitute.org/swf-news/sheikh-khalifa-restructures-adias-board/, date accessed, 17th March 2018.

159. 'Board of Directors', *Abu Dhabi Investment Authority (ADIA)*, available online, http://www.adia.ae/En/Governance/Board_Of_Directors.aspx, date accessed, 16th March 2018.

160. The Dhawahir are a strong and powerful tribe in Abu Dhabi that have a long history of alliance with the Bani Yas.

161. 'Investment Strategy and Portfolio Overview', *Annual Review 2016: A Legacy in Motion*, 2017, p.14.

162. G Luciani, 'Resources, Revenues, and Authoritarianism in the Arab World: Beyond the Rentier State?', in R Brynen, B Korany, and P Noble (eds.), *Political Liberalization and Democratization in the Arab World*, p.211.

163. KA Alsweilem, A Cummine, M Rietveld, and K Tweedie, *A Comparative Study of Sovereign Investor Models: Sovereign Fund Profiles*, The Center for International Development and the Belfer Center for Science and International Affairs, Harvard Kennedy School, Harvard, 2015, available online, https://projects.iq.harvard.edu/files/sovereignwealth/files/fund_profiles_final.pdf, date accessed, 18th March 2018, p.7.

164. Ibid.

165. 'Khalifa Issues Law Forming Abu Dhabi Investment Council', *WAM*, 12th June 2006, available online, http://wam.ae/ar/print/1395227670129, date accessed, 18th March 2018.

166. 'Investment Strategy', *Abu Dhabi Investment Council*, available online, http://www.adcouncil.ae/?page_id=41, date accessed, 18th March 2018.

167. WAM, 'CORRECTED-Abu Dhabi's crown prince is new chairman of ADIC in board revamp—WAM', *Reuters*, 22nd June 2015, available online, https://www.reuters.com/article/emirates-swf-adic/corrected-abu-dhabis-crown-prince-is-new-chairman-of-adic-in-board-revamp-wam-idUSL8N-0Z70OI20150622, date accessed, 18th March 2018.

168. The National Staff, 'Sheikh Khalifa Reshuffles Abu Dhabi Investment Council Board', *The National*, 21st June 2015, available online, https://www.the-national.ae/business/sheikh-khalifa-reshuffles-abu-dhabi-investment-council-board-1.100036, date accessed, 18th March 2018.

169. H Van Der Muelen, *The Role of Tribal and Kinship Ties in the Politics of the UAE*, p.157.

170. WAM, 'Khalifa Restructures ADIA's Board', *Emirates 24/7*, 8th April 2013, available online, https://www.emirates247.com/news/government/khalifa-restructures-adia-s-board-2013–04–08–1.501851, date accessed, 19th March 2018.

171. H Van Der Muelen, *The Role of Tribal and Kinship Ties in the Politics of the UAE*, p.157.

172. Eissa Mohamed al-Suwaidi is a board member of Abu Dhabi National Oil Company for Distribution, International Petroleum Investment Company, Abu Dhabi Fund for Development, Emirates Investment Authority, 'Board of Directors Profiles', *Abu Dhabi Commercial Bank*, available online, https://www.adcb.com/about/investorrelations/financialinformation/ARsite/2014/eissa-mohamed-al-suwaidi.html, date accessed, 19th March 2018.

173. 'Organisational Structure', *United Arab Emirates Ministry of Finance*, available online, https://www.mof.gov.ae/En/About/ocAndInstitutes/Pages/oc.aspx#, date accessed, 19th March 2018.

174. 'Board Member', *General Pension and Social Security Authority*, available online, http://gpssa.gov.ae/en/Pages/DirectorsDetails.aspx?DirectorId=13, date accessed, 19th March 2018.

175. H Van Der Muelen, *The Role of Tribal and Kinship Ties in the Politics of the UAE*, p.148.

176. S Kerr, 'UAE Central Bank Announces New Chairman', *Financial Times*, 7th November 2012, available online, https://www.ft.com/content/3d8bc29a-28d7-11e2-b92c-00144feabdc0, date accessed, 19th March 2018.

177. 'Khalifa Reshuffles Abu Dhabi Investment Council', *WAM*, 4th January 2007, available online, http://wam.ae/en/details/1395227772462, date accessed, 18th March 2018.

178. 'Khalifa bin Zayed Issues Emiri Decree Reshuffling Abu Dhabi Investment Council Board', *Emirate of Abu Dhabi Executive Council General Secretariat*, 7th April 2010, available online, https://www.abudhabi.ae/portal/public/ShowProperty?nodeId=%2FWCC%2FADEGP_ND_157028_EN&_adf.ctrl-state=asqxktyab_4, date accessed, 18th March 2018.

179. 'Board of Directors', *Abu Dhabi Investment Council*, available online, http://www.adcouncil.ae/?page_id=18, date accessed, 18th March 2018.

180. WAM, 'UAE President Issues Law Restructuring Abu Dhabi Investment Council', *Press Releases*, Mubadala, 21st March 2018, available online, https://www.mubadala.com/en/news/uae-president-issues-law-restructuring-abu-dhabi-investment-council, date accessed, 23rd March 2018.

181. 'need to be able to distribute benefits to active supporters and coalition partners, to achieve passable economic performance in order to sustain mass acquiescence, and to maintain adequate coercive capacity to get through the inevitable times when they fail to deliver', B Geddes, 'What do We Know About Democratization After Twenty Years', p.138.

182. 'Our History', *Invest AD*, available online, http://www.investad.com, date accessed, 19th March 2018.

183. KA Alsweilem, A Cummine, M Rietveld, and K Tweedie, *A Comparative Study of Sovereign Investor Models: Sovereign Fund Profiles*, p.6.

184. http://www.investad.com/board-of-director.

185. Defined by Luis Roniger 'clientelism involves asymmetric but mutually ben-eficial, open-ended transactions based on the differential control by individu-als or groups over the access and flow of resources in stratified societies'. L Roniger, *Hierarchy and Trust in Modern Mexico and Brazil*, Praeger, London, 2002, p.1, in S Hertog, *Princes, Brokers, and Bureaucrats: Oil and the State in Saudi Arabia*, p.21.

186. 'Oil, in other words, created great leeway to accommodate elites in various arenas but also permitted the creation—and funding—of important islands of bureaucratic efficiency, vertically linked to the Al Saud and no one else'. Ibid, p.17.

187. 'Our History', *Mubadala*, available online, https://www.mubadala.com/en/who-we-are/our-history, date accessed, 19th March 2018.

188. 'International Petroleum Investment Company', Credit Research, *Unicredit*, 8th March 2011, available online, https://www.research.unicreditgroup.eu/DocsKey/credit_docs_2011_114693.ashx?EXT=pdf&KEY=n03ZZLYZf5m iL7MI684NjxlHtzYjzK-LBjvcijOr3ys=, date accessed, 19th March 2018.

189. C Davidson, *Abu Dhabi: Oil and Beyond*, p.75.

190. 'Mubadala Investment Company: A Global Champion for Economic Growth in Abu Dhabi', *Mubadala*, 21st January 2017, available online, https://www.mubadala.com/en/ipic-mubadala-merger, date accessed, 19th March 2018.

191. J Everington, 'Boardroom reshuffle at IPIC', *The National*, 22nd April 2015, available online, https://www.thenational.ae/business/boardroom-reshuffle-at-ipic-1.22512, date accessed, 19th March 2018.

192. B Hope, 'Alleged 1MDB Co-Conspirators Sentenced to Prison', *Wall Street Journal*, available online, https://www.wsj.com/articles/alleged-1mdb-co-conspirators-sentenced-to-prison-11560677550, date accessed, 6th June 2021.

193. For more on this refer to T Wright and B Hope, *Billion Dollar Whale: The Man Who Fooled Wall Street, Hollywood, and the World*, Hachette Books, London, 2018.

194. Due to the fact that the IPIC only released its first 'consolidated financial state-ments in 2007', and that no other information was released pertaining to the IPIC board of directors, there can only be an illustration of the last known directors. 'Financial Information and Reports', Mubdala, available online, https://www.mubadala.com/en/investors, date accessed, 23rd March 2018.

195. 'UAE Energy Minister is New MD of Abu Dhabi's IPIC After Board Revamp', *Reuters*, 22nd April 2015, available online, https://www.reuters.com/article/emirates-ipic/uae-energy-minister-is-new-md-of-abu-dhabis-ipic-after-board-revamp-idUSL5N0XJ5AG20150422, date accessed, 19th March 2018.

196. KA Alsweilem, A Cummine, M Rietveld, and K Tweedie, *A Comparative Study of Sovereign Investor Models: Sovereign Fund Profiles*, p.7.

197. 'Our Organisational Structure', Annual Review 2016, *Mubadala*, Abu Dhabi, available online, https://www.mubadala.com/annual-review-2016/en/our-leadership, date accessed, 19th March 2018.

198. 'Board of Directors', *Mubadala*, available online, https://www.mubadala. com/en/who-we-are/board-of-directors, date accessed, 22nd March 2018.

199. S Bazoobandi, *The Political Economy of the Gulf Sovereign Wealth Funds*, pp.91– 96. KA Alsweilem, A Cummine, M Rietveld, and K Tweedie, *A Comparative Study of Sovereign Investor Models: Sovereign Fund Profiles*, p.7.

200. C Davidson, *Abu Dhabi: Oil and Beyond*, pp.80–81.

201. Data gathered from Appendix 12: Evolution of Mubadala Leadership 2008– 2018.

202. S Hertog, *Prince, Brokers, and Bureaucrats: Oil and the State in Saudi Arabia*, p.28.

203. 'Annual Report 2011', *Mubadala*, 2011.

204. 'His Excellency Dr. Sultan bin Ahmed Sultan al Jaber', *United Arab Emirates The Cabinet*, available online, https://uaecabinet.ae/en/details/cabinet-members/his-excellency-dr-sultan-bin-ahmad-sultan-al-jaber, date accessed, 23rd March 2018.

205. 'ADSB—The Company', *Abu Dhabi Ship Building (ADSB)*, available online, http://www.adsb.ae/team/homaid-abdulla-al-shimmari/, date accessed, 23rd March 2018.

206. 'Annual Report 2009', *Mubadala*, 2009.

207. 'Homaid al Shimmari', *Mubadala*, available online, https://www.mubadala. com/en/who-we-are/investment-committee/homaid-al-shimmari, date accessed, 23rd March 2018.

208. H Van Der Meulen, *The Role of Tribal and Kinship Ties in the Politics of the UAE*, p.193.

209. 'Defence Secretary Meets Abu Dhabi Crown Prince', *Ministry of Defence and The Rt Hon Sir Michael Fallon MP*, 30th October 2014, available online, https://www.gov.uk/government/news/defence-secretary-meets-abu-dhabi-crown-prince, date accessed, 23rd March 2018.

210. 'Sheikh Khalifa Approves The New 12th Cabinet of the United Arab Emirates', *United Arab Emirates: The Cabinet*, available online, https://www.uaecabinet. ae/en/details/news/sheikh-khalifa-approves-the-new-12th-cabinet-of-the-united-arab-emirates, date accessed, 23rd March 2018. He had also previously served as Secretary General of the Abu Dhabi Executive Council from 2004– 2011. He was since removed from this position by Khalifa bin Zayed when he appointed Ahmed Mubarak al Mazrouei to the position as Secretary General. 'Khalifa Appoints Ahmed al Mazrouei as Secretary General of Abu Dhabi's Executive Council', *WAM*, 23rd October 2011, available online, http://wam. ae/ar/servlet/Satellite?c=WamLocEnews&cid=1289996157259&pagename =WAM%2FWAM_E_Layout&parent=Collection&parentid=113509 9399983, date accessed, 23rd March 2018.

211. H Van Der Meulen, *The Role of Tribal and Kinship Ties in the Politics of the UAE*, p.194.

212. H Van Der Meulen, *The Role of Tribal and Kinship Ties in the Politics of the UAE*, p.164.

213. WAM, 'Khalifa Issues Emiri Decree on Abu Dhabi Accountability and Housing Authorities, Executive Committee of Abu Dhabi', *Emirates 24/7*, 19th February 2017, available online, https://www.emirates247.com/news/government/khalifa-issues-emiri-decrees-on-abu-dhabi-accountability-and-housing-authorities-executive-committee-of-abu-dhabi-2017–02–19–1.648389, date accessed, 23rd March 2018.

214. 'Member Detail', *General Secretariat of the Executive Council*, available online, https://www.ecouncil.ae/en/ADGovernment/Pages/MemberDetail.aspx?mid=7, date accessed, 23rd March 2018.

215. 'Guiding Principles', *Emirates Investment Authority*, available online, http://www.eia.gov.ae, date accessed, 23rd March 2018.

216. S Bazoobandi, *The Political Economy of the Gulf Sovereign Wealth Funds*, p.96.

217. I Bremmer, 'State Capitalism Comes of Age: The End of the Free Market?', p.44.

218. K Almezaini, 'Private Sector Actors in the UAE and Their Role in the Process of Economic and Political Reform', in S Hertog, G Luciani, and M Valeri (eds.), *Business Politics in the Middle East*, p.65.

219. E Bellin, *The Political-Economic Conundrum: The Affinity of Economic and Political Reform in the Middle East and North Africa*, p.7.

220. S Hertog, *The Private Sector and Reform in the Gulf Cooperation Council*, p.40.

6. INDUSTRIAL CONTROL

1. A Giddens, *The Consequences of Modernity*, Polity Press, Stamford, 1990, p.76.

2. I Bremmer, *The End of the Free Market: Who Wins the War Between States and Corporations?* Portfolio/Penguin, New York, 2010, p.52.

3. A Giddens, *The Consequences of Modernity*, Polity Press, Stamford, 1990, p.60.

4. M Hvidt, *Economic Diversification in GCC Countries: Past Records and Future Trends*, Kuwait Programme on Development, Governance and Globalisation in the Gulf States, London School of Economics and Political Science, January 2013, p.9. According to the United Nations (UN), there are 21 categories to the International Standard Industrial Classification (ISIC). 'Broad Structure', *International Standard Industrial Classification of all Economic Activities*, Department of Economic and Social Affairs, United Nations, Revision 4, New York, 2008, p.43.

5. M Hvidt, *Economic Diversification in GCC Countries: Past Records and Future Trends*, Kuwait Programme on Development, Governance and Globalisation in the Gulf States, London School of Economics and Political Science, January 2013, p.9.

6. M Gray, 'A Theory of "Late Rentierism" in the Arab States of the Gulf', *Occasional Paper No.7*, Center for International and Regional Studies, Georgetown University School of Foreign Service in Qatar, 2011, p.13.

7. PW Moore, 'Rents and Late Development in the Arab World', *American Political Science Association*, 5th September 2004.

8. G Gause, *Oil Monarchies: Domestic and Security Challenges in the Arab Gulf States*, Council on Foreign Relations Press, New York, 1994.

9. SD Krasner, *Structural Conflict: The Third World Against Global Liberalism*, University of California Press, London, 1985; GJ Ikenberry, 'The State and Strategies of International Adjustment, *World Politics*, Vol.39, No.1, October, 1986; J Migdal, *Strong Societies and Weak States: State-Society Relations and State Capabilities in the Third World*, Princeton University Press, Princeton, 1988.

10. R Ghazal, 'When Abu Dhabi had 30 cars', *The National*, 3rd November 2011, available online, https://www.thenational.ae/uae/when-abu-dhabi-had-30-cars-1.432812, date accessed, 29th January 2019.

11. 'United Arab Emirates', *World Health Organisation (WHO)*, available online, https://www.who.int/violence_injury_prevention/road_safety_status/2013/country_profiles/united_arab_emirates.pdf?ua=1, date accessed, 2nd February 2019.

12. A Giddens, *The Consequences of Modernity*, Polity Press, Cambridge, 1992, p.76.

13. Anthony Giddens adds to this observation by stating that 'modern industry is intrinsically based on divisions of labour, not only on the level of job tasks but on that of regional specialisation in terms of type of industry, skills, and the production of raw materials', A Giddens, *The Consequences of Modernity*, Polity Press, Cambridge, 1992, p.76.

14. Financial investments include the purchase of Manchester City Football Club (MCFC) and the management of several overseas ports by Dubai Ports World (DP).

15. 'UAE-US Trade', *Embassy of the United Arab Emirates, Washington DC*, available online, https://www.uae-embassy.org/uae-us-relations/uae-us-trade, date accessed, 5th June 2021.

16. This argument is expanded to include any source of income. For example, while Jordan has no hydrocarbon reserves, the monarchy monopolises foreign aid for its own political benefit. S Greenwood, 'Jordan's "New Bargain:" The Political Economy of Regime Security', *Middle East Journal*, Vol. 57, No.2, Spring 2003, pp.248–68.

17. D Becker, 'Bonanza Development and the New Bourgeoisie', in D Becker at al, (eds.), *Postimperialism*, Lynne Reinner, Boulder, 1987, in NN Ayubi, *Over-Stating the Arab State: Politics and Society in the Middle East*, I B Tauris, London, 2006, p.235.

18. RE Looney, *Industrial Development and Diversification of the Arabian Gulf Economies*, JAI Press, London, 1994, p.239.

19. I Bremmer, *The End of the Free Market: Who Wins the War Between States and Corporations?*, Penguin, London, 2010, p.54.

20. M Gray, 'A Theory of "Late Rentierism" in the Arab States of the Gulf', *Occasional Paper No.7*, Center for International and Regional Studies, Georgetown University School of Foreign Service in Qatar, 2011, p.7.

21. M Chatelus and Y Schemeil, 'Towards a New Political Economy of State

Industrialization in the Arab Middle East', *International Journal of Middle East Studies*, Vol.16, 1984, in NN Ayubi, *Over-Stating the Arab State: Politics and Society in the Middle East*, I B Tauris, London, 2006, p.291.

22. Mark Gasiorowski furthers this argument by saying that 'in the absence of other sources of legitimation, a regime can often gain legitimacy by carrying out popular policies', MJ Gasiorowski, 'Regime Legitimacy and National Security: The Case of Pahlavi Iran', in EE Azar and E Moon (eds.), *National Security in the Third World: The Management of Internal and External Threats*, Center for International Development and Conflict, Edward Elgar Publishing, Aldershot, 1988, p.237.

23. I Bremmer, *The End of the Free Market: Who Wins the War Between States and Corporations?*, Portfolio, Penguin, London, 2010, p.52.

24. M Gray, 'A Theory of "Late Rentierism" in the Arab States of the Gulf', *Occasional Paper No.7*, Center for International and Regional Studies, Georgetown University School of Foreign Service in Qatar, 2011, pp.21–22.

25. NN Ayubi, *Over-Stating the Arab State: Politics and Society in the Middle East*, I B Tauris, London, 2006, p.336.

26. M Gray, 'A Theory of "Late Rentierism" in the Arab States of the Gulf', *Occasional Paper No.7*, Center for International and Regional Studies, Georgetown University School of Foreign Service in Qatar, 2011, p.32.

27. Saudi Vision 2030 is a NDP created and promoted by the then Deputy Crown Prince of Saudi Arabia Muhammad bin Salman. This was created with the intention of highlighting how Saudi Arabia was aiming to develop its industrial and economic base.

28. https://www.vision2021.ae/en.

29. https://www.ecouncil.ae/PublicationsEn/economic-vision-2030-full-versionEn.pdf.

30. https://www.dubaiplan2021.ae/dubai-plan-2021/.

31. https://www.dubaiplan2021.ae/dubai-plan-2021/.

32. https://www.ecouncil.ae/PublicationsEn/plan-abu-dhabi-full-version-EN.pdf.

33. S Salama, 'UAE Outlines National Development Plan', *Gulf News*, 27th November 2018, available online, https://gulfnews.com/uae/government/uae-outlines-national-development-plan-1.60609687, date accessed, 7th February 2019.

34. KC Ulrichsen, *The Politics of Economic Reform in the Arab Gulf States*, Centre for the Middle East, Rice University, 2016, p.13.

35. CM Davidson, 'The United Arab Emirates: Economy First, Politics Second', in J Teitelbaum (ed.), *Political Liberalization in the Persian Gulf*, Hurst & Co, London, 2009.

36. H Van Der Meulen, *The Role of Tribal and Kinship Ties in the Politics of the United Arab Emirates*, PhD Thesis, Tufts University, 1997, p.94.

37. C Davidson, *Abu Dhabi: Oil and Beyond*, Hurst & Co, London, 2009, p.124.

38. Khalifa bin Zayed al-Nahyan appointed his sons Sultan and Muhammad to the ADEC in 2007 but only the latter remains part of the Council.

39. In 2007 78% of the ADEC were Bani Yas tribesman (14/18), while there were 64% in 2010 (9/14), 60% in 2016 (9/15), and 63% in 2019 (12/19).

40. M Gray, 'A Theory of "Late Rentierism" in the Arab States of the Gulf', *Occasional Paper No.7*, Center for International and Regional Studies, Georgetown University School of Foreign Service in Qatar, 2011, p.25.

41. *Federal Law No.1 of 1979*, Ministry of Finance, available online, https://www.mof.gov.ae/Ar/lawsAndPolitics/govLaws/Documents/%201979%20اتحادي%20قانون الصناعة%20-%20شئون.pdf, date accessed, 12th March 2019.

42. FS Al Shamsi, 'Industrial Strategies and Change in the UAE During the 1980s', in A Abdekarim (ed.), *Change and Development in the Gulf*, Macmillan, London, 1999, p.83.

43. *ADNOC Group Sustainability Report 2015; Taking Innovation to New Heights*, ADNOC, 2015, p.8.

44. *ADNOC Group Sustainability Report 2015; Taking Innovation to New Heights*, ADNOC, 2015, p.15.

45. HM Kumar, 'ADNOC to Spend $5bn on Capacity', *Gulf News*, 29th October 2010, available online, https://gulfnews.com/business/energy/adnoc-to-spend-5b-on-capacity-1.703468, date accessed, 11th March 2019.

46. *ADNOC Group Sustainability Report 2015: Taking Innovation to New Heights*, ADNOC, 2015, p.30.

47. This is a short-term strategy, but the long-term issue must 'make use of oil revenues to create a viable economy that will sustain a relatively high level of income after the oil era'. AA Kubursi, *Oil, Industrialization and Development In The Arab Gulf States*, Croom Helm, London, 1984, p.3.

48. S Hertog, 'Lean and Mean: The New Breed of State-Owned Enterprises in the Gulf Monarchies', in JF Seznec and M Kirk (eds.), *Industrialization in the Gulf: A Socioeconomic Revolution*, Routledge, London, 2011.

49. 'Executive Management', *ADNOC*, available online, https://www.adnoc.ae/en/about-us/executive-management, date accessed, 12th March 2019.

50. 'Khalifa Appoints Sultan Al Jaber As Director-General of ADNOC', *WAM*, 15th February 2016, available online, http://wam.ae/en/details/1395291637840, date accessed, 14th March 2019.

51. E Crooks, 'Sultan Al Jaber: changing the mindset of a 50-year-old institution', *Financial Times*, 3rd March 2019, available online, https://www.ft.com/content/48884808-3a73-11e9-b72b-2c7f526ca5d0, date accessed, 14th March 2019.

52. President approves new structure of UAE Government', *WAM*, 5th July 2020, available online, https://www.wam.ae/en/details/1395302853277, date accessed, 20th August 2020.

53. 'ADNOC Awards China's CEFC 4% Interest in ADCO Onshore Concession', Press Release, *ADNOC*, 21st February 2017, available online, https://adnoc.ae/en/news-and-media/press-releases/adnoc-onshore/2017/adnoc-awards-china-cefc-interest-in-adco-onshore-concession, date accessed, 14th March 2019.

54. 'ADNOC signs offshore concession agreements with Total', *WAM*, 18th March 2018, available online, http://wam.ae/en/details/1395302675461, date accessed, 14th March 2019.

55. 'ADCOP successfully issues US$3 billion bond', *WAM*, 6th November 2017, available online, http://wam.ae/en/details/1395302644482, date accessed, 14th March 2019.

56. 'ADNOC Distribution revenue and profit increases in 2017', *WAM*, 14th February 2018, available online, http://wam.ae/en/details/1395302667456, date accessed, 14th March 2019.

57. 'ADNOC awards Eni-PTTEP Consortium two offshore exploration blocks', *WAM*, 12th January 2019, available online, http://wam.ae/en/details/139 5302731813, date accessed, 14th March 2019.

58. 'ADNOC, BHGE form strategic partnership to grow ADNOC Drilling into fully-integrated drilling and well construction business', *WAM*, 8th October 2018, available online, http://wam.ae/en/details/1395302712590, date accessed, 14th March 2019.

59. This is again noted by Matthew Gray as one of his pillars of late rentierism. '*Feature 4: An "energy-Driven" vs. an "Energy-Centric" Economy*', M Gray, 'A Theory of "Late Rentierism" in the Arab States of the Gulf', *Occasional Paper No.7*, Center for International and Regional Studies, Georgetown University School of Foreign Service in Qatar, 2011, p.30.

60. J Gnana and S Khan, 'Regional Petchems to Grow by 60% by 2050, says ADNOC CEO', *The National*, 23rd October 2018, available online, https://www.thenational.ae/business/energy/regional-petchems-to-grow-by-60-by-2050-says-adnoc-ceo-1.783468, date accessed, 14th March 2019.

61. 'ADNOC and Mubadala to Jointly Explore Global Investment and Growth Opportunities as ADNOC Expands its Downstream Footprint', Press Releases, *Mubadala*, 14th November 2018, available online, https://www.mubadala.com/en/news/adnoc-and-mubadala-jointly-explore-global-investment-and-growth-opportunities, date accessed, 14th March 2019.

62. 'UAE Economy Set For Dh165 billion petrochemical boost', *The National*, 14th May 2018, available online, https://www.thenational.ae/business/energy/uae-economy-set-for-dh165-billion-petrochemicals-boost-1.730304, date accessed, 14th March 2019.

63. F Rahman, 'ADNOC Unveils $45bn Expansion of Ruwais Complex', *Gulf News*, 13th May 2018, available online, https://gulfnews.com/business/energy/adnoc-unveils-45b-expansion-of-ruwais-complex-1.2220790, date accessed, 14th March 2019.

64. S Kerr, 'Adnoc plots $45bn downstream investment boost', *Financial Times*, 13th May 2018, available online, https://www.ft.com/content/092a2170–56aa-11e8-bdb7-f6677d2e1ce8, date accessed, 14th March 2018.

65. 'UAE Economy Set For Dh165 billion petrochemical boost', *The National*, 14th May 2018, available online, https://www.thenational.ae/business/energy/

uae-economy-set-for-dh165-billion-petrochemicals-boost-1.730304, date accessed, 14th March 2019.

66. 'ADNOC, Saudi Aramco and India Consortium sign framework agreement to explore US$44 billion mega refinery development', *WAM*, 25th June 2018, available online, http://wam.ae/en/details/1395302696036, date accessed, 14th March 2019.

67. The clearest example is Al Ruwais within the Abu Dhabi Emirate. J Dennehy, 'Ruwais 2.0: How ADNOC is Transforming Abu Dhabi's Oil Town into a Modern City', *The National*, 10th September 2018, available online, https://www.thenational.ae/uae/government/ruwais-2-0-how-adnoc-is-transforming-abu-dhabi-s-oil-town-into-a-modern-city-1.768875, date accessed, 25th March 2019.

68. This is further verified by ADNOC itself who state that 'We are one of the world's leading energy producers, and a primary catalyst for Abu Dhabi's growth and diversification'. 'About US', *ADNOC*, available online, https://www.adnoc.ae, date accessed, 14th March 2019.

69. 'World Oil Demand', Oil Market Report, *International Energy Agency*, 15th March 2019, available online, https://www.iea.org/oilmarketreport/omrpublic/, date accessed, 25th March 2019.

70. *Sustainability Report 2015*, Emirates Nuclear Energy Corporation (ENEC), Abu Dhabi, 2015, available online, https://www.enec.gov.ae/doc/enec-sustainability-report-2015–58a2bac9d5bd5.pdf, date accessed, 30th May 2019.

71. 'Barakh nuclear power plant connects to UAE grid for first time', *The National*, 19th August 2020, available online, https://www.thenational.ae/uae/government/barakah-nuclear-power-plant-connects-to-uae-grid-for-first-time-1.1065538, date accessed, 20th August 2020.

72. M Kamrava (ed.), *The Nuclear Question in the Middle East*, Hurst & Co, London, 2012.

73. CM Davidson, 'The United Arab Emirates: Economy First, Politics Second', in J Teitelbaum (ed.), *Political Liberalization in the Persian Gulf*, Hurst & Co, London, 2009.

74. M Herb, *The Wages of Oil: Parliaments and Economic Development in Kuwait and the UAE*.

75. NA Sultan, BD Metcalfe, and D Weir, 'Building the Foundation for a Post-Oil Era: The Case of the GCC Countries', NA Sultan, BD Metcalfe, and D Weir (eds.), *The New Post-Oil Arab Gulf; Managing People and Wealth*, Saqi Books, London, 2011.

76. J Everington, 'FGB and National Bank of Abu Dhabi choose merged name: First Abu Dhabi Bank', *The National*, 2nd April 2017, available online, https://www.thenational.ae/business/fgb-and-national-bank-of-abu-dhabi-choose-merged-name-first-abu-dhabi-bank-1.643908, date accessed, 18th March 2019.

77. 'Investor Presentation', *First Abu Dhabi Bank (FAB)*, February 2019, available online, https://www.bankfab.com/-/media/fabgroup/home/about-fab/

investor-relations/pdfs/fab-investor-presentation-feb-2019.pdf?view=1, date accessed, 25ᵗʰ March 2019.

78. S Khan, 'UAE banks ADCB and UNB agree on merger and takeover of Al Hilal', *The National*, 29ᵗʰ January 2019, available online, https://www.thenational.ae/business/economy/uae-banks-adcb-and-unb-agree-on-merger-and-take-over-of-al-hilal-1.819488, date accessed, 18ᵗʰ March 2019.

79. The National Staff, 'Abu Dhabi Approves Merger of Universities and Billions in Projects', *The National*, 13ᵗʰ October 2016, available online, https://www.thenational.ae/uae/government/abu-dhabi-approves-merger-of-universities-and-billions-in-projects-1.192240, date accessed, 18ᵗʰ March 2019.

80. 'UAE President Issues Law Establishing Abu Dhabi Development Holding Company', *WAM*, 4ᵗʰ March 2018, available online, http://wam.ae/en/details/1395302671868, date accessed, 30ᵗʰ May 2019.

81. H Sayegh and A Cornwell, 'Abu Dhabi's Airports, Ports and Power Firms Moved to New Holding Company', *Reuters*, 29ᵗʰ May 2019, available online, https://www.reuters.com/article/abu-dhabi-services-holding-co/abu-dhabis-airports-ports-and-power-firms-moved-to-new-holding-company-idUSL8N2350N0, date accessed, 30ᵗʰ May 2019.

82. 'Mohammed al Suwaidi Appointed CEO of Abu Dhabi Development Holding', WAM, 19ᵗʰ May 2019, http://wam.ae/en/details/1395302763455, date accessed, 30ᵗʰ May 2019.

83. 'UAE President Issues Law Establishing Abu Dhabi Development Holding Company', *WAM*, 4ᵗʰ March 2018, available online, http://wam.ae/en/details/1395302671868, date accessed, 30ᵗʰ May 2019.

84. Reuters claim that Suwaidi is the Managing Director, but this is in contrast to WAM, the UAE's official news agency.

85. S Hertog, 'Public Industry as Tool of Rentier Economy Diversification: The GCC Case', in G Luciani (ed.), *Resource Blessed: Diversification and the Gulf Development Model*, Gerlach Press, Germany, Gulf Research Center, 2012, pp.115–139.

86. K Almezaini, 'Private Sector Actors in the UAE and their Role in the Process of Economic and Political Reform', in S Hertog, G Luciani, and M Valeri (eds.), *Business Politics in the Middle East*, p.50.

87. Khaled Almezaini looks into this in more detail. K Almezaini, 'Private Sector Actors in the UAE and their Role in the Process of Economic and Political Reform', in S Hertog, G Luciani, and M Valeri (eds.), *Business Politics in the Middle East*.

88. 'The Impact of SMEs on the UAE's Economy', *UAE Government*, 23ʳᵈ August 2017, available online, https://www.government.ae/en/information-and-services/business/crowdfunding/the-impact-of-smes-on-the-uae-economy, date accessed, 25ᵗʰ March 2015.

89. CM Davidson, 'The United Arab Emirates: Economy First, Politics Second', in J Teitelbaum (ed.), *Political Liberalization in the Persian Gulf*, Hurst & Co, London, 2009.

90. K Almezaini, 'Private Sector Actors in the UAE and their Role in the Process of Economic and Political Reform', in S Hertog, G Luciani, and M Valeri (eds.), *Business Politics in the Middle East*, p.54.

91. S Bazoobandi, *The Political Economy of the Gulf Sovereign Wealth Funds: A Case Study of Iran, Kuwait, Saudi Arabia and the United Arab Emirates*, p.75.

92. S Bazoobandi, *The Political Economy of the Gulf Sovereign Wealth Funds: A Case Study of Iran, Kuwait, Saudi Arabia and the United Arab Emirates*, p.93.

93. P Nanakorn, *The Offset Programme as a Development Tool in the UAE*, PhD Thesis, University of Exeter, 2009, p.154.

94. It is noted by Pattarnawan Nanakorn that by 2008 there were at least 33 successful joint ventures originating from the offset program. P Nanakorn, *The Offset Programme as a Development Tool in the UAE*, PhD Thesis, University of Exeter, 2009, p.142.

95. 'History and Changes in the UAE Offset Program', *Blenheim Capital Partners*, 6–7 September 2011.

96. 'Tawazun Economic Program Guideline', *Tawazun Economic Council (TEC)*, 2015/2016 Edition, available online, https://tec.tawazun.ae/wp-content/uploads/sites/2/2016/06/Tawazun-Economic-Program-Guidelines-2015-2016.pdf, date accessed, 29th March 2019.

97. 'Tawazun Economic Program Guideline', *Tawazun Economic Council (TEC)*, 2015/2016 Edition, available online, https://tec.tawazun.ae/wp-content/uploads/sites/2/2016/06/Tawazun-Economic-Program-Guidelines-2015-2016.pdf, date accessed, 29th March 2019, p.4.

98. 'About Us', *Dolphin Project*, available online, http://www.dolphinenergy.com/about, date accessed, 26th March 2019.

99. 'Better Together', *The Business Year*, UAE 2018, available online, https://www.thebusinessyear.com/uae-2018/better-together/interview, date accessed, 26th March 2019.

100. 'Yahsat Completes Thuraya Acquisition and Appoints New CEO', Press Release, *Mubadala*, 5th August 2018, available online, https://www.mubadala.com/en/news/yahsat-completes-thuraya-acquisition-and-appoints-new-ceo, date accessed, 30th March 2019.

101. 'Emirates Global Aluminium Officially Incorporated', Press Release, *Mubadala*, 7th April 2014, available online, https://www.mubadala.com/en/news/emirates-global-aluminium-officially-incorporated, date accessed, 30th March 2019.

102. 'Advanced Technology Investment Company is integrated into Mubadala Development Company', Press Release, *Mubadala*, 16th February 2011, available online, https://www.mubadala.com/en/news/advanced-technology-investment-company-integrated-mubadala-development-company, date accessed, 30th March 2019.

103. 'Russian Direct Investment Fund and Mubadala Establish co-investment program', Press Release, *Mubadala*, 21st June 2013, available online, https://www.mubadala.com/en/news/russian-direct-investment-fund-and-mubadala-establish-co-investment-fund, date accessed, 30th March 2019.

104. 'Mubadala Development Company, China Development Bank Capital (CDBD), and China's State Administration of Foreign Exchange (SAFE) establish UAE-China Joint Investment Fund', Press Release, *Mubadala*, 14ᵗʰ December 2015, available online, https://www.mubadala.com/en/news/mubadala-development-company-china-development-bank-capital-cdbc-and-chinas-state, date accessed, 30ᵗʰ March 2019.

105. 'Mubadala has invested $100 billion in U.S., eyes China: deputy CEO', *Reuters*, 10ᵗʰ December 2019, available online, https://www.reuters.com/article/us-emirates-investment-mubadala-idUSKBN1YE0GN, date accessed 5 June 2021.

106. 'Mubadala to launch $400 million European tech fund', Press Release, *Mubadala*, 13ᵗʰ June 2018, available online, https://www.mubadala.com/en/news/mubadala-launch-400-million-european-tech-fund, date accessed, 30ᵗʰ March 2019.

107. 'Masdar Invests in £1.5bn Offshore Wind Farm; Expands its Presence in the UK Wind Energy Market', Press Release, *Mubadala*, 25ᵗʰ September 2014, available online, https://www.mubadala.com/en/news/masdar-invests-15bn-offshore-wind-farm-expands-its-presence-uk-wind-energy-market, date accessed, 30ᵗʰ March 2019.

108. 'Mubadala Petroleum Starts Production at its third oil field in Thailand', Press Release, *Mubadala*, 18ᵗʰ June 2015, available online, https://www.mubadala.com/en/news/mubadala-petroleum-starts-production-its-third-oil-field-thailand, date accessed, 20ᵗʰ March 2019.

109. 'Mubadala and Trafigura create joint venture to invest in base metals', Press Release, *Mubadala*, 29ᵗʰ June 2015, available online, https://www.mubadala.com/en/news/mubadala-and-trafigura-create-joint-venture-invest-base-metals, date accessed, 30ᵗʰ March 2019.

110. 'Mubadala Petroleum completes the acquisition of a 20 percent interest in the Nour Concession in Egypt', Press Release, *Mubadala*, 9ᵗʰ December 2018, available online, https://www.mubadala.com/en/news/mubadala-petroleum-completes-acquisition-20-percent-interest-nour-concession-egypt, date accessed, 30ᵗʰ March 2019.

111. 'Mubadala puts R&D front and Center with multi-million AED commitment', Press Release, *Mubadala*, 14ᵗʰ November 2017, available online, https://www.mubadala.com/en/news/mubadala-puts-rd-front-and-center-multi-million-aed-commitment, date accessed, 30ᵗʰ March 2019.

112. 'ADEC, Boeing, and Mubadala launch afterschool program for UAE Youth', Press Release, *Mubadala*, 17ᵗʰ April 2016, available online, https://www.mubadala.com/en/news/adec-boeing-and-mubadala-launch-afterschool-program-uae-youth, date accessed, 30ᵗʰ March 2019.

113. 'With the support of Abu Dhabi Education Council, Mubadala and BAE Systems sign Cooperative Agreement to develop future Emirati talent', Press Release, *Mubadala*, 14ᵗʰ September 2015, available online, https://www.mubadala.com/en/news/support-abu-dhabi-education-council-mubadala-

and-bae-systems-sign-cooperative-agreement-develop, date accessed, 30th March 2019.

114. '42 Emirati technicians graduate from Strata's aerostructures training program', Press Release, *Mubadala*, 8th September 2014, available online, https://www.mubadala.com/en/news/42-emirati-technicians-graduate-stratas-aerostructures-training-program, date accessed, 30th March 2019.

115. 'Abu Dhabi Ship Building Launches Emirati Trainee Program', Press Release, *Mubadala*, 26th October 2016, available online, https://www.mubadala.com/en/news/abu-dhabi-ship-building-launches-emirati-trainee-program, date accessed, 30th March 2019.

116. 'Emirates Defence Industries Company Launched', *Mubadala*, 2nd December 2014, available online, https://www.mubadala.com/en/news/emirates-defence-industries-company-launched, date accessed, 18th April 2019.

117. 'Financial Information Reports', *Abu Dhabi Ship Building*, available online, http://www.adsb.ae/the-company/investors-information/financial-information-reports/, date accessed, 18th April 2019.

118. D Black, 'Warships made in Abu Dhabi to be Sold Abroad', *The National*, 16th February 2012, available online, https://www.thenational.ae/business/warships-made-in-abu-dhabi-to-be-sold-abroad-1.381429, date accessed, 18th April 2019.

119. *Military Balance 2021*, The International Institute for Strategic Studies (IISS), Routledge, London, 2021, P.371.

120. ASC Staff, 'Abu Dhabi Ship Building and Babcock sign MoU', *Middle East Logistics*, 16th September 2013, available online, https://www.logisticsmiddleeast.com/article-9191-abu-dhabi-ship-building-and-babcock-sign-mou, date accessed, 18th April 2019.

121. 'Strategic Marine and Abu Dhabi Ship Building Sign MoU', *Strategic Marine*, available online, http://www.strategicmarine.com/strategic-marine-and-abu-dhabi-ship-building-sign-mou/, date accessed, 18th April 2019.

122. 'Abu Dhabi Ship Building, Italy's Leonardo team up for naval collaboration', *Naval Today*, 19th February 2019, available online, https://navaltoday.com/2019/02/19/abu-dhabi-ship-building-italys-leonardo-team-up-for-naval-collaboration/, date accessed, 18th April 2019.

123. 'Fincantieri and Abu Dhabi Shipbuilding: Future Collaboration in the UAE', *Fincantieri*, 21st February 2019, available online, https://www.fincantieri.com/en/media/press-releases/2019/fincantieri-and-abu-dhabi-shipbuilding-future-collaboration-in-the-uae/, date accessed, 18th April 2019.

124. 'DynCorp International Awarded Maintenance Contract With UAE Land Forces', *DynCorp*, 21st December 2006, Virginia, available online, http://ir.dyn-intl.com/static-files/d94696cf-4820–45da-b164–08fab2402af5, date accessed, 18th April 2019.

125. 'DynCorp International Awarded Maintenance Contract With UAE Land

Forces', *DynCorp*, 21st December 2006, Virginia, available online, http://
ir.dyn-intl.com/static-files/d94696cf-4820–45da-b164–08fab2402af5, date
accessed, 18th April 2019.

126. 'A Message From Our CEO', *AMMROC*, available online, https://ammroc.
ae, date accessed, 18th April 2019.

127. 'BAE Systems, Ammroc to Open MRO facility in Al Ain', *Trade Arabia*, 18th
February 2019, available online, http://tradearabia.com/news/IND_351233.
html, date accessed, 18th April 2019.

128. M Selinger, 'Edge takes over AMMROC', *Jane's*, 22nd July 2020, available
online, https://www.janes.com/defence-news/news-detail/edge-takes-over-
ammroc, date accessed, 20th August 2020.

129. 'Mubadala Launches Bayanat for Mapping & Surveying', *Mubadala*, 15th
February 2011, Available online, https://www.mubadala.com/en/news/
mubadala-launches-bayanat-mapping-surveying, date accessed, 18th April 2019.

130. 'Tawazun Economic Program Industrial Development Unit', *Tawazun*,
Presentation, Abu Dhabi, July 2012.

131. 'Aerospace and defence sector diversifying Abu Dhabi's economy', *Oxford
Business Group*, available online, https://oxfordbusinessgroup.com/overview/
set-fair-sectors'-contribution-economic-diversification-set-grow-further, date
accessed, 18th April 2019.

132. 'Emirates Defence Industries Company Launched', Press Release, *Mubadala*,
2nd December 2014, available online, https://www.mubadala.com/en/news/
emirates-defence-industries-company-launched, date accessed, 30th March
2019.

133. 'EDIC adds five new defence services companies announces senior management', Press Release, *Mubadala*, 21st February 2015, available online, https://
www.mubadala.com/en/news/edic-adds-five-new-defence-services-compa-
nies-announces-senior-management, date accessed, 30th March 2019.

134. 'Aerospace and defence sector diversifying Abu Dhabi's economy', *Oxford
Business Group*, available online, https://oxfordbusinessgroup.com/overview/
set-fair-sectors'-contribution-economic-diversification-set-grow-further, date
accessed, 18th April 2019.

135. 'About Us', *EDIC*, available online, https://edic.ae/#about, date accessed,
18th April 2019.

136. A Helou, 'UAE launches 'Edge' conglomerate to address its "antiquated military industry"', *Defense News*, 6th November 2019, available online, https://
www.defensenews.com/digital-show-dailies/dubai-air-show/2019/11/06/
uae-launches-edge-conglomerate-to-address-its-antiquated-military-industry/,
date accessed, 20th August 2020.

137. 'Vision & Mission', *Tawazun*, available online, https://www.tawazun.ae/
home/about-us/vision-mission/, date accessed, 18th April 2019.

138. K Almezaini, 'Private Sector Actors in the UAE and their Role in the Process

of Economic and Political Reform', in S Hertog, G Luciani, and M Valeri (eds.), *Business Politics in the Middle East*, p.45.

139. M Gray, 'A Theory of "Late Rentierism" in the Arab States of the Gulf', *Occasional Paper No.7*, Center for International and Regional Studies, Georgetown University School of Foreign Service in Qatar, 2011, p.35.

APPENDICES

1. Ibid.
2. Frauke Heard-Bey refers to 10 of the 20 prominent sections of the Bani Yas in F Heard-Bey, p.412.
3. H Van Der Muelen, *The Role of Tribal and Kinship Ties in the Politics of the United Arab Emirates*.
4. AB Rugh, *The Political Culture of Leadership in the United Arab Emirates*, pp.30–71.
5. Ibid, p.37.
6. JG Lorrimer, *Gazetteer of the Persian Gulf, Oman, and Central Arabia*, p.464.
7. H Tammam, *Zayid bin Sultan: The Leader on the March*, Dai Nippon Printing, Tokyo, 1983.
8. AdL Rush (ed.), *Buraimi Memorial*, SA Memorial, Vol.1: 31, 1991, Slough, in ibid, p.35.
9. Ibid, p.38; JG Lorrimer, *Gazetteer of the Persian Gulf, Oman, and Central Arabia, Geographical, Statistical and Historical Edition*, Slough, 1986, p.765.
10. AdL Rush (ed.), *Buraimi Memorial*, p.55.
11. AB Rugh, *The Political Culture of Leadership in the United Arab Emirates*, p.43.
12. JG Lorrimer, *Gazetteer of the Persian Gulf, Oman, and Central Arabia*, p.768.
13. P Lienhardt, *Shaikhdoms of Eastern Arabia*, p.180.
14. AB Rugh, *The Political Culture of Leadership in the United Arab Emirates*, p.63.
15. P Lienhardt, *Shaikhdoms of Eastern Arabia*, p.181.
16. AB Rugh, *The Political Culture of Leadership in the United Arab Emirates*, p.62.
17. AdL Rush (ed.), *Buraimi Memorial*, p.92.
18. CD Davidson, 'After Shaikh Zayed: The Politics of Succession in Abu Dhabi and the UAE'.
19. 'Al Dhafra Air Base', *Air Force Central Command*, available online, https://www.afcent.af.mil/Units/380th-Air-Expeditionary-Wing/News/Tag/95930/al-dhafra-air-base/, date accessed, 8th June 2019.
20. 'Sheikh Mohammed bin Rashid attends air cadet graduation—in pictures', *The National*, 4th December 2017, available online, https://www.thenational.ae/uae/government/sheikh-mohammed-bin-rashid-attends-air-cadet-graduation-in-pictures-1.681396, date accessed, 8th June 2019.
21. K Shaheen, 'Liwa base extends defence reach', *The National*, 6th January 2011, available online, https://www.thenational.ae/uae/liwa-base-extends-defence-reach-1.564805, date accessed, 8th June 2019.

22. 'Iomax delivers first production Archangel to the UAE', *Arabian Aerospace*, 29th August 2015, available online, https://www.arabianaerospace.aero/iomax-delivers-first-production-archangel-to-the-uae.html, date accessed, 8th June 2019.

23. K Shaheen, 'Liwa base extends defence reach', *The National*, 6th January 2011, available online, https://www.thenational.ae/uae/liwa-base-extends-defence-reach-1.564805, date accessed, 8th June 2019.

24. 'Construction of Buildings for Armed Forces at Qusaiwera Air Base', *GISCO*, available online, http://www.gisco.ae/projects/construction-buildings-armed-forces-at-qusaiwera-airbase, date accessed, 8th June 2019.

25. D Cenciotti, 'The F-35 Plays Starring Role in Exercise "INIOCHOS 2019" in Greece', *The Aviationist*, 12th April 2019, available online, https://theaviation-ist.com/2019/04/12/the-f-35-plays-the-starring-role-in-exercise-iniochos-2019-in-greece/, date accessed, 8th June 2019.

26. J Nicholson, 'UAE Ground Forces unification celebrations at Zayed Military City—in pictures', *The National*, 11th January 2016, https://www.thenational.ae/uae/government/uae-ground-forces-unification-celebrations-at-zayed-military-city-in-pictures-1.187398, date accessed, 8th June 2019.

27. G Duncan, 'UAE traffic: Many roads across the Emirates slow this morning', *The National*, 30th September 2018, available online, https://www.thenational.ae/uae/transport/uae-traffic-many-roads-across-the-emirates-slow-this-morning-1.775324, date accessed, 8th June 2019.

28. 'Completed Projects; Command of Military Works Projects [CMW]), *Capriole Construction Co.LLC*, available online, http://www.capriole-construction.com/completed_projects.html, date accessed, 8th June 2019.

29. 'Projects', *Okaz Construction*, available online, http://okaz-uae.com/projects/, date accessed, 8th June 2019.

30. 'Sheikh Mohammed watches over UAE national service military exercise—in pictures', *The National*, 8th April 2018, available online, https://www.thenational.ae/uae/government/sheikh-mohammed-watches-over-uae-national-service-military-exercise-in-pictures-1.719867, date accessed, 8th June 2019.

31. 'Completed Projects; Command of Military Works Projects [CMW]), *Capriole Construction Co.LLC*, available online, http://www.capriole-construction.com/completed_projects.html, date accessed, 8th June 2019.

32. 'Completed Projects; Command of Military Works Projects [CMW]), *Capriole Construction Co.LLC*, available online, http://www.capriole-construction.com/completed_projects.html, date accessed, 8th June 2019.

33. 'Sheikh Mohammed visits military training camp', *The National*, 6th March 2017, available online, https://www.thenational.ae/uae/government/sheikh-mohammed-visits-military-training-camp-1.53577, date accessed, 8th June 2019.

34. 'Our Projects', *Time Electro & Contracting Company W.L.L*, available online,

http://www.timeelectro.ae/projectList.php?cat=14, date accessed, 8ᵗʰ June 2019.

35. 'Sheikh Mohammed bin Zayed visits military recruits at Al Manama Camp', *WAM*, 2ⁿᵈ November 2014, available online, http://wam.ae/en/details/1395271800616, date accessed, 8ᵗʰ June 2019.

36. 'Government Projects; General Head Quarters Armed Forces', *Al Badr Carpentry (ABC) L.L.C.*, available online, http://www.albadarcarpentryllc.com/general_head_quarters_armed_forces.html, date accessed, 8ᵗʰ June 2019.

37. 'Military Camps', *Al Jazirah Equipment & Technical Services*, available online, http://www.jetsemirates.ae/military.html, date accessed, 8ᵗʰ June 2019.

38. 'Military Camps', *Al Jazirah Equipment & Technical Services*, available online, http://www.jetsemirates.ae/military.html, date accessed, 8ᵗʰ June 2019.

39. 'Projects', *Okaz Construction*, available online, http://okaz-uae.com/projects/, date accessed, 8ᵗʰ June 2019.

40. 'Military Camps', *Al Jazirah Equipment & Technical Services*, available online, http://www.jetsemirates.ae/military.html, date accessed, 8ᵗʰ June 2019.

41. 'Military Camps', *Al Jazirah Equipment & Technical Services*, available online, http://www.jetsemirates.ae/military.html, date accessed, 8ᵗʰ June 2019.

42. T Ramavarman, 'French Naval Base Opens Today', *Khaleej Times*, 27ᵗʰ May 2009, available online, https://www.khaleejtimes.com/article/20090526/ARTICLE/305269881/1002, date accessed, 8ᵗʰ June 2019.

43. 'Naval Base Ghantoot', *Zublin Strabag*, available online, https://www.strabag-international.com/databases/internet/_public/content30.nsf/web30?Openagent&id=F484D4F1EF792DA8C125811B005682CC, date accessed, 8ᵗʰ June 2019.

44. 'Our Projects', *Time Electro & Contracting Company W.L.L*, available online, http://www.timeelectro.ae/projectList.php?cat=14, date accessed, 8ᵗʰ June 2019.

45. 'Government Projects; General Head Quarters Armed Forces', *Al Badr Carpentry (ABC) L.L.C.*, available online, http://www.albadarcarpentryllc.com/general_head_quarters_armed_forces.html, date accessed, 8ᵗʰ June 2019.

46. 'Projects', *Okaz Construction*, available online, http://okaz-uae.com/projects/, date accessed, 8ᵗʰ June 2019.

47. 'Government Projects; General Head Quarters Armed Forces', *Al Badr Carpentry (ABC) L.L.C.*, available online, http://www.albadarcarpentryllc.com/general_head_quarters_armed_forces.html, date accessed, 8ᵗʰ June 2019.

48. M Wallin, *U.S. Military Bases and Facilities in the Middle East*, American Security Project, June 2018.

49. 'United Arab Emirates', *The Military Balance 2009*, Routledge, London, 2009, p.269.

50. K Shaheen, 'Liwa base extends defence reach', *The National*, 6ᵗʰ January 2011, available online, https://www.thenational.ae/uae/liwa-base-extends-defence-reach-1.564805, date accessed, 8ᵗʰ June 2019.

51. 'United Arab Emirates', *The Military Balance 2009*, p.269.

52. Ibid.

53. 'Completed Projects; Command of Military Works Projects [CMW]', *Capriole Construction Co.LLC*, available online, http://www.capriole-construction.com/completed_projects.html, date accessed, 8th June 2019.

54. https://www.mocaf.gov.ae/en

55. https://www.moccae.gov.ae/en/home.aspx

56. https://www.mocd.gov.ae/en/home.aspx

57. https://mckd.gov.ae/sites/MCYCDVar/en-us/pages/home.aspx

58. http://www.mod.gov.ae/index_en.html

59. https://www.economy.gov.ae/english/Pages/default.aspx

60. https://www.moe.gov.ae/En/Pages/Home.aspx

61. https://www.moei.gov.ae/en/home.aspx

62. https://www.mfnca.gov.ae/en/

63. https://www.mof.gov.ae/en/pages/default.aspx

64. https://www.mofa.gov.ae/EN/Pages/default.aspx

65. https://government.ae

66. http://www.mohap.gov.ae/en/Pages/default.aspx

67. https://www.mohre.gov.ae/en/home.aspx

68. https://www.moid.gov.ae/en-us/pages/default.aspx

69. https://www.moi.gov.ae/en/default.aspx

70. http://ejustice.gov.ae/portal/page/portal/eJustice%20MOJ%20Portal/HomePages/Home%20Page%20HQ

71. https://www.mopa.ae/EN/TheMinister/Pages/hhmessage.aspx

72. https://www.mocd.gov.ae/en/home.aspx

73. https://www.tolerance.gov.ae/Default.aspx

74. http://wam.ae

75. http://nmc.gov.ae/ar-ae

76. https://www.tra.gov.ae/aecert/en/home.aspx

77. https://www.id.gov.ae/en/home.aspx

78. https://www.tra.gov.ae

79. http://www.du.ae/personal

80. https://www.etisalat.ae/en/index.jsp

81. https://www.virginmobile.ae

82. https://www.abudhabi.ae/portal/public/en/homepage

83. https://www.ajman.ae/en

84. http://www.dubai.ae/en/Pages/default.aspx

85. http://fujairah.ae/en/pages/default.aspx

86. https://www.rak.ae/wps/portal

87. https://www.sharjah.ae/index.aspx

88. http://egd.uaq.ae/en/home.html

89. Abu Dhabi Systems & Information Centre (ADSIC), *Annual Report 2016*, Abu Dhabi, available online, http://vpr.ae/newsletter/adsic/Annual-Report/en/index.html#p=16, date accessed, 21st January 2018.

90. Dubai Electronic Security Centre, *Dubai Cyber Security Strategy*, Version 2.0, Government of Dubai.

91. Etisalat, *Corporate Governance 2016*, Emirates Telecommunications Group Company (PJSC), pp.12–17.

92. Du, *Board of Directors*, available online, http://www.du.ae/about-us/corporate-governance/board-of-directors, date accessed, 21ˢᵗ January 2018. Du, *Annual Report 2015*, Dubai, 2015.

93. Article 30, *United Arab Emirates Constitution of 1971 with Amendments through 2004*, Abu Dhabi, Constitute Project, 1971, available online, https://www.constituteproject.org/constitution/United_Arab_Emirates_2004.pdf, date accessed, 26ᵗʰ January 2018.

94. Federal Law No.15 of 1980, available online, http://nmc.gov.ae/en-us/NMC/Lists/LawsandLegislationsList/Attachments/55/%20المطبوعات%20قانون والنشر.pdf, date accessed, 26ᵗʰ January 2018.

95. Federal Law by Decree No.3 of 2003, Regarding the Organization of Telecommunications Sector, *Telecommunications Regulatory Authority*, Abu Dhabi, Official Gazette, Edition 411, April 2004, online, https://www.tra.gov.ae/en/about-tra/legal-references/law.aspx, date accessed, 26th January 2018.

96. 'About ICA', *Federal Authority for Identity and Citizenship*, available online, https://www.id.gov.ae/en/emirates-id/about-emirates-id.aspx, date accessed, 26ᵗʰ January 2018.

97. Federal Law No. (1) of 2006, Electronic Commerce and Transactions, available online, https://www.tra.gov.ae/en/about-tra/legal-references/law.aspx, date accessed, 26th January 2018.

98. Official Gazette, Edition 485, October 2008.

99. 'Legal References', *Telecommunications Regulatory Authority (TRA)*, available online, https://www.tra.gov.ae/en/legal-references.aspx, date accessed, 26ᵗʰ January 2018.

100. S Saleem, 'Content Regulation in the UAE: "The Wolf of Wall Street"', *Al Tammimi & Co*, February 2014, available online, http://www.tamimi.com/law-update-articles/content-regulation-in-the-uae-the-wolf-of-wall-street/, date accessed 26ᵗʰ January 2018.

101. Federal Decree Law No.3 of 2012, On The Establishment of the National Electronic Security Authority, Khalifa bin Zayed Al Nahyan, Abu Dhabi, available online, http://ejustice.gov.ae/downloads/latest_laws/federal_decree_law_3_2012_en.pdf, date accessed, 20ᵗʰ January 2018.

102. Federal Decree Law No.5 of 2012, Ministry of Justice, 13ᵗʰ August 2012, available online, http://ejustice.gov.ae/downloads/latest_laws/cybercrimes_5_2012_en.pdf, date accessed, 26ᵗʰ January 2018.

103. 'Media in the UAE', *UAE Government*, available online, https://government.ae/en/media/media, date accessed, 26ᵗʰ January 2018.

104. Federal Decree Law No.7 of 2014, Ministry of Justice, 20ᵗʰ August 2014, avail-

able online, https://moj.gov.ae/documents/21128/86231/Federal%20 Law%20No%207%20of%202014%20On%20Combating%20Terrorism%20 Offences.pdf/d8e6e696-e44b-45eb-8c30-ca2cb2ff6ce5, date accessed, 26th January 2018.

105. Federal Decree Law No.2 of 2015, Ministry of Justice, 15th July 2015, available online, http://ejustice.gov.ae/downloads/latest_laws2015/FDL_2_ 2015_discrimination_hate_en.pdf, date accessed, 26th January 2018.

106. Federal Law No.11 of 2016, available online, http://nmc.gov.ae/en-us/ NMC/Lists/LawsandLegislationsList/Attachments/56/%20شأن%20تنظيم%20 واختصاصاته%20المجلس%20واختصاصات.pdf, date accessed, 26th January 2018.

107. 'UAE President Issues Federal Laws', *WAM*, 22nd July 2017, available online, http://wam.ae/en/details/1395298018406, date accessed, 26th January 2018.

108. 'Mohammed bin Rashid Issues Decision Organising Media Content', *UAE, The Cabinet*, available online, https://www.uaecabinet.ae/en/details/news/ mohammed-bin-rashid-issues-decision-organizing-media-content, date accessed, 26th January 2018.

109. Federal Law No.7 of 2014, On Combatting Terrorism Offences, 20th August 2014.

110. Board of Directors, Investment Committee, and executive level management.

111. 'Annual Report 2008', *Mubadala*, 2008.

112. 'Annual Report 2009', *Mubadala*, 2009.

113. 'Annual Report 2010', *Mubadala*, 2010.

114. 'Annual Report 2011', *Mubadala*, 2011.

115. 'Annual Report 2012', *Mubadala*, 2012.

116. 'Annual Review 2013', *Mubadala*, 2013.

117. 'Mubadala Annual Review 2014', *Mubadala*, 2014.

118. 'Annual Review 2015', *Mubadala*, available online, 2015, https://www. mubadala.com/annual-review-2015/en/our-leadership, date accessed, 23rd March 2018.

119. 'Annual Review 2016', *Mubadala*, 2016, available online, https://www. mubadala.com/annual-review-2016/en/index.html, date accessed, 23rd March 2018.

120. 'Who we Are', *Mubadala*, available online, https://www.mubadala.com/en, date accessed, 23rd March 2018.

121. 'The Executive Council, Policy Agenda 2007–2008; The Emirate of Abu Dhabi, *The Executive Council*, available online, https://eaa.gov.ae/en/docs/ policy-agenda-2007–08.pdf, date accessed, 8th February 2019.

122. 'Mohammed Reappointed Chief of Abu Dhabi Executive Council', *Gulf News*, 13th December 2010, available online, https://gulfnews.com/uae/govern- ment/mohammad-reappointed-chief-of-abu-dhabi-executive-coun- cil-1.728600, date accessed, 8th February 2019. Kareem Shaheen makes ref- erence to notable figures, such as Saeed bin Zayed, Tahnoon bin Zayed, Sultan

bin Khalifa, Ahmed bin Saif, and Rashid al Hajeri, who were left out of the ADEC. K Shaheen, 'Sheikh Hazza Appointed to Abu Dhabi Executive Council', *The National*, 13th December 2010, available online, https://www.thenational.ae/uae/government/sheikh-hazza-appointed-to-abu-dhabi-executive-council-1.553734, date accessed, 8th February 2019.

123. Amiri Decree No. (1) of 2016, *The Official Gazette*, General Secretariat of the Executive Council, 2nd Edition, 29th February 2016.

124. 'Member's Profiles', *Abu Dhabi Executive Council*, available online, https://www.ecouncil.ae/en/ADGovernment/Pages/MemberProfiles.aspx, date accessed, 8th February 2019.

125. He was previously the Director of the Private Office of MBZ. H Van Der Meulen, *The Role of Tribal and Kinship Ties in the Politics of the United Arab Emirates*, p.194.

126. Hendrik Van Der Meulen notes that the Otaibas are one of two prominent "non-tribal" merchant families 'with close long-standing ties to the Al-Nuhayyan'. H Van Der Meulen, *The Role of Tribal and Kinship Ties in the Politics of the UAE*, pp.134–135.

127. His brother, Saeed Mubarak al-Hajeri was previously on the ADIA Board of Directors.

BIBLIOGRAPHY

Books

Abdullah, M, *The United Arab Emirates: A Modern History*, Croom Helm, London, 1978.

Abu Dhabi Accountability Authority, *2015 Accountability Report*, Abu Dhabi, 2015.

Abu Dhabi Investment Authority (ADIA), 'Governance', Annual Review 2016: A Legacy in Motion, 2017.

Agathangelou, AM and Soguk, N (eds.), *Arab Revolution and World Transformations*, Taylor and Francis, London, 2013.

Ajami, F, *The Arab Predicament*, Cambridge University Press, Cambridge, 1981.

Al-Abed and Hellyer, P (eds.), *United Arab Emirates, a New Perspective*, Trident Press, London, 2001.

Al-Hajji, JMA, *Qasr al-Hosn, The History of the Rulers of Abu Dhabi 1793–1966*, Centre for Documentation and Research, Emirates Printing Press, Dubai, 2004.

Al-Naikb, R, *Education and Democratic Development in Kuwait: Citizens in Waiting*, Chatham House, London, 2015.

Al-Otaiba, MA, *Petroleum and the Economy of the United Arab Emirates*, Croom Helm, London, 1977.

Aristotle, *The Politics*, Sinclair, TA and Saunders, TJ (eds.), Penguin, London, 2000.

Arquilla, J and Ronfeldt, D, *The Emergence of Noopolitik: Toward an American Information Strategy*, RAND, Santa Monica, 1999.

Axelrod, R and Cohen, MD, *Harnessing Complexity: Organizational Implications of a Scientific Frontier*, Basic Books, New York, 2000.

Ayoob, M, *The Third World Security Predicament: State Making, Regional Conflict, and the International System*, Lynne Rienner, London, 1995.

BIBLIOGRAPHY

Ayubi, NN, *Over-Stating the Arab State: Politics and Society in the Middle East*, I B Tauris, London, 2006.

Azar, EE and Moon, C, (eds.), *National Security in the Third World: The Management of International External Threats*, Centre for International Development and Conflict, Edward Elgar, Aldershot, 1988.

Baali, F and Al-Wardi, A, *Ibn Khaldun in Islamic Thought Styles: A Social Perspective*, GH Hall, Boston, 1981.

Ball, K, Haggerty, KD and Lyon, D (eds.), *Routledge Handbook of Surveillance Studies*, Routledge, Milton Park, 2012.

Barakat, H, *The Arab World: Society, Culture, and State*, University of California Press, Berkeley, 1993.

Z Barany, *The Formative Movements That Shaped the Gulf Arab Militaries*, The Arab Gulf States Institute in Washington, Washington DC, 23rd June 2020.

Barkey, HJ (ed.), *The Politics of Economic Reform in the Middle East*, St Martin's Press, New York, 1992.

Bauman, Z and Lyon, D, *Liquid Surveillance*, Polity Press, Cambridge, 2013.

Baylis, J, Wirtz, JJ and Gray, CS, *Strategy in the Contemporary World*, Oxford University Press, Oxford, 2010.

Bazoobandi, S, *The Political Economy of the Gulf Sovereign Wealth Funds: A Case Study of Iran, Kuwait, Saudi Arabia and the United Arab Emirates*, Routledge, London, 2013.

Be'eri, E, *Army Officers in Arab Politics and Society*, Prager, London, 1970.

Beblawi, H and Luciani, G, *The Rentier State*, Croom Helm, London, 1987.

Bentham, J, *The Panopticon Writings*, Bozovic, M (ed.), Verso, London, 1995.

Bill, J and Springborg, R, *Politics in the Middle East*, New York, Addison Wesley Longman, 2000.

Bill, JA and Leiden, C, *The Middle East: Politics and Power*, Allyn and Bacon, Boston, 1974.

Billingsley, A, *Political Succession in the Arab World: Constitutions, Family Loyalties and Islam*, Routledge, London, 2009.

Booth, WC, Colomb, GG and Williams, JM, *The Craft of Research*, The University of Chicago Press, London, 2008.

Bremmer, I, *The End of the Free Market*, Portfolio/Penguin, New York/London, 2010.

Brichs, FI (ed.), *Political Regimes in the Arab World: Society and the Exercise of Power*, Routledge, London, 2013.

Brinton, C, *The Anatomy of Revolution*, Vintage, New York, 1965.

Brooks, R, *Political-Military Relations and the Stability of Arab Regimes*,

International Institute for Strategic Studies (IISS), Oxford University Press, Oxford, 1998.

Brownlee, J, *Authoritarianism in an Age of Democratization*, Cambridge University Press, New Yok, 2007.

Brynen, R, Korany, B and Noble, P (eds.), *Political Liberalization and Democratization in the Arab World, Volume 1, Theoretical Perspectives*, Lynne Rienner, Boulder, 1995.

Bull, H, *The Anarchical Society: A Study of Order in World Politics*, Columbia University Press, New York, 1977.

Buzan, B and Wæver, O and De Wilde, J, *Security: A New Framework for Analysis*, Lynn Rienner, Boulder, 1997.

Buzan, B, *People, States and Fear: An Agenda for International Security Studies in the Post-Cold War Era*, Harvester Wheatsheaf, London, 1991.

Cahill, D, Edwards, L and Stilwell, F (eds.), *Neoliberalism: Beyond the Free Market*, Edward Elgar, Cheltenham, 2012.

Chaudhry, KA, *The Price of Wealth: Economies and Institutions in the Middle East*, Cornell University Press, Ithaca, 1997.

Chehabi, HE and Linz, JJ, *Sultanistic Regimes*, John Hopkins University Press, Baltimore, 1998.

Chesterman, S, *One Nation Under Surveillance, A New Social Contract to Defend Freedom Without Sacrificing Liberty*, Oxford University Press, Oxford, 2011.

Chubin, S, Litwak, A and Plascov, *A Security in the Gulf*, The Adelphi Library 7, International Institute for Strategic Studies (IISS), Gower, Aldershot, 1982.

Cohen, ED, *Mass Surveillance and State Control: The Total Information Awareness Project*, Palgrave, New York, 2010.

Cohen, LJ and Shapiro, JP, (eds.), *Communist Systems in Comparative Perspective*, Doubleday, New York, 1974.

Cohen, S, *Visions of Social Control: Crime, Punishment, and Classification*, Polity Press, Oxford, 1985.

Collins, A (ed.), *Contemporary Security Studies*, Oxford University Press, Oxford, 2007.

Cook, MA (ed.), *Studies in the Economic History of the Middle East*, Oxford, Oxford University Press, 1970.

Cook, SA, *Ruling but Not Governing: The Military and Political Development in Egypt, Algeria, and Turkey*, John Hopkins University Press, Baltimore, 2007.

Cooke, M, *Tribal Modern: Branding New Nations in the Arab Gulf*, University of California Press, Berkeley, 2014.

Cordesman, A, *Saudi Arabia Enters the 21st Century: The Military and*

Internal Security Dimension. V. The Saudi National Guard, Center for Strategic and International Studies (CSIS), Washington, 2002.

Cordesman, AH and Al-Rodhan, KR, *Gulf Military Forces in an Era of Asymmetric Wars*, Center for Strategic and International Studies (CSIS), Praeger, London, 2006.

Dahl, RA, *Who Governs: Democracy and Power in An American City*, Yale University Press, New Haven, 2005.

Darwish, N, *The Devil We Don't Know: The Dark Side of Revolutions in the Middle East*, John Wiley & Sons, New Jersey, 2012.

Davidson, C, *The United Arab Emirates: A Study in Survival*, Lynne Rienner, London, 2004.

————, *Dubai: The Vulnerability of Success*, Oxford University Press, Oxford, 2009.

————, *Abu Dhabi Oil and Beyond*, Hurst & Co, London, 2011.

————, *After the Shaykhs: The Coming Collapse of the Gulf Monarchies*, Hurst & Co, London, 2012.

Deyo, FC (ed.), *The Political Economy of the New Asian Industrialism*, Cornell University Press, Ithaca, 1987.

Edwards, A, *Regulation and Repression*, Allen & Unwin, London, 1988.

Ehteshami, A and Wright, S, (eds.), *Reform in the Middle East Oil Monarchies*, Ithaca Press, Reading, 2008.

Eickelman, D, *The Middle East: An Anthropological Approach*, Prentice-Hall, Englewood Cliffs, 1981.

Entelis, JP (ed.), *Islam, Democracy, and the State in North Africa*, Indiana University Press, Bloomington, 1997.

Evans-Pritchard, E, *The Neur*, Oxford University Press, Oxford 1940.

————, *The Sanusi of Cyrenaica*, The Clarendon Press, Oxford, 1949.

Fenelon, KG, *The United Arab Emirates: An Economic and Social Survey*, Longman, London, 1973.

Filiu, JP, *From Deep State to Islamic State: The Arab Counter-Revolution and its Jihadi Legacy*, Hurst & Co, London 2015.

Foucault, M, *Discipline and Punish: The Birth of the Prison*, Sheridan, A, trans., Vintage, New York, 1977.

Freer, C, *Rentier Islamism: The Influence of the Muslim Brotherhood in the Gulf Monarchies*, Oxford University Press, Oxford, 2018.

Fukuyama, F, *The End of History and the Last Man*, Hamish Hamilton, London, 1992.

————, *The Origins of Political Order*, Farrar, New York, 2011.

Gaub, F and Stanley-Lockman, Z, *Defence Industries in Arab States: players and strategies*, Chaillot Papers, European Institute for Security Studies, March 2017.

BIBLIOGRAPHY

Gause, G, *Oil Monarchies: Domestic and Security Challenges in the Arab Gulf States*, Council on Foreign Relations Press, New York, 1994.

Gause, G and Yom, S, *Resilient Royals: How Arab Monarchies Hang On*, Brookings Institute, 2012.

Gause, G, 'Kings for all Seasons: How the Middle East's Monarchies Survived the Arab Spring', *Brooking Doha Centre*, Analysis Paper 8, 2013.

Gengler, J, *The Political Economy of Sectarianism in the Gulf*, Carnegie Endowment for International Peace, August 2016.

Gervais, V, *Du Pétrole à L'Armée: Les Stratégies de Construction De L'État Aux Émirats Arabes Unis*, Institut de Recherche Stratégique de l'Ecole Militaire, No.8, 2011.

Ghannam, J, *Social Media in the Arab World: Leading up to the Uprisings of 2011*, Center for International Media Assistance (CIMA), Washington, 3rd February 2011.

Ghareeb, E and al-Abed, I (eds.), *United Arab Emirates: A New Perspective*, Trident Press, London, 1997.

Giddens, A, *The Class Structure of Advanced Societies*, Hutchinson, London, 1980.

———, *The Nation-State and Violence*, Polity Press, Cambridge, 1985.

———, *The Consequences of Modernity*, Polity Press, Cambridge, 1992.

Gourevitch, P, *Politics in Hard Times: Comparative Responses to International Economic Crises*, Cornell University Press, Ithaca, 1986.

Gray, D and Henderson, SE (ed.), *The Cambridge Handbook of Surveillance Law*, Cambridge University Press, Cambridge, 2017.

Gray, M, *A Theory of 'Late Rentierism' in the Arab States of the Gulf*, Center for International and Regional Studies, Georgetown University School of Foreign Service in Qatar, Occasional Paper No.7, Doha, 2011.

Gregory, PR, *Terror by Quota, State Security from Lenin to Stalin (An Archival Study)*, Yale University Press, New Haven, 2009.

Greitens, S, *Coercive Institutions and State Violence Under Authoritarianism*, PhD Thesis, Harvard University, Boston, 2013.

GSMA, *The Mobile Economy: Arab States 2015*.

Guazzone, L and Pioppi, D (eds.), *The Arab State and Neo-Liberal Globalisation: The Restructuring of State Power in the Middle East*, Ithaca Press, Ithaca, 2012.

Haddad, B, *Business Networks in Syria: The Political Economy of Authoritarian Resilience*, Stanford University Press, Stanford, 2012.

Haggard, S and Kaufman, R (ed.), *The Politics of Economic Adjustment*, Princeton University Press, Princeton, 1995.

Haggard, S and Kaufman, RR, *The Political Economy of Democratic Transitions*, Princeton University Press, Princeton, 1995.

BIBLIOGRAPHY

Haggerty, KD and Samatas, M (ed.), *Surveillance and Democracy*, Routledge-Cavendish, Abingdon, 2010.

Hakimian, H and Moshaver, Z (eds.), *The State and Global Change: The Political Economy of Transition in the Middle East and North Africa*, Curzon, Richmond, 2001.

Halliday, F, *Mercenaries: Counter-Insurgency in the Gulf*, Spokesman, Nottingham, 1977.

——— *After the Sultans*, Saqi Books, London, 2001.

Halpern, M, *The Politics of Social Change in the Middle East and North Africa*, RAND, 1963.

Hanieh, A, *Capitalism and Class in the Gulf Arab States*, Palgrave Macmillan, New York, 2011.

Harik, I and Sullivan, D (eds.), *Privatisation and Liberalisation in the Middle East*, Indiana University Press, Bloomington, 1992.

Heard-Bey, F, *From Trucial States to United Arab Emirates: A Society in Transition*, Longman, London, 1982.

Held, D and Ulrichsen, K (eds.), *The Transformation of the Gulf: Politics, Economics and the Global Order*, Routledge, London, 2011.

Herb, M, *All in the Family: Absolutism, Revolution, and Democracy in the Middle East*, State University of New York Press, Albany, 1999.

———, *The Wages of Oil: Parliaments and Economic Development in Kuwait and the UAE*, Cornell University Press, Ithaca, 2014.

Hertog, S, Luiciani, G and Valeri, M (eds.), *Business Politics in the Middle East*, Hurst & Co, London, 2013.

Hertog, S, *Princes, Brokers, and Bureaucrats: Oil and the State in Saudi Arabia*, Cornell University Press, Ithaca, 2011.

Hertog, S, *The Private Sector and Reform in the Gulf Cooperation Council*, Research Papers, LSE Kuwait Programme, London, 2013.

Heydemann, S, *Authoritarianism in Syria: Institutions and Social Conflict, 1946–1970*, Cornell University Press, Ithaca, 1999.

Heydemann, S (ed.), *Networks of Privilege in the Middle East: The Politics of Economic Reform Revisited*, Palgrave Macmillan, Basingstoke, 2004.

Heydemann, S, *Upgrading Authoritarianism in the Arab World*, The Saban Center for Middle East Policy at the Brookings Institution, Analysis Paper 13, October 2007.

Heydemann, S and Leenders, R, (eds.), *Middle East Authoritarianisms: Governance, Contestation, and Regime Resilience in Syria and Iran*, Stanford University Press, Stanford, 2013.

Hier, SP and Greenberg, J (ed.), *The Surveillance Studies Reader*, Open University Press, Maidenhead, 2007.

Hudson, M and Kirk, M (eds.), *Gulf Politics and Economics in a Changing World*, World Scientific, London, 2014.

Hughes, CW and Meng, LY, (ed.), *Security Studies, A Reader*, Routledge, London, 2011.

Huntington, SP, *The Soldier and State*, Harvard University Press, Cambridge, 1964.

————, *The Third Wave: Democratization in the Late Twentieth Century*, University of Oklahoma Press, Norman, 1993.

————, *Political Order in Changing Societies*, Yale University Press, London, 2006.

Hurewitz, C, *Middle East Politics: The Military Dimension*, Council on Foreign Relations, Praeger, New York, 1969.

Hvidt, M, *Economic Diversification in GCC Countries: Past Records and Future Trends*, Kuwait Programme on Development, Governance and Globalisation in the Gulf States, London School of Economics and Political Science, January 2013.

Ibish, H, *The UAE's Evolving National Security Strategy*, The Arab Gulf States Institute in Washington, Washington DC, 6th April 2017.

IMF, *Economic Diversification in Oil-Exporting Arab Countries*, Annual Meeting of Arab Ministers of Finance, Manama, April 2016.

ITU, *World Telecommunication/ICT Indicators Database*, June 2016.

Jabar, FA and Dawood, H (eds.), *Tribes and Power: Nationalism and Ethnicity in the Middle East*, Saqi Books, London, 2003.

Jackson, R, *The Global Covenant: Human Conduct in a World of States*, Oxford University Press, Oxford, 2000.

Job, BL, (ed.), *The Insecurity Dilemma: National Security of Third World States*, Lynne Rienner Publishers, London, 1992.

Kagarlitsky, B, *Russian Under Yeltsin and Putin: Neo-Liberal Autocracy*, Pluto Press, London, 2002.

Kalathil, S and Boas, TC, *Open Networks, Closed Regimes: The Impact of the Internet on Authoritarian Rule*, Carnegie Endowment for International Peace, Brooking Institution Press, Washington, 2003.

Kamrava, M (ed.), *Beyond the Arab Spring: The Evolving Ruling Bargain in the Middle East*, Oxford University Press, School of Foreign Service in Qatar, Georgetown University, Oxford, 2014.

Kamrava, M, Nonneman, G, Nosova, A and Valeri, M, *Ruling Families and Business Elites in the Gulf Monarchies: Ever Closer?*, Middle East and North Africa Programme, Chatham House, November 2016.

Kant, I, *To Perpetual Peace: a Philosophical Sketch*, Hackett Publishing, Indianapolis, 2003.

Karl, TL, *The Paradox of Plenty*, University of California Press, Berkeley, 1997.

Kazim, AA, *Historic Oman to the United Arab Emirates, from 600 A.D. to 1995: An Analysis of the Making, Remaking and Unmaking of a Socio-*

Discursive Formation in the Arabian Gulf, Part 1, PhD Thesis, The American University, Washington D.C., 1996.

Kechichian, JA, *Power and Succession in Arab monarchies*, Lynne Rienner Publishers, Colorado, 2008.

Kelly, JB, *Eastern Arabian Frontiers*, Faber & Faber, London, 1964.

Khadlun, I, *The Maqqaddimah: An Introduction to History*, F Rosenthal, trans., Princeton University Press, Princeton, 2007.

Khalifa, AM, *The United Arab Emirates: Unity in Fragmentation*, Saqi Books, London, 1989.

Khoury, PS and Kostiner, J (eds.), *Tribes and State Formation in the Middle East*, University of California Press, Berkeley, 1990.

Kolkowicz, R and Korbonski, A (eds.), *Soldiers, Peasants, and Bureaucrats: Civil-Military Relations in Communist and Modernizing Societies*, Allen and Unwin, London, 1982.

Kolkowicz, R and Korbonski, A, (ed.), *Soldiers, Peasants, and Bureaucrats: Civil-Military Relations in Communist and Modernizing Societies*, Center for International and Strategic Affairs, University of California, George Allen & Unwin, London, 1982.

Korany, B and el-Mahdi (ed.), *The Arab Revolution in Egypt and Beyond*, American University of Cairo Press, Cairo, 2012.

Kostiner, J (ed.), *Middle East Monarchies: The Challenge of Modernity*, Boulder, Lynne Rienner Publishers, 2000.

Krasner, SD, *Structural Conflict: The Third World Against Global Liberalism*, University of California Press, London, 1985.

Krause, K and Williams, MC, *Critical Security Studies: Concepts and Cases*, University of Minneapolis, 1997.

Kreitmeyr-Koska, N, *Neo-Liberal Networks and Authoritarian Renewal: A Diverse Case Study of Egypt, Jordan & Morocco*, PhD Thesis, University of Tubingen, 2016.

Kristol, I, *Neoconservatism: The Autobiography of an Idea*, Simon & Schuster, New York, 1995.

Kubursi, AA, Oil, *Industrialization & Development in the Arab Gulf States*, Croom Helm, London, 1984.

Lahn, G, *Fuel, Food and Utilities Price Reforms in the GCC A Wake Up Call for Business*, Chatham House, London, Research Paper, June 2016.

Land, S, (ed.), *Zayed: A Man Who Built a Nation*, Media Prima, London, 2004.

Laquer, W, *International Fascism*, 1920–1945, Harper & Row, London, 1966.

Legrenzi, M and Momani, B (eds.), *Shifting Geo-Economic Power of the Gulf: Oil, Finance and Institutions*, Ashgate Publishing, Farnham, 2011.

Lerner, D, *The Passing of Traditional Society: Modernizing the Middle East*, Free Press of Glencoe, New York, 1958.

Lienhardt, P, *Shaikhdoms of Eastern Arabia*, Al-Shahi, A (ed.), Palgrave, Oxford, 2001.

Linz, JJ, *Totalitarian and Authoritarian Regimes*, Lynn Rienner Publishers, London, 2000.

Lipset, SM and Solari, A, (eds.), *Elites in Latin America*, Oxford University Press, Oxford, 1967.

Looney, RE, *Industrial Development and Diversification of the Arabian Gulf Economies*, JAI Press, London, 1994.

Lorimer, JG, *The Gazetteer of the Persian Gulf, Oman and Central Arabia (Part 1: Historical / Part II: Geographical and Statistical, 9 Vols)*, Archive Editions, Gerrards Cross, 1986.

——— (ed.), *The Arab State*, Routledge, London, 1990.

Luciani, G (ed.), *Resource Blessed: Diversification and the Gulf Development Model*, Gerlach Press, Germany, Gulf Research Center, 2012.

Luttwak, E, *Coup d'Etat: A Practical Handbook*, Harvard University Press, Cambridge, 1979.

Lyon, D, *Surveillance Society, Monitoring Everyday Life*, Open University Press, Buckingham, 2002.

Machiavelli, N, *The Prince*, T Parks, trans., Penguin, London, 2009.

MacQueen, B, *An Introduction to Middle East Politics*, Sage, London, 2013.

Mann, C, *Abu Dhabi, Birth of an Oil Shaykhdom*, Khayats Beirut, 1964.

Mann, M, *The Sources of Social Power: Volume II, The Rise of Classes and Nation-States, 1760–1914*, Cambridge University Press, Cambridge, 1993.

Mattei, V and Haskell, JD, (eds.), *Research Handbook on Political Economy and Law*, Edward Elgar Publishing, Cheltenham, 2015.

Maxfield, S and Schneider, BR (eds.), *Business and the State in Developing Countries*, Cornell University Press, Ithaca, 1997.

Mearsheimer, J, *The Tragedy of Great Power Politics*, Norton, New York, 2001.

Meulen, HV, *The Role of Tribal and Kinship Ties in the Politics of the United Arab Emirates*, PhD Thesis, Tufts University, 1997.

Michels, R, *Political Parties: A Sociological Study of the Oligarchical Tendencies of Modern Democracy*, The Free Press, Glencoe, 1949.

Migdal, J, *Strong Societies and Weak States: State-Society Relations and State Capabilities in the Third World*, Princeton University Press, Princeton, 1988.

Military Balance 2021, International Institute for Strategic Studies (IISS), Routledge, London, 2021.

Mills, CW, *The Power Elite*, Oxford University Press, Oxford, 2000.

Mohamedou, M, *State-Building and Regime Security: A Study of Iraq's Foreign Policy Making During the Second Gulf War*, PhD Thesis, The City University of New York, New York, 1996.

Montesquieu, *The Spirit of Laws*, Cohler, AN, Miller, BC, and Stone, HS (eds.), Cambridge University Press, Cambridge, 2000.

Moore, C, (ed.), *Authoritarian Politics in Modern Society*, Basic Books, New York, 1970.

Moore, PW, 'Rents and Late Development in the Arab World', 2004 Annual Meeting of the American Political Science Association, *American Political Science Association*, 5ᵗʰ September 2004.

Mosca, G, *The Ruling Class*, McGraw-Hill, New York, 1939.

Mullen, Chairman of the Joint Chiefs of Staff, *Joint Publication 3–0, Joint Operations*, 11ᵗʰ August 2011, Washington DC.

Munro, D, *ADNOC's CEO Institutes Seismic Shift in Corporate Strategy*, Arab Gulf States Institute in Washington Blog, 1ˢᵗ June 2016.

Nanakorn, P, *The Offset Programme as a Development Tool in the UAE*, PhD Thesis, University of Exeter, 2009.

Niblett, R (ed.), *America and a Changed World*, Chatham House, Wiley-Blackwell, London, 2010.

Nosova, A, *The Merchant Elite and Parliamentary Politic in Kuwait: The Dynamics of Business Political Participation in a Rentier State*, PhD Thesis, London School of Economics, London, 2016.

O'Donnell, G and Schmitter, P, *Transitions from Authoritarian Rule: Tentative Conclusions about Uncertain Democracies*, John Hopkins University Press, Baltimore, 1986.

O'Donnell, G, *Modernization and Bureaucratic-Authoritarianism: Studies in South American Politics*, Institute of International Studies, University of California, Berkeley, 1973.

————, *Bureaucratic Authoritarianism, Argentina 1966–1973, in Comparative Perspective*, McGuire, J, trans., University of California Press, Berkeley, 1988.

OECD, *OECD Guidelines on Corporate Governance of State-Owned Enterprises*, OECD Publishing, Paris, 2015 Edition.

Onley, J, *Britain and the Gulf Shaykhdoms, 1820–1971: The Politics of Protection*, Centre for International and Regional Studies, Georgetown University School of Foreign Service in Qatar, Doha, 2009.

Pareto, V, *The Rise and Fall of Elites: An Application of Theoretical Sociology*, Transactions Publishers, London, 1991.

Patai, R, *The Arab Mind*, Scribners, New York, 1973.

Peacock, AT, (ed.), *International Economic Papers*, Macmillan, London, 1954.

Perlmutter, A, *The Military and Politics in Modern Time*, Yale University Press, London, 1978.

————, *Modern Authoritarianism: A Comparative Institutional Analysis*, Yale University Press, New Haven, 1981.

————, *Political Roles and Military Rulers*, Frank Cass, London, 1981.

Perthes, V, (ed.), *Arab Elites: Negotiating the Politics of Change*, Lynne Rienner Publishers, London, 2004.

Peterson, JE, (ed.), *Crosscurrents in the Gulf: Arab, Regional and Global Interests, The Middle East Institute*, Routledge, London, 1988.

————, *The GCC States: Participation, Opposition, and the Fraying of the Social Contract*, Kuwait Programme on Development, Governance and Globalisation in the Gulf States, London School of Economics (LSE), London, No.26, December 2012.

Plato, *The Republic*, Ferrari, GRF, (ed.), Griffith, T, trans., Cambridge University Press, Cambridge, 2012.

Poster, P, *The Mode of Information*, University of Chicago Press, Chicago, 1990.

Posusney, MP and Angrist, MP, (eds.), *Authoritarianism in the Middle East: Regimes and Resistance*, Lynne Rienner, London, 2005.

Powell, JM, *Coups and Conflict: The Paradox of Coup-Proofing*, PhD Thesis, University of Kentucky, Kentucky, 2012.

PWC, *State-Owned Enterprises: Catalysts For Public Value Creation?*, April 2015.

Rabi, U, *Tribes and States in a Changing Middle East*, Hurst & Co, London 2016.

Reidy, DA and Riker, WJ, (eds.), *Coercion and the State*, Springer, New York, 2008.

Richet, JL (ed.), *Cybersecurity Policies and Strategies for Cyberwarfare Prevention*, IGI Global, Hershey, 2015.

Roberts, DB, *Qatar: Securing the Global Ambitions of a City-State*, Hurst & Co, London, 2017.

———— 'The Gulf Monarchies' Armed Forces at The Crossroads', *Focus Stratégique*, No.80, Ifri, May 2018.

Robertson Smith, W, *Kinship and Marriage in Early Arabia*, Kessigner, 2007.

Ross, M, 'Does Resource Wealth Cause Authoritarian Rule', The Economics of Political Violence, *World Bank Research Group*, Princeton University, March 18–19, 2000.

Rousseau, JJ, *The Social Contract and the First and Second Discourses*, Dunn, S, (ed.), New Haven, Yale University Press, 2002.

Rozanov, A, 'Who Holds the Wealth of Nations?', *Central Bank Journal*, May 2005.

Rubin, B and Keaney, TA, (ed.), *Armed Forces in the Middle East: Politics and Strategy*, BESA Studies in International Security, Frank Cass, London, 2002.

Rugh, AB, *The Political Culture of Leadership in the United Arab Emirates*, Palgrave Macmillan, Basingstoke, 2007.

Said, E, *Orientalism*, Penguin, London, 2003.

Salamé, G, *The Foundations of the Arab State*, Croom Helm, London, 1987.

Sakr, N (ed.), *Arab Media and Political Renewal*, I B Tauris, London, 2007.

Schahgaldian, N, *The Iranian Military Under the Islamic Republic*, RAND, Santa Monica, 1987.

Schlumberger, O, (ed.), *Debating Arab Authoritarianism: Dynamics and Durability in Non-Democratic Regimes*, Stanford University Press, Stanford, 2007.

Schmitt, C, *The Concept of the Political*, University of Chicago Press, Chicago, 2007.

Selvik, K and Stenslie, S, *Stability and Change in the Modern Middle East*, I B Tauris, London, 2011.

Sharabi, H (ed.), *The Next Arab Decade*, Westview Press, Boulder, 1988.

Sharabi, H, *Neopatriarchy: A Theory of Distorted Change in Arab Society*, Oxford University Press, USA, 1988.

Sherbiny, NA and Tessler, MA (eds.), *Arab Oil: Impact on the Arab Countries and Global Implications*, Praeger, New York, 1976.

Sindelar, HR and Peterson, JE, (eds.), *Crosscurrents in the Gulf: Arab, Regional and Global Interests*, The Middle East Institute, Routledge, London, 1988.

Skocpol, T, *States and Social Revolutions: A Comparative Analysis of France, Russia, and China*, Cambridge University Press, Harvard, 1979.

Smith, R, *The Utility of Force, The Art of War in the Modern World*, Penguin, London, 2006.

Snellen, I and Thaens, M (eds.), *Public Administration in the Information Age: Revisited*, Vol.19 Innovation and the Public Sector, IOS Press, Amsterdam, 2012.

Stacher, JA, *Adapting Authoritarianism: Institutions and Co-optation in Egypt and Syria*, PhD Thesis, University of St. Andrews, 2007.

Stepan, A, *The Military in Politics: Changing Patterns in Brazil*, Princeton University Press, Princeton, 1971.

————, *Authoritarian Brazil: Origins, Policies, and Future*, Yale University Press, New Haven, 1973.

Sultan, NA, Metcalfe, BD and Weir, D (eds.), *The New Post-Oil Arab Gulf: Managing People and Wealth*, Saqi Book, London, 2011.

Svolik, MW, *The Politics of Authoritarian Rule*, Cambridge University Press, Cambridge, 2012.

Tammam, H, *Zayid bin Sultan: The Leader on the March*, Dai Nippon Printing, Tokyo, 1983.

Teitelbaum, J (ed.), *Political Liberalization in the Persian Gulf*, Hurst & Co, London, 2009.

The Abu Dhabi Economic Vision 2030, The Government of Abu Dhabi, Abu Dhabi, November 2008.

The World Bank, *The Changing Wealth of Nations: Measuring Sustainable Development in the New Millennium*, Washington D.C., 2011.

Thesiger, W, *Arabian Sands*, Penguin, London, 2007.

Thomas, C, *In Search of Security: The Third World in International Relations*, Lynne Rienner, London, 1987.

Tilly, C, *From Mobilization to Revolution*, Random House, New York, 1978.

Tullock, G, *The Social Dilemma of Autocracy, Revolution, Coup D'etat, and War*, CK Rowley (ed.), The Selected Works of Gordon Tullock: Volume 8, Liberty Fund, Indianapolis, 2005.

Ulrichsen, KC, *Gulf Security: Changing Internal and External Dynamics*, The Centre for the Study of Global Governance, Kuwait Programme on Development, Governance, and Globalisation in the Gulf States, London School of Economics (LSE), London, 2009.

———, *Qatar and the Arab Spring*, Hurst & Co, London, 2014.

———, *The Politics of Economic Reform in the Arab Gulf States*, Centre for the Middle East, Rice University, 2016.

———, *The United Arab Emirates: Power, Politics, and Policymaking*, Routledge, London, 2017.

Unwin, T, *Social Media and Democracy: Critical Reflections*, Commonwealth Parliamentary Conference, Colombo, September 2012.

Useem, M, *The Inner Circle: Large Corporations and the Rise of Business Political Activity in the U.S and U.K.*, Oxford University Press, Oxford, 1986.

Valeri, M and Hertog, S (eds.), *Business Politics in the Middle East*, Hurst & Co, London, 2013.

Van Der Muelen, H, *The Role of Tribal and Kinship Ties in the Politics of the UAE*, PhD Thesis, The Fletcher School of Law and Diplomacy, Tufts University, 1997.

Wade, R, *Governing the Market: Economic Theory and the Role of Government in East Asian Industrialization*, Princeton University Press, Princeton, 1990.

Waltz, K, *Theories of International Politics*, Waveland Press, Long Grove, 2010.

Wheatcroft, A, *With United Strength, H.H Shaikh Zayid bin Sultan Al*

Nahyan, the Leader and the Nation, Emirates Center for Strategic Studies and Research (ECSSR), Abu Dhabi, 2013.

Williamson, J, (ed.), *Latin American Adjustment: How Much Has Happened?*, Institute for International Economics, 1990.

Wittfogel, KA, *Oriental Despotism: A Comparative Study of Total Power*, Yale University Press, Oxford, 1957.

Yanai, S, *Transformation of Gulf Tribal States: Elitism and the Social Contract in Kuwait, Bahrain and Dubai, 1918–1970s*, Sussex Academic Press, 2014.

Yates, D, *The Rentier State in Africa: Oil Rent Dependency and Neocolonialism in the Republic of Gabon*, Trenton, Africa World Press, 1996.

Young, K, *The Political Economy of Energy, Finance and Security in the United Arab Emirates: Between the Majlis and the Market*, Palgrave MacMillan, Basingstoke, 2014.

Zahlan, RS, *The Origins of the United Arab Emirates: A Political and Social History of the Trucial States*, The MacMillan Press, London, 1978.

Zartman, IW, (ed.), *Arab Spring: Negotiating in the Shadow of The Intifadat*, University of Georgia Press, Athens, 2015.

————, (ed.), *Elites in the Middle East*, Praeger, New York, 1980.

————, Tessler, MA, Entelis, JP, Stone, RA, Hinnebusch, RA and Akhavi, S, (eds.), *Political Elites in Arab North Africa: Morocco, Algeria, Tunisia, Libya, and Egypt*, Longman, London, 1982.

Journal Articles

'Reshuffle allows MBZ to increase Abu Dhabi's interest in UAE Federal affairs', *Gulf States News*, Vol. 40, Issue 1,010, 18th February 2016.

Abulof, U, '"Can't Buy Me Legitimacy": The Elusive Stability of Mideast Rentier Regimes', *Journal of International Relations* and Development, 2015, pp.1–25.

Al Rashedi, M, *The UAE National Security Strategy in the 21st Century*, Future Warfare Paper, United States Marine Corps School of Advanced Warfighting, Marine Corps University, Virginia, 2005.

Al-Khouri, AM, 'eGovernment Strategies: The Case of the United Arab Emirates', *European Journal of ePractice*, No.17, September 2016, pp.127–150.

Albrecht, H and Ohl, D, 'Exit, Resistance, Loyalty: Military Behaviour During Unrest in Authoritarian Regimes', *Perspective on Politics*, Vol.14, No.1, 2016.

Albrecht, H, 'The Myth of Coup-Proofing: Risk and Instances of Military Coups d'etat in the Middle East and North Africa, 1950–2013', *Armed Forces & Society*, Vol.41, No.4, 2014, pp.659–687.

————, 'Does Coup-Proofing Work? Political-Military Relations in Authoritarian Regimes Amid the Arab Uprisings', *Mediterranean Politics*, Vol. 20, No.1, 2015, pp.36–54.

AlSweilem, KA, Cummine, A, Rietveld, M and Tweedie, K, *A Comparative Study of Sovereign Investor Models: Sovereign Fund Profiles*, The Center for International Development and the Belfer Center for Science and International Affairs, Harvard Kennedy School, Harvard, 2015.

'Analysis and Recommendations', Doha Centre for Media Freedom, Doha, 2013.

Anderson, L, 'The State in the Middle East and North Africa' *Comparative Politics*, Vol. 20, No.1, October 1987, pp.1–18.

Baram, A, 'Neo-Tribalism in Iraq: Saddam Hussein's Tribal Policies 1991–96', *International Journal of Middle East Studies*, Vol. 29, No.1, February 1997.

Barari, HA, 'The Persistence of Autocracy: Jordan, Morocco and the Gulf', *Middle East Critique*, Vol. 24, No.1, 2015, pp.99–111.

Baroudi, SA, 'Sectarianism and Business Associations in Postwar Lebanon', *Arab Studies Quarterly*, Vol.22, No.4, Fall 2000, pp.81–107.

Beblawi, H, 'The Rentier State in the Arab World', *Arab Studies Quarterly*, Vol.9, No.4, Fall 1987, pp.383–398.

Bellin, E, 'The Robustness of Authoritarianism in the Middle East: Exceptionalism in Comparative Perspective', *Comparative Politics*, Vol. 36, No.2, January 2004, pp.139–157.

————, *The Political-Economic Conundrum: The Affinity of Economic and Political Reform in the Middle East and North Africa*, Middle East Series, Carnegie Papers, No.53, November 2004.

————, 'Reconsidering the Robustness of Authoritarianism in the Middle East', *Comparative Politics*, Vol.44, No.2, January 2012, pp.127–149.

Ben-Dor, G, *State, Society and Military Elites in the Middle East: An Essay in Comparative Political Sociology*, The Dayan Center for Middle Eastern and African Studies, The Shiloah Institute, Tel Aviv University, Tel Aviv, 1984.

Bennett, CJ and Raab, CD, *The Governance of Privacy, Policy Instruments in Global Perspective*, MIT Press, London, 2006.

Boone, C, 'The Making of a Rentier Class: Wealth Accumulation and Political Control in Senegal', *Journal of Development Studies*, Vol.26, No.3, pp.425–449.

Bremmer, I and Charap, S, 'The Siloviki in Putin's Russia: Who They are and What They Want', *The Washington Quarterly*, Volume 30, Number 1, Winter 2006–07, pp.83–92.

Bremmer, I, 'State Capitalism Comes of Age, The End of the Free Market?', *Foreign Affairs*, Vol.88, No.3, May/June 2009, pp.40–55.

Brodie, B, 'Strategy as a Science', *World Politics*, Vol.1, No.4, 1949, pp.467–488.

Brownlee, J, 'Hereditary Succession in Modern Autocracies', *World Politics*, Vol.59, No.4, July 2007, pp.595–628.

Brumberg, D, 'Democratization in the Arab World? The Trap of Liberalized Autocracy', *Journal of Democracy*, Vol. 13, No.44, 2002, pp.56–68.

Crystal, J, 'Authoritarianism and its Adversaries in the Arab World', *World Politics*, Vol. 46, No.2, 1994, pp.262–289.

David, SR, 'Explaining Third World Alignment', *World Politics*, Vol. 43, No.2, January 1991, pp.233–256.

Davidson, C, 'After Shaikh Zayed: The Politics of Succession in Abu Dhabi and the UAE', *Middle East Policy*, Vol.13, No.1, Spring 2006, pp.42–59.

———, 'Arab Nationalism and British Opposition in Dubai, 1920–66', *Middle Eastern Studies*, Vol.43, No.6, 2007, pp.879–892.

———, 'The Emirates of Abu Dhabi and Dubai: Contrasting Roles in the International System', *Asian Affairs*, Vol. 38, No.1, March 2007, pp.33–48.

———, 'The United Arab Emirates: Frontiers of the Arab Spring', *Open Democracy*, 8th September 2012.

Dazi-Heni, F, 'The Arab Spring Impact on Kuwaiti "Exceptionalism"', *Arabian Humanities*, Vol.4, 2015.

De Bel-Air, F, Demography, Migration, and the Labour Market in the UAE, Gulf Labour Markets and Migration (GLMM), European University Institute (EUI) and Gulf Research Center (GRC), No.7, 2015.

Deibert, R and Rohozinski, R, 'Liberation vs. Control: The Future of Cyberspace', *Journal of Democracy*, Vol.21, No.4, October 2010, pp.43–57.

Deibert, R, 'Cyberspace Under Siege', *Journal of Democracy*, Vol. 26, No.3, July 2015, pp.64–78.

Delacroix, J, 'The Distributive State in the World System', *Studies in Comparative International Development*, Vol. 15, 1980, pp.3–12.

Diamond, L, 'Liberation Technology', *Journal of Democracy*, Vol. 21, No.3, July 2010, pp.70–84.

Drysdale, A, 'Ethnicity in the Syrian Officer Corps: A Conceptualization', *Civilizations*, Vol.29, 1979, pp.359–374.

BIBLIOGRAPHY

Dye, TR and Pickering, JW, 'Governmental and Corporate Elites: Convergence and Differentiation', *The Journal of Politics*, Vol.36, No.4, November 1974, pp.900–925.

Ehteshami, A and Murphy, E, 'The Transformation of a Corporatist State', *Third World Quarterly*, Vo.17, No.4, 1996, pp.753–772.

El-Reyes, AM (ed.), *New Perspectives on Recording UAE History*, Ministry of Presidential Affairs, National Center for Documentation & Research, Abu Dhabi, 2009.

Erdmann, G and Engel, U, 'Neopatrimonialism Revisited—Beyond a Catch-All Concept', *German Institute of Global and Area Studies (GIGA)*, No.16, Hamburg, 2006.

Etzioni-Halevy, E, 'Civil-Military Relations and Democracy: The Case of the Military-Political Elites' Connection in Israel', *Armed Forces and Society*, Vol.22, Spring 1996.

C Fuchs, 'New Media, Web 2.0 and Surveillance', *Sociology Compass*, Vol.5, No.2, 2011, pp.134–147.

Geddes, B, 'Challenging the Conventional Wisdom', *Journal of Democracy*, Vol.5, No.4, October 1994, pp.104–118.

—————, 'What Do We Know About Democratization After Twenty Years', *Annual Review of Political Science*, Vol.2, 1999, pp.115–144.

Gerschewski, J, 'The Three Pillars of Stability: Legitimation, Repression, and Co-optation in Autocratic Regimes', *Democratization*, Vol.20, No.1, 2013, pp.13–38.

Greenwood, S, 'Jordan's "New Bargain:" The Political Economy of Regime Security', *Middle East Journal*, Vol. 57, No.2, Spring 2003, pp.248–268.

Haddad, B, 'Syria, the Arab uprisings, and the political economy of authoritarian resilience', *Interface: a journal for and about social movements*, Vol. 4, No.1, May 2012, pp.113–130.

Hanieh, A, 'Khaleeji-Capital: Class-Formation and Regional Integration in the Middle East Gulf', *Historical Materialism*, Vol.18, 2010, pp.35–76.

Hankla, CR and Kuthy, D, 'Economic Liberalism in Illiberal Regimes: Authoritarian Variation and the Political Economy of Trade', *International Studies Quarterly*, Vol.57, No.3, 2013, pp.492–504.

Heard-Bey, F, 'The United Arab Emirates: Statehood and Nation-Building in a Traditional Society', *Middle East Journal*, Vol.59, No.3, Democratization and Civil Society, Summer 2005, pp.357–375.

Hedges, M and Cafiero, G, 'The Future of the Muslim Brotherhood in the GCC', *Middle East Policy*, Vol.24, No.1, 2017, pp.129–153.

Herb, M, 'No Representation without Taxation?', *Comparative Politics*, Vol.37, No.3, April 2005.

————, 'A Nation of Bureaucrats: Political Participation and Economic Diversification in Kuwait and the United Arab Emirates', *International Journal of Middle Eastern Studies*, Vol.41, No.3, 2009, pp.375–339.

Hertog, S, 'Defying the Resource Curse, Explaining Successful State-Owned Enterprises in Rentier States', *World Politics*, Vol.62, No.2, April 2010, pp.262–301.

————, 'The Sociology of the Gulf Rentier Systems: Societies of Intermediaries', *Comparative Studies in Society and History*, Vol. 52, No.2, 2010, pp.1–37.

————, 'Rentier Militaries in the Gulf States: The Price of Coup-Proofing', *International Journal of Middle East Studies*, Vol. 43, No.3, 2011.

————, 'Redesigning the Distributional Bargain in the GCC', *Revolution and Revolt: Understanding the Forms and Causes of Change*, BRISMES Annual Conference 2012, London, 26–28th March 2012.

————, 'State and Private Sector in the GCC After the Arab Spring', *Journal of Arabian Studies*, Vol.3, No.2, 2014, pp.174–195.

Huntington, SP, 'The Political Modernization of Traditional Monarchies', *Daedalus*, Vol.95, No.3, 1966, pp.763–788.

————, 'The Change to Change: Modernisation, Development, and Politics', *Comparative Politics*, Vol.3, No.3, April 1971, pp.283–322.

Hurd, 'Legitimacy and Authority in International Politics', *International Organisation*, Vol.53, No.2, 1999, p.379–408.

Hvidt, M, 'The Dubai Model: An Outline of Key Development-Process Elements in Dubai', *International Journal of Middle East Studies*, Vol.41, No.3, 2009, pp.397–418.

Ikenberry, GJ, 'The State and Strategies of International Adjustment', *World Politics*, Vol.39, No.1, October 1986, pp.53–77.

Jones, CW, 'Seeing Like an Autocrat: Liberal Social Engineering in an Illiberal State', *Perspective on Politics*, Vol.13, No.1, March 2015, pp.24–41.

Kamrava, M, 'Military Professionalization and Civil-Military Relations in the Middle East', *Political Science Quarterly*, Vol.115, No.1, 2000, pp.67–92.

Konrad, KA and Mui, VL, 'The Prince—or Better No Prince? The Strategic Value of Appointing a Successor', *Journal of Conflict Resolution*, November 2016, pp.1–26.

Lazarev, V and Gregory, PR, 'Commissars and Csars: A Case Study in the Political Economy of Dictatorship', *Journal of Comparative Economics*, Vol. 1, 2003, pp.1–19.

Levitsky, S and Way, L, 'The Rise of Competitive Authoritarianism', *Journal of Democracy*, Vol.13, No.2, April 2002, pp.51–65.

BIBLIOGRAPHY

Lipset, SM, 'Some Social Requisites of Democracy: Economic Development and Political Legitimacy', *American Political Science Review*, Vol.53, No.1, March 1959, pp.69–105.

Londregan, JB and Poole, KT, 'Poverty, The Coup Trap, and the Seizure of Executive Power, *World Politics*, Vol.42, No.2, January 1990, pp.151–183.

Lucas, R, 'Monarchical Authoritarianism: Survival and Political Liberalisation in a Middle Eastern Regime Type', *International Journal of Middle Eastern Studies*, Vol. 36, No.1, 2004, pp.103–119.

Luciani, G, 'The Economic Content of Security', *Journal of Public Policy*, Vol.8, No.2, 1989, pp.151–173.

Lyon, D, 'Surveillance, Snowden, and Big Data: Capacities, Consequences, Critique', *Big Data & Society*, 2014, July–December, pp.1–13.

Makara, M, 'Rethinking Military Behaviour During the Arab Spring', *Defense & Security Analysis*, Vol.32, No.3, 2016, pp.209–223.

Mann, J, 'King Without a Kingdom: Deposed King Saud and His Intrigues', *Studia Oreintalia Electronica*, Vol.1, 2013, pp.26–40.

Mann, S, Nolan, S and Wellman, B, 'Sousveillance: Inventing and Using Wearable Computing Devices for Data Collection in Surveillance Environments', *Surveillance and Society*, Vol.1, No.3, 2003, pp.331–355.

Moore, PW and Salloukh, BF, 'Struggles Under Authoritarianism: Regimes, States, and Professional Associations in the Arab World', *International Journal of Middle East Studies*, Vol.39, No.1, February 2007, pp.53–76.

Moore, PW, 'Late Development and Rents in the Arab World', Paper presented at the Annual Meeting of American Political Science Association, Hilton Chicago and the Palmer House Hilton, Chicago, Illinois, 2nd September 2004, pp.8–11.

Moore, PW, 'Rentier Fiscal Crisis and Regime Stability: Business–State Relations in the Gulf', *Studies in Comparative International Development*, Vol.37, No.1, Spring 2002, pp.34–56.

Morozov, E, 'Whither Internet Control?', *Journal of Democracy*, Vol.22, No.2, April 2011, pp.62–74.

Murphy, E 'Agency and Space: The Political Impact of Information Technologies in the Gulf Arab States', *Third World Quarterly*, Vol.27, No.6, 2006, pp.1059–1083.

———, 'Theorizing ICTs in the Arab World: Informational Capitalism and the Public Sphere', *International Studies Quarterly*, Vol.53, No.4, 2009, pp.1131–1153.

BIBLIOGRAPHY

Nassif, H, 'Generals and Autocrats: How Coup-Proofing Predetermined the Military Elite Behavior in the Arab Spring', *Political Science Quarterly*, Vol.130, No.2, 2015, pp.245–275.

Nathan, AJ, 'Authoritarian Resilience', *Journal of Democracy*, Vol.14, No.1, 2013, pp.6–17.

Okruhlik, G, 'Rentier Wealth, Unruly Law, and the Rise of Opposition: The Political Economy of Oil States', *Comparative Politics*, Vol.31, No.3, April 1999, pp.295–315.

Perlmutter, A, 'The Praetorian State and the Praetorian Army: Toward a Taxonomy of Civil–Military Relations in Developing Polities', *Comparative Politics*, Vol.1, No.3, April 1969, pp.382–404.

Peterson, JE, 'Tribes and Politics in Eastern Arabia', *Middle East Journal*, Vol. 31, No.3, Summer 1977, pp.297–312.

———, 'The Nature of Succession in the Gulf', *Middle East Journal*, Vol.55, No.4, Autumn 2001, pp.580–601.

Pomerantsev, P, 'The Kremlin's Information War', *Journal of Democracy*, Vol.26, No.4, October 2015, pp.40–50.

Prezeworski, A and Limongi, F, 'Modernization: Theories and Facts', *World Politics*, Vol.49, No.2, January 1997, pp.155–183.

Quinlivan, JT, 'Coup-proofing: Its Practice and Consequences in the Middle East', *International Security*, Vol. 24, No.2, Fall 1999, pp.131–165.

Rabi, U, 'Oil Politics and Tribal Rulers in Eastern Arabia: The Reign of Shakhbut (1928–1966)', *British Journal of Middle Eastern Studies*, Vol.33, No.1, May 2006, pp.37–50.

Ross, M, 'The Political Economy of the Resource Curse', *World Politics*, Vol.51, No.2, 1999, pp.297–322.

———, 'Does Oil Hinder Democracy?', *World Politics*, Vol.53, No.3, April 2001, pp.325–362.

Rugh, WA, 'The United Arab Emirates: What Are the Sources of Its Stability?', *Middle East Policy*, Vol.5, No.3, Sept 1997.

Schlumberger, O, 'Structural Reform, Economic Order, and Development: Patrimonial Capitalism', *Review of International Political Economy*, Vol.15, No.4, 2008, pp.622–649.

Schwarz, R, 'The Political Economy of State-Formation in the Arab Middle East: Rentier States, Economic Reform, and Democratization', *Review of International Political Economy*, Vol.15, No.4, October 2008, pp.599–621.

Shirky, C, 'The Political Power of Social Media', *Foreign Affairs*, Vol. 90, No.1, January/February 2011, pp.28–41.

Svolik, MW, 'Power Sharing and Leadership Dynamics in Authoritarian

Regimes', *American Journal of Political Science*, Vol.53, No.2, 2009, pp.477–494.

Tétreault, MA, 'The Winter of the Arab Spring in the Gulf Monarchies', *Globalizations*, Vol. 8, No.5, pp.629–637.

Walker, C and Orttung, RW, 'Breaking the News: The Role of State-Run Media', *Journal of Democracy*, Vol.25, No.1, January 2014, pp.71–85.

Wendt, A, 'Anarchy is What States Make of It: The Social Construction of Power Politics', *International Organisation*, Vol.46, No.2, Spring 1992, pp.391–425.

Yates, A, 'Western Expatriates in the UAE Armed Forces, 1964–2015', *Journal of Arabian Studies*, Vol.6, No.2, December 2016, pp.182–200.

Yom, SL and Gause, G, 'Resilient Royals: How Arab Monarchies Hang On', *Journal of Democracy*, Vol.23, No.4, 2012, pp.74–88.

Yom, SL, 'Understanding the Durability of Authoritarianism in the Middle East', *The Arab Studies Journal*, Vol 13/14, No 2/1, Fall 2005, pp.227–233.

Zakaria, F, 'The Rise of Illiberal Democracy', *Foreign Affairs*, Vol.76, No.6, Nov/Dec 1997, pp.22–43.

Zimmerman, E, 'Towards a Causal Model of Military Coups d'Etat', *Armed Forces & Society*, Vol.5, No.3, 1979, pp.387–413.

Zukrowska, K, *The Link Between Economics, Stability and Security in a Transforming Economy*, NATO Economic Colloquium, 1999, pp.269–283.

Online Sources

'2030 Strategy', *ADNOC*, available online, https://www.adnoc.ae/en/strategy2030, date accessed, 10th March 2018.

'Abu Dhabi Water and Electric Authority', *Abu Dhabi Digital Government*, available online, https://www.abudhabi.ae/portal/public/en/departments/adwea, date accessed, 24th March 2018.

'ADNOC Restructuring Continues Apace', *The Economist Intelligence Unit (EIU)*, 20th May 2016, available online, http://country.eiu.com/article.aspx?articleid=1544237538, date accessed, 10th March 2018.

'ADSB—The Company', *Abu Dhabi Ship Building (ADSB)*, available online, http://www.adsb.ae/team/homaid-abdulla-al-shimmari/, date accessed, 23rd March 2018.

'Annual Report 2008', *Mubadala*, 2008.

'Annual Report 2009', *Mubadala*, 2009.

'Annual Report 2010', *Mubadala*, 2010.

'Annual Report 2011', *Mubadala*, 2011.

BIBLIOGRAPHY

'Annual Report 2012', *Mubadala*, 2012.

'Annual Review 2013', *Mubadala*, 2013.

'Annual Review 2015', *Mubadala*, available online, 2015, https://www. mubadala.com/annual-review-2015/en/our-leadership, date accessed, 23rd March 2018.

'Annual Review 2016', *Mubadala*, 2016, available online, https://www. mubadala.com/annual-review-2016/en/index.html, date accessed, 23rd March 2018.

'Arabic will remain a 'language of the future', Dubai ruler Says', *The National*, Abu Dhabi, 5th May 2016, available online, http://www. thenational.ae/uae/government/arabic-will-remain-a-language-of-the-future-dubai-ruler-says, date accessed 25th November 2016.

'Bahrain: Unchecked Repression', *Human Rights Watch*, 29th January 2015, available online, https://www.hrw.org/news/2015/01/29/bahrain-unchecked-repression, 14th October 2016.

'Board Member', *General Pension and Social Security Authority*, available online, http://gpssa.gov.ae/en/Pages/DirectorsDetails. aspx?DirectorId=13, date accessed, 19th March 2018.

'Board of Directors Profiles', *Abu Dhabi Commercial Bank*, available online, https://www.adcb.com/about/investorrelations/ financialinformation/ARsite/2014/eissa-mohamed-al-suwaidi.html, date accessed, 19th March 2018.

'Board of Directors', 2010 Review: Prudent Global Growth, *Abu Dhabi Investment Authority*, Abu Dhabi, 2011, available online, http://www. adia.ae/En/pr/Annual_Review_Website_2010.pdf, date accessed, 16th March 2018.

———, *Abu Dhabi Investment Authority (ADIA)*, available online, http:// www.adia.ae/En/Governance/Board_Of_Directors.aspx, date accessed, 16th March 2018.

———, *Abu Dhabi Investment Council*, available online, http://www. adcouncil.ae/?page_id=18, date accessed, 18th March 2018.

'Cabinet Member', *United Arab Emirates The Cabinet*, available online, https://uaecabinet.ae/en/details/cabinet-members/his-excellency-hussain-bin-ibrahim-al-hammadi, date accessed, 24th March 2018.

'Board of Directors', *Mubadala*, available online, https://www. mubadala.com/en/who-we-are/board-of-directors, date accessed, 22nd March 2018.

'Country Analysis Brief: United Arab Emirates', *U.S. Energy Information Administration*, 21st March 2017, available online, http://www.iberglobal.com/files/2017/emiratos_eia.pdf, date accessed, 10th March 2018.

'Defence Secretary Meets Abu Dhabi Crown Prince', *Ministry of Defence* and *The Rt Hon Sir Michael Fallon MP*, 30th October 2014, available online, https://www.gov.uk/government/news/defence-secretary-meets-abu-dhabi-crown-prince, date accessed, 23rd March 2018.

'Emirates Nuclear Energy Company (ENEC), *U.S–U.A.E Business Council*, available online, http://usuaebusiness.org/members/emirates-nuclear-energy-corporation-enec/, date accessed, 24th March 2018.

'Etihad Aviation Group', *CAPA Center For Aviation*, available online, https://centreforaviation.com/data/profiles/airline-groups/etihad-aviation-group, date accessed, 24th March 2018.

'Fund Rankings', *Sovereign Wealth Fund Institute*, June 2017, available online, https://www.swfinstitute.org/fund-rankings/, date accessed, 17th March 2018.

'Guiding Principles', *Emirates Investment Authority*, available online, http://www.eia.gov.ae, date accessed, 23rd March 2018.

'His Excellency Dr. Sultan bin Ahmed Sultan al Jaber', *United Arab Emirates The Cabinet*, available online, https://uaecabinet.ae/en/details/cabinet-members/his-excellency-dr-sultan-bin-ahmad-sultan-al-jaber, date accessed, 23rd March 2018.

'Homaid al Shimmari', *Mubadala*, available online, https://www.mubadala.com/en/who-we-are/investment-committee/homaid-al-shimmari, date accessed, 23rd March 2018.

'International Petroleum Investment Company', *Credit Research*, Unicredit, 8th March 2011, available online, https://www.research.unicreditgroup.eu/DocsKey/credit_docs_2011_114693.ashx?EXT=pdf&KEY=n03ZZLYZf5miL7MI684NjxlHtzYjzK-LBjvcijOr3ys=, date accessed, 19th March 2018.

'Investment Strategy', *Abu Dhabi Investment Council*, available online, http://www.adcouncil.ae/?page_id=41, date accessed, 18th March 2018.

'Khalifa Appoints Ahmed al Mazrouei as Secretary General of Abu Dhabi's Executive Council', *WAM*, 23rd October 2011, available online, http://wam.ae/ar/servlet/Satellite?c=WamLocEnews&cid=1289996157259&pagename=WAM%2FWAM_E_Layout&parent=Collection&parentid=1135099399983, date accessed, 23rd March 2018.

'Khalifa Appoints Mansour as ADIA Board Member', *WAM*, 8th June 2005, available online, http://wam.ae/en/details/1395227444392, date accessed, 17th March 2018.

'Khalifa Appoints Sultan al-Jaber as Director General of ADNOC', *WAM Emirates News Agency*, 15th February 2016, available online, http://wam.ae/en/details/1395291637840, date accessed, 10th March 2018.

BIBLIOGRAPHY

'Khalifa bin Zayed Issues Emiri Decree Reshuffling Abu Dhabi Investment Council Board', *Emirate of Abu Dhabi Executive Council General Secretariat*, 7th April 2010, available online, https://www.abudhabi.ae/portal/public/ShowProperty?nodeId=%2FWCC%2FADEGP_ND_157028_EN&_adf.ctrl-state=asqxktyab_4, date accessed, 18th March 2018.

'Khalifa Establishes Abu Dhabi Media Company', *WAM*, 6th June 2007, available online, http://wam.ae/en/details/1395227857102, date accessed, 24th March 2018.

'Khalifa Issues Law Forming Abu Dhabi Investment Council', *WAM*, 12th June 2006, available online, http://wam.ae/ar/print/139522767 0129, date accessed, 18th March 2018.

'Khalifa Reshuffles Abu Dhabi Investment Council', *WAM*, 4th January 2007, available online, http://wam.ae/en/details/1395227772462, date accessed, 18th March 2018.

'Khalifa Reshuffles ADIA's BoD', *WAM*, 4th January 2007, available online, http://wam.ae/en/details/1395227772438, date accessed, 17th March 2018.

'Masdar Board of Directors', *Masdar*, available online, http://www.masdar.ae/en/masdar/detail/masdar-board-of-directors, date accessed, 10th March 2018.

'Member Detail', *General Secretariat of the Executive Council*, available online, https://www.ecouncil.ae/en/ADGovernment/Pages/Member Detail.aspx?mid=7, date accessed, 23rd March 2018.

'Mubadala Annual Review 2014', *Mubadala, 2014*.

'Mubadala Investment Company: A Global Champion for Economic Growth in Abu Dhabi', *Mubadala*, 21st January 2017, available online, https://www.mubadala.com/en/ipic-mubadala-merger, date accessed, 19th March 2018.

'Organisational Structure', *United Arab Emirates Ministry of Finance*, available online, https://www.mof.gov.ae/En/About/ocAndInstitutes/Pages/oc.aspx#, date accessed, 19th March 2018.

'Our History', *Abu Dhabi National Oil Company (ADNOC)*, available online, https://www.adnoc.ae/en/about-us/our-history, date accessed, 24th March 2018.

'Our History', *Invest AD*, available online, http://www.investad.com, date accessed, 19th March 2018.

'Our History', *Mubadala*, available online, https://www.mubadala.com/en/who-we-are/our-history, date accessed, 19th March 2018.

'Our Organisational Structure', *Annual Review 2016*, Mubadala, Abu Dhabi, available online, https://www.mubadala.com/annual-review-2016/en/our-leadership, date accessed, 19th March 2018.

BIBLIOGRAPHY

'Overview', *Abu Dhabi Securities Exchange*, available online, Abu Dhabi Securities Exchange (ADX), https://www.adx.ae/English/Pages/AboutUs/Whoweare/default.aspx, date accessed, 24th March 2018.

'Ownership Information', *First Abu Dhabi Bank*, 31st December 2017, available online, https://www.nbad.com/en-ae/about-nbad/investor-relations/shareholders/ownership.html, date accessed, 24th March 2018.

'SEHA 2013 Annual Report, Delivering the Right Care for the Right Patient', *Abu Dhabi Health Services Company*, 2013.

'Sheikh Khalifa Approves The New 12th Cabinet of the United Arab Emirates', *United Arab Emirates The Cabinet*, available online, https://www.uaecabinet.ae/en/details/news/sheikh-khalifa-approves-the-new-12th-cabinet-of-the-united-arab-emirates, date accessed, 23rd March 2018.

'Sheikh Khalifa Restructures ADIA's Board', *Sovereign Wealth Fund Institute*, 9th April 2013, available online, https://www.swfinstitute.org/swf-news/sheikh-khalifa-restructures-adias-board/, date accessed, 17th March 2018.

'Sovereign Wealth Funds, Generally Accepted Principles and Practices, "Santiago Principles"', *International Working Group of Sovereign Wealth Funds*, October 2008.

'Strategy 2030', *Abu Dhabi National Oil Company (ADNOC)*, available online, https://www.adnoc.ae/en/strategy2030, date accessed, 9th March 2018.

'Supreme Petroleum Council', *ADNOC*, available online, https://www.adnoc.ae/en/about-us/supreme-petroleum-council, date accessed, 9th March 2018.

'The National Health Insurance Company', *Abu Dhabi Digital Government*, available online, https://www.abudhabi.ae/portal/public/en/departments/daman, date accessed, 24th March 2018.

'The UAE and Global Oil Supply', *UAE Embassy in Washington DC*, http://www.uae-embassy.org/about-uae/energy/uae-and-global-oil-supply, 19th January 2016.

'Top 10 Buyers and Sellers', Abu Dhabi Securities Exchange, 24th March 2018, available online, https://www.adx.ae/English/Pages/Data/ReportandCharts/ChartCenter/Top10BuyersSellersbySymbol.aspx, date accessed, 24th March 2018.

'Two Officials Take Oath Before Abu Dhabi Crown Prince', *WAM*, 6th March 2017, available online, http://wam.ae/en/details/13953 02601294, date accessed, 17th March 2018.

'UAE Energy Minister is New MD of Abu Dhabi's IPIC After Board

Revamp', *Reuters*, 22nd April 2015, available online, https://www.
reuters.com/article/emirates-ipic/uae-energy-minister-is-new-md-
of-abu-dhabis-ipic-after-board-revamp-idUSL5N0XJ5AG20150422,
date accessed, 19th March 2018.

'UAE Giant ADNOC to Consolidate Three Firms in Efficiency Drive',
Reuters, 18th October 2016, available online, https://www.reuters.
com/article/emirates-adnoc-consolidation/uae-oil-giant-adnoc-to-
consolidate-three-firms-in-efficiency-drive-idUSL8N1CO1WX
?type=companyNews, date accessed, 10th March 2018.

'What is a SWF?', *Sovereign Wealth Fund Research Institute*, available online,
https://www.swfinstitute.org/sovereign-wealth-fund/,   date
accessed, 9th March 2018.

'Who we are', *Abu Dhabi Airports Company*, available online, http://
www.adac.ae/english/who-we-are/who-we-are/, date accessed,
24th March 2018.

'Who we Are', Mubadala, available online, https://www.mubadala.
com/en, date accessed, 23rd March 2018.

Aboudi, S and Hagagy, A, 'Kuwait Opposition Win Big in Anti-Austerity
Vote', *Reuters*, 27th November 2016, available online, http://www.
reuters.com/article/us-kuwait-election-idUSKBN13M0D4,   date
accessed, 28th November 2016.

Anderson, S, 'Coercion', Zalta, EN, (ed.), *Stanford Encyclopaedia of
Philosophy*, Summer 2015, available online, https://plato.stanford.
edu/archives/sum2015/entries/coercion, date accessed 19th January
2017.

Bandow, D, 'Iran is Dangerous, But Saudi Arabia is Worse', *Forbes*, 5th
January 2016, available online, http://www.forbes.com/sites/doug-
bandow/2016/01/05/saudi-arabia-is-washington-frenemy-reckless-
riyadh-makes-mideast-more-dangerous-for-america/#2da03d
501920, date accessed, 9th January 2017.

Bin Zayed al Nahyan, H, 'Abu Dhabi Investment Authority Marks 40th
Anniversary', *Press Release*, Abu Dhabi, 21st March 2016, available
online, http://www.adia.ae/En/pr/ADIA_40th_Anniversary_Open_
Letter_Press_Release_English.pdf, date accessed, 17th March 2018.

Cordesman, AH, *Iran and the Gulf Military Balance*, Center for Strategic
and International Affairs (CSIS), Washington DC, 4th October 2016,
available online, https://www.csis.org/analysis/iran-and-gulf-mili-
tary-balance-1, date accessed, 8th July 2017.

Embassy of the United Arab Emirates in Washington D.C., 'How The
UAE is Pioneering Peaceful Civilian Nuclear Energy in the Middle
East', Smithsonian.com, 3rd January 2018, available online, https://

BIBLIOGRAPHY

www.smithsonianmag.com/sponsored/uae-pioneering-peaceful-nuclear-power-middle-east-180967322/, date accessed, 10th March 2018.

Etihad Rail Fact Sheet, available online, https://www.etihadrail.ae/sites/default/files/pdf/factsheets.pdf, date accessed, 24th March 2018.

Everington, J, 'Boardroom reshuffle at IPIC', *The National*, 22nd April 2015, available online, https://www.thenational.ae/business/boardroom-reshuffle-at-ipic-1.22512, date accessed, 19th March 2018.

Flournoy, M and Fontaine, R, 'Economic Growth is a Security Issue', *The Wall Street Journal*, 26th May 2015, available online, https://www.wsj.com/articles/economic-growth-is-a-national-security-issue-1432683397, date accessed, 4th March 2018.

Graves, L, 'Sultan al Jaber: New Man at ADNOC Helm Has the Right Energy Mix', *The National*, 16th February 2016, available online, https://www.thenational.ae/business/sultan-al-jaber-new-man-at-adnoc-helm-has-the-right-energy-mix-1.202477, date accessed, 13th April 2018.

Graves, L, 'Construction Begins at Abu Dhabi's Largest Solar Panel Field', *The National*, 4th May 2017, available online, https://www.thenational.ae/business/construction-begins-at-abu-dhabi-s-largest-solar-power-project-1.32040, date accessed, 10th March 2018.

Hanieh, A, *Neoliberalism and Autocracy—Fundamental rifts: Power, Wealth and Inequality in the Arab World*, Europe Solidaire Sans Frontières, 1st March 2015, available online, http://www.europe-solidaire.org/spip.php?article34583, date accessed, 30th September 2016.

Harb, Y, 'Bahraini Monarchy Manufactures Demographic Changes', *Al-Akhbar*, 5th April 2014, Available online, http://english.al-akhbar.com/node/19301, date accessed, 19th November 2016.

Hashem, E, 'UAE State-Owned Concerns Must Show the State Forward', *The National*, 28th June 2013, available online, https://www.thenational.ae/business/uae-state-owned-concerns-must-show-the-way-forward-1.288245, date accessed, 24th March 2018.

Hope, B 'Sheikh Hamed bin Zayed Names ADIA Chief', *The National*, 14th April 2010, available online, https://www.thenational.ae/business/sheikh-hamed-bin-zayed-named-adia-chief-1.531542, date accessed, 13th April 2018.

Hourani, A, *A History of the Arab Peoples*, Harvard University Press, Cambridge, 1991.

http://www.ourfatherzayed.ae/eng/web.html#The%20Legend%20Lives%20on, accessed 3rd November 2015.

BIBLIOGRAPHY

Kassem, M, 'Family Businesses Continue to Shun Public Listing', *The National*, 23rd November 2017, available online, https://www.the-national.ae/business/economy/family-businesses-continue-to-shun-public-listings-1.678270, date accessed, 24th March 2018.

Kerr, S, 'UAE Central Bank Announces New Chairman', *Financial Times*, 7th November 2012, available online, https://www.ft.com/content/3d8bc29a-28d7-11e2-b92c-00144feabdc0, date accessed, 19th March 2018.

McAuley, A, 'UAE President Reshuffles Supreme Petroleum Council of Abu Dhabi', *The National*, 29th March 2016, available online, https://www.thenational.ae/business/uae-president-reshuffles-supreme-petroleum-council-of-abu-dhabi-1.159318, date accessed, 9th March 2018.

O'Reilly, T, '*What Is Web 2.0*', O'Reilly Network, 2005, available online, http://www.oreillynet.com/pub/a/oreilly/tim/news/2005/09/30/what-is-web-20.html, Retrieved October 21, 2016.

Perlroth, N, 'Governments Turn to Commercial Spyware to Intimidate Dissidents', *New York Times*, 29th May 2016, available online, http://www.nytimes.com/2016/05/30/technology/governments-turn-to-commercial-spyware-to-intimidate-dissidents.html?_r=0, date accessed, 8th January 2017.

Rabil, RG, 'Why America Needs to Beware of Saudi Wuhhabism', *The National Interest*, 18th May 2015, available online, http://nationalinterest.org/feature/why-america-needs-beware-saudi-wahhabism-12906, date accessed, 9th January 2017.

Reuters, 'Qatar Hikes Salaries, Pensions for State Employees', *Arabian Business*, 7th September 2011, available online, http://www.arabianbusiness.com/qatar-hikes-salaries-pensions-for-state-employees-419346.html#.WADkt5PDTwc, date accessed 14th October 2016.

Shah, A, "Why the Arab Spring Never Came to the UAE", *TIME*, 18 July 2011, available online http://content.time.com/time/world/article/0,8599,2083768,00.html, date accessed, 1 August 2016.

The National Staff, 'Sheikh Khalifa Reshuffles Abu Dhabi Investment Council Board', *The National*, 21st June 2015, available online, https://www.thenational.ae/business/sheikh-khalifa-reshuffles-abu-dhabi-investment-council-board-1.100036, date accessed, 18th March 2018.

WAM, 'CORRECTED-Abu Dhabi's crown prince is new chairman of ADIC in board revamp—WAM', *Reuters*, 22nd June 2015, available online, https://www.reuters.com/article/emirates-swf-adic/corrected-abu-dhabis-crown-prince-is-new-chairman-of-adic-in-board-revamp-wam-idUSL8N0Z70OI20150622, date accessed, 18th March 2018.

———, 'Khalifa Issues Emiri Decree on Abu Dhabi Accountability and Housing Authorities, Executive Committee of Abu Dhabi', *Emirates 24/7*, 19th February 2017, available online, https://www.emirates247.com/news/government/khalifa-issues-emiri-decrees-on-abu-dhabi-accountability-and-housing-authorities-executive-committee-of-abu-dhabi-2017–02–19–1.648389, date accessed, 23rd March 2018.

———, 'Khalifa Restructures Supreme Petroleum Council', *Emirates 24/7*, 25th June 2011, available online, https://www.emirates247.com/news/government/khalifa-restructures-supreme-petroleum-council-2011–06–25–1.404511, date accessed, 9th March 2018.

———, 'Khalifa Restructures ADIA's Board', *Emirates 24/7*, 8th April 2013, available online, https://www.emirates247.com/news/government/khalifa-restructures-adia-s-board-2013–04–08–1.501851, date accessed, 19th March 2018.

———, 'President Khalifa Revamps Supreme Petroleum Council', *Khaleej Times*, 27th June 2011, available online, https://www.khaleejtimes.com/article/20110626/ARTICLE/306269986/1002, date accessed, 9th March 2018.

———, 'UAE President Issues Law Restructuring Abu Dhabi Investment Council', Press Releases, *Mubadala*, 21st March 2018, available online, https://www.mubadala.com/en/news/uae-president-issues-law-restructuring-abu-dhabi-investment-council, date accessed, 23rd March 2018.

———, 'UAE's ADNOC Group to Continue its Transformation, says Al Jaber', *Zawya*, 3rd January 2017, available online, https://www.zawya.com/mena/en/story/UAEs_ADNOC_Group_to_continue_its_transformation_says_Al_Jaber-WAM20170103123040071/, date accessed, 13th April 2018.

West, M, 'Just How Low Can Oil Prices Go and Who is Hit Hardest?', *BBC*, 18th January 2016, available online, http://www.bbc.co.uk/news/business-35245133, date accessed, 10th March 2018

INDEX

Note: Page numbers followed by "*n*" refer to notes, "*f*" refer to figures.

INDEX

INDEX

Davidson, Christopher, 4–5, 27, 37, 40, 41, 113, 125–6, 135–6, 148
Deibert, Ronald, 85
al-Dhaheri, Jua'an Salem, 126
Dhawahir (tribe), 28
Digital Democracy (Van Dijk), 96
Dolphin Energy, 163
Dubai, 4, 22, 30, 101, 121–2, 156
  Dubai-Sharjah independent brigades, merging of, 35
  federal military forces management between Dubai and, 34–5
  leverage oil and gas reserves, 112
  pearling industry, decline of, 26
  SWFs in, 125
  Zayed bin Sultan's proposal rejected by, 32–3
Dubai 2021 Smart City policy, 93
Dubai eGovernment, 97

economy development (UAE)
  privileged economic network, 111–12, 140–2
  See also National Oil Corporations (NOCs); Privately Owned Champions (POCs); Sovereign Wealth Funds (SWFs); State-Owned Enterprises (SOEs)
11 September 2001 terrorist attacks. *See* 9/11 attacks
Emirates Defence Industries Company (EDIC), 161, 164, 166, 167
Emirates Integrated

Telecommunications Company (EITC), 80
Emirates Investment Authority (EIA), 140
Emirates News Agency (WAM), 82, 83
Emirates Nuclear Energy Corporation (ENEC), 155, 157
eras of UAE's political history
  formation of, 30
  Iran as UAE's foremost external threat, 34
  oil discovery era, 22
  political opposition, 26–7
  political violence among UAE Elites, 23–6
  post-unification (1971–2004), 36–41
  pre-unification emirates (1761–1968), 22–9
  pre-unification UAE, threats to, 27–9
  unification difficulties, 31–3
  unification process (1968–1971), 30–6
Eritrea, 58
Etisalat, 80

Falah, Sheikh, 24
al-Falasi, Muhammad al-Bawardi, 138
Falcon Eye Surveillance system (Abu Dhabi), 93
Fatima al-Ketbi, 28–9, 40–1, 43, 115, 149
Federal Laws. *See* laws
Federal National Council (FNC), 31, 32–3
Foucault, Michel, 72
France, 58–9
Fuchs, Christian, 95

317

INDEX

laws
Council of Ministers Decree
No. 23 (2017), 90
Emiri Law 3 (1984), 134
Federal Decree Law No. 13
(2009), 140
Federal Decree Law No. 3
(2017), 102
Federal Decree Law No. 4
(2007), 140
Federal Law 1 (2006), 81
Federal Law 12 (2016), 85,
242n88
Federal Law No. 15 (1980),
89
Federal Law No. 2 (2004),
102
Federal Law No. 3 (1987),
86, 92
Federal Law No. 3 (2003), 79
Federal Law No. 3 (2012),
77, 78, 89–90
Federal Law No. 5 (2012), 89
Federal Law No. 6 (2014), 67
Federal Law No. 7 (2014), 90
Leiden, Carl, 7, 13
Lessig, Lawrence, 75–6
Limpridi-Kemou, Athina, 45,
111
Lockheed Martin Corporation,
166
Luciani, Giacomo, 128
Lyon, David, 91

al-Maktoum (Dubai ruling
family), 22, 242n83
al-Maktoum, Mana bin Rashid,
27
al-Maktoum, Mohammed bin
Rashid, 40, 137, 148
Maktoum, Sheikh Said bin, 27
Manasir (tribe), 27–8

Mann, Clarence, 23, 28
Mansour, Ahmed, 93
Marx, Gary, 73, 91–2
Mattis, James, 58
al-Mazrouei, Fares Khalaf
Khalfan, 167
al-Mazrouei, Suhail bin
Muhammad, 116, 134
MBZ. *See* al-Nahyan, Mohammed
bin Zayed (MBZ)
Meulen, Hendrik Van Der, 4–5,
35, 37, 55, 56, 125, 130
al-Mezaini, Khaled, 120, 140,
160, 161, 168
Middle East and North Africa
(MENA), 1, 2, 8, 44, 58, 109,
120, 144
Mishaghin (tribe), 28
Mohamedou, Muhammad, 9–10
Mohammed bin Rashid al-Mak-
toum Smart Majlis (Dubai
smart application), 101
Mohammed bin Zayed (MBZ).
See al-Nahyan, Mohammed bin
Zayed (MBZ)
Mubadala, 80, 125, 134–9, 161,
163–5
ADIC integration announce-
ment, 129, 133
IPIC merging with, 134
al-Mubarak, Khaldoon, 115, 139
Murphy, Emma, 96

al-Nahyan, Ahmed bin Tahnoon,
54
al-Nahyan, Ahmed bin Zayed,
126, 261n151
al-Nahyan, Hamdan bin Zayed,
129
al-Nahyan, Hamed bin Zayed,
126, 261n151
al-Nahyan, Hazza bin Zayed, 115